Грамматика в контексте

Грамматика в контексте

Russian Grammar in Literary Contexts

Benjamin Rifkin
University of Wisconsin, Madison

The McGraw-Hill Companies, Inc.

New York   St. Louis   San Francisco   Auckland   Bogotá   Caracas
Lisbon   London   Madrid   Mexico City   Milan   Montreal   New Delhi
San Juan   Singapore   Sydney   Tokyo   Toronto

This is an book.

McGraw-Hill

A Division of The McGraw·Hill Companies

Грамма́тика в конте́ксте
Russian Grammar in Literary Contexts

1 2 3 4 5 6 7 8 9 0   FGR   FGR   9 0 9 8 7 6 5

0–07–052831–4

Library of Congress Cataloging-in-Publication Data

Rifkin, Benjamin
    Grammatika v kontekste : Russian grammar in literary contexts
/ Benjamin Rifkin.
      p.   cm.
    Some text in Russian.
    Includes index.
    1. Russian language—Textbooks for foreign speakers—English.
2. Russian language—Grammar.   I. Title.
PG2129.E5R545   1996
491.78′2421—dc20   95–38613
                                   CIP

This book was set in Minion by ETP Harrison.
The editors were Thalia Dorwick, Gregory Trauth, Melissa Frazier, and E. A. Pauw.
The indexer was John Dibs.
The designer was Suzanne Montazer.
The production supervisor was Tanya Nigh.
The cover was designed by Juan Vargas.
Maps were done by Joseph Lemonnier.
Quebecor Fairfield was printer and binder.

CONTENTS

UNIT 1

Agreement   1
Согласова́ние

UNIT 2

The Verbal System: Second-conjugation Verbs   13
Глаго́льная систе́ма: Второ́е спряже́ние

UNIT 3

First-conjugation Verbs and Verbs with -ся   25
Пе́рвое спряже́ние и глаго́лы с су́ффиксом -ся

Texts: «Чёлн томле́нья», Bal'mont; «Сотру́дничать и́ли конфликтова́ть?»,
current press

UNIT 4

Stress in the Russian Verb   36
Ударе́ние в ру́сском глаго́ле

Texts: «Выхожу́ оди́н я на доро́гу», Lermontov; "Silentium!," Tiutchev

UNIT 7

The Nominative Case   73

Именительный падёж: *Кто? Что?*

Texts: Excerpt from «Бородино́», Lermontov; Excerpt from «Петербу́рг», Belyi; «Ночь, у́лица, фона́рь, апте́ка», Blok

WORKBOOK/LABORATORY MANUAL

Lexicon: Shopping for and Ordering Food
Listening Tasks
Phonetics and Intonation: Intonation Pattern 3
Exercises and Activities
Grammar Supplement: *many, some,* and *few*
Unit Glossary

UNIT 8

The Genitive Case   89

Роди́тельный падёж: *Кого́? Чего́?*

Texts: «О СПИ́Де», from current press; Excerpt from «Евге́ний Оне́гин», Pushkin; «Голуба́я тетра́дь но́мер 10», Kharms; «Ла́йза Минне́лли у ру́сских попроси́ла льда», current press

WORKBOOK/LABORATORY MANUAL

Lexicon: Nationalities and Citizenship
Listening Tasks
Phonetics and Intonation: Intonation Pattern 4
Exercises and Activities
Unit Glossary

UNIT 9

The Accusative Case 111

Вини́тельный паде́ж: *Кого́? Что?*

Texts: Excerpt from «Дя́дя Ва́ня», Chekhov; «Ло́това жена́», Akhmatova

UNIT 10

The Prepositional Case 122

Предло́жный паде́ж: *О ком? О чём?*

Texts: Excerpt from «Капита́нская до́чка», Pushkin; «Что в и́мени тебе́ моём?», Pushkin; «Па́рус», Lermontov

UNIT 17

Time Expressions 207
Выраже́ния вре́мени

WORKBOOK/LABORATORY MANUAL
Lexicon: Weather
Listening Tasks: Time Expressions
Phonetics and Intonation: **ц** and **-тся, с + ч**
Exercises and Activities
Unit Glossary

UNIT 18

The Conditional, *whether* Constructions, and Reported Speech 223
Сослага́тельное наклоне́ние и ко́свенная речь

WORKBOOK/LABORATORY MANUAL
Listening Tasks (Based on Conditional Constructions)
Lexicon: Sports
Phonetics and Intonation: **ч** and **р**
Exercises and Activities
Unit Glossary

Passive Participles   238
Страда́тельные прича́стия

WORKBOOK/LABORATORY MANUAL

Lexicon: Art, Music, Literature, and Film
Listening Tasks
Phonetics and Intonation: Russian **ж** and **ш**
Lexicon: Verbs of Memory and Perception
Exercises and Activities
Unit Glossary

Active Participles   250
Действи́тельные прича́стия

WORKBOOK/LABORATORY MANUAL

Lexicon: Talking Politics
Listening Tasks
Phonetics and Intonation: Word Initial **и**
Lexicon: *to try*
Exercises and Activities
Unit Glossary

WORKBOOK/LABORATORY MANUAL

Lexicon: Travel and Tourism

Listening Tasks

Phonetics and Intonation: Voiced and Voiceless **г** and **к**

Exercises and Activities

Unit Glossary

UNIT 24

Coming and Going: Verbs of Motion with Spatial Prefixes   307

Глаго́лы движе́ния с приста́вками

Texts: Excerpt from «Иро́ния су́дьбы (киносцена́рий)», Riazanov and Braginskii; «Де́вушка пе́ла в церко́вном хо́ре...», Blok

WORKBOOK/LABORATORY MANUAL

Lexicon: *How to get to...?*

Listening Tasks

Phonetics and Intonation: Voiced and Voiceless **д** and **т**

Exercises and Activities

Unit Glossary

UNIT 25

Bringing and Taking: Transitive Verbs of Motion   325
Перехо́дные глаго́лы движе́ния

Texts: Excerpt from «Жизнь и судьба́», Grossman; «Га́млет», Pasternak

WORKBOOK/LABORATORY MANUAL
Listening Tasks
Phonetics and Intonation: ь and ъ
Lexicon: **В ми́ре би́знеса**
Exercises and Activities
Unit Glossary

APPENDICES

**Additional listening texts and reading texts
may be found in the *Instructor's Manual*.**

To the Instructor

Грамма́тика в конте́ксте is an appropriate text for students of Russian who have completed at least one year of college-level instruction or at least two years of high-school-level instruction. The text is designed to work well with other materials and activities, such as literary readers, novels, and Russian-language films. The text may also be used on its own, should the instructor prefer to do so, since it provides adequate readings, both literary and non-literary, and instruction in phonetics and intonation, as well as a strong grammar program.

The complete *Грамма́тика в конте́ксте* package consists of the following materials:

- the student text
- a combined *Workbook/Laboratory Manual*
- an *Audiocassette Program*, coordinated with the *Laboratory Manual*
- an *Instructor's Manual/Tapescript*

Features of *Грамма́тика в конте́ксте*

The following are the distinguishing features of the *Грамма́тика в конте́ксте* program.

Modularity

Грамма́тика в конте́ксте is a modular program that allows instructors to pick and choose materials, texts, and activities from either the textbook or the *Workbook/Laboratory Manual* in a sequence that fits best with other materials used in a given course. Of course, many instructors will prefer to teach the chapters of the text sequentially, and the sequence of units as presented is pedagogically logical. But those instructors who want flexibility in an intermediate or advanced text will find it in *Грамма́тика в конте́ксте*.

Grammar is covered principally in the textbook, and vocabulary in the *Workbook*. However, instructors can use the grammar or syntax section of any unit of the textbook together with the lexicon section of any unit of the *Workbook* (or with none at all). This is because vocabulary exercises do not depend on knowledge of the textbook unit's

grammar presentation, and grammar exercises do not depend on knowledge of the
Workbook's unit vocabulary presentation. The phonetics sections of the *Laboratory
Manual* can also be covered in any sequence.

Grammar in Context

All units contain examples of the targeted grammar structures in authentic texts: literary excerpts, extracts from magazines and newspapers, proverbs, and idiomatic expressions. Reading texts by nineteenth- and twentieth-century Russian authors include works by Akhmadulina, Akhmatova, Chekhov, Lermontov, Pasternak, Pushkin, Solzhenitsyn, Tolstoy, Tsvetaeva, and many more.*

Accommodations of Learning Styles

A guiding principle of the development of **Грамма́тика в конте́ксте** is that language learners have different learning styles. Thus, some learners need to understand the theories or rules of language use, while others need to see those rules "in action." Still others need clearly defined activities to practice using targeted language structures and vocabulary. All types of students will find appropriate materials in **Грамма́тика в конте́ксте**.

From Sentences to Paragraphs

Грамма́тика в конте́ксте was prepared with an eye toward helping instructors encourage students to move beyond the discourse frame of the word or sentence. Thus, activities in the text and the *Workbook* help encourage paragraph-length expression by students, both in writing and in speech, especially in Units 5 through 25.

Organization of the Textbook

Each unit of the textbook focuses on a particular grammar topic or syntactical construction. Examples are provided in a literary or journalistic context, accompanied by clear, systematic explanations of the grammar rules that govern the topic. Translations of Russian examples are provided to a greater degree at the beginning of the book, when students are in greatest need of such support, and to a much lesser degree in the units near the end.

Both manipulative and creative exercises are provided to help students work toward

---

* Russian names are transliterated according to the Library of Congress Transliteration System (see Appendix), except for names with commonly accepted English spellings (such as Tolstoy or Yeltsin) or English spellings preferred by Russians writing their names in English (such as Aksyonov).

automatic use of the targeted structure. Exercises that promote comprehension of the structure in context always precede those in which students are required to produce the grammatical structure. Manipulative exercises in the textbook help prepare students for meaningful communicative activities. **Зада́ния** (activities) marked ✑ in each unit of the textbook are designed to promote students' active use of targeted structures in expanded discourse opportunities, either in writing or in speech.

All reading texts are accompanied by pre-reading activities to help students establish relevant schemata or expectations about what the texts might tell them. Post-reading tasks focus student attention on reading strategies as well as on both global and detail comprehension of the text. At least one of the readings in each unit is a poem that may be assigned for memorization. Students can listen to a reading of the poems in the *Audiocassette Program*. These poems are identified with cassette icons (◈). Each unit also includes a number of Russian proverbs or idiomatic expressions that illustrate the targeted language structure; these materials are appropriate for memorization by students as well.

The appendices include declension paradigms, a transliteration chart, lists of grammatical terms, classroom expressions, literary terms, and rules for the use of numbers. There are also Russian-English, English-Russian word indices and indices of literary authors and grammatical topics.

The *Грамма́тика в конте́ксте* Package of Supplementary Materials

Workbook/Laboratory Manual

The *Workbook/Laboratory Manual* offers additional practice with the grammar presented in the textbook. *Workbook* exercises are typically more challenging than those in the textbook. Each unit of the *Workbook/Laboratory Manual* also includes at least one topical lexicon (health and illness, learning and teaching, and so on), which is usually the source of the content for the listening tasks included in the *Audiocassette Program*. Some units also include a section dedicated to lexical problems, such as verbs of "using" or verbs of "remembering." *Workbook/Laboratory Manual* units conclude with a glossary that contains vocabulary from both the textbook and the *Laboratory Manual*. Vocabulary from the thematic lexicons is marked with the symbol # to facilitate the assignment of vocabulary from the textbook, the *Workbook*, or both.

The listening tasks include pre-listening activities (to help students orient themselves to the content of the listening text) as well as listening and post-listening activities that promote comprehension of main ideas and details. Some of the listening activities focus student attention on particular aspects of language usage. Post-listening activities encourage students to use the listening texts as the basis for writing or speaking activities. Each unit of the lab manual also includes a section on phonetics and intonation.

Audiocassette Program

Approximately three hours long, the *Audiocassette Program* is made available free to adopting institutions. The program can also be purchased by students.

Instructor's Manual/Tapescript

This supplement includes keys to all manipulative exercises, suggestions for additional communicative activities for pair, group, and mingling formats, and guidelines for testing, as well as a more in-depth explanation of the pedagogical assumptions and organization in *Грамма́тика в конте́ксте*. The *Instructor's Manual* also includes additional listening and reading activities, and supplementary materials.

A Few Words about Using
Грамма́тика в конте́ксте

Грамма́тика в конте́ксте is designed to provide optimal flexibility to those instructors who desire it. It may be used on its own, but it is also easily coordinated with other materials (films or readings).

The modular nature of the materials also allows instructors to "pick and choose" the grammar, texts, and activities they wish to use, without binding them to other vocabulary and grammar. Thus, instructors may require Unit 1 (agreement, both subject-verb and modifier noun) of the textbook for students who have a weak grammar background or who have forgotten a lot over the summer. Students with stronger backgrounds might easily go directly to Unit 13 of the textbook.

Instructors can also choose to present textbook units in any order. However, we recommend sequencing the units on verbs in the order in which they are presented (Units 2–6), and the units on verbs of motion in the order in which they are presented (Units 23–25), as the information in these units builds on information presented previously.

Instructors will note that the units are not of equal length, but rather are as long as required by the topics they present. For this reason, and because all classes are different, it is difficult, if not impossible, to provide a standard for how much time is needed to cover each unit. Students with a solid grammar background will be able to move quickly through the first dozen units, which review the basics. Instructors working with such students might opt to assign some or all of those units to be completed at home over the course of a week or two. Students with less than a solid grammar background will probably not be able to move so rapidly through this material and will need more reinforcement in class.

Units 14–25 present material that may be new for some if not all students, especially those who have had only one year of college-level instruction. These units may require ten to twelve contact hours for students to assimilate the concepts presented.

Acknowledgments

Special thanks go to the following instructors, whose suggestions and comments were very useful to the author in the preparation of the final manuscript for this text. The appearance of their names does not necessarily constitute an endorsement of the text or its methodology:

Diane Goldstaub, Illinois Wesleyan University
Laurie Iudin-Nelson, Luther College
Ludmila Longan, University of Michigan
Nathan Longan, Oakland University
Kevin J. McKenna, University of Vermont

I am also most grateful to my students at the University of Wisconsin-Madison and to my colleagues—James Bailey, Clare Cavanaugh, Judith Kornblatt, Harlan Marquess, and Gary Rosenshield—for their support of this project and their very helpful constructive criticism. I am also grateful to my many Russian friends and colleagues—including Anton Adassinsky, Elena Bobretsova, Nikolai Firtich, Julia Kalaushina, Boris Kalaushin of St. Petersburg; and Fatima Fedorova, Viktor Mixel'zon, Elena Rossinskaia, and Ol'ga and Aleksei Dedov of Moscow—for their encouragement of my work. I thank my colleagues, Yuri Shchegolov and Valeria Kramm, Aleksandr Dolinin and Galina Lapina, for their help with the geography of Moscow and Petersburg, respectively. I am grateful to Michael Groh and Nikita Smirnov for their photographs and I thank Vanessa Bittner for her help with geographic questions and with photography logistics. I am grateful to Galina Lapina, Liudmila Longan, Irina Odintsova, Galina Patterson, Alexander Propp, and Dan Ungurianu for their help with the manuscript. I thank Chris Putney and Tanya Nigh of McGraw-Hill for their interest and support throughout my work on this project. I am very grateful to Konstantine Klioutchkine and Glen Worthey, who proofread so well; to Melissa Frazier, whose eagle eye helped me see when I had written myself into a bind; to Liz Pauw and David Sweet, who helped put it all together; and to Thalia Dorwick and Gregory Trauth, whose patience, support, understanding, and pedagogic insight have been extremely important for the development of this book. I thank my parents, for all their support, for so many years. Lastly, I thank my wife, Lisa Fell, and my children, Nathan and Hannah, for their patience and understanding during the many long days and nights I spent working on this manuscript.

I express my deep gratitude to Emilia Hramova and to the late Konstantin Hramov, of Yale University, to whom this book is dedicated, in recognition of their love for the Russian language and enthusiasm for teaching. They were and continue to be inspiring to me and countless others.

Benjamin Rifkin
Madison, Wisconsin
November, 1995

To the Student

Since you've already completed some study of Russian, you know something about Russian grammar. However, you may feel that you haven't been able to organize what you know into a coherent system. You may also feel that you couldn't understand some of the concepts you studied previously because you didn't know enough Russian to understand how these concepts were applied in the language. This textbook will help you thoroughly review the basics of Russian grammar. As you go through it you will learn to systematize your knowledge and—I hope—become able to think less about *how* you're expressing yourself in Russian while you focus more on *what* you're expressing.

How Is *Грамма́тика в конте́ксте* Organized?

Грамма́тика в конте́ксте is a textbook package that includes a textbook, a *Workbook/Laboratory Manual*, and an *Audiocassette Program*. The material in the textbook is not necessarily linked to the material in the *Workbook*, so your instructor might want to skip around a bit, asking you, for example, to complete assignments in Unit 7 of the textbook and Unit 13 of the workbook. I encourage you to use *Грамма́тика в конте́ксте* with a three-ring binder so that when your instructor returns assignments from the *Workbook/Laboratory Manual* to you, you can place them in your binder with your class notes and compositions. This will help you keep track of your work, especially if your instructor skips back and forth between units in the textbook and the *Workbook/Laboratory Manual*.

Грамма́тика в конте́ксте focuses primarily on grammar and syntax. Each unit presents a particular grammatical or syntactical problem and provides rules for solving that problem as well as examples demonstrating how the problem is solved. You might prefer to read the explanations before the examples or the examples before the explanations. Try to vary your approach so that you can determine what works best for you.

Reading texts in each unit of the textbook feature works by classic Russian authors of the nineteenth and early twentieth centuries as well as some contemporary authors; these texts were selected because they show the grammar or syntax emphasized in the unit. I don't expect you to understand every word of the reading texts. Rather, as you read, try to understand the main ideas so that you can answer the questions in the exercises that follow the readings.

The grammar exercises in the textbook usually consist of five to ten items to prepare you for longer exercises in the *Workbook/Laboratory Manual.*

The textbook also includes some activities to help you to speak and write in longer and longer "chunks." When you first started to study Russian, sometimes you spoke and wrote just one word at a time, answering questions with minimal information. As you continued to study Russian, you probably began to speak and write in sentences and sometimes in paragraphs. Activites marked **задáния** in the textbook (and *Workbook/ Laboratory Manual*) are designed to encourage you to speak and write in paragraphs or longer. Try to use these opportunities to the fullest. It's okay to make mistakes (in fact, mistakes probably cannot be avoided entirely), but don't let that stop you from trying to express yourself in a sophisticated way in Russian.

Each unit of the *Workbook/Laboratory Manual* includes a topical lexicon (a list of words related by topic) that is usually the source of vocabulary in the listening tasks for each unit. Each unit also includes phonetics exercises (also geared to the audiocassettes) and additional exercises and activities, as well as a glossary listing the vocabulary presented in the given unit in both the *Workbook/Laboratory Manual* and the textbook. Vocabulary items drawn from the topical lexicon are always marked with the symbol #; in some instances, your instructor may assign you to memorize only vocabulary not marked with this symbol or only vocabulary marked with that symbol.

There are many strategies that can help you be a better, more efficient student of Russian. Some of them are explained in the preface to the *Workbook*, so you will want to read that preface carefully. Use those strategies and think of new ones that will work best for *you.*

Good luck!
Benjamin Rifkin
Madison, Wisconsin

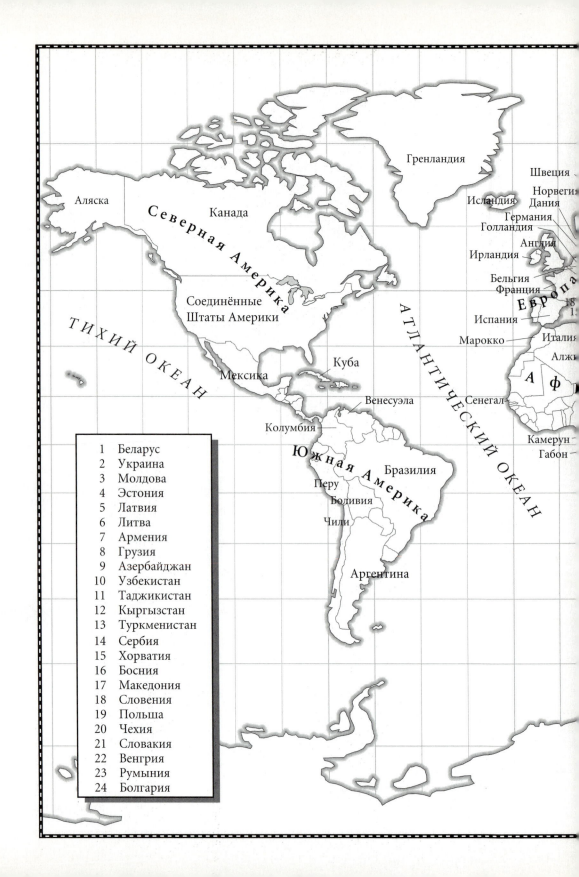

Гренландия

Швеция
Норвегия
Исландия Дания
Германия
Голландия
Англия
Ирландия

Бельгия
Франция

Европа

Испания

Италия

Алжи

Марокко

А Ф

Аляска

Канада

Северная Америка

Соединённые
Штаты Америки

Куба

ТИХИЙ ОКЕАН

Мексика

АТЛАНТИЧЕСКИЙ ОКЕАН

Сенегал

Венесуэла

Камерун
Габон

Колумбия

Южная Америка

Бразилия

Перу

Боливия

Чили

Аргентина

1	Беларус
2	Украина
3	Молдова
4	Эстония
5	Латвия
6	Литва
7	Армения
8	Грузия
9	Азербайджан
10	Узбекистан
11	Таджикистан
12	Кыргызстан
13	Туркменистан
14	Сербия
15	Хорватия
16	Босния
17	Македония
18	Словения
19	Польша
20	Чехия
21	Словакия
22	Венгрия
23	Румыния
24	Болгария

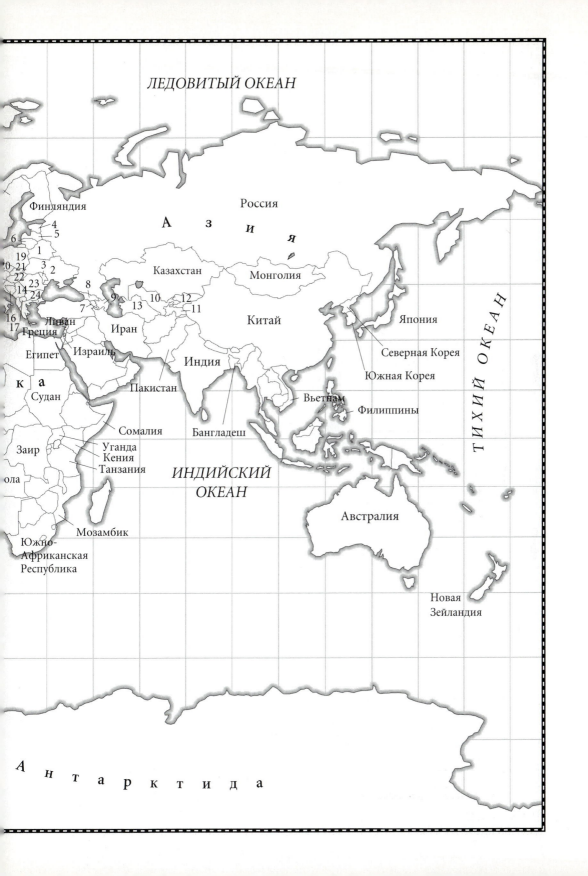

ЛЕДОВИТЫЙ ОКЕАН

Финляндия

Россия

А З И Я

4
5
6
1
19
20 21   3
22   2
14 23
24
16
17   Греция
Ливан

Казахстан

Монголия

Япония

8
9
7   10   12
13   11

Китай

Северная Корея

Южная Корея

Иран

Индия

Израиль

Египет

Пакистан

Вьетнам

Филиппины

Судан

к   а

Сомалия

Бангладеш

Заир

Уганда
Кения
Танзания

ИНДИЙСКИЙ
ОКЕАН

ола

Мозамбик

Австралия

ТИХИЙ ОКЕАН

Южно-
Африканская
Республика

Новая
Зейландия

А   н   т   а   р   к   т   и   д   а

ЛЕДОВИТЫЙ ОКЕАН

Норвегия

Финляндия

Баренцево море

Карское море

Швеция

● Мурманск

Эстония
Латвия

Финский залив

Ладожское озеро

Белое море

Печора

Обь

Енисей

Петрозаводск

● Архангельск

Литва

Псков

Нева

Санкт-Петербург

Онежское озеро

Двина

Беларус

● Вологда

● Тверь (Калинин)

Москва

Смоленск

Калуга

Москва ✪

● Кострома

Р о с с и я

Тула
● Рязань

Курск

Нижний Новгород

Пермь ●

Воронеж

Ижевск

● Екатеринбург

Казань

● Челябинск

Пенза

Самара

● Томск

Уфа

У р а л ы

Ростов-на-Дону

Волга

Саратов

Оренбург

● Омск

● Новосибирск

Чёрное море

Волгоград

Астрахань

Грузия

Кавказ

Каспийское море

Казахстан

Армения

Узбекистан

Азербайджан

Туркменистан

Кыргызстан

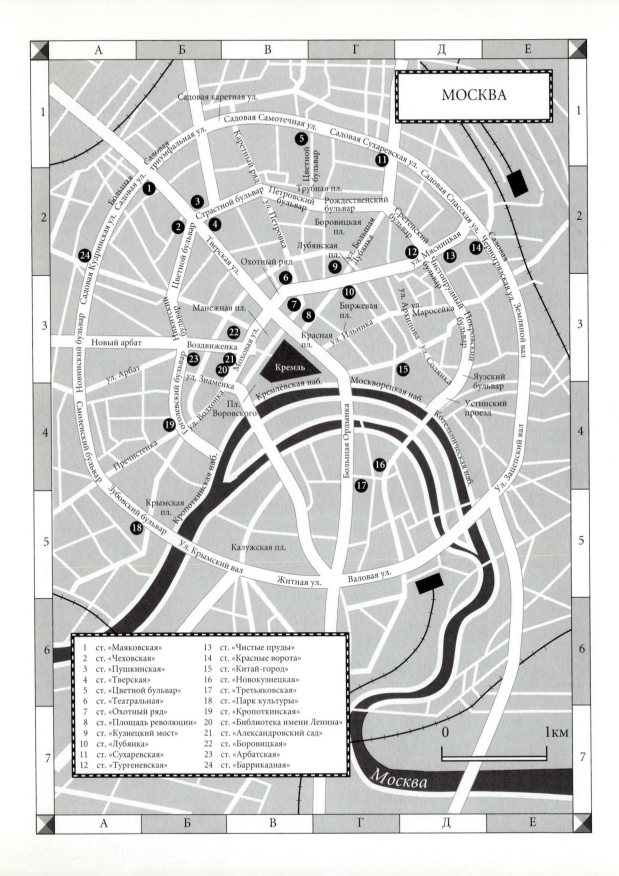

МОСКВА

Садовая каретная ул.

Садовая Самотечная ул.

Садовая Сухаревская ул. Садовая Спасская ул.

Цветной бульвар

Трубная пл.

Рождественский бульвар

Сретенский бульвар

Боровицкая пл.

Лубянская пл.

ул. Большая Лубянка

ул. Мясницкая

Чистопрудный бульвар

Черногрязская ул. Земляной вал

Садовая

Охотный ряд

Манежная пл.

Красная пл.

Биржевая пл.

ул. Ильинка

ул. Маросейка

ул. Архипова

ул. Солянка

Новый арбат

Воздвиженка

Моховая ул.

Кремль

Яузский бульвар

Устинский проезд

ул. Арбат

ул. Знаменка

Кремлёвская наб.

Москворецкая наб.

Котельническая наб.

Новинский бульвар

Никитский бульвар

Гоголевский бульвар

ул. Волхонка

Пл. Воровского

Большая Ордынка

ул. Зацепский вал

Пречистенка

Смоленский бульвар

Зубовский бульвар

Кропоткинская наб.

Крымская пл.

Калужская пл.

ул. Крымский вал

Житная ул.

Валовая ул.

Москва

Садовая Кудринская ул. Садовая ул.

Большая Садовая ул. Триумфальная ул.

Каретный ряд

Страстной бульвар

Петровский бульвар

ул. Петровка

Тверская ул.

Страстной бульвар

0 1 км

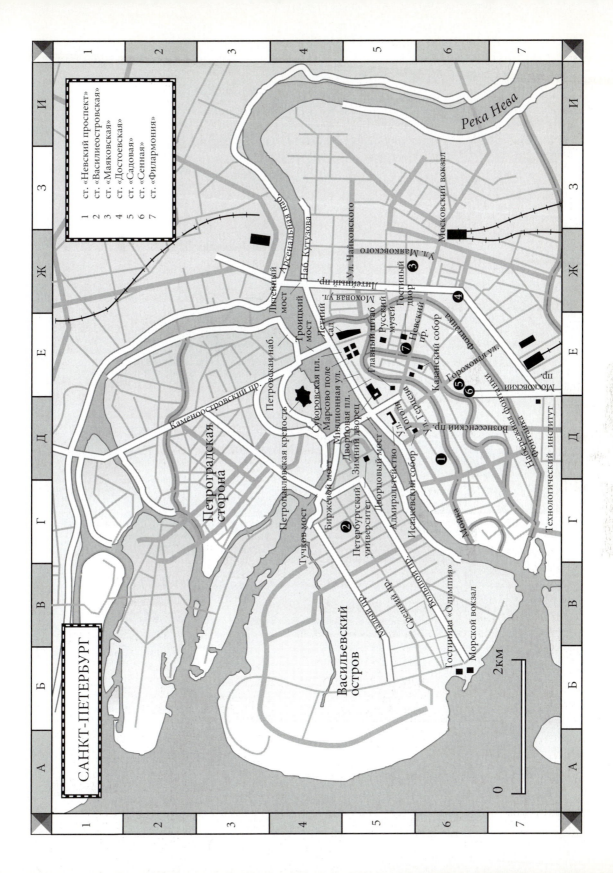

САНКТ-ПЕТЕРБУРГ

1 ст. «Невский проспект»
2 ст. «Василеостровская»
3 ст. «Маяковская»
4 ст. «Достоевская»
5 ст. «Садовая»
6 ст. «Сенная»
7 ст. «Филармония»

Река Нева

Московский вокзал

Ул. Маяковского

Ул. Чайковского

Наб. Кутузова

Арсенальная наб.

Литейный мост

Литейный пр.

Гостиный двор

Моховая ул.

Троицкий мост

Петровская наб.

Каменноостровский пр.

Петроградская сторона

Петропавловская крепость

Летний сад

Главный штаб

Русский музей

Невский пр.

Казанский собор

Гороховая ул.

Московский пр.

Набережная фонтанки

Суворовская пл.
Марсово поле
Миллионная ул.

Дворцовая пл.

Зимний дворец

Дворцовый мост

Биржевой мост

Тучков мост

Петербургский университет

Васильевский остров

Средний пр.

Большой пр.

Малый пр.

Адмиралтейство

Исаакиевский собор

ул. Герцена

ул. Гоголя

Вознесенский пр.

Мойка

Технологический институт

Гостиница «Олимпия»

Морской вокзал

0   2 км

Agreement

Согласова́ние

—Э́то действи́тельно интере́сно!

General Introduction

Russian is a highly inflected language. This means that nouns, pronouns and adjectives are declined and verbs are conjugated. Some examples may help you remember the meaning of these words. The sentences below were written by a Russian exchange student enrolled as a graduate student at an American university.

1. Мои родители живут в маленьком городе недалеко от Петербурга.

   My parents live in a small town not far from Petersburg.

2. Мать раньше работала медсестрой, а теперь работает инженером
   в небольшой лаборатории.

   [My] mother used to work as a nurse, but now works as an engineer in a small laboratory.

3. Отец—переводчик: он говорит на трёх языках.

   My father is an interpreter/translator: He speaks three languages.

4. О них я могу писать весь день.

   I could write about them all day long.

5. Я редко езжу домой к родителям, потому что нет денег; поэтому
   я им пишу каждую неделю.

   I rarely go home to my parents, because I have no money (to do so); therefore I write them every week.

6. Здесь я учусь физике и английскому языку, но я также люблю математику.

   Here I study (am a student of) physics and English (language), but I also love mathematics.

In each of the preceding sentences, note the arrows drawn from one word to another, indicating the nature of agreement between words. Now read the commentary about agreement in each sentence.

1. The possessive modifier *my* agrees with the word *parents*: Both are in the nominative case and both are plural. The verb *to live* is conjugated in the third-person plural form to agree with the subject *parents*. The phrase *a small town* is in the prepositional case because it is the object of the preposition *in* in the context of location (rather than movement in a direction). Both the noun and the adjective are

masculine and singular. Petersburg is in the genitive case as required by the preposition *from*.

2. The verb *used to work* agrees in gender (feminine) and number (singular) with the subject *mother*. The noun *nurse* is in the instrumental case (feminine, singular) as required by the verb *to work* in the context of identifying someone's profession. The verb *to work* in the second clause (following the comma) is conjugated in the third-person singular to agree with the implied subject *mother*. The noun *engineer* is in the instrumental case (masculine, singular) because it is used after the verb *to work* as explained above. (Note that this profession is a masculine noun used for both men and women.) The *small laboratory* is in the prepositional case as required by the preposition *in* in the context of location. Both the adjective and the noun are feminine and singular.

3. The two nouns in the first clause of this sentence are in the nominative case because they are the subject and the subject complement. The verb *to speak* is conjugated in the third-person singular to agree with the subject *he*. The number phrase *three languages* is in the prepositional case (plural) because it is the object of the preposition *in/on* and does not denote movement in a direction.

4. The pronoun *them* is in the prepositional case because it is the object of the preposition *about*. This pronoun, like all third person personal pronouns (he, she, it, they), takes the letter **н** when it is the object of a preposition. The verb *can* is conjugated to agree with the subject *I* (the first-person singular pronoun); this verb requires the verb that follows it to be in the infinitive form, as is the case with the verb *to write*. The time expression *all day* is in the accusative case: It is accusative masculine (inanimate) and thus identical in form to the nominative case.

5. The verb *to go* [*by vehicle*] is conjugated to agree with the subject *I*. The form of the word *home* (**домóй**) is a special directional adverb. Verbs of motion generally require that destinations be expressed in a prepositional phrase that takes either the accusative case for places or the preposition **к** and the dative case for people, as shown here. The word *money* is in the genitive case because it is negated. The verb *to write* is conjugated to agree with the subject *I*. The person written to is expressed in the dative case (the pronoun *them*). The time expression *every week* is in the accusative case, feminine singular.

6. The verbs *to study/to be a student of* and *to love* are conjugated to agree with the subject *I*. The words *physics* and *English* [*language*] are in the dative case as required by the reflexive verb *to be a student of*. The word *mathematics* is in the accusative case because it is the object of the verb *to love*.

It isn't expected that you would have been able to write these explanations yourself, or that you remember every one of the rules mentioned. But the explanations should sound familiar to you.

Before you go on, you should review some of the basic grammatical terms (parts of speech) to understand what follows.

TERM	DEFINITION, ENGLISH EXAMPLES	RUSSIAN EXAMPLES (VARIOUS GRAMMATICAL FORMS)
NOUN	Person, place, thing, or idea: Maria, students, letter, Moscow, newspaper	Мария, студéнты, письмóм, Москвý, газéтой
VERB	Action word or word denoting state of being: to be, worked, is a student, are singing, will write out, will be dancing	быть, рабóтала, ýчится, поём, напи́шут, бýдут танцевáть
ADJECTIVE	Word that modifies a noun: good, smart, all, big, these, bad, nasty	хорóший, ýмная, всей, большóе, э́тими, плохýю, злы́м
ADVERB	Word that modifies a verb: well, poorly, interestingly	хорошó, плóхо, интерéсно
PREPOSITION	Word that indicates the relation of a noun or pronoun to another noun: in, at, from, under, between	в, на, от, из, с, под, мéжду
PRONOUN	Word that takes the place of a noun: *Personal Pronouns* I, you, he, she, us, you, them *Interrogative Pronouns* who, what	я, тебя́, он, онá, нам, вас, и́ми кто, что
INTERJECTION	*Exclamation* Oh! Wow!	Ах! Ох! Эх!
CONJUNCTION	and, or, but, therefore	и, и́ли, а/но, поэ́тому

 Упражнéние 1а

Examine the dictionary assigned by your instructor for this course and find its list of abbreviations for the grammatical terms described in the chart. How does the dictionary identify nouns, verbs, adjectives, adverbs, prepositions, pronouns, interjections, and conjunctions?

 ТЕКСТ 1а

Read the "nonsense poem" by Khlebnikov that is built on word play revolving around the root **смех/смей**, meaning *laughter*.

Pre-reading Task

What is a "nonsense poem"? Why do we write them and why do we read them? As you read, think of any nonsense poems in English with which you could compare this one.

Заклятие смéхом[1]

О, рассмéйтесь, смехачи́!
О, засмéйтесь смехачи́!
Что смею́тся смехáми, что смея́нствуют
     смея́льно.
 О, засмéйтесь усмея́льно!
О рассмéшищ надсмея́льных—смех усмéйных
     смехачéй!
О иссмéйся рассмея́льно, смех надсмéйных
     смеячéй!
 Смéйево, смéйево,
Усмéй, осмéй, смéшики, смéшики.
 Смею́нчики, смею́нчики:
О рассмéйтесь, смехачи́!
О, засмéйтесь, смехачи́!

В. В. Хлéбников, 1910

[1] *Incantation by laughter*

Post-reading Task

After you read the text through twice, try to identify the parts of speech of the underlined words. Remember that many of the words in this poem are "made up" by the poet.

ТЕКСТ 16

Read the famous text below (the opening of L. N. Tolstoy's *Anna Karenina*) about how a family and its servants react to a husband's affair.

Pre-reading Task

Write down two or three things you expect to read about, given the preceding information. Then write down two or three words you expect to find in the text.

Все счастли́вые[1] сéмьи похóжи друг на дрýга, кáждая несчастли́вая[2] семья́ несчáстлива по-своéму.[3]
   Всё смешáлось[4] в дóме Облóнских. Женá узнáла,[5] что муж был в свя́зи[6] с бы́вшею в их дóме францýженкою-гувернáнткой, и объяви́ла[7] мýжу, что не мóжет жить с ним в однóм дóме. Положéние[8] это

[1] *happy*
[2] *unhappy*
[3] *in its own way*
[4] *was confused*
[5] *found out*
[6] *affair*
[7] *announced*
[8] *situation*

продолжа́лось уже́ тре́тий день и мучи́тельно чу́вствовалось и сами́ми супру́гами,[9] и все́ми чле́нами семьи́, и домоча́дцами.[10] Все чле́ны семьи́ и домоча́дцы чу́вствовали, что нет смы́сла в их сожи́тельстве[11] и что на ка́ждом посто́ялом дворе́[12] случа́йно соше́дшиеся лю́ди[13] бо́лее свя́заны ме́жду собо́й, чем они́, чле́ны семьи́ и домоча́дцы Обло́нских. Жена́ не выходи́ла из свои́х ко́мнат, му́жа тре́тий день не́ было до́ма.

Л. Н. Толсто́й, «А́нна Каре́нина», 1877

[9] чу́вствовалось... *was felt by the spouses themselves*
[10] все́ми... *all the members of the family and servants*
[11] *cohabitation*
[12] посто́ялом... *inn*
[13] случа́йно... *people who have come together randomly*

10

Post-reading Tasks

1. Draw arrows in the passage to indicate how each underlined word agrees with other words or the preposition that governs it. On a separate piece of paper identify the part of speech of each underlined word.
2. How does the narrator convey that the confusion in the Oblonsky home had gone on for three days? (What verb and time expression are used to convey this information?)
3. How many times does the narrator use the words *family*, *home*, and *servants* in this short passage? Why do you think the narrator repeats these words so many times?
4. Rewrite the passage by setting it in a middle-class family in your hometown today.

Gender°

род

Russian has three genders: masculine, feminine, and neuter. Every noun in Russian is assigned one of these genders according to the rules shown in the chart below.

МУЖСКО́Й РОД (*Masculine*)	ЖЕ́НСКИЙ РОД (*Feminine*)	СРЕ́ДНИЙ РОД (*Neuter*)
All nouns ending in a consonant Some nouns ending in soft sign All nouns referring to males, including names and relationships with "typically" feminine endings: па́па, дя́дя, Ми́ша, Па́ша.	All nouns ending in -**a** or -**я** except those denoting males and those ending in -**мя** (which are neuter) All nouns ending in -**чь**, -**шь**, -**жь**, and -**щь** Some nouns ending in soft sign	All nouns ending in -**о**, -**е** or -**ё** All nouns ending in -**мя**: и́мя, вре́мя Many foreign words that are indeclinable

There are, of course, many exceptions to these general rules. Here are the most common.

- The word **ко́фе** is masculine.

- The words **челове́к**, **друг**, **врач**, and **до́ктор** are masculine and take masculine adjectives even when referring to women: **Она́—хоро́ший челове́к.**
- The words **сирота́** (*orphan*), **пла́кса** (*crybaby*), **пья́ница** (*drunkard*), and **уби́йца** (*murderer*) are of common gender. They may be either masculine or feminine depending on the context: **Он ужа́сный пья́ница. Она́ то́же ужа́сная пья́ница!**

Remember how to ask and answer questions about the gender of nouns.

> Како́го ро́да э́то сло́во?
> Мужско́го/Же́нского/Сре́днего ро́да.

✳ Упражне́ние 16

Referring to the gender chart, identify the gender of each of the nouns listed below. Note that the nouns in the left-hand column are singular, while the nouns in the right-hand column are plural. To determine the gender of the plural nouns, you must consider their singular form!

1. студе́нт
2. письмо́
3. студе́нтка

4. профессора́
5. до́чери
6. заня́тия

PART 3
Hard and Soft Endings

To determine which case endings you need to use for any noun or adjective, you must first determine whether that noun or adjective has a hard or soft stem. In order to do this, you must recall how to recognize hard- and soft-stem endings. The Russian alphabet consists of thirty-three letters, of which ten are vowels (**а, я, о, ё, у, ю, э, е, ы, и**), twenty-one are consonants (**б, в, г, д, ж, з, й, к, л, м, н, п, р, с, т, ф, х, ц, ч, ш, щ**), and two are neither vowels nor consonants (**ь, ъ**). Of the twenty-one consonants, three are always hard, three are always soft, and fifteen may be either hard or soft depending on the context in which they occur.

> Group 1: Always Hard   ж, ш, ц
> Group 2: Always Soft   й, ч, щ
> Group 3: Hard or Soft   All Others

If a noun or adjective stem (that part of the word that precedes the grammatical case and gender ending) ends in a hard consonant, it is a hard-stem noun or adjective; if it ends in a soft consonant, it is a soft-stem noun or adjective. How, then, can you tell if a stem is hard or soft if it ends with a consonant of Group 3? You must look at the letter following that consonant.

Твёрдые согла́сные°

hard consonants

Group 3 consonants are *hard* if they are

- followed by a hard-series vowel (**а**, **о**, **у**, **э**, **ы**): **окно́**
- word-final: **стол**
- followed by another hard consonant: **стол**

Мя́гкие согла́сные°

soft consonants

Group 3 consonants are *soft* if they are

- followed by the soft sign: **мать**
- followed by a soft-series vowel (**я**, **ё**, **ю**, **е**, **и**): **и́мя**
- followed by another soft consonant: **борщ**

✵   Упражне́ние 1в

Referring to the chart and explanations, determine whether the stem of each word below is hard (**Т**) or soft (**М**) and mark them accordingly.

1. студе́нт
2. письмо́
3. студе́нтка

4. профессора́
5. до́чери
6. заня́тия

✵   Упражне́ние 1г

Compare your answers from **Упражне́ния 1б** with those of **Упражне́ния 1в** and determine whether there is any relationship between the gender of a noun and its hard or soft stem.

PART 4

The Case System

Russian has six cases, as shown in the following chart.

ENGLISH CASE NAME	RUSSIAN CASE NAME 1	RUSSIAN CASE NAME 2
NOMINATIVE	имени́тельный	кто? что?
ACCUSATIVE	вини́тельный	кого́? что?
GENITIVE	роди́тельный	кого́? чего́?
DATIVE	да́тельный	кому́? чему́?
PREPOSITIONAL	предло́жный	о ком? о чём?
INSTRUMENTAL	твори́тельный	кем? чем?

Russians refer to these cases using either the actual case name (Case Name 1) or a shorthand for the case name that consists of the declension, in the given case, of the interrogative pronouns *who* and *what*.

Later, we will review the endings for each case and the basic constructions that require the use of that case. Now, however, we need to recall the structure of the case system as a whole. Most important, adjectives must agree in case, gender, and number (singular or plural) with the nouns they modify.

Remember how to ask and answer questions about case.

> В како́м падеже́ стои́т э́то сло́во?
> Оно́ стои́т в имени́тельном/вини́тельном/роди́тельном/да́тельном/ предло́жном/твори́тельном падеже́.

✳ Упражне́ние 1д

In the sentences below, identify the case and the number (singular or plural) of each underlined noun + adjective phrase; if the phrase is singular, identify its gender (masculine, feminine, or neuter) as well. Use the declension charts in the Appendix to help you identify the endings. English translations are provided to help make the task easier.

	SENTENCE	CASE	NUMBER/ GENDER
1.	Она́ живёт в <u>небольшо́м го́роде</u>. *She lives in a small city.*		
2.	Ми́ша сейча́с говори́т со <u>свои́м ста́ршим бра́том</u>. *Misha is talking with his older brother.*		
3.	Они́ пи́шут <u>свое́й ма́тери</u> три ра́за в ме́сяц. *They write to their mother three times a month.*		
4.	В э́том го́роде нет <u>хоро́ших музе́ев</u>. *There aren't any good museums in this city.*		
5.	На <u>сле́дующей неде́ле</u> мы е́дем в Москву́. *We're going to Moscow next week.*		
6.	В про́шлом году́ мы бы́ли в <u>двух бы́вших сове́тских респу́бликах</u>. *Last year we were in two former Soviet republics.*		

Saying

Лихá бедá—начáло.

A beginning is a terrible misfortune.
[The beginning is the hardest part.]

The Verbal System

Russian has three tenses and two aspects as depicted below.

	ПРОШÉДШЕЕ ВРÉМЯ (*Past Tense*)	NONPAST TENSES	
		НАСТОЯ́ЩЕЕ ВРÉМЯ (*Present Tense*)	БУДУ́ЩЕЕ ВРÉМЯ (*Future Tense*)
НЕСОВЕРШÉННЫЙ ВИД (*Imperfective Aspect*)	[онá] писáла *was writing*	[онá] пи́шет *is writing*	[онá] бу́дет писáть *will be writing*
СОВЕРШÉННЫЙ ВИД (*Perfective Aspect*)	[онá] написáла *wrote out*	Ø	[онá] напи́шет *will write out*

Russian verb forms must agree in person and number with the subject noun or pronoun in the so-called nonpast forms (i.e., present and future tenses for the imperfective verbs, future tense for the perfective verbs). In the past tense, Russian verbs must agree in gender and/or number with the subject noun or pronoun. The imperfective future is a "compound tense" consisting of two words, one of which is a "helping" or "auxiliary" verb, much like the English form *will do*. All Russian tenses are simple verb forms except the imperfective future.

In order to understand the conjugation system, you must recall the personal pronouns with which the verb forms must agree.

	ЕДИ́НСТВЕННОЕ ЧИСЛÓ (*Singular*)	МНÓЖЕСТВЕННОЕ ЧИСЛÓ (*Plural*)
ПÉРВОЕ ЛИЦÓ (*First Person*)	я	мы
ВТОРÓЕ ЛИЦÓ (*Second Person*)	ты	вы
ТРÉТЬЕ ЛИЦÓ (*Third Person*)	он, онá, онó	они́

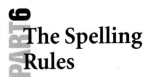   Упражнéние 1e

Circle the subject of each sentence and draw an arrow to the verb with which the subject agrees. If the subject is a pronoun, identify it as first, second, or third person, singular or plural; if the subject is a noun, find the pronoun that matches it and then identify that pronoun as above. Next, identify the tense and aspect of the verb.

1. Онá живёт в небольшóм гóроде.
   Pronoun:

   Verb:

2. Звонúли Юра и Пóля.
   Pronoun:

   Verb:

3. Олéг нам расскáжет об э́том.
   Pronoun:

   Verb:

4. Вы не знáете, гдé здесь туалéт?
   Pronoun:

   Verb:

5. Зáвтра я бýду весь день лежáть в постéли.
   Pronoun:

   Verb:

PART 6
The Spelling Rules

Russian has three simple spelling rules you should memorize!

---

1. After **г, к, х, ж, ч, ш, щ**, never write **ы**, write **и** instead.
2. After **г, к, х, ж, ч, ш, щ, ц**, never write **ю** or **я**, write **у** or **а** instead.
3. After **ж, ч, ш, щ, ц**, never write unstressed **о**, write **е** instead.
Exceptions: Foreign words (especially place names), including **шоколáд, брошюра, шофёр, парашют**.

※   Упражнéние 1ё

According to the three spelling rules, fill in the blanks with the missing letters, choosing from the letters given.

1. ы/и   Как_____е хорóш_____е кни́г_____!
What great books!

2. о/е   Я óчень люблю́ Достоéвск_____го! Он мой люби́мый писáтель.
I really love Dostoevsky! He's my favorite writer.

3. у/ю   Антóн! У меня́ высóкая температýра. Я идý к врач_____́.
Anton! I have a high temperature. I'm going to the doctor's.

4. а/я   У меня́ нет мóдного плащ_____́: нáдо купи́ть нóвый плащ.
I don't have a fashionable raincoat: I'll have to buy a new one.

5. а/я   Эти студéнты ýч_____тся в Пенсильвáнском университéте.
These students are enrolled at the University of Pennsylvania.

6. о/е   Онá знáет хорóш_____го специали́ста.
She knows a good specialist.

7. о/е   Вчерá мы бы́ли в пéрвый раз в Больш_____́м теáтре.
Yesterday we were in the Bolshoi Theater for the first time.

The Verbal System:
Second-conjugation Verbs

Глаго́льная систе́ма: Второ́е спряже́ние

Интервью́ с ветера́ном би́твы Сталингра́да.

PART 1 General Introduction: First or Second Conjugation?

Russian verbs may be grouped into three general classes:

- first-conjugation, or **-ут/-ют**, verbs (the **они** form ending of the verb)
- second-conjugation, or **-ат/-ят**, verbs (the **они** form ending)
- truly irregular verbs, of which there are only four in the entire Russian language!

There is one important rule to remember about verbs of the first and second conjugations: It is *often* impossible to tell from the infinitive whether a verb belongs to the first- or second-conjugation class.

First-conjugation verbs feature the vowel **-e-** or **-ё-** in every conjugated (nonpast) form except the **я** and **они** forms, which have the vowel **-у-** or **-ю-**; some first-conjugation verbs include **читáть** (**читáю, читáешь, читáют**); **писáть** (**пишý, пи́шешь, пи́шут**); **пить** (**пью, пьёшь, пьют**); **идти́** (**идý, идёшь, идýт**).

Second-conjugation verbs feature the vowel **-и-** in every conjugated (nonpast) form except the **я** form (which has **-у** or **-ю**) and the **они** form (which has the vowel **-а-** or **-я-**). Some second-conjugation verbs include **говори́ть** (**говорю́, говори́шь, говоря́т**); **лежáть** (**лежý, лежи́шь, лежáт**); **смотрéть** (**смотрю́, смо́тришь, смо́трят**); **купи́ть** (**куплю́, кýпишь, кýпят**).

Don't trust the infinitive, except for the four types of verbs shown below, which are among the most common verb types.

Four Predictable Infinitives

1. **-овать/-евать**   *Always first conjugation* with syllabic alternation **-уй-**: **сове́товать, сове́тую, сове́туешь, сове́туют**

2. **-нуть**   *Always first conjugation*: **верну́ться, верну́сь, вернёшься, верну́тся**, or **привы́кнуть, привы́кну, привы́кнешь, привы́кнут**

3. **-ывать/-ивать**   *Always first conjugation*: **расскáзывать, расскáзываю, расскáзываешь, расскáзывают** and *always imperfective aspect*

4. polysyllabic **-ить**   *Always second conjugation*: **купи́ть, куплю́, кýпишь, кýпят**. (Note that verbs of this type must be polysyllabic; monosyllabic verbs ending in **-ить** are first-conjugation verbs, such as **жить, живý, живёшь, живýт**, or **пить, пью, пьёшь, пьют**.)

Except for these four verb types, it is impossible to predict the conjugation of a Russian verb on the basis of the infinitive alone.

Many American students of Russian overgeneralize about verbs whose infinitives end in **-ать** or **-ять**; they believe that the conjugation pattern for such infinitives is analogous to that of **читáть** or **теря́ть**. This is not necessarily true! Consider the conjugation of each of the following verbs.

	ждать (*to wait*)	**дава́ть** (*to give*)	**крича́ть** (*to shout*)	**стоя́ть** (*to stand*)	**снять** (*to remove*)
я	жду	даю́	кричу́	стою́	сниму́
ты	ждёшь	даёшь	кричи́шь	стои́шь	сни́мешь
он/а́	ждёт	даёт	кричи́т	стои́т	сни́мет
мы	ждём	даём	кричи́м	стои́м	сни́мем
вы	ждёте	даёте	кричи́те	стои́те	сни́мете
они́	ждут	даю́т	крича́т	стоя́т	сни́мут
ИМПЕРАТИ́В	жди(те)!	дава́й(те)!	кричи́(те)!	сто́й(те)!	сними́(те)!

As you can see from this chart, just because an infinitive ends in **-ать** or **-ять** doesn't mean that it is a first-conjugation verb (unless it is really an **-овать/-евать** or **-ывать/-ивать** verb). The only way you can be sure of the conjugation is to check it in your textbook or a good reference book.

Furthermore, just because an infinitive ends in **-ить/-ыть** or **-еть** doesn't mean that it is a second-conjugation verb. Consider the conjugation of each of the following verbs.

	уме́ть (*to be able*)	**смотре́ть** (*to watch*)	**пить** (*to drink*)	**жить** (*to live*)	**откры́ть** (*to open*)
я	уме́ю	смотрю́	пью	живу́	откро́ю
ты	уме́ешь	смо́тришь	пьёшь	живёшь	откро́ешь
он/а́	уме́ет	смо́трит	пьёт	живёт	откро́ет
мы	уме́ем	смо́трим	пьём	живём	откро́ем
вы	уме́ете	смо́трите	пьёте	живёте	откро́ете
они́	уме́ют	смо́трят	пьют	живу́т	откро́ют
ИМПЕРАТИ́В	уме́й(те)!	смотри́(те)!	пе́й(те)!	живи́(те)!	откро́й(те)!

As you can see from this chart, just because an infinitive ends in **-ить/-ыть** or **-еть** doesn't mean that it is a second-conjugation verb.

✳ Упражне́ние 2a

Look at the verbs in the glossaries of Units 1 and 2 in the *Workbook*. Which verbs are first conjugation and which are second conjugation?

PART 2
Second-conjugation Verbs

Second-conjugation verbs have a limited range of patterns that makes them easier for many students to learn. (That's why this book presents the second-conjugation verbs first.) A "prototype" for each pattern is presented below, but first there is one basic rule you should remember about second-conjugation verbs concerning consonantal mutation. A consonantal mutation is the term that describes the transformation of one consonant, usually found in the infinitive, into another consonant found in one or more of the conjugated forms of the verb. If a second-conjugation verb has a consonantal mutation, then the mutation will occur in the **я** form *only*. The consonantal mutation will *not* occur in the imperative form.

COMMON SECOND-CONJUGATION MUTATION TYPES		
IN THE INFINITIVE	IN THE NONPAST*	SECOND-CONJUGATION VERBS
с	ш	спроси́ть: спрошу́, спро́сишь, спро́сят
з	ж	вози́ть: вожу́, во́зишь, во́зят
д	ж	ви́деть: ви́жу, ви́дишь, ви́дят
ст	щ	чи́стить: чи́щу, чи́стишь, чи́стят
т	ч	заме́тить: замечу́, заме́тишь, заме́тят
б	бль	люби́ть: люблю́, лю́бишь, лю́бят
в	вль	лови́ть: ловлю́, ло́вишь, ло́вят
м	мль	знако́мить: знако́млю, знако́мишь, знако́мят
п	пль	купи́ть: куплю́, ку́пишь, ку́пят

* Remember, nonpast verb forms are the conjugated verb forms (present tense of imperfective verbs and future tense of perfective verbs).

Note that in all second-conjugation verbs, mutations occur *only* in the **я** form, as in the examples above. Furthermore, the soft sign used in the last four mutation types indicates that the "epenthetic **л**" (the **л** that appears in the mutated form) is soft, as evidenced by the soft-series vowel **ю** that follows this letter.

There are a limited number of types of verbs of the second conjugation. A few verbs of each prototype are listed to help you recognize the range of patterns among second-conjugation verbs.

Second-conjugation Prototypes

In the list below, key features of each prototype are emphasized. Note that all second-conjugation verbs that have mutations will feature the mutation in the **я** form *only*.

1. проси́ть   *to request:* прошу́, про́сишь, про́сят, проси́л, проси́ла, проси́ли, проси́(те)!

OTHER EXAMPLES

говори́ть   *to say:* говор**ю́**, говори́шь, говоря́т

гото́вить   *to prepare, to cook:* гото́в**лю**, гото́вишь, гото́вят

купи́ть   *to buy:* куп**лю́**, ку́пишь, ку́пят

люби́ть   *to like, to love:* люб**лю́**, лю́бишь, лю́бят

знако́мить   *to acquaint:* знако́м**лю**, знако́мишь, знако́мят

вози́ть   *to transport by vehicle:* вож**у́**, во́зишь, во́зят

води́ть   *to lead on foot:* вож**у́**, во́дишь, во́дят

	отве́тить	*to answer:* отве́**ч**у, отве́тишь, отве́тят
	хвали́ть	*to praise:* хва**лю́**, хва́лишь, хва́лят
2.	смотре́ть	*to watch:* смот**рю́**, смо́тришь, смо́трят, смотре́л, смотре́ла, смотре́ли, смотри́(те)!

OTHER EXAMPLES

	ви́деть	*to see:* ви́**ж**у, ви́дишь, ви́дят
	висе́ть	*to be hanging:* ви**шу́**, виси́шь, вися́т
	лете́ть	*to fly, unidirectional:* ле**чу́**, лети́шь, летя́т
3.	держа́ть	*to hold:* дер**жу́**, де́р**жи**шь, де́р**жа**т, держа́л, держа́ла, держа́ли, держи́(те)!

OTHER EXAMPLES

	слы́шать	*to hear:* слы́**ш**у, слы́**ши**шь, слы́**ша**т
	крича́ть	*to shout:* кри**чу́**, кри**чи́**шь, кри**ча́**т
	лежа́ть	*to lie:* ле**жу́**, ле**жи́**шь, ле**жа́**т

Exceptions

4.	спать	*to sleep:* сплю, спишь, спят, спал, спала́, спа́ли, спи(те)!
5.	стоя́ть	*to stand:* стою, стои́шь, стоя́т, стоя́л, стоя́ла, стоя́ли, сто́й(те)!
6.	боя́ться	*to fear:* бою́сь, бои́шься, боя́тся, боя́лся, боя́лась, боя́лись, бо́йся/бо́йтесь!

The verbs **стоя́ть** and **боя́ться** are the only two second-conjugation verbs with infinitives ending in **-ять, -яться**. All other verbs whose infinitives end in **-ять** or **-яться** are first-conjugation verbs (like **взять** and **теря́ться**).

✳ Упражне́ние 2б

Create a section in your notebook dedicated to verb conjugation. Set aside a page for each prototype and its conjugation. For each verb write down the infinitive, imperative, nonpast forms, and past-tense forms. Note the stress pattern of each verb, because the stress patterns of verbs for each prototype do vary. Add to this list as you continue with this book.

✳ Упражне́ние 2в

Look at the second-conjugation verbs in the *Workbook* glossaries for Units 1 and 2 and divide them into the three major prototypes listed here.

✳ Упражне́ние 2г

Which second-conjugation prototypes have mutations? Which second-conjugation verbs have infinitives that might look like first-conjugation verbs?

Saying

Лю́бишь ката́ться, люби́ и са́ночки вози́ть.

If you like to go sledding, you should enjoy pulling the sled uphill.
[If you want to hear the music, you have to pay the piper.]

ТЕКСТ 2a

Read the excerpt from Chekhov's play *The Seagull* in which Treplev, the son of an actress, talks with his uncle (his mother's brother) about whether his mother loves him and whether she likes the play he has written.

Pre-reading Task

Given the topics of this text (acting, mother and son relations), what words and ideas do you expect to find in it?

ТРЕПЛЁВ. ...Психологи́ческий курьёз—моя́ мать...здесь, в дере́вне,[1]... она́ скуча́ет и зли́тся,[2] и все мы—её враги́,[3] все мы винова́ты.[4] Зате́м она́ суеве́рна,[5] бои́тся трёх свече́й,[6] трина́дцатого числа́. Она́ скупа́.[7] У неё в Оде́ссе в ба́нке се́мьдесят ты́сяч—э́то я зна́ю наве́рное. А попроси́ у неё взаймы́,[8] она́ ста́нет пла́кать.[9]

5 СО́РИН. Ты вообрази́л,[10] что твоя́ пье́са[11] не нра́вится ма́тери, и уже́ волну́ешься[12] и всё. Успоко́йся, мать тебя́ обожа́ет.[13]

ТРЕПЛЁВ. (*обрыва́я у цветка́ лепестки́.*[14]) Лю́бит—не лю́бит, лю́бит— не лю́бит, лю́бит—не лю́бит. (*Смеётся.*) Ви́дишь, моя́ мать меня́ не лю́бит. Ещё бы![15] Ей хо́чется[16] жить, люби́ть, носи́ть све́тлые 10 ко́фточки,[17] а мне уже́ два́дцать пять лет, и я постоя́нно напомина́ю ей,[18] что она́ уже́ не молода́. Когда́ меня́ нет, ей то́лько три́дцать два го́да, при мне[19] же со́рок три, и за э́то она́ меня́ ненави́дит.[20] Она́ зна́ет та́кже, что я не признаю́[21] теа́тра. Она́ лю́бит теа́тр, ей ка́жется, что она́ 15 слу́жит челове́честву, свято́му иску́сству,[22] а по-мо́ему, совреме́нный теа́тр—э́то рути́на, предрассу́док.[23]

А. П. Че́хов, «Ча́йка», 1896

[1] *in the countryside*
[2] *gets bored and angry*
[3] *enemies*
[4] *guilty*
[5] *superstitious*
[6] трёх... *three candles*
[7] *miserly*
[8] *loan*
[9] ста́нет... *begins to cry*
[10] *imagined*
[11] *play*
[12] *are worried*
[13] *adores*
[14] обрыва́я... *ripping off the petals of a flower one by one*
[15] *If only!*
[16] Ей... *She feels like*
[17] све́тлые... *bright sweaters*
[18] постоя́нно... *constantly remind her*
[19] при... *in my presence*
[20] за... *hates me for this*
[21] *recognize (respect)*
[22] слу́жит... *serves humanity, sacred art*
[23] рути́на... *routine, prejudice*

Post-reading Tasks

1. What do you think the word **курьёз** means, given the context in which it is used? Hint: What part of speech is this word?
2. What are Treplev's mother's superstitions? Does your culture share the same superstitions?
3. Write a summary of Treplev's characterization of his mother.
4. Note whether each underlined verb in the passage is a first-conjugation, second-conjugation, or irregular verb, then identify the conjugation prototype for second-conjugation verbs, using a dictionary or other reference book as necessary.
5. Assume the point of view of someone famous and write a paragraph describing your relationship with a parent or sibling.

✳ Упражне́ние 2д

Look at the list of infinitives below and use a reference book or the glossary to determine the prototype to which the verbs belong.

1. учи́ться
2. веле́ть
3. останови́ть
4. принадлежа́ть
5. молча́ть
6. носи́ть

ТЕКСТ 2б

The text below is a short article giving instructions on training a Caucasian shepherd puppy.

Pre-reading Task

What would be your recommendations on training a dog? List three important points.

Начина́я занима́ться со щенко́м,[1] запо́мните три пра́вила:[2] нельзя́ крича́ть, бить, торопи́ть.[3] Он не воспринима́ет[4] крик, озлобля́ется,[5] е́сли его́ бьют, и по́лностью отключа́ется,[6] е́сли торо́пят.

5   Наприме́р. Вы обуча́ете щенка́ кома́нде сади́ться.[7] Споко́йным, чётким го́лосом произнеси́те[8] кома́нду, покажи́те кусо́чек ла́комства, зажа́тый у вас в ладо́ни,[9] и подожди́те.[10] Кавка́зская овча́рка снача́ла ду́мает и то́лько по́сле [э́того] выполня́ет[11] [кома́нду].

10   Е́сли при отрабо́тке[12] како́й-либо кома́нды вы сорвали́сь,[13]

[1] начина́я... *Beginning to work with a puppy*
[2] запо́мните... *remember 3 rules*
[3] нельзя́... *don't yell, hit/beat or hurry*
[4] не... *doesn't understand*
[5] *gets angry (mean)*
[6] по́лностью... *completely tunes out*
[7] Вы... *You're teaching your puppy the command to sit*
[8] Споко́йным... *with a calm, even voice, pronounce*
[9] покажи́те... *show a tasty treat hidden in your palm*
[10] *wait*
[11] *carry it out*
[12] при... *as you're working out*
[13] *you broke form*

удáрили[14] собáку, считáйте, что в течéние мéсяца, как
мúнимум,[15] онá éту комáнду выполнять не бýдет. Потомý что
собáка дýмает: «Я началá чтó-то дéлать, а меня за éто[16]
удáрили». Пóсле тогó как вы научúли собáку однóй какóй-
либо комáнде, похвалúте[17] её, отпустúте побéгать.[18]

[14] *hit (struck)*
[15] в... *for a month at least*
[16] за... *for this/that*
[17] *praise*
[18] отпустúте... *let her out to run*

15

Post-reading Tasks

1. Two different words are used to refer to the dog being trained in the text above. What are these words? (Why is the dog sometimes referred to with masculine and sometimes feminine third-person pronouns?)
2. What are the three most important rules in training a dog?
3. If you break one of the rules and hit a dog while trying to train it, what are the likely results?
4. Note whether each underlined verb in the passage is a first-conjugation, second-conjugation, or irregular verb. Then, for second-conjugation verbs, identify the prototype, using a dictionary or other reference book as necessary.
5. Write a paragraph or two continuing the topic of how to train a dog or why you agree or disagree with the author of this text.

Irregular Verbs

The truly irregular verbs are neither first- nor second-conjugation verbs. First-conjugation verbs are presented in the next unit. Before we turn to those verbs, the four irregular verbs are listed and conjugated for you here.

ИНФИНИТИ́В	хоте́ть *(to want)*	дать *(to give)* *(perfective)*	бежа́ть *(to run)* *(unidirectional)*	есть *(to eat)*
я	хочу́	дам	бегу́	ем
ты	хо́чешь	дашь	бежи́шь	ешь
он, она́, оно́	хо́чет	даст	бежи́т	ест
мы	хоти́м	дади́м	бежи́м	еди́м
вы	хоти́те	дади́те	бежи́те	еди́те
они́	хотя́т	даду́т	бегу́т	едя́т
ИМПЕРАТИ́В	Ø	да́й(те)!	беги́(те)!	е́шь(те)!
ПРОШЕ́ДШЕЕ ВРЕ́МЯ	хоте́л хоте́ла хоте́ли	дал дала́ да́ли	бежа́л бежа́ла бежа́ли	ел е́ла е́ли

✳ Упражне́ние 2е

Fill in the blanks with the necessary forms of the missing verbs, choosing verbs from the chart of irregular verbs above.

1. Я о́чень (*want*) _____ пойти́ в кино́!
2. Ты ка́ждый день говори́шь, что ты (*want*) _____ идти́ в кино́!
3. Мы все (*want*) _____ пойти́ в кино́!
4. Вы не (*want*) _____ пойти́ в кино́?
5. Неуже́ли Са́ша и Па́ша не (*want*) _____ пойти́ в кино́?!

6. Когда́ ты мне (*will give*) _____ э́ту кни́гу?
7. Я тебе́ её (*will give*) _____ за́втра.
8. Она́ мне (*will give*) _____ кни́гу за́втра.
9. Когда́ вы нам (*will give*) _____ де́ньги?
10. Они́ вам (*will give*) _____ де́ньги че́рез неде́лю.

11. Куда́ ты (*are running*) _____, Са́ша?
12. Я (*am running*) _____ на рабо́ту, я о́чень опа́здываю.
13. Мы все опа́здываем, мы все (*are running*) _____ на рабо́ту.
14. Нет, они́ (*are running*) _____ в кино́: но́вый италья́нский фильм начина́ется в кинотеа́тре «Ви́тязь» в семь часо́в.
15. А вот (*is running*) _____ О́ля на ста́нцию метро́! Интере́сно, куда́ она́ е́дет?

16. Мы вегетариа́нцы, мы не (*eat*) _____ никако́го мя́са.
17. А вы ры́бу (*eat*) _____?
18. Я (*eat*) _____ ры́бу.
19. А О́ля и ры́бы не (*eat*) _____.
20. Анто́н! Предста́вьте себе́! Э́ти америка́нцы не (*eat*) _____ никако́го мя́са!

RUSSIAN

Saying

На ловца́ и зверь бежи́т.

The animal runs right to the hunter.
[Speak of the devil!]

PART 4 Passive Constructions

In English, passive constructions are generally considered awkward. Compare these sentences.

> Active: Sarah fixed the car yesterday.
> Passive: The car was fixed by Sarah yesterday.

In Russian, however, passive constructions are very idiomatic. They are used much more frequently than in English and are not considered awkward. There are several different kinds of passive constructions in Russian.

1. Third-person plural (**они́**) form of the verb with an implicit subject

Сейча́с **стро́ят** но́вую шко́лу на на́шей у́лице.	*A new school is being built on our street now.*
За́втра **бу́дут говори́ть** об э́том.	*It will be discussed tomorrow.*
Говоря́т, что они́ влюби́лись.	*It's said (people are saying) that they fell in love.*
Мне **сказа́ли**, что они́ разошли́сь.	*I was told that they broke up.*

2. A reflexive verb in third-person singular or plural form without a subject

Счита́ется, что э́то—оди́н из лу́чших институ́тов.	*This is considered to be one of the best institutes.*
Ду́мается, что кто́-нибудь пое́дет туда́ в командиро́вку.	*It's thought that someone will go there on a business trip.*

3. A past passive participle (discussed in Unit 19) with a logical subject in the instrumental case (called the "agent" of the action)

Э́та кни́га **была́ напи́сана** мое́й тётей.	*This book was written by my aunt.*
Сла́йды, **сде́ланные** на́шим преподава́телем в Сиби́ри, **бу́дут пока́заны** сего́дня в четы́ре часа́.	*The slides taken by our teacher in Siberia will be shown today at 4:00.*

 ТЕКСТ 2в

Read the excerpt from Akhmatova's narrative poem "Requiem," written in memory of the victims of Stalin's terror.

Pre-reading Task

What words and phrases do you think you might find in a poem about the victims of Stalin's terror? Make some predictions and see if you're right.

Опя́ть помина́льный прибли́зился час.[1]
Я ви́жу, я слы́шу, я чу́вствую вас:
И ту, что едва́ до окна́ довели́,[2]
И ту, что роди́мой не то́пчет земли́,[3]
И ту, что, краси́вой тряхну́в голово́й,[4]
Сказа́ла: «Сюда́ прихожу́, как домо́й».
Хоте́лось бы всех поимённо назва́ть,[5]
Да о́тняли спи́сок, и не́где узна́ть.[6]
Для них соткала́ я широ́кий покро́в[7]
Из бе́дных, у них же подслу́шанных слов.[8]
О них вспомина́ю[9] всегда́ и везде́,[10]
О них не забу́ду и в но́вой беде́,[11]
И е́сли зажму́т мой изму́ченный рот,[12]
Кото́рым кричи́т стомильо́нный наро́д,
Пусть так же они́ помина́ют[13] меня́
В кану́н[14] моего́ помина́льного дня.
А е́сли когда́-нибудь в э́той стране́
Воздви́гнуть заду́мают па́мятник мне,[15]
Согла́сье на э́то даю́ торжество́,[16]
Но то́лько с усло́вьем[17]—не ста́вить его́
Ни о́коло мо́ря,[18] где я родила́сь:
После́дняя с мо́рем разо́рвана связь,[19]
Ни в ца́рском саду́ у заве́тного пня,[20]
Где тень безуте́шная[21] и́щет меня́,
А здесь, где стоя́ла я три́ста часо́в
И где для меня́ не откры́ли засо́в.[22]
Зате́м что и в сме́рти блаже́нной[23] бою́сь
Забы́ть громыха́ние чёрных мару́сь,[24]
Забы́ть, как посты́лая хло́пала дверь[25]
И вы́ла стару́ха,[26] как ра́неный зверь.[27]
И пусть с неподви́жных и бро́нзовых век
Как слёзы струи́тся подта́явший снег,[28]
И го́лубь тюре́мный пусть гу́лит вдали́,[29]
И ти́хо иду́т по Неве́ корабли́.[30]

А. А. Ахма́това, «Ре́квием», 1940

[1] помина́льный... *the death memorial is near*
[2] И... *and the woman whom they were barely able to bring to the window [of the sentry]*
[3] что... *who is no longer alive [who doesn't tramp her native earth]*
[4] краси́вой... *tossing her pretty head of hair*
[5] Хоте́лось... *I'd like to list them all by name*
[6] Да... *the list was taken away, and there is nowhere to find out*
[7] соткала́... *I wove a broad tapestry*
[8] Из... *from the poor words I heard from them*
[9] *recall*
[10] *everywhere*
[11] но́вой... *a new catastrophe*
[12] е́сли... *if my tortured mouth should be gagged*
[13] *remember*
[14] В... *on the eve*
[15] Воздви́гнуть... *conceive of putting up a monument to me*
[16] Согла́сье... *I agree to this ceremony*
[17] то́лько... *only on the condition*
[18] Ни... *not near the sea*
[19] После́дняя... *my last tie with the sea is severed*
[20] Ни... *not in the Tsar's garden near the sacred stump*
[21] тень... *an inconsolable shadow*
[22] *the iron bars*
[23] сме́рти... *blessed death*
[24] громыха́ние... *the roaring of the Black Marias [cars used by secret police]*
[25] как... *how the awful door slammed*
[26] вы́ла... *old woman howled*
[27] ра́неный... *wounded beast*
[28] пусть... *from my still bronze eyelids may the melting snow flow like tears*
[29] го́лубь... *may a prison dove coo in the distance*
[30] ти́хо... *as ships sail quietly on the [river] Neva*

Post-reading Tasks

1. Where does the poet suggest her monument be set up?
2. The first line of the poem includes a reference to the anniversary of a death. Find the Russian word that means *anniversary* or *remembrance* and look for other words in the poem with the same root.

3. Who uses the poet's tortured mouth?
4. Whom does the poet ask to remember her?
5. Find all the passive constructions in the excerpt and identify their type.
6. Find all the second-conjugation verbs in the poem and identify their prototype.

✳   Упражнёние 2ё

Translate the paragraph below with passive constructions into idiomatic English.

В газётах мнóго пи́шут о погóде, когдá в при́нципе нýжно говори́ть не о погóде, а о кли́мате. Мне сказáли, что меня́ется мировóй кли́мат. Говоря́т, что земля́ постепéнно теплéет. В кни́ге, напи́санной Ни́ной Михáйловной Фёдоровой, óчень интерéсное обсуждéние проблéм кли́мата. Считáется, что э́та кни́га—однá из лýчших на тéму кли́мата. Всем, комý интерéсны таки́е вопрóсы, совéтуют прочитáть э́ту кни́гу.

✳   Упражнёние 2ж

Make a list of all the "connecting" words and phrases you can find in the texts of Units 1 and 2, such as *because*, *but*, *in the first place*, *then*, and so forth. Next to each connecting word or phrase, write out the clause or sentence in which they are used. Keep this list in your notebook and add to it as you continue with this book.

First-conjugation Verbs and Verbs with *-ся*

Пе́рвое спряже́ние и глаго́лы с су́ффиксом *-ся*

Андре́евы:
Лю́ба (с ко́шкой «Мотя»), Людми́ла
(с соба́кой «А́льба»), Жо́ра.

PART 1 First-conjugation Verbs

First-conjugation verbs have a larger range of patterns than do second-conjugation verbs. A prototypical verb for each pattern is presented below, but first there are a couple of rules you should remember about first-conjugation verbs.

1. Some first-conjugation verbs may have a syllabic alternation, in which one syllable in the infinitive is altered in the conjugated forms: **совéтовать → совéтую, давáть → даю́, пить → пью, открыть → откро́ю**.

2. If a first-conjugation verb has a consonantal mutation, then the mutation occurs in each conjugated form of the verb and in the imperative. (A consonantal mutation is the term given to describe the transformation of one consonant, usually found in the infinitive, into another consonant found in one or more of the conjugated forms of the verb.) Exception: for all infinitives ending in **-чь**, there is no mutation in the **они́** form or the imperative.

MOST COMMON FIRST-CONJUGATION MUTATION TYPES		
IN THE INFINITIVE	IN THE NONPAST	FIRST-CONJUGATION VERBS
с	ш	писáть: пишу́, пи́шешь, пи́шут
з	ж	сказáть: скажу́, скáжешь, скáжут
ск	щ	искáть: ищу́, и́щешь, и́щут
ч	г/ж	мочь: могу́, мо́жешь, мо́гут
к	ч	плáкать: плáчу, плáчешь, плáчут
т	ч	шептáть: шепчу́, шéпчешь, шéпчут
LESS COMMON FIRST-CONJUGATION MUTATION TYPES		
х	ш	махáть: машу́, мáшешь, мáшут
д	ж	глодáть: гложу́, гло́жешь, гло́жут
б	бль	колебáть: колéблю, колéблешь, колéблют
м	мль	дремáть: дремлю́, дрéмлешь, дрéмлют
п	пль	сы́пать: сы́плю, сы́плешь, сы́плют

First-conjugation Prototypes

In the list below, key features of each prototype are emphasized.

Very Common Prototypes

1. совéт**ова**ть   *to advise:* совéт**ую**, совéт**у**ешь, совéт**ую**т, совéтовал, совéтовала, совéтовали, совéт**уй**(те)!

This prototype also includes the many verbs whose infinitives end in **-евать**, such as

танц**ева́**ть   *to dance:* танц**у́**ю, танц**у́**ешь, танц**у́**ют, танцева́л, танцева́ла, танцева́ли, танцу́й(те)!
Note the importance of the spelling rule for this verb.

This prototype also includes one verb most commonly used in the imperative.

здра́вств**ова**ть   *to be healthy:* здра́вству**ю**, здра́вству**е**шь, здра́вству**ю**т, здра́вствовал, здра́ствовала, здра́ствовали, здра́вству**й**(те)!

2.   де́лать   *to do:* де́ла**ю**, де́ла**е**шь, де́ла**ю**т, де́лал, де́лала, де́лали, де́лай(те)!

This prototype also includes the many verbs whose infinitives end in **-ывать**, such as

откр**ыва́**ть   *to open:* откр**ыва́**ю, откр**ыва́**ешь, откр**ыва́**ют, откр**ыва́**л, откр**ыва́**ла, откр**ыва́**ли, откр**ыва́**й(те)!

3.   дава́ть   *to give:* даю, даёшь, дают, дава́л, дава́ла, дава́ли, **дава́**й(те)!

4.   вер**ну́ть**ся   *to return:* вер**ну́**сь, вер**нё**шься, вер**ну́**тся, вернулся, верну́лась, верну́лись, верни́сь/верни́тесь!

Common Prototypes

5.   пис**а́**ть   *to write:* пишу́, пи́шешь, пи́шут, писа́л, писа́ла, писа́ли, пиши́(те)!

OTHER EXAMPLES

сказ**а́**ть   *to say, tell:* скажу́, ска́жешь, ска́жут, сказа́л, сказа́ла, сказа́ли, скажи́(те)!

пла́к**а**ть   *to cry:* пла́чу, пла́чешь, пла́чут, пла́кал, пла́кала, пла́кали, (не) пла́**чь**(те)!

6.   стать   *to become:* ста́**ну**, ста́**не**шь, ста́**ну**т, стал, ста́ла, ста́ли, ста́**нь**(те)!

7.   уме́ть   *to be able:* уме́**ю**, уме́**е**шь, уме́**ю**т, умёл, умёла, умёли, умёй(те)!

8.   откр**ы́**ть   *to open:* откр**о́**ю, откр**о́**ешь, откр**о́**ют, откры́л, откры́ла, откры́ли, откр**о́**й(те)!

9.   ве**сти́**   *to lead:* веду́, ведёшь, веду́т, вёл, вела́, вели́, веди́(те)!

10. **жить** *to live (Infinitives of this prototype must be monosyllabic.*)*:
    живу́, живёшь, живу́т, жил, жила́, жи́ли, живи́(те)!

11. **пить** *to drink (Infinitives of this prototype must be monosyllabic.*)*:
    пью, пьёшь, пьют, пил, пила́, пи́ли, пей(те)!

12. **ждать** *to wait:* жду, ждёшь, ждут, ждал, ждала́, жда́ли, жди(те)

13. **взять** *to take:* возьму́, возьмёшь, возьму́т, взял, взяла́, взя́ли,
    возьми́(те)!

OTHER EXAMPLES

нача́ть *to begin:* начну́, начнёшь, начну́т, на́чал, начала́, на́чали,
    начни́(те)!

поня́ть *to understand:* пойму́, поймёшь, пойму́т, по́нял, поняла́,
    по́няли, пойми́(те)!

14. **приня́ть** *to accept:* приму́, при́мешь, при́мут, при́нял, приняла́,
    при́няли, прими́(те)!

15. **везти́** *to transport by vehicle:* везу́, везёшь, везу́т, вёз,† везла́, везли́,
    вези́(те)!

16. **привы́к(ну)ть** *to get used to (suffix -ну- drops in past tense):* привы́кну,
    привы́кнешь, привы́кнут, привы́к,† привы́кла, привы́кли,
    привы́кни(те)!

Less Common Prototypes

17. **жать** *to squeeze, to shake [hands]:* жму, жмёшь, жмут (ру́ку), жал,
    жа́ла, жа́ли, жми́(те)!

18. **дуть** *to blow:* ду́ю, ду́ешь, ду́ют, дул, ду́ла, ду́ли, дуй(те)!

19. **печь** *to bake:* пеку́, печёшь, пеку́т, пёк,† пекла́, пекли́, пеки́(те)!

20. **бере́чь** *to save:* берегу́, бережёшь, берегу́т, берёг,† берегла́, берегли́,
    береги́(те)!‡

21. **умере́ть** *to die:* умру́, умрёшь, умру́т, у́мер,† умерла́, у́мерли, умри́(те)!

22. **коло́ть** *to pierce:* колю́, ко́лешь, ко́лют, коло́л, коло́ла, коло́ли,
    коли́(те)!

---

* Except for infinitives with a prefix or suffix: **прожи́ть, напи́ться**.

† Note that the masculine singular past-tense form of these prototypes has no л.

‡ The verb **мочь** also belongs to this prototype, but it has one slight irregularity: its stress pattern. Unlike the standard stress pattern for this prototype, as demonstrated by the verb **бере́чь**, the stress pattern in **мочь** is irregular in that it is shifting in the nonpast: **я могу́, ты мо́жешь, она́ мо́жет, мы мо́жем, вы мо́жете, они́ мо́гут, он мог, она́ могла́, они́ могли́.** This verb has no imperative form.)

Упражне́ние 3а

Look at the verbs in the glossaries for Units 1 through 3. Find all the verbs that are first-conjugation verbs and determine their prototype.

ТЕКСТ 3а

Read the text below, a poem by the symbolist poet Bal'mont about a boat tossed around in the sea as night falls.

Pre-reading Task

Try reading the poem out loud and think about the sounds in the poem. What relationship might the sounds have to the meaning of the poem?

Чёлн томле́нья

Ве́чер. Взмо́рье. Вздо́хи ве́тра.
Велича́вый во́зглас волн.
Бли́зко бу́ря. В бе́рег бьётся
Чу́ждый ча́рам чёрный чёлн.

Чу́ждым чи́стым ча́рам сча́стья,
Чёлн томле́нья, чёлн трево́г
Бро́сил бе́рег, бьётся с бу́рей,
И́щет све́тлых снов черто́г.

Мчи́тся взмо́рьем, мчи́тся мо́рем,
Отдава́ясь во́ле волн.
Ме́сяц ма́товый взира́ет,
Ме́сяц го́рькой гру́сти полн.

У́мер ве́чер. Ночь черне́ет.
Ро́пщет мо́ре. Мра́к растёт.
Чёлн томле́нья тьмой охва́чен.
Бу́ря во́ет в бе́здне вод.

К. Д. Бальмо́нт, 1894

The Skiff of Languor

Evening. The seashore. The sighs of the wind.
The majestic voice of the waves.
The storm is near. Against the shore there beats
A black skiff alien to charms.

Alien to the pure charms of happiness,
The skiff of languor, the skiff of uneasiness
Abandoned the shore, struggles with the storm,
Seeks the mansion of bright dreams.

It rushes along the seashore, it rushes along the sea,
Giving itself up to the will of the waves.
The dull moon looks on,
The bitter moon full of sorrow.

The evening has died. Night becomes black.
The sea murmurs. The gloom grows.
The skiff of languor is encompassed by darkness.
The storm howls in the abyss of waters.

Post-reading Tasks

1. Write a one-sentence summary in English of each stanza of the poem.
2. Find all the words that contain the letters **щ** and **ч**.

3. What do you think the density of these sounds in the poem might mean?
4. Identify the prototypes for each of the underlined verbs in the poem. Try to determine the infinitive for each of the underlined verbs.
5. Try to write a poetic translation of this poem, preserving the sound qualities and rhyme pattern.

ТЕКСТ 3б

Read the psychological self-quiz on competitiveness and cooperativeness in the workplace.

Pre-reading Task

Think about yourself and your own behavior. What do you do when you find yourself involved in a conflict? Are you ready to compromise, or do you seek to maintain your position no matter what the cost? Do you handle conflict well, or do you try to avoid it?

Какой стиль в деловых отношениях характерен для вас, вы узнаете, ответив на вопросы теста.[1] Каждый пункт теста оцените по[2] пятибалльной шкале:

     1—совсем не согласен/согласна[3]

5   2—не согласен/согласна

     3—скорее согласен/согласна

     4—согласен/согласна

     5—полностью согласен/согласна[4]

1. Я человек принципиальный и никогда не меняю[5] своей позиции.

10 2. Мне сложно отстаивать[6] свою позицию, даже если я точно знаю, что прав/á.

3. Трачу много времени на поиски общих точек соприкосновения.[7]

4. Для меня важнее сохранить[8] хорошие отношения, даже если приходится жертвовать[9] своими интересами.

15 5. Я отзываюсь[10] на предложения других, но сам не склонен[11] проявлять инициативу.

6. Из любого[12] конфликта я выхожу победителем.[13]

7. Я избегаю напряжённых[14] ситуаций, хотя дело от этого может пострадать.[15]

20 8. Пересматриваю[16] свою точку зрения, почувствовав в ходе обсуждения[17] свою неправоту.

---

[1] ответив... *having answered the questions in the test*
[2] Каждый... *evaluate each point according to*
[3] совсем... *completely disagree*
[4] полностью... *completely agree*
[5] *change*
[6] *maintain (defend)*
[7] Трачу... *waste a lot of time on the search for points in common*
[8] *preserve*
[9] *sacrifice*
[10] *respond*
[11] *inclined*
[12] *any*
[13] *victor*
[14] *tense (stressful)*
[15] *suffer*
[16] *reconsider*
[17] почувствовав... *having come to feel in the course of discussion*

9. Мно́го вре́мени я уделя́ю[18] пробле́мам други́х и ча́сто забыва́ю о себе́.

10. Я легко́ соглаша́юсь уступи́ть,[19] е́сли и друго́й поступа́ет так же.[20]

11. Продолжа́ю спор до тех пор, пока́ собесе́дник не вы́нужден[21] бу́дет приня́ть мою́ то́чку зре́ния.

12. Я добива́юсь[22] эффекти́вных результа́тов, когда́ рабо́таю под руково́дством бо́лее о́пытного[23] партнёра.

13. С удово́льствием проявля́ю инициати́ву в примире́нии сторо́н.[24]

14. Е́сли э́то сде́лает друго́го счастли́вым,[25] даю́ ему́ возмо́жность настоя́ть на своём.[26]

15. Ча́сто я соглаша́юсь на пе́рвое же усло́вие,[27] кото́рое ведёт к урегули́рованию пробле́мы в отноше́ниях.[28]

Тепе́рь поста́вьте ря́дом с ци́фрами, обознача́ющими ни́же но́мер утвержде́ния, соотве́тствующий балл и подсчита́йте их су́мму:[29]

Сопе́рничество[30]—1, 6, 11;
Избега́ние[31]—2, 7, 12;
Сотру́дничество[32]—3, 8, 13;
Приспособле́ние[33]—4, 9, 14;
Компроми́сс—5, 10, 15.

Стиль счита́ется вы́раженным,[34] е́сли су́мма ба́ллов превыша́ет[35] 10.

[18] dedicate
[19] соглаша́юсь... *agree to yield*
[20] поступа́ет... *does the same*
[21] пока́... *until my partner is compelled*
[22] achieve
[23] под... *under the direction of a more experienced*
[24] в... *reconciliation of the different sides*
[25] Е́сли... *If it makes the other person happy*
[26] возмо́жность... *the opportunity to have his own way*
[27] condition
[28] урегули́рованию... *resolution of a problem in relations*
[29] поста́вьте... *write down the score for each question next to the number of that question and then add up the totals for each category*
[30] Competition
[31] Evasion
[32] Cooperation
[33] Facilitation
[34] expressed (manifested)
[35] exceeds

Post-reading Tasks

1. Given the context of the passage, what do you think the words **пятиба́лльной шкале́** and **балл** mean?

2. Can you find the Russian word that means *not rightness* in the text? What is the root of the word and what are its prefixes and suffixes?

3. What is the verb used with the Russian word meaning *initiative*? What do you think this verb means?

4. What is the root of the Russian word meaning *reconciliation*?

5. What is the root of the Russian word meaning *to insist* that is used in the expression *to have one's own way*?

6. Pretend that you are a psychologist and you have just given this test to a famous individual. Present a short oral or written report on your findings to your colleagues.

7. Identify the conjugation prototype of the underlined verbs in the passage. Some may be first-conjugation, second-conjugation, or irregular verbs.

8. Identify the possible conjugation prototypes of the verbs with double underline. Then consult a dictionary to determine which of the possible conjugation prototypes you have identified is the actual one.

RUSSIAN

Saying

Кто ме́ньше толку́ет, тот ме́ньше тоску́ет.

He who talks less grieves less.
[Ignorance is bliss.]

✳ Упражне́ние 3б

Examine the following list of verbs. Check their conjugation patterns in a good reference book. Then assign them a number from the list of first-conjugation prototypes.

1. мыть
2. зашйть
3. нача́ть

4. начина́ть
5. везтй
6. жечь

RUSSIAN

Saying

Цыпля́т по о́сени счита́ют.

Count the chicks in the fall (when they're old enough to survive).
[Don't count your chickens before they hatch.]

✳ Упражне́ние 3в

Now that you have assigned each of the preceding verbs to a prototype, provide the following forms for each of the verbs: **я, ты, они́**; past tense—**он, она́, они́**; imperative.

✳ Упражне́ние 3г

Set aside one page in your notebook for each of the more common prototypes of first-conjugation verbs. Write out the full conjugation of the prototype verb and then keep a running list of verbs that are similar to this prototype as you continue your study of Russian. Add to the list of second-conjugation verbs you started in the previous unit.

✳ Упражне́ние 3д

Answer the questions below for each first-conjugation prototype and record your answers on a page in your notebook dedicated to first-conjugation verbs.

1. Does this verb prototype feature a mutation? If so, in what conjugated forms does it occur?
2. Does this verb prototype feature a shifting stress pattern in either the nonpast or past-tense forms? If so, in which?

3. Does this verb prototype feature a syllabic alternation?
4. Which verb prototypes feature mutations?
5. Which verb prototypes feature shifting stress patterns in the nonpast?
6. Which verb prototypes feature shifting stress patterns in the past tense?

PART 2
Verbs with the Ending -*ся*

The ending -**ся** is sometimes attached to Russian verbs. This ending can have one of five different functions.

1. The verb ending -**ся** can mean *oneself*: The action of the verb is "reflected" onto the subject of the verb.

бри́ться	*to shave (oneself)*
купа́ться	*to bathe (oneself)*

Кири́лл Анато́льевич бре́ется то́лько два ра́за в неде́лю.	*Kirill Anatol'evich shaves only twice a week.*
Ле́том мы ча́сто купа́емся на э́том о́зере.	*In the summer we often bathe (swim around) in this lake.*

2. A verb ending in -**ся** can mean an action that is "reciprocal" for two or more subjects.

договори́ться	*to agree (with one another)*
познако́миться	*to become acquainted (with one another)*

Еле́на и О́льга договори́лись пойти́ к Зинаи́де Па́вловне.	*Elena and Ol'ga agreed to go see Zinaida Pavlovna.*
Мы познако́мились с Андре́ем Миха́йловичем у Татья́ны Жуко́вской.	*We became acquainted with Andrei Mikhailovich at Tat'iana Zhukovskaia's.*

3. A transitive verb (one that takes a direct object) which ends in -**ся** can be used in a passive construction.

рассма́триваться	*to be examined*
проверя́ться	*to be checked*

Сейча́с же рассма́тривается вопро́с о приватиза́ции заво́да.	*The question of privatizing the factory is being examined right now.*
Все его́ пла́ны проверя́ются на са́мом высо́ком у́ровне.	*All his plans are checked on the highest level.*

4. A verb ending in **-ся** can have a meaning completely different from the same verb without this ending.

сойти́	*to get off or down*
сойти́сь	*to come together (from different points)*
собира́ть	*to gather, collect*
собира́ться	*to plan, get together*
Я сойду́ на сле́дующей.	*I'm getting off at the next (stop).*
Мы сойдёмся у Петра́ Никола́евича.	*We'll meet at Petr Nikolaevich's.*
Филатели́сты собира́ют ма́рки.	*Philatelists collect stamps.*
Мы собира́лись пое́хать в Петербу́рг, но не смогли́.	*We were planning to go to Petersburg, but couldn't go.*

5. A verb ending in **-ся** can have its own meaning and have no related verb without the **-ся** ending.

смея́ться	*to laugh*
наде́яться	*to hope*
Почему́ вы смеётесь? Ра́зве э́то заба́вно?!	*Why are you laughing? Do you think this is funny?*
Мы о́чень наде́емся, что она́ смо́жет прие́хать.	*We really hope that she'll be able to come.*

Spelling of the -ся *Ending*

When the **-ся** ending is attached to a verb, it is spelled either **-ся** or **-сь** depending on the last letter before the ending. If the last letter is a vowel, the ending is spelled **-сь** in the **я** and **вы** forms, in some imperatives, and in some of the past-tense forms.

я бре́юсь	я договорю́сь
вы бре́етесь	вы договори́тесь
они́ бри́лись	они́ договори́лись
я купа́юсь	я познако́млюсь
вы купа́етесь	вы познако́митесь
они́ купа́лись	они́ познако́мились

If the last letter is a consonant or the soft sign, the ending is spelled **-ся** in the infinitive, the **ты** and **он/она́** forms, some imperatives, and some of the past-tense forms.

бри́ться	**купа́ться**
ты бре́ешься	ты купа́ешься
он/она́ бре́ется	он/она́ купа́ется
он бри́лся	он купа́лся

The key exceptions to this spelling rule are for the participles and verbal adverbs formed from infinitives ending in **-ся**; these exceptions are discussed in Units 19 through 21.

✳   Упражне́ние 3е

Examine all the verbs in the glossaries for Units 1 through 3 and find all the verbs with the **-ся** ending. Then determine to which of the five categories they belong.

✳   Упражне́ние 3ё

Continue your list of all the connecting words and phrases (such as *because, but, in the first place, then,* and so forth) with those you can find in the texts of this unit. Next to each connecting word or phrase, write out the clause or sentence in which they are used. Keep this list in your notebook and add to it as you continue with this book.

Stress in the
Russian Verb

Ударе́ние в ру́сском глаго́ле

Театра́льный кио́ск.

PART 1 Stress in the Russian Verb

Most Russian words have only one lexical stress (except for compound words, such as **ме́ждунаро́дный**, or some foreign words, especially place names, such as **Нью-Йо́рк**). The lexical stress in a Russian word is in many ways similar to the lexical stress in an English word: Compare the pronunciation of the English words *execute* and *executive*. In both words, one of the vowel sounds receives extra attention in pronunciation. The same thing happens in the pronunciation of Russian words. In addition to this extra attention for stressed vowels, unstressed vowels in Russian are reduced. For example, compare the pronunciation of the words **хорошо́**, **хоро́ший**, **Москва́**, and **ро́за**.

Regular Russian verbs have, primarily, two basic stress patterns for the past tense and the nonpast tense. Remember, the nonpast forms of a verb are the conjugated forms of the verb: the present tense of imperfective verbs and the future tense of perfective verbs. The two basic stress patterns may be called "stable" and "shifting."

Stable Stress in the Nonpast

If a verb has stable stress in the nonpast, or conjugated, forms, the stress is fixed on one particular syllable. The syllable with the stress may be the stem of the verb or the ending. The stress in all the conjugated forms of the verb is the same as the stress in the infinitive.

STABLE STEM-STRESS IN NONPAST		STABLE END-STRESS IN NONPAST	
сде́лать:	сде́лаю, сде́лаешь, сде́лают	жить:	живу́, живёшь, живу́т
рабо́тать:	рабо́таю, рабо́таешь, рабо́тают	говори́ть:	говорю́, говори́шь, говоря́т
уви́деть:	уви́жу, уви́дишь, уви́дят	закрича́ть:	закричу́, закричи́шь, закрича́т

A verb with stable stress in the nonpast may also have stable stress in the past, but beware: It may well have shifting stress in the past.

RUSSIAN Saying

Без труда́ не вы́нешь и ры́бку из пруда́.

Without effort you won't be able to get a single fish out of the pond.
[No pain, no gain.]

Shifting Stress (Regressive Stress) in the Nonpast

If a verb has shifting or regressive stress in the nonpast, or conjugated, forms, the stress falls on the same final syllable in the infinitive, imperative, and **я** forms of the verb, and then moves one syllable closer to the beginning of the verb for all the other conjugated forms.

сказа́ть	*to say:* я скажу́, ты ска́жешь, они́ ска́жут, скажи́(те)!
писа́ть	*to write:* я пишу́, ты пи́шешь, они́ пи́шут, пиши́(те)!
купи́ть	*to buy:* я куплю́, ты ку́пишь, они́ ку́пят, купи́(те)!
останови́ть	*to stop (something/someone):* я остановлю́, ты остано́вишь, они́ остано́вят, останови́(те)!
ходи́ть	*to go (multidirectional):* я хожу́, ты хо́дишь, они́ хо́дят, ходи́(те)!
плати́ть	*to pay:* я плачу́, ты пла́тишь, они́ пла́тят, плати́(те)!

A verb with shifting stress in the nonpast must have stable stress in the past.

Stable Stress in the Past

If a verb has stable stress in the past tense, the stress is fixed either on the stem of the verb or on the past-tense ending. If the stress is fixed on the past-tense ending, it will fall on the stem of the verb in the masculine singular past-tense form. Stable end-stress is commonly found among many verbs of motion.

STABLE STEM-STRESS IN PAST		STABLE END-STRESS IN PAST	
сде́лать:	сде́лал, сде́лала, сде́лали	пойти́:	пошёл, пошла́, пошли́
рабо́тать:	рабо́тал, рабо́тала, рабо́тали	привести́:	привёл, привела́, привели́
уви́деть:	уви́дел, уви́дела, уви́дели	мо́чь:	мог, могла́, могли́

A verb with stable stress in the past may also have stable stress in the nonpast, but beware: It may well have a shifting stress in the nonpast instead.

Shifting Stress in the Past

If a verb has shifting stress in the past tense, the stress falls on the same syllable in the masculine, neuter, and plural forms of the past tense, but shifts to the ending for the feminine past tense. This pattern is most common with verbs similar to the prototype **приня́ть** but occurs in other verbs as well.

приня́ть	он при́нял, они́ при́няли	она́ приняла́
взять	он взял, они́ взя́ли	она́ взяла́

жить	он жил, они́ жи́ли	она́ жила́
пить	он пил, они́ пи́ли	она́ пила́
дать	он дал, они́ да́ли	она́ дала́

A verb with shifting stress in the past tense must have stable stress in the nonpast. If you look at the conjugated forms of the preceding verbs, you'll see that all of them have stable stress in the nonpast forms.

✳ Упражне́ние 4а

Review the sample conjugation patterns given in Units 2 and 3 and determine whether there are any correlations between shifting or stable stress in the past or nonpast and conjugation class (first or second conjugation).

✳ Упражне́ние 4б

Using the glossary for Units 1 through 4, find two examples of each of the four stress patterns for verbs.

RUSSIAN   Saying

Из пе́сни сло́ва не вы́кинешь.

You can't toss words out of a song.
[One has to take the bad with the good.]

ТЕКСТ 4а

This poem by Lermontov is one of the most famous in Russia. Virtually every Russian knows this poem by heart because most children memorize it in school.

Pre-reading Task

This poem is known by its first line: "Alone, I go out onto the road..." Imagine standing on a road at night alone under a starry sky. What would you think about?

Выхожу́ оди́н я на доро́гу;	Alone, I go out onto the road.
Сквозь тума́н кремни́стый путь блести́т;	The stony way glistens through the mist;
Ночь тиха́. Пусты́ня вне́млет Бо́гу,	The night is still, the wilderness listens to God,
И звезда́ с звездо́ю говори́т.	And star speaks with star.

В небеса́х торже́ственно и чу́дно!
Спит земля́ в сия́нье голубо́м. . .
Что же мне так бо́льно и так тру́дно?
Жду ль чего́? Жале́ю ли о чём?

Уж не жду от жи́зни ничего́ я,
И не жаль мне про́шлого ничу́ть;
Я ищу́ свобо́ды и поко́я!
Я б хоте́л забы́ться и засну́ть!

Но не тем холо́дным сно́м моги́лы...
Я б жела́л наве́ки так засну́ть,
Чтоб в груди́ дрема́ли жи́зни си́лы,
Чтоб дыша́ вздыма́лась ти́хо грудь;

Чтоб всю ночь, весь день мой слух леле́я,
Про любо́вь мне сла́дкий го́лос пел,
На́до мной чтоб, ве́чно зелене́я,
Тёмный дуб склоня́лся и шуме́л.

М. Ю. Ле́рмонтов, 1841

All is solemn and wonderful in the sky;
The earth is sleeping in a pale blue radiance. . .
Why then do I feel so much pain and heaviness?
Am I waiting for something? Do I regret anything?

I expect nothing more from life,
And I don't regret the past at all.
I seek freedom and peace;
I would like to find oblivion and fall asleep. . .

But not with that cold sleep of the grave:
I would like to fall asleep forever
So that the forces of life would slumber in my breast,
So that, breathing, my breast would gently heave;

So that delighting my ear all night and all day,
An enchanting voice would sing to me of love;
So that, above me, eternally green,
A dark oak would bend and rustle.

Post-reading Tasks

1. Find all the words that relate to nature: What is the image of nature in the poem?
2. Find all the words that relate to sleep and rest: What is the notion of sleep in the poem?
3. Identify the stress patterns of all the underlined verbs in the poem.
4. Write a paragraph-long summary in Russian of the meaning of the poem.
5. Think up a title for the poem.

ТЕКСТ 4б

This poem, "Silentium," by Tiutchev, is another famous poem many Russians know by heart.

Pre-reading Task

Before you read the poem, think of three images you associate with silence and three reasons to keep silent. As you read, see if Tiutchev makes the same associations and offers the same reasons.

Silentium!

Молчи́, скрыва́йся и тай[1]
И чу́вства, и мечты́ свои́[2]—
Пуска́й в душе́вной глубине́
Встаю́т и захо́дят оне́[3]
5   Безмо́лвно,[4] как звёзды в ночи́,—
Любу́йся и́ми[5]—и молчи́.

Как се́рдцу вы́сказать себя́?[6]
Друго́му как поня́ть тебя́?[7]
Поймёт ли он, чем ты живёшь?
10   Мысль изречённая есть ложь.[8]
Взрыва́я, возмути́шь ключи́,[9]—
Пита́йся и́ми[10]—и молчи́.

Лишь жить в само́м себе́ уме́й[11]—
Есть це́лый мир в душе́ твое́й
15   Таи́нственно-волше́бных дум;[12]
Их оглуши́т нару́жный шум,[13]
Дневны́е разгоня́т лучи́,[14]—
Внима́й их пе́нью[15]—и молчи́!...

Ф. И. Тю́тчев, 1829

[1] Молчи́... *Be silent, hide, and conceal*
[2] И... *Your own feelings and daydreams*
[3] Пуска́й... *in the depths of your soul may they rise and set*
[4] *silently*
[5] Любу́йся... *Enjoy (admire) them*
[6] Как... *How can the heart have its say?*
[7] Друго́му... *How can another understand you?*
[8] Мысль... *A thought which is spoken is a lie*
[9] Взрыва́я... *Stirring them up, you cloud the springs*
[10] Пита́йся... *Be nourished by them*
[11] Лишь... *Be able to live within yourself*
[12] Есть... *There is a whole world in your soul of secret and magical thoughts*
[13] Их... *They are muffled by external noise*
[14] Дневны́е... *The rays of daylight disperse them*
[15] Внима́й... *Hear their singing*

Post-reading Tasks

1.   Find all the references to nature and determine if they are associated with silence in the poem.
2.   Identify the infinitives for all the underlined verbs and determine their stress pattern.
3.   What is the infinitive of the Russian verb meaning *to admire* in the first stanza?
4.   Write a three-sentence summary of the poet's attitude toward showing one's feelings.
5.   Write a paragraph explaining why you agree or disagree with the poet's point of view.

✳   Упражне́ние 4в

Continue your list of all the connecting words and phrases (such as *because*, *but*, *in the first place*, *then*, and so forth) with those you can find in the texts of this unit. Next to each connecting word or phrase, write out the clause or sentence in which they are used. Keep this list in your notebook and add to it as you continue with this book.

✳   Упражне́ние 4г

Review the lists of first- and second-conjugation verbs you started in Units 2 and 3. Note the stress pattern of each verb.

UNIT 5

Aspect
Вид глаго́лов

Собира́ются друзья́.

PART 1 General Introduction

Russian verbs generally come in pairs of imperfective and perfective verbs. The opposition between an imperfective verb and its perfective mate is not an equal balance for all pairs. In some pairs, one verb is used far more frequently than the other. Moreover, the meaning of each verb in a pair may differ. For instance, the imperfective verb **поступа́ть** means *to apply (for admission to a school)*, while its perfective mate, **поступи́ть**, means *to matriculate or enroll*. Similarly, the imperfective verb **сдава́ть** (**экза́мен**) means *to take a test*, while its perfective mate, **сдать** (**экза́мен**) means *to pass a test*.

It is important to recognize that there is a limited number of criteria that require the use of the perfective verb, while the number of criteria requiring the use of the imperfective verb is much greater.

> In making the choice between aspects, you should always ask yourself first: "Can I use the perfective verb here?" If the answer is no, then you know to use the imperfective verb. It is important to bear in mind the definition of the perfective verb.
>
> The perfective verb is used to describe a single event in its entirety:
>
> - the result of that verb is still in effect
> - the event is described with respect to a particular time (not in general)*

Here are some circumstances that would require a perfective verb in Russian; the underlined verbs would be translated into Russian with a perfective verb.

1. Did you read the poem the teacher assigned yesterday?
2. I was on my way to Vika's place, but I didn't see the furniture store where I was supposed to turn left.
3. I will write the letter tomorrow.
4. Please tell me about your trip!
5. She opened the window (and the window is still open at this time).

Here are some circumstances that would require an imperfective verb in Russian; the underlined verbs would be translated into Russian with an imperfective verb.

---

* Forsythe, John. *A Grammar of Aspect: Usage and Meaning in the Russian Verb.* (Cambridge: Cambridge University Press, 1970), p. 6.

6. I have never read *War and Peace.*
7. I have driven down this street a million times, but I never saw the furniture store that must have been there all along!
8. I'm going to be writing letters all day long tomorrow.
9. They are always telling some poor unsuspecting soul about their trip to Khabarovsk.
10. She opened the window (and the window is now closed at this time).

Note that because the perfective aspect must be used to describe single events summed up in their entirety with respect to a particular point in space or time, the English verbal ending *-ing* (progressive tenses) always requires the imperfective aspect. Some adverbs require the imperfective as well.

✳ Упражне́ние 5a

Explain why the perfective verb cannot be used in the English examples 6 through 10.

Aspect and Adverbs

Some adverbs require a verb of a particular aspect, while others may use verbs of one aspect more frequently than the others.

ADVERBS REQUIRING THE IMPERFECTIVE

всегда́	*always*
ча́сто	*frequently*
иногда́	*sometimes*
ре́дко	*rarely*
до́лго	*for a long time*
це́лую неде́лю, весь день, и. т. д.	*the entire week, all day, etc. (accusative time expressions of duration)*

ADVERBS ASSOCIATED WITH (BUT NOT NECESSARILY REQUIRING) THE PERFECTIVE

наконе́ц	*finally*
вдруг	*suddenly*

ADVERBS REQUIRING THE IMPERFECTIVE IN THE PAST TENSE, THE PERFECTIVE IN THE FUTURE

когда́-нибудь	*ever*
никогда́	*never*

Вы когда́-нибудь чита́ли «Войну́ и мир»?	*Have you ever read War and Peace?*
Я когда́-нибудь сде́лаю э́то.	*I'll do that sometime.*
Они́ никогда́ не замеча́ли э́тот рестора́н.	*They never noticed that restaurant.*
Я вас бо́льше никогда́ не уви́жу!	*I'll never see you again!*

Aspect and Verbs of Beginning, Continuing, and Ending

Verbs that mean *to begin*, *to continue*, *to end* or *to finish* always take an imperfective infinitive.

Мы ско́ро начнём чита́ть рома́н «А́нна Каре́нина».	*We will soon begin to read the novel Anna Karenina.*
Они́ продолжа́ют обсужда́ть э́тот вопро́с.	*They are continuing to discuss this question.*
Вы уже́ ко́нчили рабо́тать над э́тим?	*Have you already finished working on that?*

PART 2
Aspect in the Future Tense

In choosing the correct aspect in the future tense, you need to consider some of the following questions.

- Is this a single event or more than one event?
- Is this a single event in a series of consecutive events?
- Is this event summed up in its entirety?
- Will this event lead to a particular result?
- Is this event best described as a process that will take place in the future or a general background to some other single event?

Consider these Russian sentences in which perfective verbs have been emphasized.

1.	За́втра, когда́ мы **прие́дем**, мы **расска́жем** вам о пое́здке.	*Tomorrow, as soon as we arrive, we'll tell you about our trip.*
2.	Они́ **войду́т** в кварти́ру, **включа́т** свет, и мы все **закричи́м**: «Поздравля́ем»!	*They'll come into the apartment, turn on the light, and we'll all yell "Congratulations!"*
3.	Она́ всё **зако́нчит** и **пойдёт** домо́й.	*She'll finish up everything and go home.*
4.	Вам не хо́лодно? Я **закро́ю** окно́.	*Aren't you cold? I'll close the window.*
5.	Я **пригото́влю** обе́д, пока́ он бу́дет печа́тать докла́д.	*I'll make dinner while he's typing up the report.*

Now consider these Russian sentences, in which imperfective verbs have been emphasized.

6.	В ка́ждом го́роде мы **бу́дем расска́зывать** о но́вых америка́нских фи́льмах.	*In each city we'll talk about the new American films.*

7. Ста́рые жильцы́ оста́вили здесь таку́ю грязь! Мы **бу́дем** до́лго **убира́ть** на́шу но́вую кварти́ру.

   The former tenants left such filth here! We'll be cleaning our new apartment for a long time.

8. На но́вой рабо́те она́ обы́чно **бу́дет конча́ть** рабо́ту в пять часо́в.

   At her new job she will usually finish work at 5:00.

9. Когда́ де́тям бу́дет хо́лодно, я всегда́ **бу́ду закрыва́ть** окно́.

   When the children are cold I will always close the window.

10. Я пригото́влю обе́д, когда́ он **бу́дет печа́тать** докла́д.

    I'll make dinner, while he's typing up the report.

✳ Упражне́ние 5б

Explain why the perfective cannot be used for examples 6 through 10.

RUSSIAN

Saying

Поспеши́шь—люде́й насмеши́шь.

If you rush, people will laugh at you.
[Haste makes waste.]

✳ Упражне́ние 5в

For each of the sentences numbered 6 through 10, change the meaning of the sentence in some way to require the substitution of a perfective verb for the emphasized imperfective verb.

ТЕКСТ 5а

Read this excerpt from the novel *School for Fools* by Sokolov. The narrator (who is quite eccentric) is looking at a young girl with a dog and takes a rather unique (and, perhaps, disturbing) view of her life as it might unfold.

Pre-reading Task

What events might you predict for the life of a typical woman? What about for the life of a typical man? Do you think there are any differences between the two? Why or why not?

Я уви́дел ма́ленькую де́вочку, она́ вела́ на верёвке[1] соба́ку—
обыкнове́нную, просту́ю соба́ку—они́ шли в сто́рону
ста́нции. Я знал, сейча́с де́вочка идёт на пруд,[2] она́ бу́дет
купа́ться и купа́ть свою́ просту́ю соба́ку, а зате́м мину́ет[3]
ско́лько-то лет, де́вочка ста́нет взро́слой[4] и начнёт жить
взро́слой жи́знью: вы́йдет за́муж, бу́дет чита́ть серьёзные
кни́ги, спеши́ть и опа́здывать на рабо́ту, покупа́ть ме́бель,[5]
часа́ми говори́ть по телефо́ну, стира́ть чулки́,[6] гото́вить есть
себе́ и други́м, ходи́ть в го́сти и пьяне́ть[7] от вина́, зави́довать[8]
сосе́дям и пти́цам, следи́ть за метеосво́дками,[9] вытира́ть
пыль,[10] счита́ть копе́йки[11], ждать ребёнка,[12] ходи́ть к
зубно́му,[13] отдава́ть ту́фли в ремо́нт, нра́виться мужчи́нам,
смотре́ть в окно́ на проезжа́ющие автомоби́ли, посеща́ть
конце́рты и музе́и, смея́ться, когда́ не смешно́, красне́ть,[14]
когда́ сты́дно, пла́кать, когда́ пла́чется, крича́ть от бо́ли,
стона́ть от прикоснове́ний люби́мого,[15] постепе́нно седе́ть,[16]
кра́сить ресни́цы и во́лосы,[17] мыть ру́ки пе́ред обе́дом, а
но́ги—пе́ред сном,[18] плати́ть пе́ни,[19] распи́сываться в
получе́нии перево́дов,[20] листа́ть журна́лы,[21] встреча́ть на
у́лицах ста́рых знако́мых, выступа́ть на собра́ниях, хорони́ть
ро́дственников,[22] греме́ть посу́дой на ку́хне,[23] про́бовать
кури́ть,[24] переска́зывать сюже́ты фи́льмов, дерзи́ть
нача́льству,[25] жа́ловаться,[26] что опя́ть мигре́нь, выезжа́ть за́
город и собира́ть грибы́,[27] изменя́ть му́жу,[28] бе́гать по
магази́нам, смотре́ть салю́ты,[29] люби́ть Шопе́на, нести́
вздор,[30] боя́ться пополне́ть,[31] мечта́ть о пое́здке за грани́цу,[32]
ду́мать о самоуби́йстве,[33] руга́ть неиспра́вные ли́фты,[34]
копи́ть на чёрный день,[35] петь рома́нсы, ждать ребёнка,
храни́ть[36] да́вние фотогра́фии, продвига́ться по слу́жбе,[37]
визжа́ть от у́жаса,[38] осужда́юще кача́ть голово́й,[39] се́товать на
бесконе́чные дожди́,[40] сожале́ть об утра́ченном,[41] слу́шать
после́дние изве́стия по ра́дио, лови́ть[42] такси́, е́здить на юг,
воспи́тывать дете́й,[43] часа́ми проста́ивать[44] в очередя́х,
непоправи́мо старе́ть,[45] одева́ться по мо́де, руга́ть
прави́тельство,[46] жить по ине́рции,[47] пить карвало́л,[48]
проклина́ть му́жа,[49] сиде́ть на дие́те,[50] уходи́ть и
возвраща́ться, кра́сить гу́бы, не жела́ть ничего́ бо́льше,
навеща́ть[51] роди́телей, счита́ть, что всё ко́нчено, а та́кже—что
вельве́т (дра́пбати́стшёлкси́тецсафья́н[52]) о́чень практи́чный,
сиде́ть на бюллете́не,[53] лгать[54] подру́гам и ро́дственникам,
забыва́ть обо всём на све́те, занима́ть де́ньги,[55] жить, как
живу́т все, и вспомина́ть да́чу, пруд и просту́ю соба́ку.

А. В. (Са́ша) Соколо́в, «Шко́ла для дурако́в», 1976

[1] rope (leash)
[2] pond
[3] goes by (time)
[4] adult
[5] furniture
[6] стира́ть... wash stockings
[7] become inebriated
[8] envy
[9] следи́ть... follow the weather reports
[10] вытира́ть... do the dusting
[11] счита́ть... count kopecks (pennies)
[12] ждать... expect a baby (be pregnant)
[13] ходи́ть... see the dentist
[14] blush
[15] стона́ть... moan at the touch of (her) lover
[16] постепе́нно... go grey gradually
[17] кра́сить... put on mascara and dye (her) hair
[18] пе́ред... before bed (sleep)
[19] плати́ть... pay fines
[20] распи́сываться... sign in receipt of money
[21] листа́ть... leaf through magazines
[22] хорони́ть... bury relatives
[23] греме́ть... make noise with the dishes in the kitchen
[24] про́бовать... try smoking
[25] дерзи́ть... be impudent to the boss(es)
[26] complain
[27] mushrooms
[28] изменя́ть... be unfaithful to her husband
[29] fireworks displays
[30] нести́... talk nonsense (rubbish)
[31] боя́ться... be afraid of gaining weight
[32] мечта́ть... dream about a trip abroad
[33] suicide
[34] руга́ть... curse broken elevators
[35] копи́ть... save for a rainy day
[36] keep
[37] продвига́ться... get promoted at work
[38] визжа́ть... scream in horror
[39] осужда́юще... nod her head in condemnation
[40] се́товать... lament incessant rains
[41] сожале́ть... regret that which has been wasted or lost
[42] catch
[43] воспи́тывать... raise kids
[44] wait (stand)
[45] непоправи́мо... age irreparably
[46] руга́ть... curse the government
[47] жить... live by inertia (or "on auto-pilot")
[48] пить... take tranquilizers
[49] проклина́ть... curse her husband
[50] сиде́ть... diet
[51] visit
[52] (made-up word consisting of several different kinds of fabric)
[53] сиде́ть... have a medical excuse so as not to go to work
[54] lie
[55] занима́ть... borrow money

Post-reading Tasks

1. Make a chart of the stages of this girl's life and put three events or activities in each stage.
2. Underline all the verbs in the passage: What is the aspect of the majority of these verbs? What is the author's purpose in using this aspect?
3. Pick out five expressions from the text that you'd like to add to your own personal vocabulary.
4. Write a long paragraph describing the future of a boy, using the text above as a model. Use imperfective verbs as appropriate to indicate events that repeat with regularity in his life.

Saying

Что посе́ешь, то и пожнёшь.

As ye sow, so shall ye reap.

ТЕКСТ 56

Read the excerpt from Solzhenitsyn's novel *The First Circle*. Nerzhin, a scientist who is a prisoner in a camp for scientists working on special projects including one involving cryptography, is talking with one of his jailers, Trofimovich.

Pre-reading Task

Make some predictions about the topic of conversation between a prisoner and one of his jailers. How are they likely to use the future tense? Which aspect are they likely to use and why?

—Пётр Трофи́мович! А вы...сапоги́[1] уме́ете шить[2]?

—Как вы сказа́ли?

—Я говорю́: *сапоги́* вы меня́ шить не нау́чите? Мне бы вот сапоги́ научи́ться шить.[3]

5 —Я, прости́те, не понима́ю...

—Пётр Трофи́мович! В скорлупе́[4] вы живёте! Мне ведь, око́нчу срок, е́хать в глуху́ю тайгу́, на ве́чную ссы́лку.[5] Рабо́тать я рука́ми ничего́ не уме́ю—как проживу́? Там медве́ди бу́рые.[6] Там Леона́рда Э́йлера фу́нкции ещё три мезозо́йских э́ры

10 никому́ не пона́добятся.[7]

[1] boots
[2] sew (make)
[3] Мне... *I would like to learn how to sew boots*
[4] shell
[5] Мне... *After I finish my sentence, I'll have to go to the deep taiga in eternal exile*
[6] медве́ди... *brown bears*
[7] Там... *no one will need Leonhard Euler's functions for another three mesosoic eras there*

—Что вы говори́те, Не́ржин? В слу́чае успе́ха рабо́ты вас
как крипто́графа досро́чно освободя́т, сни́мут суди́мость,[8]
даду́т кварти́ру в Москве́...

—Сни́мут суди́мость! —зло воскли́кнул Не́ржин,[9] и глаза́
15 его́ су́зились.[10] Да отку́да вы взя́ли,[11] что я хочу́ э́той пода́чки:[12]
хорошо́ рабо́тал, так мол освобожда́йся[13]?! Мы тебя́ *проща́ем!*[14]
Нет, Пётр Трофи́мович!—и он отпу́щенным и потому́
утяжелённым па́льцем постуча́л по лакиро́ванной
пове́рхности сто́лика,[15]—не с того́ конца́![16] Пусть призна́ют
20 сперва́, что за о́браз мы́слей нельзя́ сажа́ть[17]—а там и *мы*
посмо́трим—проща́ем ли!

А. И. Солжени́цын, «В кру́ге пе́рвом», 1968

8 В... *In the event of the success of [your] work as a cryptograph you'll be released early, your convictions will be removed from your record*
9 зло... *exclaimed Nerzhin maliciously*
10 глаза́... *his eyes narrowed*
11 Да... *Where did you get it in your head*
12 *sop (miserable pittance, paltry dole)*
13 мол... *well, be free*
14 Мы... *we forgive you*
15 он... *he knocked with his relaxed and therefore heavy finger against the polished surface of the desk*
16 не... *you've got it all backwards*
17 Пусть... *First let them admit that for one's way of thinking one cannot (should not) be sent to jail*

Post-reading Tasks

1. What does the jailer offer Nerzhin? Why doesn't Nerzhin accept this deal?
2. Find all the words that might be relevant to the topic "dissident."
3. Identify all the future-tense verbs and determine their aspect.
4. Write a short letter from Petr Trofimovich to Nerzhin dated after the collapse of the Soviet Union.

   Упражне́ние 5г

In the following sentences, circle the correct verb in the parentheses and be prepared to explain why. The imperfective option is given first, the perfective second.

1. Э́то о́чень дли́нный рома́н. Я (бу́ду чита́ть/прочита́ю) его́ три дня.
   This is a very long novel. I'll be reading it for three days.

2. Мы вам сра́зу (бу́дем расска́зывать/расска́жем) о Москве́, как то́лько (бу́дем возвраща́ться/вернёмся) в Калифо́рнию.
   We'll tell you about Moscow as soon as we return to California.

3. Она́ нашла́ но́вую рабо́ту недалеко́ от на́шей кварти́ры. Тепе́рь она́ (бу́дет заходи́ть/зайдёт) к нам ча́сто!
   She found a new job not far from our apartment. Now she'll be dropping by to see us often!

4. Оле́г сказа́л, что у него́ боли́т голова́ и что он (бу́дет принима́ть/при́мет) аспири́н.
   Oleg said that his head hurts and that he's going to take aspirin.

5. Я узна́ла, что я диабе́тик. Тепе́рь я бо́льше не (бу́ду есть/съем) са́хара.
   I found out that I'm diabetic. Now I won't eat any more sugar.

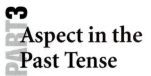

Зада́ние 5a

Prepare a short oral or written presentation to answer each of the following questions. Be sure to use aspect consistently in your answers!

Что вы бу́дете де́лать в суббо́ту и воскресе́нье?	*What will you be doing on Saturday and Sunday?*
Что вы сде́лаете за́втра ве́чером?	*What will you complete tomorrow evening?*

"For the sake of argument . . ."

Note that the perfective future-tense forms of the verbs **допусти́ть**, **предположи́ть**, and **сказа́ть** are used as part of rhetorical structures in making an argument.

Допу́стим, что вы пра́вы, тогда́ нам не ну́жно е́хать туда́.	*Let's say that you're right, then we don't have to go there.*
Предполо́жим, что Ири́на Макси́мовна всё сде́лает.	*Let's assume that Irina Maksimovna will do everything.*
Ска́жем, что Ви́тя не найдёт реше́ния; тогда́ придётся ему́ помо́чь.	*Let's say (for the sake of argument) that Vitia won't find a solution (to the problem); then we will have to help him.*

PART 3 Aspect in the Past Tense

For the past tense you should ask some of the same questions in order to choose the correct aspect of the verb.

- Is this a single event or more than one event?
- Is this a single event in a series of consecutive events (perfective) or is it an event that took place simultaneously with some other event (imperfective)?
- Is this event summed up in its entirety?
- Did this event lead to a particular result still in effect?*
- Is the very occurrence of the event (imperfective) emphasized more than its result (perfective)?
- Is this event best described as a process that took place or a general background to some other single event?

---

* Some English expressions, such as *I forget* and *I am tired*, use the present tense, while their Russian counterparts use the past tense of the perfective verb: **Я забы́л/а**, **Я уста́л/а**. These Russian expressions convey the idea that the speaker has forgotten something or that the speaker has become tired, respectively, and that the results of these events remain in effect: The information is forgotten, the speaker is tired.

Moreover, in negated past-tense sentences (that is, sentences with verbs with the negative particle **не**), we must also consider whether the negated event was *intended* to have taken place (perfective) or whether there was no such intention (imperfective).

Intention plays a very important role in determining the aspect of verbs in negative sentences in the past tense. For instance, consider each of the following scenarios.

1. "Vika, I'm calling from a pay phone on University Prospect. You said to turn left at the furniture store, and I drove up and down the strip for a mile, but I didn't see the furniture store."

2. "Vika, I've been living on this street for ten years, and you know, I never noticed that there was a furniture store here!"

If we translated these scenes into Russian, the underlined verb phrase in scenario 1 would need a perfective verb: **увйдел/а**. In scenario 1, the speaker clearly intended to see the furniture store, because he or she knew that that was where to make the left turn. Somehow, however, the speaker missed it.

In scenario 2, an imperfective verb would have to be used to translate *never noticed*, because it was clearly never the speaker's intention to see the furniture store.

Consider two more scenarios.

3. "Lara, I didn't read the assignment for today. Could you tell me what it was about?"
4. "Lara, I swear I didn't take your notes!"

A Russian speaker conveying the message of scenario 3 would use a perfective verb, because the reading had been assigned for that day and on some level the speaker intended to do the reading; at least he or she knows that someone (presumably the teacher) expected him or her to have that intention.

Scenario 4 would require an imperfective verb, because the speaker would want it to be clear that he or she had no intention of taking Lara's notes. A perfective verb would create a very odd impression, as if, although the speaker didn't take Lara's notes, he or she nonetheless wanted to.

Saying

RUSSIAN

Москва́ не сра́зу стро́илась.

Moscow wasn't built right away.
[Rome wasn't built in a day.]

Verbs of beginning and ending in the past tense are *usually* perfective when they refer to the beginning or ending of a single event or action. These verbs still take an imperfective (second) infinitive.

Ле́на **начала́** рабо́тать над э́тим в семь часо́в.　　　*Lena began working on this at 7:00.*

Ви́тя ско́ро **ко́нчил** гото́вить обе́д, и все се́ли за стол.	*Vitia soon finished making dinner, and everyone sat down at the table.*

Verbs of beginning and ending in the past tense that refer to a habitual or customary action are imperfective because they do not refer to the beginning or ending of a single event or action. These verbs still take an imperfective (second) infinitive.

Ле́на **обы́чно** начина́ла рабо́тать над э́тим в семь часо́в.	*Lena usually began working on this at 7:00. (Every day or frequently this project would be part of Lena's schedule for 7:00.)*
Ви́тя **ра́ньше** конча́л чита́ть газе́ту до обе́да.	*Vitia used to finish reading the paper before lunch. (The implication is that something has changed in Vitia's routine.)*

Remember also to use imperfective verbs to refer to a process or event that used to occur with some frequency. The English words *used to* or *would* in the sense of *previously used to* are cues for the imperfective aspect in Russian.

О́ля Остро́вская ра́ньше рабо́тала здесь, но тепе́рь рабо́тает в друго́м ме́сте.	*Olia Ostrovskaia used to work here, but now she works somewhere else.*
Ка́ждый раз когда́ поднима́лась э́та те́ма, Сла́ва говори́л шёпотом, потому́ что ему́ бы́ло сты́дно.	*Every time the topic would come up, Slava would speak in a whisper because he was ashamed.*

Consider these Russian sentences in which perfective verbs have been emphasized.

1.	У Мари́и вчера́ **родила́сь** до́чка!	*Maria had a baby girl yesterday!*
2.	Она́ **откры́ла** дверь, **вошла́** в ко́мнату и **се́ла** за стол.	*She opened the door, entered the room, and sat down at the table.*
3.	Ты, что, с ума́ **сошёл**?!	*Have you gone mad?*
4.	Мы **пое́дем** в Во́логду по́сле пра́здников и **поговори́м** с дире́ктором на э́ту те́му.	*We'll go to Vologda after the holidays and talk with the director about this question.*
5.	—Вы **прочита́ли** весь расска́з?	*—Did you read the entire story?*
	—Я не **успе́ла**, я весь день гото́вилась к экза́мену по фи́зике.	*—I didn't have time (to read the entire story): I was studying for a physics test all day.*

Now consider these Russian sentences in which imperfective verbs have been emphasized.

6.	День **подходи́л** к концу́: па́па **лежа́л** на дива́не и **ду́мал** о рабо́те.	*The day was coming to an end: Dad was lying on the couch and thinking about work.*

Оле́г мне ... с пе́рвого взгля́да
а) нра́вился
б) понра́вился

7. Студе́нты **стоя́ли** в коридо́ре и **кури́ли**, когда́ вдруг к ним подошла́ Ле́на Андре́ева.

The students were standing in the hallway and smoking when Lena Andreeva suddenly came up to them.

когда+1, past – imperf

8. —Вы когда́-нибудь **чита́ли** «Войну́ и мир»?
    —Коне́чно, **чита́ла**.

—Have you ever read War and Peace?
—Of course I've read (it).

9. Они́ ещё не на́чали **рабо́тать** над но́вым прое́ктом: они́ ещё не ко́нчили **говори́ть** о ста́ром!

They still haven't begun to work on the new project: They still haven't finished talking about the old (one).

10. Мы с роди́телями о́чень ча́сто **переезжа́ли**, когда́ я была́ ма́ленькая—до сих пор я не **люблю́** до́лго **жить** на одно́м ме́сте.

My parents and I moved a lot when I was little: To this day I don't like to live for a long time in one place.

 Упражне́ние 5д

Explain why the particular aspect was used in examples 1 through 10.

> **Saying**
>
> Зна́ет ко́шка, чьё мя́со съе́ла.
>
> *The cat knows whose meat she's eaten.*
> *[A guilty conscience needs no accuser.]*

ТЕКСТ 5в

Read the excerpt from the novella *This Is Moscow Speaking* by Arzhak (Daniel'). The narrator is explaining how he spent some time at a dacha with friends.

Pre-reading Task

Write down five things you imagine a Russian might do at a dacha in summer. Do the characters in this story do any of these things?

Мы сиде́ли в саду́, на да́че. Накану́не[1] все мы, прие́хавшие[2] на
де́нь рожде́ния к И́горю, кре́пко вы́пили,[3] шуме́ли допоздна́[4] и,
наконе́ц, улегли́сь в по́лной уве́ренности,[5] что проспи́м до
полу́дня;[6] одна́ко за́городная тишина́ разбуди́ла нас часо́в в семь
утра́.[7] Мы подняли́сь[8] и дру́жно ста́ли соверша́ть вся́кие неле́пые
посту́пки:[9] бе́гали в одни́х тру́сиках[10] по алле́йкам, подтя́гивались
на турнике́[11] (бо́льше пяти́ раз никто́ так и не суме́л
подтяну́ться), а Володька Маргу́лис да́же окати́лся водо́й из
коло́дца,[12] хотя́ как всем бы́ло изве́стно, по утра́м он никогда́ не
умыва́лся,[13] ссыла́ясь[14] на то, что опа́здывает на рабо́ту.

Н. Аржа́к [Ю. М. Даниэ́ль], «Говори́т Москва́», 1960–1961

[1] *The evening before*
[2] *those who had arrived*
[3] *drank a lot (of alcohol)*
[4] шуме́ли... *made noise until late*
[5] улегли́сь... *got settled down in full confidence*
[6] проспи́м... *sleep until noon*
[7] за́городная... *suburban silence woke us around seven* A.M.
[8] *got up*
[9] ста́ли... *began to do all kinds of crazy (absurd) things*
[10] бе́гали... *ran around in just swimming trunks*
[11] подтя́гивались... *did pull-ups*
[12] окати́лся... *poured water from the well over himself*
[13] *washed up*
[14] *explaining*

Post-reading Tasks

1. Make a list of all the characters mentioned and write down one personality trait or detail for each.
2. Identify the aspect of all the underlined verbs.
3. Write a paragraph about what you and your friends might do if you were to visit someone's cabin in the woods.

✳ Упражне́ние 5e

In the following sentences, choose the correct verb in the parentheses and be prepared to explain why. Consult the English translations of each sentence to make sure you understand the context.

1. Оле́г до́лго (писа́л/написа́л) письмо́; наконе́ц, он его́ (писа́л/написа́л), и мы
вме́сте пошли́ на по́чту.
Oleg was writing the letter for a long time; finally he finished writing it, and we went to the post office together.

2. Вчера́ А́нна не (чита́ла/прочита́ла) материа́лы в уче́бнике, кото́рые ей
(задава́ла/задала́) преподава́тельница.
Anna didn't read the materials in the textbook that her teacher had assigned.

3. Они́ продолжа́ли упо́рно (повторя́ть/повтори́ть), что они́ э́того не
(де́лали/сде́лали): в тот день они́ бы́ли в Петербу́рге!
They stubbornly continued to repeat that they hadn't done it: On that day they had been in Petersburg!

4. Михаи́л (смотре́л/посмотре́л) телеви́зор, когда́ А́нна (гото́вила/ пригото́вила)
обе́д: зна́чит ли э́то, что он плохо́й муж?
Mikhail was watching television while Anna was making dinner: Does that mean he's a bad husband?

5. Бори́с Никола́евич (выходи́л/вы́шел) из кварти́ры, когда́ он вдруг (ви́дел/уви́дел) своего́ ста́рого нача́льника, Михаи́ла Серге́евича.
Boris Nikolaevich was coming out of his apartment when he suddenly caught sight of his old boss, Mikhail Sergeevich.

6. Та́ня (запира́ла/заперла́) кварти́ру, (кла́ла/положи́ла) ключи́ в карма́н и ушла́ на рабо́ту.
Tania locked up her apartment, put the keys in her pocket, and left for work.

7. А́лла Миха́йловна начала́ (иска́ть/поиска́ть) очки́ му́жа.
Alla Mikhailovna began to look for her husband's glasses.

8. Вы когда́-нибудь (чита́ли/прочита́ли) «Войну́ и мир»?
Have you ever read War and Peace?

9. Мари́я ча́сто (приходи́ла/пришла́) домо́й с рабо́ты в семь часо́в, но неда́вно она́ перешла́ на но́вую рабо́ту и (начина́ла/начала́) (приходи́ть/прийти́) домо́й ра́ньше.
Maria often used to come home from work at seven o'clock, but recently she switched to a new job and began to come home earlier.

10. Ми́ша (реша́л/реши́л) стать вегетариа́нцем и (переста́ва́л/ переста́л) (есть/съесть) мя́со.
Misha decided to become a vegetarian and stopped eating meat.

ТЕКСТ 5г

Read the excerpt from Vasil'eva's book *Wives of the Kremlin*, which all Moscow was reading and talking about in 1994. In this excerpt, Vasil'eva discusses several of the hypotheses surrounding the mysterious death of Stalin's second wife, Nadezhda Allilueva, dwelling on the possibility that Stalin killed her or had her killed.

Pre-reading Task

What are some of the words you might expect to find in a text about possible murder or suicide? Make a list of these words in English or Russian and look for them as you read the text.

Бы́ло две ве́рсии сме́рти Аллилу́евой: уби́йство и самоуби́йство.[1] В пе́рвой три предположе́ния: уби́та сами́м Ста́линым,[2] уби́та охра́нниками,[3] уби́та сообщниками.[4] Ка́ждая ве́рсия распада́ется[5] ещё на не́сколько. Вот основны́е:[6]

5   „Ста́лин сам уби́л её из ре́вности.[7] Она́ завела́ рома́н со свои́м па́сынком Я́ковом.[8] Он заста́л их.[9] С ней распра́вился на

[1] уби́йство... *murder and suicide*
[2] уби́та... *she was killed by Stalin himself*
[3] *by guards*
[4] *by her own accomplices*
[5] *breaks down into*
[6] *fundamental [ones]*
[7] *jealousy*
[8] завела́... *began an affair with her own stepson (Stalin's son) Jacob*
[9] Он... *He caught them (in the act)*

ме́сте,[10] а сы́ну сказа́л, что отомсти́т позднее́.[11] Поэ́тому-то он и Я́кова из неме́цкого пле́на не вы́зволил".[12]

„Ста́лин уби́л её как своего́ полити́ческого проти́вника.[13] Она́ возмуща́лась[14] его́ поли́тикой, коллективиза́цией, а он не мог э́того слу́шать—пра́вда глаза́ ко́лет".[15]

„Ста́лин приказа́л[16] её уби́ть, что́бы самому́ не мара́ть рук,[17] узна́в, что она́ полити́чески измени́ла[18] ему́—вошла́ в гру́ппу враго́в наро́да,[19] была́ така́я гру́ппа „девяно́ста двух".

„Она́ действи́тельно была́ в оппози́ции, входи́ла в гру́ппу, враждéбную[20] Ста́лину. Соо́бщники,[21] боя́сь, что она́ преда́ст[22] их, убра́ли её".[23]

„Ста́лин приказа́л охра́не её уби́ть, она́ надое́ла ему́[24] ре́вностью, и вообще́, они́ уже́ давно́ не жи́ли как муж и жена́. Она́ меша́ла[25] ему́ жить, как он хоте́л,—пить вино́ и гуля́ть с балери́нами".

„В Аллилу́еву стреля́ли[26]—спасти́[27] её бы́ло невозмо́жно. Истека́ющая кро́вью,[28] она́ сказа́ла: „Это Ио́сиф [Ста́лин]. Не прости́л,[29] что я заступи́лась[30] за На́дю Кру́пскую [жену́ Ле́нина], когда́ она́ проси́ла ми́ловать.[31] Свое́й руко́й, сам...".[32]

В э́той невозмо́жной ве́рсии меня́, коне́чно же, привлекло́ появле́ние и́мени Наде́жды Константи́новны [Кру́пской, жены́ Ле́нина][33] ря́дом с траге́дией друго́й Наде́жды...Сообща́я слу́хи, я не даю́ им оце́нок.[34] Могу́ лишь сказа́ть, что все они́ представля́ются мне далёкими от и́стины.[35]

Л. Васи́льева, «Кремлёвские жёны», 1994

10 С... *He took care of her on the spot*
11 отомсти́т... *that he would take revenge later*
12 неме́цкого... *didn't liberate from German imprisonment*
13 полити́ческого... *political opponent*
14 *was indignant about*
15 пра́вда... *truth hurts (pierces the eyes)*
16 *ordered*
17 самому́... *not to soil (stain) his own hands*
18 *betrayed*
19 враго́в... *enemies of the people*
20 *hostile (to Stalin)*
21 *accomplices, confederates*
22 *betray*
23 убра́ли... *got rid of her*
24 она́... *he got sick of her*
25 *disturbed*
26 В... *they shot Allilueva*
27 *save*
28 Истека́ющая... *bleeding to death*
29 Не... *didn't forgive*
30 *spoke out for (on behalf of)*
31 *to have mercy*
32 Свое́й... *with his own hand, he himself*
33 меня́...привлекло́... *the appearance of the name of Krupskaya attracted me*
34 *any evaluation*
35 все... *they all seem far from the truth*

Post-reading Tasks

1. How many of the words that you listed in the pre-reading task did you find in the text?
2. Summarize each version of Allilueva's death in three to five words in English or Russian.
3. Write another version or possible explanation for the death of Allilueva.
4. Write a paragraph explaining why you think one version is most likely.
5. Identify the aspect of each underlined verb in the text and explain the reason for the author's choice of that aspect.

§ Зада́ние 56

Prepare a three-minute talk to answer each of the following questions. Be sure to use aspect consistently in your answers! **Что вы де́лали про́шлым ле́том (и́ли: во вре́мя кани́кул)? Что вы сде́лали в суббо́ту и воскресе́нье на про́шлой неде́ле?**

PART 4 Aspect in the Infinitive

As discussed previously, verbs of beginning, continuing, and ending take an imperfective infinitive. This rule also applies to verbs that refer to learning how to do something (such as **учи́ться/научи́ться**) or to becoming accustomed to doing something (such as **привыка́ть/привы́кнуть**).

Где же вы так хорошо́ научи́лись **говори́ть** по-ру́сски?	*Where did you learn to speak Russian so well?*
Я никогда́ не **привы́кну** води́ть маши́ну!	*I'll never get used to driving a car!*

When constructions with **на́до, ну́жно, до́лжен/должна́/должны́** are used *in the negative,* the *imperfective* infinitive is generally used (unless the action involved is one that no one would want to do).

1.	Не на́до **чита́ть** э́ту статью́.	*There is no need to read this article.*
2.	Она́ не должна́ так бы́стро **говори́ть**, когда́ чита́ет ле́кции.	*She shouldn't speak so quickly when giving lectures.*

In other instances, there is no hard and fast rule governing the aspect of the infinitive. The aspect of the infinitive is often determined by the context: Is the speaker referring to a single event summed up in its entirety or not?

3.	Тебе́ на́до сего́дня **написа́ть** письмо́ ма́тери!	*You have to write a letter to your mother today!*
4.	Тебе́ на́до **писа́ть** ма́тери раз в неде́лю.	*You have to write your mother once a week.*

In example 3, the perfective infinitive is used because the speaker is talking about a single letter (and a single act of letter writing) for a single time (today), while in example 4, the imperfective infinitive is used because the speaker is talking about a general rule requiring the writing of more than one letter (more than one act of letter writing) with reference to frequency (once a week).

With the word **нельзя́** or constructions with **не (с)мочь**, the imperfective infinitive is used to express that something is forbidden, while the perfective infinitive is used to express that something is physically impossible.

нельзя́ + imperfective = forbidden
нельзя́ + perfective = physically impossible

5.	Они́ не мо́гут **отвеча́ть** на э́тот вопро́с.	*They can't answer this question (they are forbidden to do so; they may know the answer, but for some reason they are not allowed to answer).*

6. Они́ не мо́гут **отве́тить** на э́тот вопро́с.

They can't answer this question (because they don't know the answer; if they knew the answer, they would be able to answer it).

7. Нельзя́ **говори́ть** на э́ту те́му с ним!

It is forbidden to talk about this topic with him!

8. Жаль, что нельзя́ **рассказа́ть** ему́ об э́том сего́дня: он вернётся то́лько в пя́тницу.

It's a shame that (we) can't tell him about this today (because he's not here): He's coming back only on Friday.

✳ Упражне́ние 5ё

Reread examples 5 through 8 above and identify the aspect of the emphasized verb in each sentence. Then explain why that aspect is the correct one, given the rules for the selection of aspect in the infinitive.

✳ Упражне́ние 5ж

Select the aspectually correct form of the infinitive from the options provided in the parentheses below. Then identify which rule supports your choice. (Note that the imperfective infinitive is always provided first in each pair.)

1. Нам на́до (чита́ть/прочита́ть) э́тот расска́з на за́втра.
   We have to read this story for tomorrow.

2. Нам на́до (чита́ть/прочита́ть) э́ти материа́лы на ру́сском языке́.
   We have to read these materials in Russian.

3. Не на́до (отвеча́ть/отве́тить) на их письмо́: пусть А́нна э́то сде́лает сама́.
   It's not necessary to answer their letter: Let Anna do it herself.

4. Нельзя́ (отвеча́ть/отве́тить) на их письмо́: мы не хоти́м, что́бы они́ узна́ли об э́том!
   We can't answer their letter: We don't want them to find out about this!

5. Я не смогу́ (отвеча́ть/отве́тить) на их письмо́: я не зна́ю, о чём они́ спра́шивают.
   I can't answer their letter: I don't know what they are asking about.

6. На́до сего́дня (расска́зывать/рассказа́ть) ей об э́том!
   We have to tell her about this today!

7. Не на́до (расска́зывать/рассказа́ть) ей об э́том!
   It's better not to tell her about this!

8. Нельзя́ (расска́зывать/рассказа́ть) ей об э́том, а то она́ рассе́рдится на нас!
   You can't tell her about this or else she'll get angry at us.

9. Нельзя́ (расска́зывать/рассказа́ть) ей об э́том сего́дня, потому́ что она́ ещё в О́мске.

   You can't tell her about this today, because she's still in Omsk.

10. Оле́г не смо́жет (расска́зывать/рассказа́ть) ей об э́том, потому́ что он не зна́ет всю исто́рию.

   Oleg can't tell her about this because he doesn't know the whole story.

Aspect in the imperative is discussed in the next unit.

✳ Упражне́ние 5з

Continue your list of all the connecting words and phrases (such as *because*, *but*, *in the first place*, *then*, and so forth) with those you can find in the texts of this unit. Next to each connecting word or phrase, write out the clause or sentence in which they are used. Keep this list in your notebook and add to it as you continue with this book.

✳ Упражне́ние 5и

Add the verbs of this unit to your lists of first- and second-conjugation verbs and note the stress pattern of each verb.

 ТЕКСТ 5д

The text below is a poem by Maiakovskii about the end of a relationship.

Pre-reading Tasks

What do you think the narrator of the poem might talk about when he is unable to sleep in the middle of the night after recently ending a relationship? Make some predictions and see if you're right. As you read, try to determine if the narrator still loves the woman referred to in the poem.

Уже́ второ́й.[1] Должно́ быть, ты легла́.[2]
В ночи́ Млечпу́ть серебряной Око́ю.[3]
Я не спешу́,[4] и мо́лниями телегра́мм
Мне не́зачем тебя́ буди́ть и беспоко́ить.[5]

Как говоря́т, инциде́нт испе́рчен.[6]
Любо́вная ло́дка разби́лась о бы́т.[7]
С тобо́й мы в расчёте.[8] И не́ к чему пе́речень
взаи́мных боле́й, бед и оби́д.[9]

[1] Уже́... *It's after 1 A.M.*
[2] Должно́... *It must be that you have already gone to sleep*
[3] Млечпу́ть... *the Milky Way is like the silver Oka (river in Moscow)*
[4] *hurry*
[5] мо́лниями... *there's no reason for me to wake you up and trouble you with the lightning speed of telegrams*
[6] *(pun: word invented from words exhausted or completed and peppered)*
[7] Любо́вная... *the boat of love has crashed on daily life*
[8] С... *We're even*
[9] не́... *There's no need for a list of mutual pains, woes, and offenses*

Ты посмотри, кака́я в ми́ре тишь.[10]
10   Ночь обложи́ла не́бо звёздной да́нью.[11]   —2
Ночь обложи́ла не́бо звёздной да́нью.[11]

В таки́е вот часы́[12] встаёшь[13] и говори́шь
века́м,[14] исто́рии и мирозда́нью.[15]

В. В. Мая́ко́вский, 1930

[10] *silence*
[11] *обложи́ла... has exacted from the sky a starry tribute*
[12] *В... At just such times*
[13] *get up*
[14] *to the ages*
[15] *all creation*

Post-reading Tasks

1. Write a two-sentence summary of the poem.
2. Find all the references to money in the poem. How are love and the night compared to a financial relationship?
3. Determine the aspect of all the underlined verb forms and explain the reason for the aspectual choice.
4. Assume the point of view of the woman referred to in the poem and write a response to the narrator about what she was doing and thinking after 1:00 A.M. that night and how she views her relationship with the narrator.

The Imperative

Императи́в

—Прия́тного аппети́та!

PART 1

General
Introduction

The imperative (**императи́в**)* is the form of the verb used to convey a command. In English, for example, we can say "Please answer the phone" or "Let me do that for you," using imperatives to convey our wishes. In Russian there are four kinds of imperatives.

First Person:	Дава́йте я э́то сде́лаю.	*Let me do that.*
	Дава́йте (мы) э́то сде́лаем.	*Let us do that.*
Second Person:	Сде́лай(те) э́то!	*Do that!*
Third Person:	Пусть он/а́ э́то сде́лает.	*Let him/her do that.*
	Пусть они́ э́то сде́лают.	*Let them do that.*
Indirect:	Она́ хо́чет, чтобы мы э́то сде́лали.	*She wants us to do that.*
	Она́ сказа́ла, чтобы мы э́то сде́лали.	*She told us to do that.*

The first- and third-person imperatives and the indirect imperative are rather simple; they are presented in Part 4 of this unit. The second-person imperative requires special attention and is the focus of Part 2.

PART 2

Formation of the
Second-person Imperative

The second-person imperative must be formed in a special manner as outlined below. Start with the **они́** form of the verb.

1. If the **они́** form of the verb ends in **-ают** or **-яют**, (except for verbs whose infinitives end in **-авать**, as explained in step 7), remove the **-ют** and add **-й(те)**.

   Use this approach even for verbs whose infinitives end in **-овать** or **-евать**.

ду́мают	теря́ют
ду́ма-ют	теря́-ют
ду́май(те)	теря́й(те)
сове́туют	вою́ют
сове́ту-ют	вою́-ют
сове́туй(те)	вою́й(те)

2. If the **они́** form of the verb does *not* end in **-ают** or **-яют**, remove the grammatical third-person ending, and then:

пи́ш-ут	говор-я́т
ста́н-ут	гото́в-ят

3. If the stem ends in a single consonant *and* the verb has end-stress in the **я** form, as in these examples, add **-й(те)**.

пиши́(те)	говори́(те)

4. If the stem ends in a single consonant, but the verb does *not* have end-stress in the **я** form, as in these examples, add **-ь(те)**.

стань(те)	гото́вь(те)

---

* Some instructors call it **фо́рма повели́тельного наклоне́ния**.

5. If the stem ends in a single consonant, but the verb is perfective and has the prefix **вы́-**, then add unstressed **-и(те).**

6. If the stem ends in a double consonant, then add unstressed **-и(те).**

вы́йти	вы́сказать
вы́йд-ут	вы́скаж-ут
вы́йди(те)	вы́скажи(те)
по́мнить	чи́стить
по́мн-ят	чи́ст-ят
по́мни(те)	чи́сти(те)

7. For verbs with infinitives in **-дава́ть**, **-става́ть**, and **-знава́ть**, form the imperatives from the infinitive: drop **-ть** and add **-й(те).**

дава́ть	встава́ть
дава́-ть	встава́-ть
дава́й(те)	встава́й(те)

8. Exceptional verbs (and verbs like them) are listed here by infinitive.

бить:	бе́й(те)	дать:	да́й(те)
есть:	е́шь(те)	лечь:	ля́г(те)
пить:	пе́й(те)	ехать:	езжа́й(те)

9. The following verbs have no imperatives.

ви́деть	мо́чь
слы́шать	хоте́ть

Saying

Век живи́, век учи́сь.

Live for an age, learn for an age.
[Live and learn.]

❈   Упражне́ние 6а

Form second-person imperatives from the verbs below.

	INFINITIVE	**они́** FORM	IMPERATIVE
1.	сде́лать	сде́лают	
2.	прочита́ть	прочита́ют	
3.	заказа́ть	зака́жут	
4.	гото́вить	гото́вят	
5.	писа́ть	пи́шут	
6.	иска́ть	и́щут	

❈   Упражне́ние 6б

То́ля is the nine-year-old son of a friend of yours. You've been asked to look after him, but you had to step out for a few minutes just when you expected him home from school. You've got to leave a note with instructions telling him what to do. Because he's only nine, all your commands should be in the **ты** form. Write out sentences from the phrases below using imperative forms. Do not change the aspect of the assigned verbs! (Rules for selecting the aspect of the imperative are presented later.)

взять пече́нье и молоко́ из холоди́льника	*to take cookies and milk from the refrigerator*
вы́пить стака́н молока́ и съесть пече́нье	*to drink up a glass of milk and eat up the cookies*
не смотре́ть телеви́зор	*not to watch television*
пригото́вить уро́к на за́втра	*to prepare his lesson for tomorrow*
написа́ть письмо́ дру́гу	*to write a letter to a friend*
дать соба́ке пое́сть	*to give the dog something to eat*
никого́ не впуска́ть в кварти́ру	*not to let anyone into the apartment*
никому́ не звони́ть по телефо́ну	*not to call anyone on the telephone*
не открыва́ть дверь	*not to open the door*
не волнова́ться—я ско́ро верну́сь	*not to worry: I'll be back soon*

[handwritten margin note: вы́пей]

[handwritten margin note: обо́ху]

ТЕКСТ 6a

In this poem by the symbolist poet Belyi, the narrator has a somewhat bitter attitude toward Russia.

Pre-reading Task

What might you expect to find in a poem about America by a patriot? By someone who is embittered?

Дово́льно: не жди, не наде́йся[1]—
Рассе́йся, мой бе́дный наро́д![2]
В простра́нстве пади́ и разбе́йся[3]
За го́дом мучи́тельный год![4]

5 Века́ нищеты́ и безво́лья.[5]
Позво́ль[6] же, о ро́дина мать,
В сыро́е, в пусто́е раздо́лье,[7]
В раздо́лье твоё прорыда́ть:[8]—

Туда́, на равни́не горба́той,[9]—
10 Где ста́я зелёных дубо́в[10]
Волну́ется ку́пой подъя́той,[11]
В косма́тый свине́ц облако́в,[12]

[1] Дово́льно... *Enough: Don't wait, don't hope*
[2] Рассе́йся... *Disperse, my poor people!*
[3] пади́... *fall and shatter in space*
[4] За... *year after torturous year*
[5] Века́... *Centuries of poverty and subjugation*
[6] *Let me*
[7] В... *In your damp and empty expanse*
[8] *sob my heart out*
[9] Туда́... *There, on the hunched prairie*
[10] Где... *Where a flock of green oaks*
[11] Волну́ется... *waves like a raised clump*
[12] В... *To the shaggy lead of the clouds*

15

Где по́ полю О́торопь ры́щет,
Восста́в сухору́ким кусто́м,[13]
И в ве́тер пронзи́тельно сви́щет
Ветви́стым свои́м лоскуто́м.[14]

20

Где в ду́шу[15] мне смо́трят из но́чи,
Подня́вшись над се́тью бугро́в,[16]
Жесто́кие, жёлтые о́чи
Безу́мных твои́х кабако́в,—[17]
Туда́,—где смерте́й и боле́зней
Лиха́я прошла́ колея́,[18]—
Исче́зни[19] в простра́нство, исче́зни,
Росси́я, Росси́я моя́!

А. Бе́лый, 1908

[13] Где... *Where Terror roams the field rising up like a bush with withered limbs*
[14] И... *and into the wind whistles penetratingly with the rag of its branches*
[15] в... *into my soul*
[16] Подня́вшись... *Having arisen over the range of hills*
[17] Жесто́кие... *cruel, yellow eyes of your mad taverns*
[18] где... *where the evil track of deaths and diseases has passed*
[19] *Disappear!*

Post-reading Tasks

1. Find all the words that relate to nature: What is the image of nature in the poem?
2. Find all the words related to the image of the motherland in the poem.
3. Identify all the imperatives in the poem and determine their infinitive forms.
4. Write a paragraph-long summary in Russian of the meaning of the poem.
5. Think up a title for the poem.

PART 3

Aspect in the Second-person Imperative

There are two basic rules governing aspectual choice for the second-person imperative:

1. Positive commands to execute a single action are expressed with a perfective imperative.

Прочита́йте э́ти материа́лы на за́втра, пожа́луйста!	*Read these materials for tomorrow, please!*
Откро́йте, пожа́луйста, окно́!	*Open the window, please!*
Расскажи́те нам о Москве́!	*Tell us about Moscow!*

Exception: Positive commands to execute actions in general are expressed with an imperfective imperative.

На заня́тиях говори́те по-ру́сски!	*Speak Russian in class!*

В Москве́ не ходи́те в шо́ртах!*	*Don't go around in shorts in Moscow!*
Мо́йте ру́ки пе́ред едо́й!	*Wash your hands before eating.*

2. Negative commands are generally expressed with an imperfective imperative.

Не кури́те!	*Don't smoke!*
Не опа́здывайте!	*Don't be late!*
Не ври́те!	*Don't lie!*

There are three basic exceptions to these rules.

a. Positive commands that are really polite invitations ("Sit down!" or "Have a piece of cake!") are expressed with an imperfective imperative.

Заходи́те к нам когда́-нибудь, пожа́луйста!	*Please come and see us sometime!*
Входи́те, пожа́луйста!	*Please come in!*
Раздева́йтесь, пожа́луйста!	*Please take off your coat!*
Проходи́те, пожа́луйста!	*Please walk through (the entryway into the living room).*
Сади́тесь, пожа́луйста!	*Please sit down!*
Бери́те конфе́т, пожа́луйста!	*Please take some candy!*
Е́шьте пиро́г, пожа́луйста!	*Eat some pie, please!*
Приходи́те к нам ещё раз, пожа́луйста!	*Please come visit us again!*

b. Negative commands to warn against doing something that no one would want to do are expressed with a perfective imperative.

Не упади́те! Здесь ско́льзко!	*Don't fall! It's slippery here!*
Не потеря́йте де́ньги!	*Don't lose the money!*
Не забу́дьте сда́чу!	*Don't forget your change!*

c. Positive commands that must convey urgency or are repeated before they are implemented are expressed with an imperfective imperative. Beware: This may be rude!

Включа́йте телеви́зор! Переда́ча уже́ начала́сь!	*Turn on the TV! The program has already begun!*
Откро́йте окно́! Открыва́йте же окно́!	*Open the window! Open the window already!*
Да́йте, пожа́луйста, немно́го бума́ги. Ну, дава́йте наконе́ц немно́го бума́ги!	*Give me some paper please. Well, give me some paper already!*

---

* The taboo on wearing shorts is fading under increasing fashion influence from the West.

§   Зада́ние 6а

Imagine going to visit a Russian friend at home. Remember that Russians are generally very hospitable and love having guests. Write out a dialogue between you and your friend in which he or she asks you to come in, take off your coat, walk through the entryway, sit down, have some tea, pie, or candy, and come again. Practice this dialogue out loud and act out what your Russian friend is asking you to do after each polite command. Memorize your dialogue together with all the actions that go with it.

✳   Упражне́ние 6в

Select the aspectually correct form of the imperative from the options provided in the parentheses below. Then identify which rule (1 or 2) or which exception (a, b, or c) supports your choice. (Note that the imperfective imperative is always provided first in each pair.)

1. (Чита́йте/Прочита́йте) пе́рвое предложе́ние.
    Read the first sentence.

2. (Включа́йте/Включи́те) телеви́зор. Ну, (включа́йте/включи́те) же телеви́зор!
    Turn on the television. Well, turn on the television already!

3. Не (отвеча́йте/отве́тьте) на их письмо́: пусть А́нна э́то сде́лает сама́.
    Don't answer their letter: Let Anna do it herself.

4. (Пиши́те/Напиши́те) э́то сло́во на доске́.
    Write this word on the blackboard.

5. Не (забыва́йте/забу́дьте) свои́ ве́щи!
    Don't forget your things!

RUSSIAN

Saying

Ищи́ ве́тра в по́ле.

Look for the wind in a field.
[Look for a needle in a haystack.]

PART 4

First- and Third-person and Indirect Imperatives

single = pf
repeat or neg. = impf

As you may have noticed from the examples in Part 1 of this unit, third-person imperatives are not difficult. They involve only the use of the word **пусть** with the appropriately conjugated verb (of the appropriate aspect).

Пу́сть Та́ня Дубро́вская э́то сде́лает.	*Let Tania Dubrovskaia do it.*
Пусть де́ти игра́ют, пока́ мы чита́ем газе́ту.	*Let the children play while we read the newspaper.*
Пусть Андре́й бу́дет гото́вить обе́д на сле́дующей неде́ле.	*Let Andrei prepare dinner next week.*

Special expressions are used when referring to God.

Не дай Бо́г, он бо́лен ра́ком!	*God forbid he's sick with cancer!*
Дай вам Бог здоро́вья и сча́стья!	*May God grant you health and happiness!*

The first-person singular imperatives are also not difficult, involving only the use of the word **дава́й(те)** with the appropriately conjugated verb (of the appropriate aspect).

Дава́йте я э́то сде́лаю.	*Let me do that.*
Дава́й я пригото́влю обе́д, а ты пока́ отдохни́.	*Let me make dinner while you rest/relax.*
Дава́й я буду гото́вить обе́д на э́той неде́ле.	*Let me prepare dinner every day this week.*

The first-person plural imperative requires the use of **дава́йте** with either the imperfective infinitive or the **мы** form of the perfective or imperfective future, depending on the aspectual context.

Дава́йте не бу́дем говори́ть об э́том.	*Let's not talk about this.*
Дава́йте говори́ть то́лько по-ру́сски.	*Let's talk only in Russian (in general).*
Дава́йте расска́жем им об э́том.	*Let's tell them about this (a single topic of conversation).*

VERB FORMS USED IN дава́йте CONSTRUCTIONS		
	Дава́йте (мы) *(Let's…)*	**Дава́йте (я)** *(Let me…)*
POSITIVE: ONE EVENT	perfective: **мы** form	perfective: **я** form
POSITIVE: MANY EVENTS	imperfective future: **мы бу́дем** + imperfective infinitive	imperfective future: **я бу́ду** + imperfective infinitive
NEGATIVE: ONCE	**не** + imperfective infinitive	**не** + imperfective infinitive
NEGATIVE: MANY TIMES	imperfective future: (**мы**) **не бу́дем** + imperfective infinitive	imperfective future: **я не бу́ду** + imperfective infinitive

Упражне́ние 6г

Complete the following sentences with the correct form of the verb. Note that the imperfective form always comes first in the pair of options in parentheses.

1. Дава́йте сейча́с же (чита́ть/прочита́ем) письмо́ от Па́ши.
   Let's read the letter from Pasha right away.

2. Дава́йте не (чита́ть/прочита́ем) письмо́ сейча́с: дава́йте (ждать/подождём),
   пока́ не придёт О́ля.
   Let's not read the letter now: Let's wait until Olia comes.

3. Дава́йте тогда́ (смотре́ть/посмо́трим) телеви́зор, пока́ не придёт О́ля.
   In that case let's watch television until Olia comes.

4. Дава́йте не (смотре́ть/посмо́трим) телеви́зор; дава́йте лу́чше
   (убира́ть/уберём) ко́мнату и (гото́вить/пригото́вим) обе́д.
   Let's not watch television; instead let's clean up the room and make dinner.

5. Дава́йте я (убира́ть/уберу́) ко́мнату, но пусть Ди́ма (гото́вить/пригото́вит)
   обе́д.
   Let me clean up the room, but let Dima make dinner.

Indirect Imperative

The indirect imperative usually involves a form of **хоте́ть** or **сказа́ть**, the word
что́бы, and the past-tense form of the verb denoting the desired action or the use of
the subjunctive form.

Япо́нцы хотя́т, что́бы ру́сские наконе́ц о́тдали Кури́льские острова́.	*The Japanese want the Russians to return the Kurile islands finally.*
Ру́сские сказа́ли, что́бы япо́нцы переста́ли говори́ть на э́ту тему.	*The Russians told the Japanese to stop talking about this issue.*
Они́ бы реши́ли э́тот вопро́с!	*If only they would resolve this issue!*

Упражне́ние 6д

Now imagine that you are writing a letter to a friend and you want to mention the instructions you left for **То́ля** in **Упражне́ние 6б**. Use the constructions **Я хоте́л(а), что́бы он...** and **пото́м я сказа́л(а), что́бы он...** to convey the essence of your instructions with indirect commands.

ТЕКСТ 6б

This poem was written by Akhmatova and depicts a relationship between the narrator
and Russia that is different from the one in **Текст 6а**.

Pre-reading Task

How do you think Russians might have felt when their country was invaded (by the French or the Germans)?

> Мне го́лос был.[1] Он звал уте́шно,[2]
> Он говори́л: «Иди́ сюда́,
> Оста́вь свой край глухо́й и гре́шный,[3]
> Оста́вь Росси́ю навсегда́.
> 5 Я кровь от рук твои́х отмо́ю,[4]
> Из се́рдца вы́ну чёрный стыд,[5]
> Я но́вым и́менем покро́ю
> Боль пораже́ний и оби́д».[6]
> Но равноду́шно и споко́йно[7]
> 10 Рука́ми я замкну́ла слух,[8]
> Чтоб э́той ре́чью недосто́йной
> Не оскверни́лся ско́рбный дух.[9]
>
>   А. А. Ахма́това, 1917

[1] Мне... *I heard a voice*
[2] Он... *it called to me in comfort (consolation)*
[3] Оста́вь... *Leave (abandon) your dark and sinful land*
[4] Я... *I will wash the blood from your hands*
[5] Из... *I'll remove the black shame from your heart*
[6] Я... *I'll cover with a new name the pain of defeats and offenses*
[7] Но... *But indifferently and calmly*
[8] Рука́ми... *I covered my ears with my hands*
[9] Чтоб... *so that this unworthy speech would not defile my mournful spirit*

Post-reading Tasks

1. Write a two-sentence summary in Russian on the meaning of the poem.
2. What events may have prompted Akhmatova to write this poem?
3. Find all the imperatives in the poem and determine their infinitive forms.
4. Compare this poem to the one in **Текст 6a** by Belyi. Do the poems share any common images or ideas?   *65-66 do as 3*
5. Think up a title for the poem.

✳   Упражне́ние 6е

Reread **Текст 4б** and identify all the imperative forms in the poem. Find the infinitive forms of all the imperatives.   *41*

ТЕКСТ 6в

The following text gives recommendations for people with high blood pressure.

Pre-reading Task

How's your blood pressure? What do doctors recommend we do to keep our blood pressure low? What happens if blood pressure gets too high?

Как же пра́вильно пита́ться при гипертони́ческой боле́зни[1]?

Начнём с со́ли.[2] Ограни́чивайте[3] её употребле́ние[4] при гипертони́ческой боле́зни. Гото́вьте пи́щу без со́ли и лишь слегка́ доса́ливайте уже́ пригото́вленные блю́да.[5] Если ну́жно, улучша́йте вкус[6] несолёной и́ли недосо́ленной пи́щи, испо́льзуя лимо́нную кислоту́, зе́лень укро́па и́ли петру́шки.[7]

Гипертони́ческая боле́знь и артеросклеро́з взаимосвя́заны.[8] Гипертони́я спосо́бствует разви́тию[9] артеросклеро́за и в то же вре́мя сама́ нере́дко возника́ет на его́ фо́не,[10] причём да́же у молоды́х люде́й. Учи́тывайте э́ту осо́бенность при лече́бном пита́нии.[11] Уменьша́йте потребле́ние живо́тных жиро́в,[12] заменя́я их расти́тельными масла́ми.[13] Избега́йте[14] та́кже употребле́ния проду́ктов, содержа́щих[15] холестери́н в больши́х коли́чествах,[16]— пе́чени, по́чек, мозго́в, жи́рных сорто́в мя́са, яи́чных желтко́в.[17]

[1] пита́ться... *eat (take nourishment) when one has high blood pressure*
[2] *salt*
[3] *limit*
[4] *use*
[5] доса́ливайте... *add salt to dishes that have already been cooked*
[6] улучша́йте... *improve the taste*
[7] испо́льзуя... *using lemon, dill, or parsley*
[8] *are related*
[9] спосо́бствует... *promotes the development*
[10] возника́ет... *arises on the background of arterosclerosis*
[11] Учи́тывайте... *Keep this particularity in mind as you plan your diet*
[12] Уменьша́йте... *Reduce the use of animal fats*
[13] заменя́я... *replacing them with vegetable oils*
[14] *avoid*
[15] *containing*
[16] В... *in large quantities*
[17] пе́чени... *liver, kidneys, brains, fatty kinds of meat, and egg yolks*

Post-reading Tasks

1. Summarize the recommendations in English. Add a few more of your own.
2. Look for the Russian words meaning *limit* and *reduce*. Can you recognize the roots in these words? (Hint: Think of the Russian words for *border* or *frontier* and *less*.)
3. Reread the text and find as many imperatives as you can: Underline the imperatives.   7
4. What is the aspect of the imperatives? Why are the imperatives of this aspect?
5. Pretend that you have a Russian friend whose father has high blood pressure and arteriosclerosis. She has written you for advice concerning her father's diet. Write her a letter, summarizing the information in this text. Be sure to transform the imperatives from second person to third person imperatives with **пусть** or **что́бы**.
6. Write a paragraph on the dietary restrictions for diabetics under the title: **Пита́ние при са́харном диабе́те**.

✳ Упражне́ние 6ё

Continue your list of all the connecting words and phrases (such as *because, but, in the first place, then,* and so forth) with those you can find in the texts of this unit. Next to each connecting word or phrase, write out the clause or sentence in which they are used. Keep this list in your notebook and add to it as you continue with this book.

✳ Упражне́ние 6ж

Add the verbs of this unit to your lists of first- and second-conjugation verbs and note the stress pattern of each verb.

The Nominative Case

Имени́тельный паде́ж: *Кто? Что?*

На ры́нке.

PART 1 General Introduction

As we discussed in Unit 1, Russian is a highly inflected language. In order to know which case to use in any given context, you will have to memorize the case requirements of all verbs and prepositions. Russian has particular rules about the cases governing nouns, adjectives, and pronouns that are the objects of verbs and prepositions. There is no rhyme or reason why a verb or preposition requires a particular case except that Russians have communicated this way for centuries. Why, for example, do we English speakers say *to think something through* or *to think something up*? Why not say *to think something out* or *to think something down*? It's important to memorize the verbs and their conjugations together with the cases so that you can use them correctly.

✻   Упражнéние 7a

Examine the glossaries in the *Workbook* for Units 1 through 6 to determine how case information is provided. Compare the case information with the case names in the Appendix and in Unit 1.

The nominative case (**имени́тельный падéж: *кто? что?***) is used for nouns, adjectives, and pronouns that are the subject of the clause in which they occur or that are the subject complement of verbs such as **есть** (when it means *to be*) and, in some constructions, **быть** (also *to be*).

1. **Па́вел Кири́ллович и Ири́на Андрéевна** зайдýт чéрез час.

   Pavel Kirillovich and Irina Andreevna will drop by in an hour.

2. **Тама́ра Васи́льевна** прекра́сно говори́т по-англи́йски.

   Tamara Vasil'evna speaks English splendidly.

3. В на́шем го́роде есть **хоро́ший универма́г**.

   There's a good department store in our city.

4. Э́то была́ **Мари́на**.

   It was Marina.

In examples 1 and 2, the emphasized words are the nominative case subjects of the verbs *to drop by* and *to speak*, whereas in examples 3 and 4, the nominative case subject complements (Marina, good department store) of the verb *to be* are emphasized.

Before going on, review in Unit 1 ~~сtp стр 6,7~~

- the determination of the gender of nouns
- the determination of whether a noun's stem is hard or soft

✳ Упражнéние 7б

Answer the questions.

1. What is the gender of the following nouns?
   собáка   мóре   кот   ночь   письмó
2. Determine whether the stems of these nouns are hard or soft.
3. Which of the nouns are animate and which are inanimate?

RUSSIAN **Saying**

Не всё то зóлото, что блестѝт.

Not all that glistens is gold.

PART 2 Regular Plural Endings

Nominative case plural adjectives end in either **-ые** or **-ие** depending on whether they are attached to a hard or soft stem or whether any of the three spelling rules apply (see Unit 1, Part 6): **хорóшие, плохѝе, интерéсные, скýчные, ужáсные, богáтые.** The rules regarding nouns are somewhat more complicated.

CATEGORY OF NOUN	PLURAL ENDING	EXAMPLES
Hard-stem masculine and feminine nouns such as **студéнт,* газéта**	-ы	студéнты,* газéты
Soft-stem masculine or feminine nouns such as **словáрь, тётя***	-и	словарѝ, тёти*
Hard-stem neuter nouns such as **окнó, письмó**	-а	óкна, пѝсьма
Soft-stem neuter nouns such as **здáние, упражнéние**	-я	здáния, упражнéния

* This is an animate noun. Animate nouns include people and animals, living or deceased.

ТЕКСТ 7a

Read the first three stanzas of Lermontov's ballad "Borodino." A young Russian soldier is asking an older soldier (whom he calls "Uncle") about the decisive battle against

Napoleon that took place in Borodino immediately preceding Napoleon's capture of
Moscow and the great fire of 1812.

Pre-reading Task

What sort of relationships tend to develop between young soldiers and old ones? Are
these relationships between soldiers different from those between young people and
old people generally? Do you know any books or movies in which young and old come
together?

[handwritten: молодой]

    —Скажи́-ка,[1] дя́дя, ведь не да́ром[2]
Москва́, спалённая пожа́ром,[3]
    Францу́зу отдана́?[4]
Ведь бы́ли ж схва́тки боевы́е,[5]
5   Да, говоря́т, ещё каки́е!
Неда́ром по́мнит вся Росси́я
    Про[6] день Бородина́!

[handwritten: старый]

    —Да, бы́ли лю́ди в на́ше вре́мя,
Не то, что ны́нешнее пле́мя:[7]
10   Богатыри́[8]—не вы!
Плоха́я им доста́лась до́ля:[9]
Немно́гие верну́лись с по́ля...
Не будь на то Госпо́дня во́ля,[10]
    Не о́тдали б Москвы́!

15   Мы до́лго мо́лча отступа́ли,[11]
Доса́дно[12] бы́ло, бо́я[13] жда́ли,
    Ворча́ли[14] старики́:
«Что ж мы? на зи́мние кварти́ры?[15]
Не сме́ют, что ли, команди́ры
20   Чужи́е изорва́ть мунди́ры
    О ру́сские штыки́?»[16]...

               М. Ю. Ле́рмонтов, 1837

[handwritten notes: фатализм / найти судьбу / решить ч'ю судьбу / идти навстречу / своей жизни]

[1] particle softening the imperative
[2] in vain
[3] спалённая... burned up, consumed by fire
[4] given away
[5] схва́тки... military battles
[6] about (colloq.)
[7] ны́нешнее... contemporary tribe, people
[8] knights, heroes
[9] fate, destiny
[10] Не... If it hadn't been for God's will
[11] мо́лча... silently retreated
[12] sad, depressing
[13] the battle
[14] grumbled
[15] на... off to winter quarters
[16] Чужи́е... tear off others' uniforms on the points of Russian bayonets

Post-reading Tasks

1. Summarize in one or two sentences in Russian the nature of the conflict between
   the older soldier and the younger soldier.
2. Find all the singular or plural words in the nominative case and underline them.
3. Identify the gender of these underlined words.

4. How does the older soldier say that the soldiers of his generation are heroes and that the younger soldiers of today are not?
5. Why does the older soldier think that Moscow was surrendered to the French and then consumed in fire? What might the younger soldier believe about the causes of this catastrophe? Write a response in Russian (in prose or verse) from the younger soldier to the older soldier's argument.

✳ Упражне́ние 7в ✓

Identify the gender of each noun and determine whether its stem is hard or soft. Then provide the plural form.

NOUN	GENDER	STEM	PLURAL FORM
1. учи́тельница			
2. со́лнце			
3. музе́й			
4. письмо́*			
5. самолёт			

* This word has a stress shift in the nominative plural.

RUSSIAN **Saying**

Не до́рог пода́рок, а дорога́ любо́вь.

It's not the present that's dear, it's the love.
[It's the thought that counts.]

ТЕКСТ 7б

The following text is from the prologue to Belyi's novel *Petersburg*. In this excerpt, the narrator tries to describe the importance of Petersburg in the Russian Empire.

Pre-reading Task

What is particular about your town or city that makes it different from any other? How would you describe it? Write a description of your town or city and note the verbs you use. What verbs do we tend to use for definitions?

Что есть Ру́сская Импе́рия на́ша?

Ру́сская Импе́рия на́ша есть географи́ческое еди́нство,[1] что зна́чит: часть изве́стной плане́ты.[2] И Ру́сская Импе́рия заключа́ет:[3] во-пе́рвых[4]—вели́кую, ма́лую, бе́лую и черво́нную Русь;[5] во-вторы́х—грузи́нское, по́льское, каза́нское и астраха́нское ца́рство;[6] в-тре́тьих, она́ заключа́ет... Но—про́чая, про́чая, про́чая.[7]

Ру́сская Импе́рия на́ша состои́т из мно́жества городо́в:[8] столи́чных, губе́рнских, уе́здных, зашта́тных; и да́лее:[9] из первопресто́льного гра́да и ма́тери гра́дов ру́сских.[10]

Град первопресто́льный—Москва́; и мать гра́дов ру́сских есть Ки́ев.

Петербу́рг, и́ли Са́нкт-Петербу́рг, и́ли Пи́тер (что—то́ же[11]) по́длинно принадлежи́т[12] Росси́йской Импе́рии. А Ца́рьград, Константи́ноград (и́ли, как говоря́т, Константино́поль[13]) принадлежи́т по пра́ву насле́дия.[14] И о нём распространя́ться не бу́дем.[15]

Распространи́мся бо́лее о Петербу́рге: есть—Петербу́рг, и́ли Са́нкт-Петербу́рг, и́ли Пи́тер (что—то́ же). На основа́нии тех же сужде́ний[16] Не́вский Проспе́кт[17] есть петербу́ргский Проспе́кт.

Не́вский Проспе́кт облада́ет рази́тельным сво́йством:[18] он состои́т из простра́нства для циркуля́ции пу́блики;[19] нумеро́ванные дома́ ограни́чивают его́;[20] нумера́ция идёт в поря́дке домо́в,—и по́иски ну́жного до́ма весьма́ облегча́ются.[21] Не́вский Проспе́кт, как и вся́кий[22] проспе́кт, есть публи́чный Проспе́кт; то́ есть: проспе́кт для циркуля́ции пу́блики (не во́здуха,[23] наприме́р); образу́ющие его́ боковы́е грани́цы дома́ суть[24]—гм...да: для пу́блики. Не́вский Проспе́кт по вечера́м освеща́ется[25] электри́чеством. Днём же Не́вский Проспе́кт не тре́бует освеще́ния.

Не́вский Проспе́кт прямолине́ен[26] (говоря́ ме́жду на́ми[27]), потому́ что он—европе́йский проспе́кт; вся́кий же европе́йский проспе́кт есть не просто́й проспе́кт, а (как я уже́ сказа́л) проспе́кт европе́йский, потому́ что...да...

A. Бе́лый, «Петербу́рг», 1912–1916

[1] *unit*
[2] *часть... part of a certain planet*
[3] *includes*
[4] *in the first place*
[5] *вели́кую... Great Russia (Russia), Little Russia (Ukraine), White Russia (Belarus), and Red Russia*
[6] *грузи́нское... the Kingdoms of Georgia, Poland, Kazan', and Astrakhan*
[7] *and so on and so on*
[8] *состои́т... consists of a multitude of cities*
[9] *столи́чных... capital and provincial (of various levels); and furthermore*
[10] *первопресто́льного... the city of the first throne (of the first Russian monarchy) and the mother of all Russian cities*
[11] *что... which is one and the same*
[12] *по́длинно... genuinely belongs to*
[13] *Constantinople (now Istanbul)*
[14] *принадлежи́т... belongs to Russia by the right of inheritance*
[15] *о... we won't talk any more about it*
[16] *На... On the basis of these same arguments*
[17] *Nevskii Prospect (the most important street in Petersburg)*
[18] *Не́вский... Nevskii Prospect has a unique quality*
[19] *состои́т... it consists of space for the circulation of the public*
[20] *нумеро́ванные... numbered buildings define it*
[21] *по́иски... searches for a particular building are made much easier*
[22] *any*
[23] *not air*
[24] *образу́ющие... the buildings that form the side borders of it are*
[25] *is lit by*
[26] *rectilinear*
[27] *confidentially, just between us*

Post-reading Tasks

1. Write the main idea of each paragraph of Belyi's prologue in English.
2. Reread the text and determine the kind of audience the narrator might be addressing.
3. What is the tone of the text?

4. What are the two most important geometric figures of the text and how do they relate to each other?

5. What is the relationship between Petersburg and Russia according to this text?

6. Underline all the words in the nominative case. Circle those that are the subject of the sentence in which they occur. Of those you did not circle, identify the verbs (or implied verbs) for which they are the subject complement.

7. Given the meaning of **освещáется** (*is lit by*), what do you think **освещéние** means?

8. Given the meaning of **во-пéрвых**, what do you think **во-вторы́х** and **в-трéтьих** mean?

9. Write a paragraph or two in Russian describing New York, Los Angeles, or Washington, D.C., in relation to the United States, using this text as a model.

PART 3
Irregular Plural Endings

1. There are many common nouns that have an irregular plural ending in the nominative case.

Mothers and daughters: **мать → мáтери, дочь → дóчери**
Brothers, husbands, and sons: **брат → брáтья, муж → мужья́,**
   сын → сыновья́
✓ Children: **ребёнок → дéти**
People: **человéк → лю́ди**
Friends: **друг → друзья́**
Chairs: **стул → сту́лья**

2. Many nouns have a stress shift in the nominative plural.

женá	жёны	*wife/wives*
сестрá	сёстры	*sister/s*
дéло	делá	*matter/s*
слóво	словá	*word/s*
ногá	нóги	*leg/s*
рукá	рýки	*arm/s*
окнó	óкна	*window/s*
письмó	пи́сьма	*letter/s*

3. Many nouns have a "fleeting vowel" that drops out before the declension ending is added.

америкáнец	америкáнцы	*American/s*
канáдец	канáдцы	*Canadian/s*

4. Many masculine nouns take the ending **-á/-я** in the nominative plural. Although the ending **-á/-я** may make these nouns look feminine singular, they remain masculine, because the gender is determined by the nominative singular ending.

áдрес	адресá	*address/es*
дóктор	докторá	*doctor/s*
глаз	глазá	*eye/s*
гóлос	голосá	*voice/s*
гóрод	городá	*city/cities*
дом	домá	*building/s*
нóмер	номерá	*number/s or hotel room/s*
профéссор	профессорá	*professor/s*
учúтель	учителя́	*schoolteacher/s*

5. Some masculine nouns ending in **-анин/-янин** take the ending **-ане/-яне**.

граждани́н	гра́ждане	*citizen/s*
россия́нин	россия́не	*citizen/s of the Russian Federation**

6. Substantives: Some nouns are adjectival in form and take plural adjectival endings.

знакóмый	знакóмые	*acquaintance/s*
учёный	учёные	*scholar/s*
больнóй	больны́е	*patient/s*
взрóслый	взрóслые	*adult/s*
живóтное	живóтные	*animal/s*
бýлочная	бýлочные	*bakery/bakeries*

7. Many nouns, especially foreign borrowings, are indeclinable: They do not change form in any case. The only way you can determine the case of these words is from the adjective that modifies them or from other contextual clues. The following nouns are neuter, unless otherwise noted.

рáдио	*radio*
метрó	*metro, subway*
пальтó	*overcoat*
кафé	*cafe*
кóфе (м.)	*coffee*
меню́	*menu*
такси́	*taxi*
бюрó	*office*
кинó	*the movies, the film industry, a movie theater*

---

* Not necessarily ethnic Russians, but people of any nationality who are citizens of the Russian Federation, e.g., Ukrainians, Tatars, Chechens, Karelians, and so forth.

8. Some nouns exist only in singular form.

мéбель (f.)	*furniture*
одéжда	*clothing*

9. And some words exist only in plural form.

брюки	*pants*
дéньги	*money*
нóжницы	*scissors*
очкú	*eyeglasses*
óвощи	*vegetables*
пóхороны	*funeral*
щи	*cabbage soup*
шáхматы	*chess*

RUSSIAN

Saying

Друзья́ познаю́тся в беде́.

In bad times you know who your true friends are.
[A friend in need is a friend indeed.]

✳   Упражнéние 7г

Identify the gender of each noun and determine whether its stem is hard or soft. Then provide the plural form.

NOUN	GENDER	STEM	PLURAL FORM
1. стул			*стýлья*
2. друг*			*друзья́*
3. учёный			*учёные*
4. мать			*мáтери*
5. отéц†			*отцы́*

* This word has a stress shift in the nominative plural.
† This word is end stressed.

✳   Упражнéние 7д

Review the nouns in **Упражнéние 7г** and make a list of those that are inanimate.

❋   Упражне́ние 7е

Imagine a Russian tourist who enthusiastically responds to everything he or she sees. Using the following adjectives and the nouns, create sentences the tourist might say following the model. Make sure your adjectives agree in number and gender with the nouns they modify. Choose from the list of adjectives below or come up with your own.

Adjectives: хоро́ший, плохо́й, интере́сный, ску́чный, большо́й, ма́ленький, мо́дный, старомо́дный, совреме́нный, (не)краси́вый, удиви́тельный, гря́зный, чи́стый.

Nouns: дома́, газе́та, учителя́, гра́ждане, больны́е, бу́лочные, метро́, ме́бель, карто́фель, оде́жда, очки́, о́вощи, профессора́, студе́нтка, такси́, учёный, и́мя, города́, пи́сьма, сёстры, бра́тья.

ОБРАЗЕ́Ц: Каки́е интере́сные дома́!

PART 4
Two Irregular Noun Groups and One Irregular Noun

You probably noticed that the first examples of irregular plural nouns, **мать** and **дочь**, take the infix **-ер-** before the regular ending. This infix appears throughout the declension except the nominative and accusative singular.

мать, дочь		
CASE	**SINGULAR**	**PLURAL**
NOMINATIVE	мать, дочь	ма́тери, до́чери
ACCUSATIVE	мать, дочь	матере́й, дочере́й
GENITIVE	ма́тери, до́чери	матере́й, дочере́й
PREPOSITIONAL	ма́тери, до́чери	матеря́х, дочеря́х
DATIVE	ма́тери, до́чери	матеря́м, дочеря́м
INSTRUMENTAL	ма́терью, до́черью	матеря́ми, дочерьми́

The neuter nouns **и́мя** and **вре́мя** behave similarly to **мать** and **дочь**. These nouns take the infix **-ен-** in all cases except the nominative and accusative singular. Depending on the stress for the given case, this infix may also be spelled **-ён-**.

и́мя, вре́мя		
CASE	**SINGULAR**	**PLURAL**
NOMINATIVE	и́мя, вре́мя	им**ена́**, врем**ена́**
ACCUSATIVE	и́мя, вре́мя	им**ена́**, врем**ена́**
GENITIVE	и́м**ени**, вре́м**ени**	им**ён**, врем**ён**
PREPOSITIONAL	и́м**ени**, вре́м**ени**	им**ен**а́х, врем**ен**а́х
DATIVE	и́м**ени**, вре́м**ени**	им**ен**а́м, врем**ен**а́м
INSTRUMENTAL	и́м**ен**ем, вре́м**ен**ем	им**ен**а́ми, врем**ен**а́ми

Also, note that the masculine word **путь** (*path*, *way*) has a mixed declension, feminine in the singular of the genitive, prepositional, and dative cases.

путь		
CASE	**SINGULAR**	**PLURAL**
NOMINATIVE	путь	пути́
ACCUSATIVE	путь	пути́
GENITIVE	пути́	путе́й
PREPOSITIONAL	пути́	путя́х
DATIVE	пути́	путя́м
INSTRUMENTAL	пут**ём**	путя́ми

Упражне́ние 7ё

Imagine that you have some friends who are very negative about everything. Whatever you show them, whatever you tell them about, they always respond, "What terrible. . . !" or "Such awful. . . !" Use the following nouns to form sentences according to the model **Каки́е ужа́сные . . .** Or create a similar sentence of your choice. Be sure to check whether each noun is singular feminine (ending in **-а/-я**), plural neuter, or plural masculine before making up your sentences.

1. города́
2. кварти́ра
3. дома́
4. газе́та
5. номера́ (в гости́нице)

Упражне́ние 7ж

Using the nouns in **Упражне́ние 7ё**, write new sentences showing the singular form of the plural nouns and the plural form of the singular nouns.

PART 5

Numbers

Numbers are used in the nominative case when they govern a noun or noun phrase that is the subject of the sentence.

1.	В за́ле сиде́ла **одна́** ти́хая студе́нтка.	*One quiet student was sitting in the auditorium.*
2.	**Три** студе́нта ти́хо говори́ли ме́жду собо́й.	*Three students were quietly talking among themselves.*

It is important to note that although the numbers in the preceding sentences are in the nominative case, the noun or noun phrase they govern is not necessarily in the nominative. The noun is, in fact, governed by the number and is in the genitive case (as in example 2), *unless* the number is 1 or ends in 1 such as 21, 31, 41, and so forth (as in example 1). (The rules concerning the use of nouns governed by numbers are presented in Unit 8.)

Review the nominative case forms of number nouns (**оди́н**, **два**, etc.) in the Appendix.

Number adjectives (ordinal numbers: **пе́рвый**, **второ́й**, etc.) are formed from number nouns (cardinal numbers). They are used in the neuter singular form to answer the question **Како́е сего́дня число́?** (*What's today's date?*).

1.	Сего́дня тре́тье ноября́.	*Today is the third of November.*
2.	Вчера́ бы́ло девятна́дцатое ма́я.	*Yesterday was the nineteenth of May.*
3.	За́втра бу́дет два́дцать второ́е января́.	*Tomorrow will be the twenty-second of January.*

Note that in compound numbers (such as 62 or 96), only the last digit of the adjective is declined (as in example 3). The previous digits are written and pronounced as nouns. Review the number adjectives in the Appendix.

✳   Упражне́ние 7з

Practice saying out loud the following numbers as nouns and then as neuter adjectives.

1	19	31
4	21	1.007*
12	22	1.994
14	24	2.540
17	28	

---

* Russians use a period to set off thousands (except when giving the year, in which case no punctuation is used, as in English), and commas where North Americans use a decimal point to set off whole numbers from numbers less than 1.

✳   Упражне́ние 7и

Practice asking the date with the following different responses as answers. Remember to use the neuter adjective for the date.

Како́е сего́дня число́? Сего́дня ...

2	10	18
3	11	19
4	12	20
5	13	21
6	14	30
7	15	31
8	16	
9	17	

Introduction to Subordination

One of the most important characteristics of good speech and writing is the use of complex and compound sentences to connect simple sentences.

1. She is my friend. She works in a hospital. She is a nurse. Her name is Anne. She likes classical music.

These sentences are all technically correct, but they may seem "primitive" to the adult native speaker of English, who would use subordination.

2. My friend Anne, who works as a nurse in a hospital, likes classical music.

The clause in the middle of example 2 is called a subordinate clause. One idea ("works as a nurse in a hospital") is "subordinated" to another ("My friend Anne likes classical music"). Subordinate clauses in English and in Russian make your speech and writing sound more sophisticated to native speakers of both languages.

There are many different ways of subordinating clauses in Russian, but three of the most important use the words **кото́рый**, **кто**, and **что**.

Кото́рый is a relative pronoun that declines as an adjective. It means *that, which,* or *who/whom*. It agrees in gender and number with the antecedent to which it refers, but its case is determined by the clause in which it is used.

3. Мое́й подру́ге А́нне, кото́рая рабо́тает медсестро́й в больни́це, нра́вится класси́ческая му́зыка.
My friend Anne, who works as a nurse in a hospital, likes classical music.

4. Мы говори́ли со **Смирно́выми**, кото́рые то́лько что купи́ли но́вый компью́тер.
We were talking with the Smirnovs, who just bought a new computer.

Кото́рый is used with antecedents, which are nouns. In examples 3 and 4, the antecedents are in bold. Note that **кото́рый** agrees in number and gender with each of the antecedents (**А́нна** = feminine and singular = **кото́рая**; **Смирно́вы** = plural = **кото́рые**), but the case of the antecedent is not necessarily the same as the case used for **кото́рый**. **Мое́й подру́ге А́нне** is in the dative case because it agrees with the **нра́вится** construction, but **кото́рая** is in the nominative case because it is the subject of the clause in which it occurs. **Смирно́выми** is in the instrumental case because it is the object of the preposition **со** (*with*), but **кото́рые** is in the nominative case because it is also the subject of the clause in which it occurs.

 Упражне́ние 7й

Use **кото́рый** clauses to connect each pair of simple sentences. The word **кото́рый** requires the nominative case in every instance.

1. Мы идём к Та́не. Та́ня хорошо́ зна́ет Ми́шу.
2. Ива́н рабо́тает в инжене́рном институ́те. Инжене́рный институ́т нахо́дится недалеко́ отсю́да.
3. Ири́на Вита́льевна написа́ла но́вую кни́гу. Её кни́га получи́ла большо́й приз.
4. Пе́тя получи́л письмо́ от Андре́евых. Андре́евы живу́т в Каза́ни.
5. Тама́ре о́чень нра́вится но́вое ра́дио. Э́то ра́дио хорошо́ принима́ет сигна́лы из Петербу́рга.

Whereas the word **кото́рый** is used with antecedents that are nouns, the words **кто** and **что** are used with antecedents that are pronouns (animate and inanimate, respectively).

Ва́ся бои́тся **всех**, **кто** говори́т с акце́нтом.	*Vasia is afraid of everyone who speaks with an accent.*
Ра́я взяла́ **всё**, **что** им бы́ло ну́жно, и пошла́ на рабо́ту.	*Raia took everything that they needed and left for work.*

Like **кото́рый**, the case of **кто** and **что** is determined by the clause in which it occurs but **кто** is always masculine singular,* and **что** neuter singular.

Ве́ра помога́ет **всем**, **кому́** мы не мо́жем помога́ть.	*Vera helps everyone whom we cannot help.*
Бо́ря забыва́ет **всё**, **о чём** ему́ не напомина́ют.	*Boria forgets everything about which he is not reminded.*

An easy way to remember how to use these two constructions is as follows.

все, кто	*everyone who*
всё, что	*everything that/which*

---

* Colloquially **кто** may be used with plural verbs when the antecedent is plural: **Мы поговори́ли со все́ми, кто там бы́ли** (*We spoke with all those who were there*).

✳ Упражнéние 7к

Fill in the blanks with **кто** or **что** as required by context.

1. Дúма берёт всё, _____ емý даю́т.
2. Лéра доверя́ет всем, _____ говорúт хорошó об Андрéе.
3. Галúна Андрéевна забы́ла обо всём, _____ ей бы́ло нýжно.
4. Мы говорúли со всéми, _____ был на собрáнии.
5. Там бы́ли все, _____ хорошó знал Дмúтрия.

 ТЕКСТ 7в

Memorize this short poem by Blok.

Pre-reading Task

Have you ever had the feeling of being frozen in time?

Ночь, ýлица, фонáрь,[1] аптéка,[2]
Бессмы́сленный и тýсклый свет.[3]
Живú ещё хоть[4] чéтверть вéка[5]—
Всё бýдет так. Исхóда[6] нет.

Умрёшь[7]—начнёшь опя́ть сначáла,
И повторúтся всё, как встарь:[8]
Ночь, ледяня́я рябь[9] канáла,
Аптéка, ýлица, фонáрь.

А. А. Блок, 1912

[1] *streetlamp*
[2] *pharmacy*
[3] тýсклый... *dreary light*
[4] *at least, if only*
[5] *of a century*
[6] *solution, outcome, way out*
[7] *You'll die*
[8] И... *everything will be repeated as of old*
[9] ледяня́я... *icy ripples*

Post-reading Tasks

1. Write a one-sentence summary of the poem.
2. Blok did not give this poem a title. After you read it, try to come up with a title.
3. If the word **смысл** means *meaning, sense, idea,* or *thought,* what do you think **бессмы́сленный** means?
4. Find the Russian word for *pharmacy* in the text. Think of an English word with the same meaning that has some of the same letters as the Russian word.
5. Find the two words in the poem whose roots are *numerical* and define them.
6. The poet seems to be saying that everything will always be the same, but is it?
7. Write a one-paragraph response to the poem in Russian, describing what the same scene might be like today.

✳   Упражнѐние 7л

Continue your list of all the "connecting" words and phrases (such as *because*, *but*, *in the first place*, *then*, and so forth) with those you can find in the texts of this unit, especially in **Текст 7б.** Next to each connecting word or phrase, write out the clause or sentence in which they are used. Keep this list in your notebook and add to it as you continue with this book.

✳   Упражнѐние 7м

Add the verbs of this unit to your lists of first- and second-conjugation verbs and note the stress pattern of each.

✳   Упражнѐние 7н

In Unit 1 you were told to dedicate a page in your notes to the nominative case. On that page write out some of the lists of regular plural forms explained above as well as some of the more common exceptions. Then make a list of all the verbs that take nominative case complements (as described above and demonstrated in **Текст 7б**).

есть, (суть!)

до

The Genitive Case

Роди́тельный паде́ж: *Кого́? Чего́?*

Э́ти же́нщины пою́т ру́сские
наро́дные пе́сни.

89

PART 1 Usage

The genitive case (**роди́тельный паде́ж:** *кого́? чего́?*), one of the most frequently used cases, has many applications.

1. to express possession

    Э́то маши́на **мое́й ма́тери**.   *This is my mother's car.*

2. to express *of* or to answer the question **чей?** (*whose?*)

    Э́то Валенти́на Васи́льевна,   *This is Valentina Vasil'evna, the*
        дире́ктор **на́шего клу́ба**.   *director of our club.*

    —Чьи э́то де́ньги?   —*Whose money is this?*
    —Э́то де́ньги **Мари́ны   —*This is Marina Pavlovna's money*
        Па́вловны**.   *(the money of Marina Pavlovna).*

3. to express measures and quantities after the words **ско́лько, не́сколько, мно́го, немно́го,** and **ма́ло**

    Здесь о́чень *мно́го* **книг**, а там   *There are a lot of books here, but*
        бы́ло то́лько *не́сколько*   *there were only a few magazines*
        журна́лов.   *there.*

4. to express lack or negation

    У них *не́ было* **никаки́х де́нег**.   *They didn't have any money.*
    Его́ *нет* до́ма.   *He's not home.*

5. to express the direct object of a negated verb

    Они́ *не писа́ли* **никаки́х пи́сем**.   *They didn't write any letters.*

6. to express the date when something happened

    Они́ уе́хали **четвёртого ма́рта**.   *They left on March fourth.*

7. Certain verbs, including **боя́ться** and **избега́ть/избежа́ть** always take the genitive case, while other verbs, such as **тре́бовать** and **иска́ть**, take the genitive case only when the object of the verb is abstract (rather than concrete or specified).

    Э́тот ма́льчик *бои́тся* **соба́к**.   *This boy is afraid of dogs.*
    Она́ *избега́ет* **э́того вопро́са**.   *She's avoiding this question.*
    Профе́ссор *тре́бует* **тишины́**.   *The professor demands silence.*
    Э́тот мужчи́на *и́щет* **сча́стья**.   *This man is looking for happiness.*

    but

    Я *тре́бую* **э́ту кни́гу**.   *I demand this book.*
    Э́тот мужчи́на *и́щет* **жену́**.   *This man is looking for his wife.*

8. with certain prepositions, such as **без, вро́де, для, до, из, кро́ме, о́коло, от, по́сле, с(о),** and **у**

Он прие́хал *без* **по́мощи.**	He arrived without help.
Э́то *вро́де* **маши́ны** «универса́л».	It's sort of (like) a station wagon.
Э́то пода́рок *для* **мое́й подру́ги.**	This is a present for my (girl)friend.
Дава́йте зайдём в кафе́ *до* **фи́льма.**	Let's go to a café before the film.
Они́ *из* **Росси́и.**	They're from Russia.
Все там бы́ли, *кро́ме* **А́нны.**	Everyone was there except Anna.
Она́ стоя́ла *о́коло* **Ки́ры.**	She was standing near Kira.
Мы пришли́ сюда́ *от* **Со́ни.**	We came here from Sonia's place.
Мы пойдём к Са́ше *по́сле* **рабо́ты.**	We'll go to Sasha's after work.
Она́ ушла́ *с* **рабо́ты.**	She left (from) work.*
Я бу́ду стоя́ть *у* **телефо́на.**	I'll be standing by the telephone.

9. to express *from* (**отку́да?**) with the prepositions **из, с,** and **от**

Мы прие́хали *из* **Аме́рики.**	We came from America.
Вот Лари́са Петро́вна: она́ сейча́с идёт домо́й *с* **ле́кции.**	There's Larisa Petrovna: She's coming home now from the lecture.
Анто́н ушёл *от* **свое́й жены́,** и́ли, мо́жет быть, она́ ушла́ *от* **него́:** я то́чно не зна́ю.	Anton left his wife, or maybe she left him: I don't know for sure.

Use **из** in those constructions that normally take **в** for the destination in a *going to* construction:

Мы идём *в* **теа́тр** → Мы сейча́с идём *из* **теа́тра.**	We're going to the theater. → Now we're coming from the theater.

Use **с** in those constructions that normally take **на** for the destination in a *going to* construction:

Мы идём *на* **по́чту.** → Мы сейча́с идём *с* **по́чты.**	We're going to the post office. → Now we're coming from the post office.

Use **от** in those constructions that convey *going away* from a person or a person's home, the direct opposite of *going to* constructions with **к** and the dative case:

Мы идём *к* **Ната́ше.** → Мы идём *от* **Ната́ши.**	We're going to Natasha's house. → We're coming from Natasha's house.

---

* The preposition **с** takes the genitive only when it means *from* or *down off of.* The same preposition takes the instrumental case when it means *with.*

10.   to express *being at someone's home* with the preposition **y**

Вчера́ мы бы́ли в гостя́х *y*   Yesterday we were at Emiliia
Эми́лии Константи́новны.   Konstantinovna's place.

11.   after the numbers 2–4, 22–24, 32–34, and so on: genitive singular noun *and* genitive plural adjective if noun is masculine or neuter; nominative plural adjective if noun is feminine

У Мари́ны *две́* **у́мные до́чери**.   Marina has two smart daughters.
У Па́ши *два* **спосо́бных бра́та**.   Pasha has two talented brothers.

after the numerals 5–20, 25–30, 35–40, and so on: genitive plural noun and adjective

В на́шем го́роде *пять* **интере́сных**   In our city there are five interesting
  музе́ев.   museums.
Мы е́хали *де́сять* **часо́в** на   It took us 10 hours by car and,
  маши́не и наконе́ц прие́хали.   finally, we arrived.

12.   to express the notion *some* (partitive genitive)

Да́йте пожа́луйста **хле́ба**.   Please give me some bread.
Вы́пейте **ча́ю**.   Have a drink of tea.

Many nouns have a special partitive form for this usage: **сыр/сы́ру, рис/ри́су, са́хар/са́хару, чай/ча́ю**.

13.   in certain connecting phrases

С **одно́й стороны́**..., но *с* **друго́й**   On the one hand..., but on the other
  стороны́...   hand...
С **мое́й то́чки зре́ния**... (*С* **то́чки**   From my point of view... (From
  зре́ния А́нны...)   Anna's point of view...)

ТЕКСТ 8a

This excerpt is from an article about people with HIV and AIDS in Russia and the Russian health policy toward the AIDS crisis.

Pre-reading Task

What do you know about AIDS? Is AIDS a problem in Russia? Write down as many words as you can think of, in either English or Russian, that you associate with this disease.

В своё вре́мя президе́нт США Р. Ре́йган на вопро́с журнали́стов отве́тил, что СПИД[1]—э́то пробле́ма гомосексуали́стов, наркома́нов и проститу́ток и им сами́м необходи́мо её реша́ть.[2] Билл Кли́нтон в свое́й инаугурацио́нной ре́чи[3] заяви́л, что СПИД[4]—глоба́льная пробле́ма челове́чества[5] и реши́ть её необходи́мо сообща́.[6] К сожале́нию, конста́тация э́того фа́кта[7] для Аме́рики не́сколько запозда́ла:[8] там уже́ бо́лее одного́ проце́нта населе́ния[9] инфици́ровано ВИЧем.[10]

Росси́йская ситуа́ция по своему́ проло́гу в чём-то схо́дна с америка́нской.[11]...Коли́чество больны́х СПИ́Дом[12] в Росси́и по сравне́нию с други́ми стра́нами[13] пока́ о́чень невелико́. Действи́тельно, по све́дениям ВОЗ,[14] в ми́ре в настоя́щее вре́мя[15] инфици́ровано бо́лее 13 млн. [трина́дцати миллио́нов] челове́к. Согла́сно прогно́зам число́ их возрастёт[16] к 2000 го́ду до 40 млн [сорока́ миллио́нов]. В не́которых стра́нах Центра́льной А́фрики ВИЧ зараже́но,[17] по ра́зным подсчётам,[18] от пяти́десяти до семи́десяти проце́нтов населе́ния, носи́телями инфе́кции[19] явля́ется тре́тья часть бере́менных же́нщин.[20]

...Нам всем необходи́мо осозна́ть, что безразли́чное и́ли негати́вное отноше́ние о́бщества к су́дьбам ВИЧ-позити́вных[21]—э́то пряма́я угро́за дальне́йшего распростране́ния СПИ́Да.[22] В сме́рти[23] больны́х СПИ́Дом дете́й их ма́тери справедли́во обвиня́ют госуда́рство.[24] Ведь и́менно в госуда́рственном лече́бном заведе́нии, в результа́те престу́пной хала́тности находя́щегося на госуда́рственной слу́жбе медици́нского персона́ла,[25] наступа́ет инфици́рование[26] дете́й смерте́льным ви́русом...

...Я выступа́ю от и́мени доброво́льного благотвори́тельного о́бщества[27] в подде́ржку[28] национа́льной програ́ммы по СПИ́ду «Мы и вы», где явля́юсь отве́тственным секретарём.[29]

Почему́ «Мы и вы»? Во-пе́рвых,[30] в борьбе́ со СПИ́Дом[31] должны́ принима́ть уча́стие[32] все, как здоро́вые,[33] так и ВИЧ+. Во-вторы́х, мы счита́ем, что пробле́мы э́ти не явля́ются то́лько медици́нскими, и потому́ мы за равнопра́вный[34] диало́г с госуда́рством. И, в-тре́тьих, пробле́мы СПИ́Да не явля́ются специфи́ческими росси́йскими пробле́мами и тре́буют интегра́ции с мировы́м соо́бществом.[35] Отсю́да—две руки́, протя́нутые[36] друг к дру́гу,[37] на на́шей эмбле́ме.

[1] *AIDS*
[2] *им... they themselves have to solve it*
[3] *в... in his inaugural address*
[4] *СПИД = синдро́м приобретённого иммуннодефици́та*
[5] *of mankind, of humanity*
[6] *all together*
[7] *конста́ция... the mere statement of this fact*
[8] *не́сколько... is somewhat late*
[9] *of the population*
[10] *инфици́ровано... is infected with HIV*
[11] *Росси́йская... The Russian situation in its prologue is in some ways similar to the American*
[12] *Коли́чество... The number of AIDS patients*
[13] *по... in comparison with other countries*
[14] *по... according to information from the WHO (World Health Organization)*
[15] *в... at present*
[16] *Согла́сно... according to the predictions their number will grow*
[17] *infected*
[18] *по... according to various calculations*
[19] *носи́телями... carriers of the infection*
[20] *тре́тья... one third of all the pregnant women*
[21] *безразли́чное... the indifferent or negative attitude of society toward the fate(s) of HIV-positive people*
[22] *пряма́я... is a direct threat of the greater spread of AIDS*
[23] *В... In the death*
[24] *их... their mothers fairly accuse the government*
[25] *в... in a state medical institution as a result of criminal negligence of the medical personnel in state service*
[26] *наступа́ет... the infection takes place*
[27] *Я... I speak on behalf of a volunteer charitable society*
[28] *в... in support of*
[29] *явля́юсь... I am the executive secretary*
[30] *In the first place*
[31] *в... in the struggle with (against) AIDS*
[32] *принима́ть... take part*
[33] *healthy (HIV negative)*
[34] *on equal footing*
[35] *с... with the world community*
[36] *stretched out*
[37] *друг... one to another*

ВИРУС

Post-reading Tasks

1. In Russian summarize the text in three sentences: Who is the author (what organization does he represent?) and what does he consider to be among the most serious problems of the AIDS crisis in Russia?
2. Find all the words that express *fatal* or *lethal*. What are their roots?
3. Make a list of all the words you can find that are English cognates.
4. The underlined words and phrases are in the genitive case. Determine the reason for the use of the genitive case from the list in Part 1.
5. Why did the members of the author's organization choose its name? Provide at least two reasons in Russian.
6. Write a paragraph in Russian describing AIDS policy in your city or state.

Singular Endings

Here are the singular endings for adjectives and nouns in the genitive case.

HARD-STEM ADJECTIVES			
	MASCULINE	**FEMININE**	**NEUTER**
NOMINATIVE CASE	прекра́сный	прекра́сная	прекра́сное
GENITIVE CASE	прекра́сного	прекра́сной	прекра́сного
SOFT-STEM ADJECTIVES			
	MASCULINE	**FEMININE**	**NEUTER**
NOMINATIVE CASE	после́дний	после́дняя	после́днее
GENITIVE CASE	после́днего	после́дней	после́днего
HARD-STEM NOUNS			
	MASCULINE	**FEMININE**	**NEUTER**
NOMINATIVE CASE	стол	газе́та	письмо́
GENITIVE CASE	стола́	газе́ты	письма́
SOFT-STEM NOUNS			
	MASCULINE	**FEMININE**	**NEUTER**
NOMINATIVE CASE	учи́тель	тётя	мо́ре
GENITIVE CASE	учи́теля	тёти	мо́ря

EXCEPTION

Masculine nouns with feminine endings take feminine endings:

(дéдушка) Это друзья́ нашего дéдушки.

 TEKCT 86

In this stanza from Pushkin's novel in verse, *Eugene Onegin*, the narrator warns his readers to keep a watchful eye on their wives and daughters when they head out for a ball.

Pre-reading Task

What would you warn parents about their children's behavior at a party? What do you think a nineteenth-century man would have warned a mother in a similar situation?

Во дни весéлий[1] и желáний
Я был от бáлов без умá:
Вернéй[2] нет мéста для признáний[3]
Или вручéния[4] письмá.
5   О вы, почтéнные супрýги[5]!
Вам предложý свои́ услýги;[6]
Прошý мою́ замéтить рéчь:
Я вас хочý предостерéчь.[7]
Вы тáкже, мáменьки, пострóже[8]
10   За дочерьми́ смотри́те вслед:[9]
Держи́те прямо свой лорнéт[10]!
Не то...не то, избáви Бóже![11]
Я это потомý пишý,
Что уж давнó я не грешý.[12]

А. С. Пýшкин,
«Евгéний Онéгин», 1833

[1] *fun, amusement*
[2] *better*
[3] *confessions*
[4] *the handing over*
[5] *husbands*
[6] *services*
[7] *to warn*
[8] *more carefully*
[9] смотри́те... *watch after*
[10] *lorgnettes (glasses)*
[11] *Не... If not... if not, then God deliver (us from what might happen)!*
[12] *sin (verb)*

Post-reading Tasks

1. Write a three-sentence summary in Russian of the narrator's warning.
2. Why is the narrator warning his readers?
3. Find three noun phrases in the genitive singular. Write these phrases out.
4. Write a prose response in Russian from the point of view of a woman who trusts her daughter, a man who trusts his wife, or a trustworthy daughter or wife.

✳   Упражне́ние 8а

Provide the genitive case form of each word or phrase to complete the sentence **Здесь нет сейча́с...**

1. интере́сная шко́ла
2. плохо́е письмо́
3. большо́й институ́т
4. у́мная студе́нтка
5. у́мный студе́нт

PART 3 Plural Endings

The plural endings for nouns and adjectives in the genitive case are the same as those endings for animate nouns in the accusative case, as described in Unit 9. Note that the spelling of the bold words in each pair of sentences is the same, but that the cases are different because of different meaning and grammatical context.

ACCUSATIVE	GENITIVE
Я о́чень люблю́ **э́тих дете́й**.	**Дете́й** здесь нет: они́ уже́ пошли́ в шко́лу.
I love these children very much.	*The children are not here: They already left for school.*
ACCUSATIVE	GENITIVE
Я ви́жу **ва́ших сестёр**.	**Ва́ших сестёр** здесь нет: они́ пошли́ домо́й.
I see your sisters.	*Your sisters are not here: They went home.*
ACCUSATIVE	GENITIVE
Я понима́ю **э́тих молоды́х специали́стов**.	**Специали́стов** здесь нет: они́ уже́ в лаборато́рии.
I understand these young specialists.	*The specialists are not here: They are already at the laboratory.*

Before we introduce the plural noun endings in the genitive case, it is important to remind you of the concept of the "zero ending." Masculine nouns that end in a consonant in the nominative case, such as **дом** and **стол**, are said to have zero endings. The symbol for zero ending is **Ø**. The endings are given here, and they are summed up in the declension charts in the Appendix.

Masculine nouns ending in **-ч, -ш, -щ, -ж,** and **-ь** in the nominative singular end in **-ей** in the genitive plural.*

> Здесь нет никаки́х врачéй, карандашéй, плащéй, ножéй, словарéй, учителéй.

All other masculine nouns ending in **∅** or **-й** in the nominative singular end in **-ов/-ев** in the genitive plural case.†

> Здесь нет никаки́х столо́в, учéбников, кана́дцев, музéев.

Feminine nouns ending in **-ия** and neuter nouns ending in **-ие** in the nominative case take a genitive plural ending in **-ий.**

> лаборато́рия, консервато́рия, зда́ние, упражнéние →
> лаборато́рий, консервато́рий, зда́ний, упражнéний.

Neuter nouns ending in **-о, -е,** and **-мя** in the nominative singular have a genitive ending in **∅.** Some neuter nouns have filler vowels, such as those emphasized here.

> Здесь нет никаки́х о́кон, пи́сем, знамён, имён.

Feminine nouns ending in **-а** and **-я** in the nominative singular have a genitive ending in **∅.** Some feminine nouns also have filler vowels, such as those emphasized here.

> Здесь нет никаки́х жéнщин, дéвушек, сестёр, кни́г, газéт, ма́рок, лаборато́рий.

Feminine nouns ending in **-ь** in the nominative singular end in **-ей** in the genitive plural.

> Здесь нет никаки́х матерéй, дочерéй, площадéй, тетра́дей.

There are many exceptions to these genitive plural patterns.

Masculine and neuter nouns ending in **-ья** in the nominative plural end in **-éй** in the genitive plural. Note there is *no* soft sign in the spelling of this ending.

> Здесь нет никаки́х мужéй, сыновéй.

Masculine and neuter nouns ending in **-ья** in the nominative plural end in **-ьев** in the genitive plural. Note there *is* a soft sign in the spelling of this ending.

> Здесь нет никаки́х бра́тьев, сту́льев, пéрьев.

There are many exceptions to these rules, including:

1. For some nouns, the genitive plural form is identical to the nominative singular form: **солда́т, глаз, раз.**

---

* In nouns that take this genitive case ending the soft sign is deleted.
† In the rest of this book, hard-stem endings will be given first, soft-stem endings second. Note that soft-stem endings are used when spelling rules prevent the use of the hard stem, as is the case with the adjective **хоро́ший.**

2. The word **челове́к** (*person*) has two genitive plural forms: **челове́к** and **люде́й**. The first is used with numbers that take the genitive plural and the words **ско́лько** and **не́сколько**. The second is used with the words **мно́го** and **ма́ло**.

3. Words that occur only in the plural must be memorized.

де́ньги	→	де́нег
ша́хматы		ша́хмат
по́хороны		похоро́н
щи		щей
о́вощи		овоще́й
де́ти		дете́й
часы́		часо́в
очки́		очко́в
брю́ки		брюк

4. Some nouns are simply irregular and must also be memorized.

сосе́д→сосе́дей, мо́ре→море́й, по́ле→поле́й, дя́дя→дя́дей, тётя→тётей

※ Упражне́ние 8б

Write out your own chart for the regular endings of nouns and adjectives (masculine, feminine, and neuter, and singular and plural for both hard- and soft-stem nouns) in the genitive case. Compare your chart with those in this book to make sure that it is accurate.

※ Упражне́ние 8в

Reread **Текст 8а** and find five noun phrases in the genitive plural case. Write these phrases out on a separate piece of paper.

※ Упражне́ние 8г

Provide the genitive case form of each word or phrase to complete the sentence **Здесь нет сейча́с...**

1. хоро́шие профессора́
2. интере́сные шко́лы
3. блестя́щие студе́нты
4. мои́ сёстры
5. ва́ши бра́тья

※ Упражне́ние 8д

Make a list of five to ten items you have purchased in the last two weeks, including food, clothing, school supplies, and so forth. Write down how much you paid (**плати́ть/заплати́ть**) for each item, being careful to use the correct genitive case forms for the words **до́ллар** (**оди́н до́ллар, два до́ллара, пять до́лларов**) and **цент** (**оди́н цент, два це́нта, пять це́нтов**).

ОБРАЗЕ́Ц: Я обы́чно плачу́ 50 це́нтов за газе́ту.

Я заплати́ла 4 до́ллара за э́ту кни́гу.

✳   Упражне́ние 8е

Reverse the direction of the following sentences, replacing the preposition and changing from the accusative case to the genitive case as required.

ОБРАЗЕ́Ц: Мы сейча́с идём в теа́тр. →

Мы сейча́с идём **из теа́тра**.

1. Они́ е́дут на Украи́ну.*
2. Мы уе́хали в Москву́. («Мы прие́хали...»)
3. Бо́ря е́дет в Петербу́рг.
4. О́ля уе́хала в Хаба́ровск. («О́ля прие́хала...»)
5. Э́ти студе́нты иду́т на ле́кцию.

✳   Упражне́ние 8ё

Complete the sentences with the special partitive genitive forms as required by the context.

1. Да́йте мне, пожа́луйста, ещё (чай)...
2. Бери́те ещё (шокола́д)...
3. Не хо́чешь (са́хар)...?
4. Мо́жно, пожа́луйста, (рис)...?
5. Я бы хоте́ла ещё (сыр)..., пожа́луйста.

Personal Pronouns

PART 4

Review the declension of the personal pronouns in the genitive case in **Табли́ца 12** in the Appendix.

Remember that the third-person genitive personal pronouns (**его́, её, их**) sometimes acquire the letter **н**. This letter is added whenever the personal pronoun is the object of a preposition.

It is important to distinguish between personal pronouns in the accusative and genitive cases and possessive modifiers **его́, её, их** (*his, her, their*), which look the same but differ in meaning. Compare the meanings of these words in the following exam-

---

* Current usage now allows **в Украи́ну**.

ples: In each pair of sentences, the sentences on the left feature a personal pronoun, while the sentences on the right feature a possessive pronoun that may look like the same word. (Compare the English word *her* in the two sentences: "I saw her" and "I saw her sister.")

PERSONAL PRONOUNS	POSSESSIVE PRONOUNS
Они́ бы́ли у **него́** в гостя́х в Петербу́рге.	Они́ бы́ли у **его́** сестры́ в гостя́х в Петербу́рге.
They were at his place in Petersburg.	*They were at his sister's place in Petersburg.*
Мы ча́сто хо́дим к **ней**.	Мы ча́сто хо́дим к **её бра́ту**.
We often go to visit her.	*We often go to visit her brother.*
Мы уже́ говори́ли с **ни́ми** об э́том.	Мы уже́ говори́ли с **их преподава́телем** об э́том.
We already spoke with them about this.	*We already spoke with their teacher about this.*

If you're not sure whether a word is a personal pronoun in the accusative or genitive case or a possessive pronoun, try substituting other Russian words of the same grammatical category to see which one fits best: To test for other personal pronouns in the accusative and genitive cases, try using **меня́**, **тебя́**, **нас**, **вас**; to test for possessive pronouns, try using **моего́/мое́й/мои́х**, **твоего́/твое́й/твои́х**, **на́шего/на́шей/на́ших**, **ва́шего/ва́шей/ва́ших**.

❉   Упражне́ние 8ж

In the preceding examples circle the prepositions that govern the emphasized pronouns.

❉   Упражне́ние 8з

Fill in the blanks with the correct form of the personal pronoun.

1. Вчера́ мы бы́ли у (они́) _____ в гостя́х; нам бы́ло о́чень ве́село.
2. Э́то кни́га для (он) _____.
3. Когда́ (вы) _____ не́ было, мы реши́ли пойти́ в кино́.
4. —Мари́на до́ма?
   —Нет, (она́) _____ сейча́с здесь нет.
5. Мы ча́сто быва́ем у (она́) _____.

ТЕКСТ 8в

This very short story was written by the absurdist writer Kharms in 1937.

Pre-reading Tasks

What do you know about Russia in the late 1930s? Think about the relevance of the history of the period as you read Kharms's story.

Голубáя тетрáдь[1] нóмер 10

Жил одúн рúжий[2] человéк, у котóрого нé было глаз и ушéй. У негó нé было и волóс, так что рúжим его называáли услóвно.[3]

Говорúть он не мог, так как у негó нé было рта.[4] Нóса тóже у негó нé было.

У негó нé было дáже рук и ног. И животá[5] у негó нé было, и спинú[6] у негó нé было, и хребтá[7] у негó нé было, и никакúх внýтренностей[8] у негó нé было. НИЧЕГÓ НÉ БЫЛО! Так что непонáтно, о ком идёт речь.[9]

Уж лýчше мы о нём не бýдем бóльше говорúть.[10]

Д. И. Хармс, 1937

[1] Голубáя... *Blue notebook*
[2] *redheaded*
[3] рúжим... *calling him a redhead was a convention*
[4] *mouth*
[5] *stomach*
[6] *back*
[7] *spine, backbone*
[8] *internal organs*
[9] о... *about whom we're talking*
[10] Уж... *It would be better for us not to talk about him anymore*

Post-reading Tasks

1. Write a two-sentence summary of the text in Russian.
2. Find all the words and expressions in the genitive case (singular and plural, including pronouns) and write them out. Then identify the reason they are in the genitive case.
3. Identify the nominative case singular and plural forms of all the words and expressions you found in the genitive case.
4. Write a paragraph about a mystery man or woman in American society, using the text as a model.
5. Write a response from the redheaded man to the description in the text. Why might he complain about it?
6. Write a paragraph explaining the importance of the date the text was written.

Last Names

Russian last names that end in **-ов/-ев** or **-ын/-ин** decline in the genitive singular as nouns for men but as adjectives for women. These names also decline as adjectives in the plural.

Асáнов	Это машúна Асáнова.
Асáнова	Это машúна Асáновой.
Асáновы	Это машúна Асáновых.

Солжени́цын	Э́то маши́на Солжени́цына.
Солжени́цына	Э́то маши́на Солжени́цыной.
Солжени́цыны	Э́то маши́на Солжени́цыных.

Women's last names that end in a consonant do not decline at all.

female: А́ндрея Смит   Э́то маши́на А́ндреи Смит.
male: Андре́й Смит   Э́то маши́на Андре́я Сми́та.

✳ Упражне́ние 8и

Complete the sentences with the correct form of the last names indicated.

Э́то маши́на...

1. Серге́й Па́влов
2. Ири́на Па́влова
3. Па́вловы
4. Ди́ма Ри́вкий
5. А́нна Ри́вкина
6. Ри́вкины

имя = noun

Saying

Нет ды́ма без огня́.

No smoke without fire.
[Where there's smoke, there's fire.]

PART 6
Possession:
есть and *нет*

English generally uses the verb *to have* as the primary means for expressing possession: the subject of the verb is the person or thing which possesses something and the object of the verb is the thing possessed. Russian uses a very different construction for most expressions of possession, whether positive or negative. A person who possesses or lacks something concrete (not abstract) is identified in the construction **у кого́**, whereas the thing possessed is expressed in the nominative case.

1. **У Андре́я есть** маши́на.   *Andrei has a car.*

When the expression of possession given in example 1 is put in the past or future tense, the verb agrees *not* with the person who possesses, but with the thing possessed, as in examples 2 and 3.

2. У Андре́я **была́** маши́на.   *Andrei had a car.*
3. У Андре́я **бу́дет** маши́на.   *Andrei will have a car.*

In the present tense version of these expressions, the word **есть** is used *only* when the existence of the object is emphasized, as in example 1.

4. У Андре́я **кра́сная** маши́на.   *Andrei has a red car.*
5. У Андре́я **ма́ленькая** маши́на.   *Andrei has a small car.*

Example 4 answers the question, "What *color* is Andrei's car?," while example 5 answers the question, "Is Andrei's car *big or small*?" Both examples 4 and 5 imply the speaker's understanding that Andrei does have a car, and the fact of the car's existence is not in question.

A slightly different construction is used to express possession of things by things.

6. **В университе́те** есть (име́ется) компью́терный це́нтр.   *The university has a computer center.*
7. **На но́вой по́чте** бу́дут больши́е о́кна.   *The new post office will have large windows.*
8. **В Му́рманске** бы́ло мно́го кинотеа́тров и теа́тров.   *Murmansk used to have a lot of movie theaters and theaters.*

In examples 6 to 8, the university, post office, and Murmansk all possess things. When inanimate objects "possess" something, Russian requires the prepositional case of the noun that is the logical subject and **в** or **на** depending on the noun, rather than the **у кого** construction used for people. In such constructions the word **име́ется** or **име́ются** may be used (for a more formal style).

To express possession of an abstraction (such as *happiness, opportunity,* or *honor*), the verb **име́ть** is used as in examples 9 and 10.

9. **Я име́ю честь** предста́вить вам Ири́ну Влади́мировну Андре́еву.   *I have the honor of introducing you to Irina Vladimirovna Andreeva.*
10. **Она́ уже́ име́ла возмо́жность** познако́миться с ва́шей рабо́той.   *She already had an opportunity to become acquainted with your work.*

When expressing the lack of possession, Russians use the genitive case for the thing which is lacked. (Examples 11 to 20 are negations of examples 1 to 10.)

11. У Андре́я **нет маши́ны**.   *Andrei does not have a car.*
12. У Андре́я **не́ было маши́ны**.   *Andrei did not have a car.*
13. У Андре́я **не бу́дет маши́ны**.   *Andrei will not have a car.*
14. У Андре́я **нет кра́сной маши́ны**.   *Andrei does not have a red car.*

15.	У Андрéя **нет мáленькой машѝны.**	*Andrei does not have a small car.*
16.	В университéте **нет (не имéется) компьютерного цéнтра.**	*The university does not have a computer center.*
17.	На нóвой пóчте **не бýдет óкон.**	*The new post office will not have windows.*
18.	В Мýрманске **нé было ни кинотеáтров, ни теáтров.**	*Murmansk had neither movie theaters, nor theaters.*
19.	**Я не имéл чéсти** познакóмиться с вáми рáньше.	*I haven't had the opportunity of becoming acquainted with you earlier.*
20.	Онá **не бýдет имéть возмóжности** познакóмиться с вáми.	*She won't have the opportunity to become acquainted with you.*

The word **есть** is *never* used in constructions expressing the lack of possession. The expressions of lack of possession always feature a genitive-case construction of the objects which are lacking. In the past tense, note also the stress in the expression **нé было**. Lastly, expressions of the lack of possession of more than one object (as in example 18) use a *neither/nor* type construction with **ни** + genitive ... **ни** + genitive.

✻ Упражнéние 8й

Fill in the blanks as required below.

1. У Сóни (will have) _____ дéньги, когдá онá закóнчит институт бизнéса, потомý что онá хорóший предпринимáтель.

2. Рáньше у неё (did not have) _____ дéнег и онá чáсто просѝла дéньги у друзéй и знакóмых.

3. Её родѝтели (did not have) _____ возмóжности мнóго зарабáтывать в совéтское врéмя, но дéньги в то врéмя не имéли такóе значéние, какóе онѝ тепéрь имéют.

4. В институте, где ýчится Сóня, (has) _____ отделéние, котóрое занимáется устрóйством выпускникóв на рабóту.

5. Сóня (has) _____ отлѝчные перспектѝвы (*prospects*) на бýдущее!

✻ Упражнéние 8к

Translate the following sentences into Russian.

1. Anton and Maria have a large apartment which has all the conveniences of modern life (**все удóбства совремéнной жѝзни**).

2. They have all the latest video technology (**вся послéдняя вѝдео-тéхника**), but they don't have a compact-disk player (**плéйер**) or a telephone answering machine (**áвто-отвéтчик**).

3. Previously they didn't have such luxuries (**ро́скоши**) in their life, but then they had an opportunity to invest money (**вложи́ть де́ньги**) in a good investment fund (**инвестицио́нный фонд**) during the privatization process (**во вре́мя приватиза́ции**).
4. This investment fund has good managers (**ме́неджеры**). *имеется*

PART 7
Subordination:
то/что and *то/как* Clauses

То/что and **то/как** clauses may be called the "hinges" of the Russian language. They are used to connect clauses to constructions that require the declension of a noun phrase or pronoun.

Моя́ мать занима́ется тем, что звони́т лю́дям по телефо́ну и про́сит их купи́ть страхо́вку «Аул-Стейт».	*My mother works in telemarketing for All State Insurance.*
Она́ удивля́ется тому́, что мно́гие не име́ют никако́й страхо́вки.	*She is surprised at the fact that many people have no insurance whatsoever.*
Мы все лю́бим мать за то, что она́ и рабо́тает, и занима́ется до́мом.	*We all love our mother because she both works and takes care of our house.*
По́сле того́, как мы всё убира́ем, мать начина́ет рабо́тать для фи́рмы «Аул-Стейт».	*After we clean up everything, mom starts to work for All State.*
Мать, одна́ко, всё вре́мя бои́тся того́, что она́ не дости́гнет но́рмы для свое́й рабо́ты.	*Mom, however, is always afraid that she might not "make the quota" at work.*

✳ Упражне́ние 8л

Fill in the blanks with the correct form of the words **то/что**, then translate the sentences.

1. Он избежи́т _____, _____ она́ ему́ предло́жит.   *того, что*
2. В э́том го́роде нет _____, _____ нам ну́жно.   *того, что*
3. Он бои́тся _____, _____ мо́жет произойти́ за́втра.   *того, что*
4. Мы избега́ем _____, _____ говоря́т на таки́х встре́чах.   *того, что о чём*
5. Я бою́сь _____, _____ они́ боя́тся.   *того, чего*

PART 8

Numbers

You have already read about how numbers may require the words that follow them to take the genitive case.

1. Здесь два больши́х музе́я.   *There are two large museums here.*
2. Там бы́ло пять интере́сных профессоро́в.   *There were five interesting professors there.*

Numbers themselves may be in the genitive case if required by the grammatical context in which they occur.

3. Без э́тих двух больши́х музе́ев, наш го́род был бы неинтере́сным.   *Without these two large museums our city would not be interesting.*
4. Мы избега́ем э́тих пяти́ профессоро́в.   *We are avoiding these five professors.*
5. На́ша семья́ состои́т из семи́ челове́к.   *Our family consists of seven people.*

In example 3, the expression *two large museums* is in the genitive case because it is the object of the preposition *without*, while in example 4, the expression *these five professors* is in the genitive case because it is governed by the verb *to avoid*, which requires the genitive case. In example 5, the words *seven persons* (*people*) are in the genitive case because they are the object of the preposition **из**.

 One of the most common uses of the genitive case with numbers is for times and dates. The genitive case of dates (using the number adjective) has already been discussed (see p. 90).

6. Она́ улета́ет четвёртого сентября́.   *She's leaving on September fourth.*

Memorize the names of the months and their genitive case form.

NOMINATIVE CASE	GENITIVE CASE
янва́рь	января́
февра́ль	февраля́
март	ма́рта
апре́ль	апре́ля
май	ма́я
ию́нь	ию́ня
ию́ль	ию́ля
а́вгуст	а́вгуста
сентя́брь	сентября́
октя́брь	октября́
ноя́брь	ноября́
дека́брь	декабря́

Expressions of clock time sometimes require the genitive case of the number noun or cardinal number. Review the chart of number nouns in the Appendix.   *Таб 16   355-56*

Use the genitive case form of the number noun (cardinal number) whenever the entire expression including the numeral is governed by a preposition or verb that takes the genitive case.

1.	Мы заплати́ли о́коло **двухсо́т ты́сяч** рубле́й за э́то.	*We paid about two hundred thousand rubles for this.*
2.	В да́нном слу́чае врачи́ боя́тся **восемна́дцати** ра́зных инфе́кций.	*In this instance the doctors fear eighteen different infections.*
3.	Она́ нас встре́тит без **десяти́** семь.	*She'll meet us at ten of seven (6:50).*

Russians use the genitive case of the number adjective (ordinal number) when talking about a date with the year, omitting the century if it is the current one.*

1.	Она́ родила́сь в ма́е (ты́сяча девятьсо́т) **шестьдеся́т второ́го го́да.**	*She was born in May of '62.*
2.	Мы полу́чим но́вые материа́лы в ию́не (ты́сяча девятьсо́т) **девяно́сто шесто́го го́да.**	*We'll get the new materials in June of '96.*
3.	Ре́йган был в пе́рвый раз и́збран президе́нтом в ноябре́ (ты́сяча девятьсо́т) **восьмидеся́того го́да.**	*Reagan was elected president for the first time in November of '80.*

Note that in compound numbers (such as 62 and 96), only the last digit of the adjective is declined. The preceding digit is written and pronounced as a noun. Memorize the number adjectives (ordinal numbers) and their genitive case forms for use in such constructions. (See **Табли́ца 17** in the Appendix.)   *357-8*

✳   Упражне́ние 8м

Provide the missing form of the number in parentheses as required by grammatical context. Some of the missing numbers are nouns (cardinal numbers), others are adjectives (ordinal numbers). Write out all numbers as words.

Это кварти́ра мои́х (3) _____ сестёр. (2) _____ из них нет сейча́с до́ма, но ста́ршая сестра́, Ни́на, нам откро́ет дверь. Мла́дшие сёстры уе́хали в Петербу́рг (12) _____ октября́ к дя́де, кото́рый о́чень бо́лен. Он бои́тся свои́х (2) _____ сосе́дей, и поэ́тому о́чень рад, что прие́хали его́ племя́нницы помога́ть. Ни́на сейча́с рабо́тает с иностра́нной делега́цией: делега́ты из (40) _____ ра́зных стран. Кро́ме (6) _____ из них, все говоря́т по-ру́сски. Это удиви́тельно! У (4) _____ из них бы́ли пробле́мы с гости́ницей, но Ни́на помогла́ им всем.

Трёх; Двух
12-го; двух

сороковы́х
шести́
четырёх

---

* When specifying only the year, the prepositional case is used. See Unit 10.

Упражнéние 8н

Prepare a short presentation describing when some important historical or personal events took place or will take place. Use the complete date (day, month, and year).

RUSSIAN

Saying

Не имéй сто рублéй, а имéй сто друзéй.

Don't possess a hundred rubles, possess a hundred friends.
[Friends are what matter most in life.]

ТЕКСТ 8г

This excerpt is from an article about an impending concert appearance of Liza Minnelli in Moscow.

Pre-reading Task

What do Americans like to know about famous people? Do you think Russians would be interested in the same information? Look at the title of the text. Why do you think ice might be so important that it is in the title? What do you expect the author's attitude to Liza Minnelli to be, based on your reading of the title?

Лáйза Миннéлли у рýсских попросúла льда.[1]

«У меня в нóмере должны́ быть: блок[2] “Мáрльборо”, 18 бéлых бáнных [полотéнец][3] и 12 бéлых полотéнец для рук, гримёр,[4] две костюмéрши и перевóдчица»—крáтко описáла свои непритязáтельные трéбования америкáнская сýпер-звездá Лáйза Миннéлли.[5] Певúца прибýдет[6] в Москвý четвёртого ию́ня, шестóго и седьмóго вы́ступит[7] в Концéртном зáле “Россúя” и девя́того улетúт в Тýрцию.

Прогрáмма гастрóлей покá согласóвывается нáшей и америкáнской сторонáми.[8] Но, естéственно, звездé не избежáть традицио́нных экскýрсий по террито́рии Кремля́, Крáсной плóщади и Алмáзному фóнду.[9] Крóме того,[10] Миннéлли желáет посетúть воéнное подразделéние.[11] Организáторы визúта ужé ведýт переговóры с óпытной в общéнии с эстрáдными звёздами Тамáнской дивúзией.[12] Миннéлли свóдят и в ресторáн “Серéбряный век”.[13]

...На приёмах,[14] устрáиваемых в честь звезды́,[15] не бýдет

---

[1] some ice
[2] carton
[3] бáнных... bath towels
[4] makeup artist
[5] крáтко... the American superstar Liza Minnelli briefly described her unpretentious demands
[6] will arrive
[7] will perform
[8] Прогрáмма... The program of the tour is still being worked out by our and the American sides
[9] Алмáзному... State Collection of Jewels (crowns, etc.)
[10] Furthermore
[11] воéнное... military division
[12] ведýт... are conducting negotiations with the Taman division, which is experienced in relations with stage stars
[13] свóдят... will also be taken to the "Silver Age" Restaurant
[14] На... at receptions
[15] устрáиваемых... held, set up in honor of the star

спиртно́го. В ка́честве горячи́тельных[16] напи́тков на столы́
вы́ставят то́лько пи́во. Как оказа́лось, в её тру́ппе де́сять
вегетариа́нцев, что вы́звало не́которые сло́жности[17] в
плани́ровании меню́. Пра́вда, его́ приме́рный набро́сок уже́
20 существу́ет:[18] регуля́рно две больши́е буты́лки фрукто́вой воды́
"Гэйторэ́йд", ко́фе, чай, молоко́ (сла́дкое и ни́зкой жи́рности),
диети́ческая и проста́я "Ко́ка-Ко́ла", две ба́нки натура́льного мёда,
сыр, кре́кер, фрукто́вые ша́рики,[19] апельси́новый и клю́квенный
25 сок, минера́льная вода́, 12 больши́х...стака́нов и мно́го-мно́го
льда.[20] Наде́емся, что на голосовы́х свя́зках э́то ника́к не
отрази́тся.[21]

[16] warming (ironic)
[17] что... which generated some complications
[18] его... a first draft of it (the menu) already exists
[19] фрукто́вые... fruit balls (melon balls)
[20] мно́го... a lot of ice
[21] Наде́емся... We hope that this will not affect her vocal chords in any way

Post-reading Tasks

1. Make a schedule for Liza Minnelli, indicating her arrival and departure dates from Moscow and the dates she will perform.
2. Make a shopping list for Liza Minnelli. What food items will you need to have on hand for her hotel room while she's staying in Moscow?
3. Find all the words in the genitive case and determine the reason they are in the genitive case. Then find all the number expressions and determine their case.
4. How does the author express the difference between two kinds of Coca-Cola? Between the two kinds of milk?
5. Given the verb form **существу́ет**, what do you think the infinitive of this verb might be? Why?
6. What is the author's attitude to trips to Red Square and the Kremlin? Why?
7. What is the author's attitude to Liza Minnelli? Why do you think so?
8. Russians generally don't drink iced beverages, believing that they are likely to lead to infections of the upper respiratory tract. How does this cultural phenomenon enter into the author's view of Minnelli?
9. Imagine that you are one of the people responsible for Liza Minnelli's stay in Moscow. Prepare an oral presentation or a composition describing your impressions of the superstar's visit and her demands on your staff.

♪ Зада́ние 8а

Write a composition or prepare an oral presentation beginning with the phrase **Я бою́сь того́, что...** or **Когда́ я бы́л/а́ ма́леньким/ма́ленькой, я боя́лся/боя́лась того́, что...**

♪ Зада́ние 8б

Write a composition or prepare an oral presentation beginning with the phrase **Я избега́ю таки́х ситуа́ций, когда́...**

§   Зада́ние 8в

Prepare a three-minute talk or write a composition in which you discuss what you can't live without or what you think students want to avoid at your school and why.

Saying

От копе́ечной све́чи Москва́ загоре́лась.

Moscow burned down from a candle worth one kopeck.
[A small leak will sink a great ship.]

※   Упражне́ние 8о

Continue your list of all the connecting words and phrases (such as *because*, *but*, *in the first place*, *then*, and so forth) with those you can find in the texts of this unit. Next to each connecting word or phrase, write out the clause or sentence in which they are used. Keep this list in your notebook and add to it as you continue with this book.

※   Упражне́ние 8п

Add the verbs of this unit to your lists of first- and second-conjugation verbs, noting the stress pattern of each verb as you do so.

※   Упражне́ние 8р

In Unit 1 you were told to dedicate a page of your notes to the genitive case. Write out the genitive case endings on that page. Then write out some sentences with genitive case constructions. Lastly, write up a list of all the verbs and the prepositions that take the genitive case (as listed in this unit). Be sure to distinguish the verbs and the prepositions that *can* take the genitive case from those verbs and prepositions that *must* take the genitive case.

[handwritten notes in red:]

из текстов :

8о   что; к сожалению; по сравнению с чем; действительно; по сведениям кого; согласно чему; ведь; в результате чего; почему; во-первых; потому; во-вторых; в-третьих; отсюда; потому, что; так что; так как; непонятно, уж лучше; но; естественно; кроме того; как оказалось; правда.

стр 92   с одной стороны; с другой стороны, с (чьей) точки зрения.

The Accusative Case

Винительный падёж: *Когó? Что?*

Готóвится чай.

Usage

The accusative case (**вини́тельный паде́ж:** *кого́? что?*) is used quite often. The singular endings for neuter and inanimate masculine nouns and the plural endings for all inanimate nouns are the same in the accusative case as they are in the nominative case.* The endings for singular animate masculine nouns in the accusative case are identical, in most instances, to the endings for these nouns in the genitive case; the endings for all plural animate nouns in the accusative case are the same as the endings for these nouns in the genitive case. This coincidence of case endings is why the second Russian name for the accusative case (**кого́? что?**) combines one of the words for the genitive case (**кого́?**) with one of the words for the nominative case (**что?**).

Here are some of the most common uses of the accusative case.

1. As the direct object of many verbs in several different contexts including the verb **сто́ить** (*to cost*).
2. With the prepositions **в, на, за,** and **под** in the context of movement in a direction (answering the question **куда́?**). It is not used when the destination is a person or a person's home.†
3. With the prepositions **на, за,** and **че́рез** in time expressions.‡
4. For time expressions indicating duration or repetition.
5. In certain constructions with many verbs, including **игра́ть во что** (*to play a game or sport*), **серди́ться на кого́ за что** (*to get angry at someone for something*), **жа́ловаться на кого́/что? кому́?** (*to complain about someone or something to someone*), **наде́яться на кого́/что?** (*to rely on someone or something*), and **крича́ть на кого́/что?** (*to yell at someone or something*). The accusative case is used in the construction **похо́ж (похо́жа, похо́жи) на кого́/что** (*similar [in appearance or in some other way if specified] to*), and **обижа́ться/оби́деться на кого́/что за что?** (*to be/get offended at someone for some reason*).
6. With many common verbs expressing relationships between people, such as **люби́ть кого́?** (*to love someone*), **ненави́деть кого́?** (*to hate someone*), **уважа́ть кого́?** (*to respect someone*), **понима́ть кого́?** (*to understand someone*), **влюбля́ться в кого́?** (*to fall in love with someone*). The accusative case is used without prepositions with the verb **ждать кого́?/что?** (*to wait*) when the person or

---

* Inanimate nouns are "things" that are not alive and have never been living, such as chairs, tables, books, rocks, and spatulas. Plants are also considered inanimate nouns. Animate nouns are "living beings," such as friends, cousins, parents, dogs, cats.

† The preposition **к** and the dative case are used for this type of construction: **Я сейча́с иду́ к Ната́ше.** The dative case is presented in Unit 11.

‡ If an accusative time expression involves a numeral, often only the numeral itself is in the accusative. The noun phrase that follows the numeral is governed by the numeral (and is therefore often in the genitive or some other case).

thing awaited is concrete (e.g., *Anton* or *the bus*), not abstract (such as *happiness* or *inflation*).

7. In two important "connecting" phrases, **несмотря́ на что/несмотря́ на то, что...** (*despite something, despite the fact that...*) and **на вся́кий слу́чай** (*just in case*).

Consider these examples.

1. Мы **поста́вили** пусты́е буты́лки **под** стол.	*We put the empty bottles under the table.*
2. Роди́тели ча́сто **се́рдятся на** свои́х дете́й.	*Parents often get angry at their children.*
3. Ты всё вре́мя **жа́луешься** свои́м друзья́м **на** гости́ницу.	*You're always complaining to your friends about the hotel.*
4. Не **кричи́те на** него́!	*Don't yell at him!*
5. Мы **е́здим в** Во́логду ка́ждую неде́лю.	*We go to Vologda every week.*
6. Э́тот журна́л **сто́ит** ты́сячу рубле́й.*	*This magazine costs a thousand rubles.*
7. Мы **пое́дем на** о́зеро Байка́л **на** неде́лю.	*We're going to Lake Baikal for a week (we'll spend a week at Lake Baikal after we get there).*
8. Они́ хорошо́ **игра́ют в** хокке́й.	*They play hockey well.*
9. Мы **наде́емся на** Ни́ну: она́ нам помо́жет!	*We're relying on (depending on) Nina: She'll help us!*
10. Та́ня всё вре́мя **влюбля́ется в** спортсме́нов!	*Tania is always falling in love with athletes!*
11. С э́того моме́нта Пётр Ильи́ч **возненави́дел** нас: он нас не **понима́ет**.	*Piotr Il'ich began to hate us from that moment: He doesn't understand us.*
12. Зинаи́да Па́вловна о́чень **похо́жа на** свою́ мать.	*Zinaida Pavlovna looks a lot like her mother.*
13. Мы **ждём** Бори́са Петро́вича.	*We're waiting for Boris Petrovich.*
14. **Несмотря́ на** плоху́ю пого́ду, мы **пойдём в** парк.	*Despite the bad weather, we're going to the park.*
15. **Несмотря́ на** то, что вы сказа́ли, я всё равно́ **куплю́** э́ту маши́ну.	*Despite what you've said, I'm going to buy this car anyway.*

Упражне́ние 9а

Assign to each example one of the seven uses of the accusative case.

* The number **ты́сяча** (*thousand*) requires the genitive case of the noun it governs.

PART 2 Singular Endings

In the accusative case,

1. Masculine inanimate adjectives end in **-ый (-óй)/-ий**.
2. Masculine animate adjectives end in **-ого/-его**.
3. Neuter adjectives end in **-ое/-ее**.
4. Feminine adjectives end in **-ую/-юю**.
5. All masculine and neuter inanimate nouns have the same endings as in the nominative.
6. All masculine animate nouns end in **-a/-я**, except masculine nouns ending in **-a/-я** in the nominative, such as **дéдушка**, end in **-y/-ю**:

    Мы слýшаем ýмного **дéдушку**.

7. All feminine nouns end in **-y/-ю**, except feminine nouns ending in **-ь** in the nominative, such as **часть**, have the same endings as in the nominative.

    Мы читáем интерéсную **часть** кнúги.

Note that for all inanimate masculine and neuter nouns and the adjectives that modify them, the accusative is the same as the nominative; for animate masculine nouns and the adjectives that modify them, the accusative is the same as the genitive. The exception to this rule is masculine animate nouns ending in **-a/-я** in the nominative, which take feminine endings. Finally, note that for feminine nouns ending in **-ь**, the accusative is the same as the nominative.

RUSSIAN Saying

Рыбáк рыбакá вúдит издалекá.

A fisherman can recognize another fisherman from far away.
[It takes one to know one./Birds of a feather flock together.]

ТЕКСТ 9a

Read the following excerpt from Chekhov's play *Uncle Vania*. One character, Sonia, talks about her unrequited love.

Pre-reading Task

Have you ever experienced unrequited love? Did you tell anyone about it? Why or why not? What do you think Sonia will say about her feelings? How do you think she copes with them?

СО́НЯ. Нет! (*огля́дывается, что́бы взгляну́ть на себя́ в зе́ркало.*)[1] Нет! Когда́ же́нщина некраси́ва, то ей говоря́т: «У вас прекра́сные во́лосы»...Я его́ люблю́ уже́ шесть лет, люблю́ бо́льше, чем свою́ мать; я ка́ждую мину́ту слы́шу его́, чу́вствую пожа́тие его́ руки́;[2] и я смотрю́ на дверь, жду, мне всё [вре́мя] ка́жется, что он сейча́с войдёт. И вот, ты ви́дишь, я всё прихожу́ к тебе́, что́бы поговори́ть о нём. Тепе́рь он быва́ет здесь ка́ждый день, но не смо́трит на меня́, не ви́дит...Это тако́е страда́ние![3] У меня́ нет никако́й наде́жды, нет, нет! (*В отча́янии.*)[4] О Бо́же, пошли́ мне си́лы[5]...Я всю ночь моли́лась...Я ча́сто подхожу́ к нему́, сама́ загова́риваю[6] с ним, смотрю́ ему́ в глаза́...У меня́ уже́ нет го́рдости,[7] нет сил владе́ть собо́ю[8]...Не удержа́лась и вчера́ призна́лась[9] дя́де Ва́не, что люблю́...

А. П. Че́хов, «Дя́дя Ва́ня», 1899

[1] огля́дывается... *looks back to look at herself in the mirror*
[2] пожа́тие... *pressure of his hand*
[3] *suffering*
[4] В... *In despair*
[5] *O God, send me strength*
[6] *begin to talk*
[7] *pride*
[8] владе́ть... *to be in control of myself*
[9] Не... *couldn't restrain myself and yesterday confessed*

Post-reading Tasks

1. Summarize Sonia's speech in two or three sentences in Russian.
2. Find five noun phrases in the accusative singular or accusative inanimate plural (the same as the nominative case plural) and write them out on a separate piece of paper.
3. Write a response to Sonia.

ТЕКСТ 96

The following poem by Akhmatova is entitled "Lot's Wife." According to the Bible, God decided to destroy the wicked city of Sodom, saving only Lot and his family; but as they were fleeing, Lot's wife looked back at Sodom and God turned her into a pillar of salt as punishment.

Pre-reading Task

Biblical interpretations have generally portrayed Lot's wife as empty-headed and foolish for stopping to look back at Sodom. Why do you think she did it? Why might Akhmatova sympathize with her action?

Ло́това жена́

И пра́ведник[1] шёл за посла́нником[2] Бо́га,
Огро́мный и све́тлый, по чёрной горе́.
Но гро́мко жене́ говори́ла трево́га:[3]
Не по́здно, ты мо́жешь ещё посмотре́ть

[1] *righteous man*
[2] *messenger*
[3] *alarm, worry, fear*

5 На кра́сные ба́шни[4] родно́го Содо́ма,
   На пло́щадь, где пе́ла, на двор, где пряла́,[5]
   На о́кна пусты́е высо́кого до́ма,
   Где ми́лому му́жу дете́й родила́.

   Взгляну́ла,[6]—и, ско́ваны[7] сме́ртною бо́лью,
10 Глаза́ её бо́льше смотре́ть не могли́;
   И сде́лалось те́ло прозра́чною[8] со́лью,
   И бы́стрые но́ги к земле́ приросли́.[9]

   Кто же́нщину э́ту опла́кивать[10] бу́дет?
   Не ме́ньшей ли мни́тся она́ из утра́т?[11]
15 Лишь[12] се́рдце моё никогда́ не забу́дет
   Отда́вшую[13] жизнь за еди́нственный взгляд.[14]

                    А. А. Ахма́това, 1922–1924

[4] *towers*
[5] *wove*
[6] *took a glance*
[7] *pierced*
[8] *transparent*
[9] *grew into*
[10] *mourn*
[11] *He... Doesn't she seem the least important of all that was lost*
[12] **то́лько**
[13] *one who gave up*
[14] *glance*

Post-reading Tasks

1. List the things that Lot's wife thought she would miss as she contemplated leaving her home.
2. Write a prose paraphrase of the poem in Russian.
3. Circle any religious words or phrases in the poem.
4. Find five noun phrases in the accusative singular or accusative inanimate plural (the same as the nominative case plural) and write them out.
5. Write about the life of Lot's wife from her point of view.

✳   Упражне́ние 9б

Put the phrases in the accusative case to complete the sentence **Я жа́луюсь на...**

ОБРАЗЕ́Ц: э́тот профе́ссор →

            Я жа́луюсь на э́того профе́ссора.

1. э́та интере́сная шко́ла
2. э́та интере́сная жи́знь
3. э́тот большо́й институ́т
4. э́та у́мная студе́нтка
5. э́тот у́мный студе́нт
6. э́тот но́вый слова́рь

Plural Endings

Inanimate Nouns

The plural endings for inanimate nouns in the accusative case are exactly the same as they are in the nominative case. Adjectives that modify plural inanimate nouns in the accusative case are also the same as nominative case plural adjectives. Review the nominative case plural endings in Unit 7 before doing **Упражнéние 9в**.

 Упражнéние 9в

Complete the sentence **Я óчень люблю́...** or **Я не люблю́...** with the plural form of the noun phrases. Be careful to check spelling rules and stress shifts in the nouns.

> ОБРАЗÉЦ: зелёная рýчка →
>
>   Я óчень люблю́ зелёные рýчки.

1. хорóшее письмó
2. большóе окнó
3. интерéсная кни́га
4. такóй цветóк
5. нóвый компью́тер «Макинтóш»

Saying

Я готóв/а сквозь зéмлю провали́ться.

I'm ready to drop through the earth (from embarrassment).

Animate Nouns

The plural endings for animate nouns in the accusative case are the same as they are in the genitive case as described in Unit 8.

 Упражнéние 9г

Answer the question **Кто обижáется на...?** with the plural form of the noun phrases. Remember to review the spelling rules.

> ОБРАЗÉЦ: мои́ роди́тели → Я рéдко обижáюсь на мои́х роди́телей.

1. твои друзья́
2. э́ти ба́бушки
3. хоро́шие преподава́тели
4. больши́е соба́ки
5. у́мные профессора́

Personal Pronouns

The accusative case personal pronouns are the same as the genitive case personal pronouns. Note that when the third-person personal pronouns (**его́**, **её**, **их**) are the object of a preposition, they also take on the letter **н-**: **в/на него́**, **в/на неё**, **в/на них**.

Я о́чень наде́юсь на **неё**.	*I am really relying (depending) on her.*
Я ча́сто жа́луюсь на **него́**.	*I often complain about him.*
Я о́чень сержу́сь на **них**.	*I am really angry at them.*

Review the personal pronouns in **Табли́ца 12** in the Appendix.

Last Names

Russian last names that end in **-ов/-ев** or **-ын/-ин** decline in the accusative singular as nouns for both men and women. The plural endings for both men and women are adjectival.

Аса́нов	Мы хорошо́ зна́ем Аса́нова.
Аса́нова	Мы хорошо́ зна́ем Аса́нову.
Аса́новы	Мы хорошо́ зна́ем Аса́новых.
Солжени́цын	Мы хорошо́ зна́ем Солжени́цына.
Солжени́цына	Мы хорошо́ зна́ем Солжени́цыну.
Солжени́цыны	Мы хорошо́ зна́ем Солжени́цыных.

Women's last names that end in a consonant do not decline at all.

male: Андре́й Смит	Мы хорошо́ зна́ем Андре́я Сми́та.
female: А́ндрея Смит	Мы хорошо́ зна́ем А́ндрею Смит.

✱ Упражне́ние 9д

Complete the sentence with the correct form of the names.

Я не зна́ю...

1. Михаи́л Горбачёв
2. Раи́са Горбачёва
3. Горбачёвы
4. Бори́с Е́льцин
5. Е́льцины

§ Зада́ние 9а

Write a paragraph or prepare a presentation that begins with **Я сержу́сь на мои́х сосе́дей (преподава́телей, роди́телей), когда́ они́...**

§ Зада́ние 9б

Write a paragraph or prepare a presentation that begins with **Я люблю́ (*и́ли* ненави́жу *и́ли* уважа́ю) мои́х сосе́дей (преподава́телей, знако́мых), когда́ они́...**

§ Зада́ние 9в

Prepare a three-minute talk in which you discuss what you think students complain about the most. Use the verb **жа́ловаться (жа́луюсь, жа́луешься, жа́луются на что? кому́?).**

Numbers

Numbers are in the accusative case when they are governed by a preposition that requires the accusative or when they are the direct object of a verb that requires the accusative.

1. Мы ви́дели то́лько **одну́** студе́нтку на конце́рте.

   We saw only one student at the concert.

2. Она́ ви́дела **двух** студе́нтов на конце́рте.

   She saw two students at the concert.

3. Я сейча́с чита́ю **три** ра́зные кни́ги.

   I'm reading three different books now.

The number 1 (**оди́н/одна́/одно́**) is a modifier and agrees in case and gender with the noun it modifies, as demonstrated in example 1. Numbers ending in 1 (21, 31, 41, 51, and so forth) are subject to the same rule. All other numbers are treated as nouns and use the genitive/accusative form when the noun phrase they govern is animate (as in example 2), or the nominative/accusative form when the noun phrase they govern is inanimate (as in example 3).

The accusative case forms of the number nouns modifying inanimate nouns are the same as the nominative case number nouns except for the feminine form of numbers 1 and 1,000.

одна́→одну́
ты́сяча→ты́сячу

Accusative case forms of the number nouns 2, 3, and 4, when modifying animate nouns, are the same as the genitive case forms, such as **двух**, **трёх**, and **четырёх**. The accusative case forms of the number nouns 5 through 20, when modifying animate nouns, behave as feminine nouns ending in a soft sign, i.e., they do not change.

The accusative number adjectives are the same as the nominative number adjectives for inanimate nouns in the masculine and neuter and the same as the genitive number adjectives for animate masculine nouns; the feminine accusative number adjectives have the accusative feminine adjectival ending **-ую** or **-юю**. Remember that in compound numbers, such as 62 or 96, only the last digit of the adjective is declined. The previous digits are written and pronounced as nouns:

Он жа́луется на два́дцать второ́го солда́та.	*He is complaining about the twenty-second soldier.*

Review the number nouns and their corresponding adjectives in the Appendix.

✳ Упражне́ние 9e

Imagine that you are hiring someone to work at an information booth on your campus. All the applicants for the position are foreign women who have different accents. Use the numbers to identify the applicants and practice saying which women you understood and which you didn't. Then imagine that all the applicants are foreign men with different accents.

ОБРАЗЕ́Ц: Я пло́хо понима́л/а _____ же́нщину. →

Я пло́хо понима́л/а пе́рвую же́нщину.

2	8	14
3	9	17
4	12	18
7	13	19
5	11	1
6	31	20
30	15	21
10	16	

❇   Упражнéние 9ё

Continue your list of all the "connecting" words and phrases (such as *because*, *but*, *in the first place*, *then*, and so forth) with those you can find in the texts of this unit. Next to each connecting word or phrase, write out the clause or sentence in which they are used. Keep this list in your notebook and add to it as you continue with this book.

❇   Упражнéние 9ж

Add the verbs of this unit to your lists of first- and second-conjugation verbs, noting the stress pattern of each verb as you do so.

❇   Упражнéние 9з

Write out the accusative case endings on the page in your notes dedicated to the accusative case. Then write out some example sentences with accusative case constructions. Lastly, write up a list of all the verbs and the prepositions that take the accusative case (as listed in this unit). Be sure to distinguish the verbs and the prepositions that *can* take the accusative case from those verbs and prepositions that *must* take the accusative case.

The Prepositional Case

Предло́жный паде́ж: *О ком? О чём?*

На цвето́чном ры́нке: 8-го ма́рта.

Usage

The prepositional case (**предло́жный паде́ж: *о ком? о чём?***) is so named because it is the only case that must always take a preposition, unlike the other cases. This case is also called the locative case because it answers the question *In what location?* or **где?** The prepositional case is used in several different contexts.

1. to show location

    Где живу́т Домбро́вские? Они́
    живу́т **в** кварти́ре № 15.

    Where do the Dombrovskiis live?
    They live in apartment 15.

2. as the object of either the preposition **в** or **на** when they do not express movement in a direction

    В чём де́ло? Де́ло **в** том, что он
    ничего́ не де́лает.

    What's the problem? The problem is
    he doesn't do anything.

3. as the object of the preposition **о** meaning *about* or *concerning*

    Вчера́ мы говори́ли **о** свое́й
    пое́здке в Петербу́рг.

    Yesterday we talked about our own
    trip to Petersburg.

4. as the object of the preposition **при** meaning *under the auspices, in the presence of,* or *during the reign or administration of*

    Это музе́й иску́сств **при**
    Аризо́нском университе́те.

    This is the museum of arts under the
    auspices of the University of
    Arizona.

    Не говори́те так **при** де́тях!

    Don't speak like that in front of the
    children!

    У него́ была́ хоро́шая рабо́та **при**
    Горбачёве.

    He had a good job during
    Gorbachev's administration.

5. as the object of either the preposition **в** or **на** in certain idiomatic expressions

    игра́ть **на** музыка́льном
    инструме́нте

    to play a musical instrument

    жени́ться **на** ком (**на** како́й
    де́вушке)

    to marry someone (said of a man
    marrying a woman)

    наста́ивать **на** чём

    to insist on something

    сомнева́ться **в** чём

    to doubt something

6. in certain "connecting" phrases

    во-пе́рвых, **во**-вторы́х,
    в-тре́тьих...

    in the first place, second, third...

в тако́м слу́чае	*in that case*
в виду́ того́, что...	*in light of the fact that...*
де́ло **в** том, что...	*the point is that...*

ТЕКСТ 10a

Read the excerpt from Pushkin's novella *The Captain's Daughter*, set in the late eighteenth century.

Pre-reading Task

In this excerpt, the narrator describes his parents' background. What kinds of words and expressions do you expect to find?

Оте́ц мой Андре́й Петро́вич Гринёв в мо́лодости свое́й[1] служи́л при гра́фе[2] Ми́нихе и вы́шел в отста́вку[3] премье́р-майо́ром в 17...году́.[4] С тех пор жил он в свое́й Симби́рской дере́вне, где и жени́лся на деви́це[5] Авдо́тье Васи́льевне Ю.,[6]
5   до́чери бе́дного та́мошнего дворяни́на.[7] Нас бы́ло де́вять челове́к дете́й....

А. С. Пу́шкин, «Капита́нская до́чка», 1836

[1] в... *in his youth*
[2] служи́л... *served under Count...*
[3] в... *and retired*
[4] премье́р-майо́ром... *at the rank of first major in the year 17... (the narrator doesn't specify the actual year, only the century)*
[5] *lass, maiden*
[6] *the narrator doesn't specify his mother's maiden or birth name*
[7] та́мошнего... *local (adjective derived from the adverb* **там**) *nobleman, aristocrat*

Post-reading Tasks

1. Write a two-sentence summary of the text.
2. Identify the reason the underlined words and phrases are in the prepositional case.
3. Write a paragraph about your own family's background, using this text as a model.

PART 2 Singular and Plural Endings

In the prepositional case:

1. All singular masculine and neuter adjectives end in **-ом/-ем**.
2. Singular feminine adjectives end in **-ой/-ей**.
3. Masculine nouns ending in **-ий** in the nominative, such as **Дми́трий**, end in **-и**.

   Мы говори́ли о Дми́трии.

4. Neuter nouns ending in **-ие** in the nominative, such as **зда́ние**, end in **-и**.

   Мы ра́ньше рабо́тали в э́том зда́нии.

5. Neuter nouns ending in **-мя** in the nominative, such as **и́мя**, end in **-и**.

    Они́ поговоря́т об э́том и́мени.

6. Feminine nouns ending in **-ия** in the nominative, such as **Фра́нция**, end in **-и**.

    Она́ живёт во Фра́нции.

7. Feminine nouns ending in **-ь** in the nominative, such as **жизнь**, end in **-и**.

    Мы говори́м о его́ жи́зни.

8. All other singular masculine, feminine, and neuter nouns end in **-e**. The one exception is certain masculine nouns—such as **сад, год, лес, пол, рот, снег, час, шкаф,** and **край**—used with prepositions **в** and **на** in the sense of location only end in **-у́/-ю́**.

    Макси́м сейча́с в де́тском саду́.
    В про́шлом году́ мы е́здили в Москву́.
    Они́ сейча́с в лесу́.
    Игру́шка лежа́ла на полу́.

    These words have regular prepositional case endings when used in other grammatical contexts.

    Мы говори́м о са́де, ле́се, сне́ге, шка́фе.

    With the exception of the special **-у́/-ю́** locative ending, the stress of the prepositional case form is generally the same as that of the nominative case form in the singular.

9. All plural adjectives end in **-ых** or **-их**.
10. All plural nouns end in **-ах** or **-ях**.

RUSSIAN

Saying

Э́то ви́дно, как на ладо́ни.

It's as visible as if it were in the palm of your hand.
[It's as plain as the nose on your face.]

The stress of the prepositional case plural form is *generally* the same as that of the nominative case plural form. However, when there is a stress shift in the genitive plural, the stress of the prepositional case plural form is generally not the same as that of the nominative case form: **вещь** (nom. sing.: *thing*), **ве́щи** (nom. pl.), **веще́й** (gen. pl.), **веща́х** (prep. pl.).

RUSSIAN

Saying

Не в деньга́х сча́стье.

Happiness is not in money.
[Money can't buy you happiness.]

❋   Упражне́ние 10a

Put the noun phrases in the prepositional case to answer the question **Где же вы бы́ли?** Do not change the number of the noun phrases from singular to plural.

ОБРАЗЕ́Ц: Где же вы бы́ли?

большо́й го́род →

Мы бы́ли в большо́м го́роде.

1. Росси́я
2. глубо́кий снег
3. интере́сная шко́ла
4. большо́е зда́ние
5. э́тот музе́й
6. Кра́сная пло́щадь (на)
7. Кремль

❋   Упражне́ние 10б

Put the noun phrases in the prepositional case to answer the question **О чём вы говори́ли?** or **О ком вы говори́ли?** Do not change the number of the noun phrases from plural to singular.

ОБРАЗЕ́Ц: О чём вы говори́ли? О ком вы говори́ли?

больши́е города́ →

Мы говори́ли о больши́х города́х.

1. интере́сные студе́нты
2. спосо́бные преподава́тельницы
3. у́мные спортсме́нки
4. ру́сские имена́
5. голубы́е моря́

PART 3 Personal Pronouns

Memorize the declension of the personal pronouns, as presented in **Табли́ца 12** in the Appendix.

Because the prepositional case is always used with a preposition, the prepositional case forms of the third-person personal pronouns (**нём**, **ней**, **них**) always start with the letter **н**.

✳ Упражне́ние 10в

Fill in the blanks with the correct form of the personal pronoun.

1. Вчера́ ве́чером говори́ли то́лько о (вы) _____.
2. Ра́зве вы сомнева́етесь во (я) _____?
3. Я ничего́ хоро́шего не ви́жу в (он) _____.
4. Почему́ вы всё вре́мя говори́те то́лько о (мы) _____?
5. В (она́) _____ есть тала́нт.
6. Мы расска́зывали о (они́) _____ весь ве́чер!

PART 4 Last Names

Russian last names that end in **-ов/-ев** or **-ын/-ин** decline in the prepositional case as adjectives for individual women and groups of people, but as nouns for individual men.

Аса́нов	Мы говори́м об Аса́нове.
Аса́нова	Мы говори́м об Аса́новой.
Аса́новы	Мы говори́м об Аса́новых.
Солжени́цын	Мы говори́м о Солжени́цыне.
Солжени́цына	Мы говори́м о Солжени́цыной.
Солжени́цыны	Мы говори́м о Солжени́цыных.

Women's last names that end in a consonant do not decline at all.

male: Андре́й Смит	Мы говори́м об Андре́е Сми́те.
female: А́ндрея Смит	Мы говори́м об А́ндрее Смит.

✳ Упражне́ние 10г

Complete the sentence with the correct form of the names.

Ру́сские демокра́ты сомнева́ются в

1. Михаи́л Горбачёв
2. Раи́са Горбачёва
3. Горбачёвы
4. Бори́с Е́льцин
5. Е́льцины

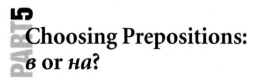

Choosing Prepositions: *в* or *на*?

In general speech, without special circumstances, Russian nouns are coupled with either **в** or **на** when used to express location. You must memorize the preposition that goes with each noun. Because nouns taking **в** far outnumber those taking **на**, it is most efficient to memorize the nouns that take **на**.

COMMON NOUNS TAKING **на**

на у́лице	на мо́ре
на вокза́ле	на Ку́бе
на ста́нции	на Украи́не*
на рабо́те	на Кавка́зе
на по́чте	на Аля́ске
на стадио́не	на седьмо́м (пе́рвом) этаже́
на конце́рте	на заня́тиях

Some nouns take either **в** or **на** depending on the intended meaning.

в столе́	на столе́
in the drawer, table	*on the table*
в углу́	на углу́
in the corner (inside)	*on the corner (outside)*
во дворе́	на дворе́
in the yard, courtyard	*outside (on the street)*
в уро́ке	на уро́ке
in the lesson in the book	*at class*
в ле́кции	на ле́кции
(words, ideas) in the lecture	*at the lecture (people present)*
в о́пере	на о́пере
in the opera (said of a performer	*at the opera (said of an audience*
or of a stretch of music)	*member)*

---

* Currently, **в Украи́не** is acceptable.

в зда́нии

in the building

на зда́нии

on the building's rooftop

✳ Упражне́ние 10д

Answer the questions in complete Russian sentences.

1. Где живу́т (и́ли жи́ли) ва́ши роди́тели?
2. Где живу́т (и́ли жи́ли) ва́ши ба́бушки и де́душки?
3. Где жи́ли ва́ши пре́дки (*ancestors*)?
4. Где вы живёте?
5. Рабо́таете ли вы? Е́сли да, то где вы рабо́таете?

§ Зада́ние 10а

Choose one of the questions in **Упражне́ние 10д** and write a longer composition in response.

RUSSIAN

Saying

Быть на седьмо́м не́бе (от сча́стья).

To be in seventh heaven (from happiness).

---

§ Зада́ние 10б

Prepare a three-minute presentation in which you talk about all the different places in which you (or your parents or friends) have lived. You may want to use the verb **переезжа́ть/перее́хать (отку́да? куда́?)** (*to move [from one home or residence to another]*).

§ Зада́ние 10в

Prepare a short presentation describing when some important historical or personal events took place or will take place. Use only the year as a time reference.

§ Зада́ние 10г

Make a list of four of the most famous opinionated people you can think of and write a short scene in which they argue a particular point. Use the expressions **Я наста́иваю (он/а́ наста́ивает) на том, что...** and **Я сомнева́юсь в том, что...** as many times as you can in your scene.

ТЕКСТ 10б

In this poem by Pushkin, the narrator laments that his name will ultimately mean nothing to his beloved.

Pre-reading Task

What's in a name? What different names do your friends or parents use to refer to you? Do these names have any special meaning for you?

Что в и́мени тебе́ моём?[1]
Оно́ умрёт,[2] как шум печа́льный
Волны́,[3] плесну́вшей в бе́рег да́льный,[4]
Как звук ночно́й в лесу́ глухо́м.[5]

Оно́ на па́мятном листке́[6]
Оста́вит мёртвый след,[7] подо́бный
Узо́ру на́дписи надгро́бной[8]
На непоня́тном языке́.

Что в нём? Забы́тое давно́[9]
В волне́ньях но́вых и мяте́жных,[10]
Твое́й душе́ не даст оно́
Воспомина́ний чи́стых, не́жных.[11]

Но в день печа́ли, в тишине́[12]
Произнеси́ его́ тоску́я;[13]
Скажи́: есть па́мять обо мне,[14]
Есть в ми́ре се́рдце, где живу́ я...[15]

А. С. Пу́шкин, 1830

[1] Что... *What is my name to you?*
[2] *It (My name) will die*
[3] как... *as the sad sound of a wave*
[4] плесну́вшей... *washing up on a distant shore*
[5] звук... *nocturnal sound in a mute forest*
[6] на...*in an album of memories*
[7] Оста́вит... *will leave a dead trace*
[8] подо́бный... *like the design of a carving on a tombstone*
[9] Забы́тое... *Long forgotten*
[10] В... *in new and exciting emotions*
[11] Твое́й... *It will not give your soul any pure or tender memories*
[12] *silence*
[13] Произнеси́... *utter it in anguish (grief)*
[14] есть... *there is memory of me*
[15] Есть... *there is a heart in the world in which I live*

Post-reading Tasks

1. Rewrite the poem, changing the word order to make the text more understandable (although less poetic).
2. Write a two-sentence summary of the poem in Russian.
3. Circle all the references to the narrator's name.
4. Underline all the words and phrases in the prepositional case. Identify their nominative case forms.
5. Find all the words that convey *sad* or *sadness*.
6. Find the two words related to the notion of *wave(s)*.

7. Write a prose response from a woman to whom this poem might have been addressed.
8. Give the poem a title.

ТЕКСТ 10в

This poem, "The Sailboat" by Lermontov, is one of the most famous in Russian poetry.

Pre-reading Task

The poem describes a sailboat out at sea. As you read, think what the sailboat might represent.

Па́рус

Беле́ет[1] па́рус одино́кой[2]
В тума́не[3] мо́ря голубо́м!...
Что и́щет он в стране́ далёкой?[4]
Что ки́нул он в краю́ родно́м[5]?..

5   Игра́ют во́лны—ве́тер сви́щет,[6]
И ма́чта гнётся и скрыпи́т...[7]
Увы́,[8]—он сча́стия[9] не и́щет
И не от сча́стия бежи́т!

10   Под ним струя́ светле́й лазу́ри,[10]
Над ним луч со́лнца золото́й...[11]
А он, мяте́жный,[12] про́сит бу́ри,[13]
Как бу́дто[14] в бу́рях есть поко́й[15]!

М. Ю. Ле́рмонтов, 1832

[1] whitens, gleams white
[2] all alone, lonely
[3] fog
[4] в... in a distant land
[5] ки́нул... abandoned in his home, native place
[6] ве́тер... wind whistles
[7] ма́чта... mast bends and groans
[8] alas
[9] happiness
[10] Под... the stream of water beneath it is brighter than azure
[11] луч... a golden ray of sun
[12] rebellious
[13] про́сит... seeks the storm
[14] Как... as if
[15] peace, tranquillity

Post-reading Tasks

1. Write a summary of the poem in two or three sentences in Russian or draw a picture of the scene described in the poem.
2. Find all the expressions in the prepositional case and determine why they are in that case.
3. Find all the verbs in the poem and determine their conjugation prototype.
4. Write a paragraph from the point of view of a storm nearing the sailboat.

PART 6 Numbers

Numbers are in the prepositional case if required by grammatical context.

1. Мы бы́ли в трёх ра́зных города́х. — *We were in three different cities.*
2. Они́ служи́ли при пяти́ президе́нтах. — *They served under five presidents.*

In example 1, *three different cities* is in the prepositional case because it is the object of the preposition *in*. In example 2, *five presidents* is in the prepositional case because it is governed by the preposition *under*.

You should memorize the prepositional case form of numbers 1 through 20, but you need only recognize the form for the other numbers.

Упражне́ние 10е

Provide the missing form of the number as required by grammatical context. Some of the missing numbers are nouns, others are adjectives. Write out all numbers as words.

В про́шлом году́ мы е́здили в Евро́пу. Мы бы́ли в Евро́пе 14 дней. За э́то вре́мя мы о́чень мно́го ви́дели. Мы бы́ли в (7) _____ ра́зных стра́нах, (4) _____ столи́чных города́х, (12) _____ други́х города́х, (20) _____ истори́ческих музе́ях. Мы да́же пла́вали на (2) _____ корабля́х по трём река́м. К сожале́нию, мы о́чень ма́ло по́мним, потому́ что мы всё вре́мя ду́мали то́лько о своём расписа́нии!

Russians use the prepositional case of the number adjective to state the year an event took place (or will take place) when they do not specify the date or the month.

1. Она́ родила́сь в **шестьдеся́т второ́м году́**. — *She was born in '62.*
2. Мы полу́чим но́вые материа́лы в **девяно́сто шесто́м году́**. — *We'll get the new materials in '96.*
3. Ре́йган был в пе́рвый раз и́збран президентом в **восьмидеся́том году́**. — *Reagan was elected president for the first time in '80.*

Note that in compound numbers, such as 62 or 96, only the last digit of the adjective is declined. The previous digits are written and pronounced as nouns. Memorize the number adjectives and their prepositional case forms.

Упражне́ние 10ё

Continue your list of all the "connecting" words and phrases (such as *because*, *but*, *in the first place*, *then*, and so forth) with those you can find in the texts of this unit. Next to each connecting word or phrase, write out the clause or sentence in which they are used. Keep this list in your notebook and add to it as you continue with this book.

✳ Упражнéние 10ж

Add the verbs of this unit to your lists of first- and second-conjugation verbs, noting the stress pattern of each verb as you do so.

✳ Упражнéние 10з

Write out the prepositional case endings on the page in your notes dedicated to the prepositional case. Then write out some sentences with prepositional case constructions. Lastly, write up a list of all the verbs and the prepositions that take the prepositional case (as listed in this unit). Be sure to distinguish the verbs and the prepositions that *can* take the prepositional case from those verbs and prepositions that *must* take the prepositional case.

The Dative Case

Дáтельный падéж: *Комý? Чемý?*

Не сорúть.

Usage

The dative case (**да́тельный паде́ж**: *кому́? чему́?*) is most frequently used for words that serve as the indirect object in a sentence. It is also used in modal expressions and impersonal constructions, which will be explained below. In the following examples, words requiring use of the dative case are boldfaced, while words in the dative case are italicized.

1. for indirect objects

    —*Кому́* вы **да́ли** журна́л?

    —*To whom did you give the magazine?*

    —Мы **да́ли** э́тот журна́л *Анто́ну.*

    —*We gave the magazine to Anton.*

2. to express age

    —Ско́лько *ему́* **лет**?

    —*How old is he?*

    —Я не зна́ю, ско́лько *ему́* **лет**, но *ей* **15 лет**.

    —*I don't know how old he is, but she's 15.*

    —Я ду́мала, что *ей* уже́ **16 лет**!

    —*I thought she was already 16!*

    —Нет, *ей* **испо́лнится** 16 лет то́лько в сле́дующем году́.

    —*No, she turns 16 only next year.*

    —А я была́ уве́рена, что *ей* **испо́лнилось** 16 лет в январе́!

    —*And I was certain that she had turned 16 in January!*

3. in impersonal constructions

    Ива́ну бы́ло **ску́чно** на ле́кции.

    Ivan was bored at the lecture.

    Мне о́чень **прия́тно** познако́миться с ва́ми.

    It's a pleasure for me to meet you (to make your acquaintance).

4. in modal expressions

    Мне **на́до** э́то сде́лать.

    I have to do this.

    Студе́нтам **нельзя́** здесь обе́дать.

    Students are not allowed to eat lunch here.

    Э́тим студе́нтам **нужны́** бу́дут де́ньги.

    These students will need money.

    Лифт сего́дня не рабо́тает: *нам* **прихо́дится** поднима́ться пешко́м.

    The elevator isn't working today: We have to go upstairs by foot.

    Мари́и Андре́евне всегда́ **удаётся** достава́ть биле́ты.

    Maria Andreevna always manages to get tickets.

5.   with certain verbs

Мы всегда́ **помога́ем** *свои́м* *роди́телям.*	We always help our parents.
Нам о́чень **понра́вились** э́ти профессора́.	We liked these professors a lot.
Они́ **у́чатся** *ру́сскому языку́.*	They are students of Russian.
Она́ уже́ **рассказа́ла** *нам* об э́том.	She told us about this already.
Сейча́с Со́ня *ему́* **ска́жет**, что она́ лю́бит друго́го.	Sonia's going to tell him now that she loves someone else.
Мы **позвони́м** *ему́* за́втра на рабо́ту.	We'll call him tomorrow at work.
Я о́чень **удивля́юсь** *э́тому.*	I'm very surprised at (by) that.

6.   with prepositions **к** and **по**

Я иду́ **к** *Ма́ше.*	I'm going to Masha's place.
Мы ещё не привы́кли **к** *э́тому* *кли́мату.*	We still haven't become accustomed to this climate.
За́втра бу́дет хоро́шая переда́ча **по** *телеви́зору.*	There's going to be a good program on television tomorrow.
Она́ большо́й специали́ст **по** *э́тому вопро́су.*	She's a big specialist in this area.
За́втра у меня́ экза́мен **по** *матема́тике.*	I have a math exam tomorrow.

7.   with the noun **па́мятник**

Э́то **па́мятник** *Пу́шкину.*	This is a monument to Pushkin.

8.   with the adjectives **подо́бный** (short and long form) and **благода́рен** (usually in short form)

Э́то **подо́бно** *той кни́ге,* кото́рую мы ви́дели на про́шлой неде́ле.	This is similar to the book that we saw last week.
Там бы́ло всё: и икра́, и блины́, и пельме́ни и *тому́* **подо́бное.**	Everything was there: caviar and bliny and pel'meni and so forth.
Мы *вам* о́чень **благода́рны.**	We are very grateful to you.

9.   in the expression **сла́ва Бо́гу**

Сла́ва *Бо́гу* он вы́здоровел.	Thank God he recovered (from his illness).

10.   in certain "connecting" phrases

по *ме́ре* того́, как...	inasmuch as...
су́дя **по** *тому́,* что...	judging by the fact that...
по *сле́дующей причи́не,* **по** *сле́дующим причи́нам...*	for the following reason(s)...
благодаря́ *тому́,* что...	owing to the fact that...

Comments on Constructions Requiring the Dative Case

1. Note that the verb used in impersonal constructions does not agree with the subject for whom the condition exists. If the sentence is in the present tense, no verb is used (there is no present tense of the verb *to be*); if the sentence is in the past or future tenses, the verb **быть** is in the third-person neuter form (**бы́ло, бу́дет**).

2. The words **на́до** and **ну́жно** are used only with a verbal infinitive, never with a noun, to express the need to do something. In order to express the need for something, you must use the words **ну́жен/нужна́/ну́жно/нужны́**, which must agree in gender and number with the thing needed.

Мне ну́жен но́вый слова́рь.	*I need a new dictionary.*
Мне нужна́ но́вая маши́на.	*I need a new car.*
Мне ну́жно но́вое пальто́.	*I need a new overcoat.*
Мне нужны́ но́вые ключи́.	*I need new keys.*

Note that this expression uses no verb at all in the present tense, while in the past and the future tenses the verb *to be* must agree in gender and number with the thing needed.

Мне ну́жен был но́вый слова́рь.	*I needed a new dictionary.*
Мне нужна́ была́ но́вая маши́на.	*I needed a new car.*
Мне ну́жно бу́дет но́вое пальто́.	*I will need a new overcoat.*
Мне нужны́ бу́дут но́вые ключи́.	*I will need new keys.*

The verb **приходи́ться/прийти́сь** is used to convey the idea that someone is compelled to do something because of unforeseen (and usually unpleasant) circumstances.

The words **до́лжен/должна́/должны́** are *not* modals and do not take the dative case, although they do convey necessity or obligation, frequently implying a moral obligation. These words are used with the nominative case of the person who should or ought to do something.

Со́ня должна́ помога́ть ма́тери, но она́ не хо́чет.	*Sonia should help her mother (in general), but she doesn't want to.*
Со́не на́до помо́чь ма́тери сего́дня.	*Sonia has to help her mother today.*

3. The verb **нра́виться/по-** requires the dative case of the person who likes or liked something. The verb must agree with the nominative case form of the thing or person liked. (Use **люби́ть + инфинити́в** when you want to say *to like to do something*.)

—Мне нра́вится э́тот фильм.	*—I like that film.*
—Он вам понра́вится.	*—You'll like it (the film).*
—Нам понра́вились э́ти кни́ги.	*—We liked those books.*
—Я люблю́ чита́ть таки́е кни́ги.	*—I like to read such books.*

The past tense of the imperfective verb is used to convey that something or someone is no longer liked:

Мне тогда́ нра́вились таки́е   *At that time I used to like such books.*
кни́ги.

4. Use the dative case with most verbs of communication, including **сказа́ть** and **рассказа́ть** (**кому́? о чём?**), but *not* with **спроси́ть/спра́шивать** (**кого́? о чём**).

5. Use the verb **звони́ть/по-** with the dative case of the person called, but use this verb with the accusative case after a preposition for the place to which the telephone call is made.

Мы ча́сто звони́м ей **в Ту́лу.**   *We often call her in Tula.*
Я сейча́с позвоню́ **в кинотеа́тр.**   *I'll call the movie theater.*

6. Use the preposition **к** and the dative case of the person to describe movement to someone's home or place.

Мы ча́сто хо́дим к Мари́и   *We often go to visit Maria*
Анато́льевне.   *Anatol'evna.*

Saying

RUSSIAN

Всему́ своё вре́мя.

Everything in its own time.

ТЕКСТ 11а

Read the excerpt from L. N. Tolstoy's *War and Peace*, which describes how Anna Pavlovna, who is having a party, brings all her guests to meet her aunt.

Pre-reading Task

What's your guess: How would these guests feel about meeting Anna Pavlovna's elderly aunt? As you read, think about how Tolstoy conveys the guests' feelings. How quickly do you know if your guess is right?

—Вы не вида́ли[1] ещё, —и́ли: —Вы не знако́мы с ma tante[2]?—
говори́ла А́нна Па́вловна приезжа́вшим гостя́м[3] и весьма́ серьёзно
подводи́ла[4] их к ма́ленькой стару́шке в высо́ких ба́нтах,[5]
вы́плывшей[6] из друго́й ко́мнаты, как ско́ро ста́ли приезжа́ть
5   го́сти, называ́ла их по и́мени, ме́дленно переводя́[7] глаза́ с го́стя на
ma tante, и пото́м отходи́ла.

[1] *seen*
[2] *my aunt (French)*
[3] приезжа́вшим... *guests who were arriving*
[4] *led them up to*
[5] *ribbons*
[6] *who had swum out*
[7] *shifting*

> Все го́сти соверша́ли обря́д приве́тствования[8] <u>никому́</u> не изве́стной, <u>никому́</u> не интере́сной и не ну́жной тётушки. А́нна
> Па́вловна с гру́стным, торже́ственным уча́стием[9] следи́ла[10] за их приве́тствиями, молчали́во одобря́я[11] их. Ma tante <u>ка́ждому</u>[12]
> говори́ла в одни́х и тех[13] же выраже́ниях о его́ здоро́вье,[14] о своём здоро́вье и о здоро́вье её Вели́чества,[15] кото́рое ны́нче[16] бы́ло,
> сла́ва Бо́гу, лу́чше. Все подходи́вшие,[17] из прили́чия не выка́зывая поспе́шности,[18] с чу́вством облегче́ния от испо́лненной тяжёлой
> обя́занности[19] отходи́ли от стару́шки, чтоб уж весь ве́чер ни ра́зу[20] не подойти́ к ней.
>
> Л. Н. Толсто́й, «Война́ и мир», 1869

[8] соверша́ли... *completed the ritual of greeting*
[9] гру́стным... *sad, solemn, involvement, participation*
[10] *followed*
[11] молчали́во... *silently approving*
[12] *to each guest*
[13] в... *in one and the same*
[14] его́... *his (the guest's) health*
[15] *majesty (empress)*
[16] *lately*
[17] *who approached*
[18] прили́чия... *sense of decency not showing any rush, hurry*
[19] облегче́ния... *relief at a burdensome responsibility fulfilled*
[20] ни... *not even once*

Post-reading Tasks

1. Summarize the text in three sentences in Russian.
2. Find all the different words that refer to the aunt.
3. Find all the words meaning *duty* or *obligation*.
4. Identify the reason the underlined words and phrases are in the dative case using the numbered list of uses of the dative case.
5. Rewrite the text, describing a party in America today.
6. Write a paragraph from the point of view of one of the guests or the aunt.

✳ Упражне́ние 11а

Fill in the blanks with the correct form of the words in parentheses.

1. Со́не (needed) _____ де́ньги.
2. Им (needed) _____ пое́хать в Москву́.
3. Дми́трию (needed) _____ но́вая маши́на.
4. Мне (will need) _____ де́ньги.
5. Им (will need) _____ пое́хать в Москву́.
6. Мари́и (will need) _____ но́вая маши́на.

✳ Упражне́ние 11б

Fill in the blanks with the correct form of the words **ве́село, гру́стно, ску́чно, интере́сно, хорошо́, пло́хо, хо́лодно,** and **тепло́**.

1. Та́не (was merry, had fun) _____ в Петербу́рге.
2. Им (will be cold) _____ в Сиби́ри.
3. Дми́трию (is warm) _____: откро́й окно́.
4. Мне (will be interesting) _____ на ле́кции.
5. Вам (was sad) _____, когда́ вы бы́ли в О́мске?
6. Мари́и (was bored) _____ на собра́нии.

PART 2
Singular and Plural Endings

The dative case has very regular endings, with few exceptions.

1. Masculine and neuter singular adjectives end in **-ому/-ему**.
2. Feminine singular adjectives end in **-ой/-ей**.
3. Masculine and neuter nouns end in **-у/-ю**, including

    - masculine nouns ending in **-ий** in the nominative, such as **Дми́трий**:

      Мы да́ли кни́гу Дми́трию.

    - neuter nouns ending in **-ие** in the nominative, such as **зда́ние**:

      Мы ещё не привы́кли к э́тому зда́нию.

    except for

    - masculine nouns ending in **-а/-я** in the nominative, such as **па́па**. These nouns take feminine endings.

      Мы всегда́ помога́ем па́пе.

4. Feminine nouns end in **-е**, except for

    - feminine nouns ending in **-ия** in the nominative, such as **Фра́нция**, end in **-и**:

      Она́ уже́ привы́кла к Фра́нции.

    - feminine nouns ending in **-ь** in the nominative, such as **жизнь**, end in **-и**:

      Мы уже́ привы́кли к э́той жи́зни.

5. All plural adjectives end in **-ым/-им**.
6. All plural nouns end in **-ам/-ям**.

Singular feminine case endings in the dative case are the same as they are in the prepositional.

The stress of the dative case plural form is *generally* the same as that of the nominative case plural form; the stress of the dative case plural form is generally not the same as that of the nominative case form when there are stress shifts in the genitive plural as well: **ве́щь** (nom. sing., *thing*), **ве́щи** (nom. pl.), **веще́й** (gen. pl.), **веща́м** (dat. pl.).

RUSSIAN Saying

Дарёному коню́ в зу́бы не смо́трят.

Don't look a gift horse in the teeth.
[Don't look a gift horse in the mouth.]

❋ Упражнéние 11в

Fill in the blanks with the correct form of the word in parentheses.

1. Мы чáсто помогáем (мать) _____.
2. Они́ ужé óтдали кни́гу (моя́ сестрá) _____.
3. Я обязáтельно передáм э́ту информáцию (Мари́я Васи́льевна) _____.
4. (Антóн Николáевич) _____ нáдо бýдет купи́ть э́ту кни́гу.
5. (Наш учи́тель) _____ по (рýсский язы́к) _____ нýжно купи́ть нóвый компью́тер.

PART 3 Personal Pronouns

Review the declension of the personal pronouns in **Табли́ца 12** in the Appendix.

Remember that third-person personal pronouns (**емý, ей, им**) in the dative case acquire the letter **н-** when preceded by a preposition (**к, по**): **немý, ней, ним.**

❋ Упражнéние 11г

Fill in the blanks with the correct form of the personal pronoun.

1. Ты (они́) _____ помóжешь э́то сдéлать?
2. Мóйка—óчень краси́вый канáл в Петербýрге. Всегдá прия́тно гуля́ть по (он) _____, осóбенно в «бéлые нóчи».
3. (Мы) _____ óчень нрáвится э́тот учéбник и поэ́тому мы чáсто рабóтаем по (он) _____.
4. (Онá) _____ нáдо бýдет купи́ть э́ту кни́гу.

RUSSIAN Saying

Большóму кораблю́—большóе плáвание.

A great ship—deep waters.
[Someone of great talent needs great responsibilities.]

PART 4 Last Names

Russian last names that end in **-ов/-ев** or **-ын/-ин** decline in the dative case as adjectives for individual women and groups of people, but as nouns for individual men.

Аса́нов	Аса́нову на́до э́то сде́лать.
Аса́нова	Аса́новой на́до э́то сде́лать.
Аса́новы	Аса́новым на́до э́то сде́лать.
Солжени́цын	Солжени́цыну на́до э́то сде́лать.
Солжени́цына	Солжени́цыной на́до э́то сде́лать.
Солжени́цыны	Солжени́цыным на́до э́то сде́лать.

Women's last names that end in a consonant do not decline at all.

female: Áндрея Смит	Áндрее Смит на́до э́то сде́лать.
male: Андрей Смит	Андре́ю Сми́ту на́до э́то сде́лать.

 Упражне́ние 11д

Complete the sentence with the correct form of the names.

(Кому́?) на́до э́то сде́лать.

1. Мари́на Андре́ева
2. Серге́й Андре́ев
3. Андре́евы
4. Та́ня Сини́цына
5. Бо́ря Сини́цын
6. Сини́цыны

✳ Упражне́ние 11е

One of the most common uses of the dative case is with the expression **на́до** to mean *must* or *has, have to* with an infinitive. Use the names to write instructions to various individuals as shown in the model.

ОБРАЗЕ́Ц: Влади́мир Петро́вич Ту́пин / купи́ть но́вую маши́ну →

Влади́миру Петро́вичу Ту́пину на́до купи́ть но́вую маши́ну.

1. Анто́н Никола́евич Зи́пкин / пое́хать в Петербу́рг
2. Зинаи́да Васи́льевна Па́влова / прийти́ в 8 утра́
3. Мари́я Серге́евна Фёдорова / написа́ть докла́д
4. Дми́трий Алексе́евич / убра́ть ку́хню
5. Са́ша / пригото́вить уро́к

PART 5

Special Impersonal Constructions: *есть когда́* and *не́когда*

The English construction *There is, was, will be someone for someone to* (*talk to, work with, borrow money from, etc.*) is translated into Russian by a special construction consisting of **есть** for the present tense and **быть** for the past and future tenses accompanied by the infinitive of the action to be performed and a form of the pronoun **кто**. An analogous construction is used with the pronoun **что** for sentences like *There is, was, will be something for someone to* (*complain about, write about, think about, etc.*). Note that the logical subject is in the genitive. Here are some example sentences.

У неё есть с кем (по)говори́ть.	*There is someone for her to talk to.*
У него́ есть кому́ (на)писа́ть.	*There is someone for him to write to.*
У них бы́ло куда́ идти́ (пойти́).	*They had someplace to go.*
У Алексе́я бу́дет на что жа́ловаться.	*Aleksei will have something to complain about.*
У Ири́ны бы́ло о чём (на)писа́ть.	*Irina had something to write about.*

If the sentence is negated to say *There isn't, wasn't, won't be something for someone to* (*complain about, write about, think about, etc.*), a special pronoun will be used: **не́где, не́куда, не́когда, не́чем, не́чему, не́чего, не́зачем**. Note that in negative sentences the logical subject is in the dative. Here are some example sentences.

Ей не́ с кем бы́ло (по)говори́ть.	*There was no one for her to talk to.*
Ему́ не́кому бы́ло (на)писа́ть.	*There was no one for him to write to.*
Им не́чего бы́ло боя́ться.	*There was nothing for them to be afraid of.*
Им не́куда бы́ло торопи́ться.	*They had nowhere to hurry off to.*
Мне не́чего сказа́ть ему́.	*There's nothing for me to say to him.*
Мне не́когда бы́ло говори́ть с ним.	*There was no time for me to talk with him.*
Вам не́зачем бу́дет расска́зывать об э́том.	*There will be no reason for you to talk about this.*

RUSSIAN Saying

Да́льше е́хать не́куда.

There's nowhere to go from here.
[There's no place to go but up.]

✳ Упражне́ние 11ё

This story is about the Petrovs, a Russian family living in Moscow, and Paul Bellin, an American who is their boarder for the summer. Fill in the blanks with the correct form of the words in parentheses.

1. Э́тим ле́том Петро́вы сдаю́т ко́мнату америка́нскому стажёру Па́ше. К сожале́нию кварти́ра о́чень ма́ленькая, и Па́ше (has no place) _____ занима́ться.

2. Па́ша всё-таки о́чень дово́лен свое́й рабо́той, и когда́ он вернётся домо́й в Аме́рику, у него́ бу́дет (about something) _____ расска́зывать свои́м друзья́м.

3. Са́ша, сын Петро́вых, большо́й лентя́й. Па́ша ча́сто замеча́ет, как Са́ша сиди́т и смо́трит в окно́. Са́ша счита́ет, что ему́ (there's nothing) _____ де́лать.

4. Когда́ Па́ша спра́шивает Са́шу, почему́ он ничего́ не де́лает, Са́ша всегда́ отвеча́ет, что все его́ друзья́ уе́хали на да́чу на це́лое ле́то, и поэ́тому ему́ (то есть Са́ше) (has no one with whom) _____ игра́ть.

5. Па́ша дово́льно ма́ло обща́ется с Лари́сой Петро́вой, Са́шиной ма́мой, потому́ что она́ и рабо́тает фи́зиком в институ́те, и хо́дит за поку́пками, и гото́вит за́втрак, обе́д и у́жин, и убира́ет кварти́ру ка́ждый день и стира́ет. Лари́са безу́мно занята́ и о́чень устаёт. Ей (has no time) _____ разгова́ривать с америка́нскими стажёрами.

6. К сча́стью, Па́ша о́чень хоро́ший челове́к, о́чень отве́тственный (*responsible*) челове́к. Иногда́ Па́ша остаётся до́ма с Са́шей и смо́трит за ним. Хотя́ ра́ньше Лари́са и Алёша (Лари́син муж) о́чень ре́дко гуля́ли ве́чером, э́тим ле́том они́ иногда́ хо́дят в кино́ и́ли в теа́тр ве́чером, потому́ что у них есть (someone with whom) _____ оста́вить Са́шу.

7. Алёша большо́й зану́да (*nerd*) и ча́сто жа́луется, что им (there's nowhere) _____ идти́. А Лари́са споко́йно (но упо́рно) расска́зывает о но́вых фи́льмах и спекта́клях, кото́рые они́ могли́ бы посмотре́ть.

8. Когда́ они́ ухо́дят ве́чером, Алёша всегда́ жа́луется, что им (there's no reason) _____ гуля́ть по го́роду в э́то вре́мя, когда́ по телеви́зору передаю́т чемпиона́т по футбо́лу.

9. Са́ша ещё ма́ленький, и поэ́тому, когда́ ухо́дят его́ роди́тели, он пла́чет. Па́ша его́ утеша́ет (*consoles*) и говори́т Са́ше, что ему́ (there's nothing) _____ боя́ться.

✳ Упражне́ние 11ж

Rewrite this story in past-tense and future-tense versions, writing out only the **не́когда** constructions in Russian; you need not copy out the rest of the story by hand.

Saying

RUSSIAN

Как по ма́слу.

As smoothly as on butter.
[*Like clockwork.*]

PART 6
хочу́, хо́чется,
хоте́л/а бы

There are three different ways to use the verb **хоте́ть/захоте́ть** to express desires:

1. by simply conjugating the verb: This is most direct, but may sometimes come across as rude.

Я хочу́ пое́сть.	*I want to have a bite to eat.*
Она́ хоте́ла во́ду.	*She wanted water.*
Они́ прие́дут и сра́зу захотя́т докуме́нты.	*They'll come and will want the documents right away.*

2. by using the impersonal construction **хоте́ться/захо́теться** with the dative case of the person who wants to do something: This is less forceful, and less likely to be interpreted as rude. This expression may be completed with either an infinitive or an object in the genitive case.

Мне хо́чется пое́сть.	*I feel like having a bite to eat.*
Ей хоте́лось воды́.	*She felt like having some water.*
Им захо́чется уви́деть докуме́нты.	*They'll feel like seeing the documents.*
Нам вдруг захоте́лось пи́ццы, и мы отпра́вились в пиццери́ю.	*We suddenly felt like having some pizza and set off for the pizzeria.*

3. by using the subjunctive **хоте́л/а бы**: This is the most deferential and polite of the three different constructions.

Я хоте́ла бы пое́сть.	*I would like to have a bite to eat.*
Она́ хоте́ла бы воды́.	*She would like to have some water.*
Они́ хоте́ли бы уви́деть докуме́нты.	*They would like to see the documents.*

✳ Упражне́ние 11з

Fill in the blanks using one of the expressions *to want* described above.

1. Я (want) _____ пойти́ в кино́ сего́дня ве́чером.
2. Тебе́ не (feel like) _____ пойти́ в кино́ со мной?
3. Она́ (would like) _____ пойти́ в теа́тр.
4. Ему́ наве́рно (will feel like) _____ пойти́ на футбо́л.
5. Они́ (would like) _____ посмотре́ть но́вый мексика́нский сериа́л по телеви́зору.
6. Кири́ллу Анато́льевичу вдруг (felt like) _____ сыгра́ть в ша́хматы, и поэ́тому пошёл в парк.

ТЕКСТ 11б

This excerpt is from the introduction to Pushkin's narrative poem "The Bronze Horseman."

Pre-reading Task

What do you know about the founding of Petersburg? Or about Peter the Great? Write down three facts.

На берегу́ пусты́нных волн[1]
Стоя́л *он*,[2] дум вели́ких полн,[3]
И вдаль гляде́л.[4] Пред ним широ́ко
Река́ несла́ся;[5] бе́дный чёлн
По ней стреми́лся одино́ко.[6]
По мши́стым, то́пким берега́м
Черне́ли и́збы здесь и там,[7]
Прию́т убо́гого чухо́нца;[8]
И лес, неве́домый луча́м
В тума́не спря́танного со́лнца,
Круго́м шуме́л.[9]
        И ду́мал он:
Отсе́ль грози́ть мы бу́дем шве́ду,[10]
Здесь бу́дет го́род заложён[11]
Назло́ надме́нному сосе́ду.[12]
Приро́дой здесь нам суждено́
В Евро́пу проруби́ть окно́,[13]
Ного́ю твёрдой стать при мо́ре.[14]
Сюда́ по но́вым им волна́м
Все фла́ги в го́сти бу́дут к нам,
И запиру́ем на просто́ре.[15]

                А. С. Пу́шкин,
        «Ме́дный вса́дник», 1833

[1] На... *On the bank of desolate waves*
[2] *Peter the Great*
[3] дум... *full of great thoughts*
[4] вдаль... *looked into the distance*
[5] Пред... *the river flowed broadly before him*
[6] бе́дный... *a poor skiff sailed all alone on it (the river)*
[7] По... *little black huts were scattered along the mossy swampy banks*
[8] Прию́т... *the refuge of the poor Finn*
[9] лес... *the forest, unknown to the rays of the sun hidden in the fog, murmured all around*
[10] Отсе́ль... *from here we will threaten the Swede*
[11] бу́дет... *A city will be founded*
[12] Назло́... *to defy our impudent neighbor*
[13] Приро́дой... *Nature has decreed that here we will cut open a window to Europe*
[14] Ного́ю... *We will take a firm stand at the sea*
[15] запиру́ем... *We shall feast in the vast space*

Post-reading Tasks

1. Write a three-sentence summary of the excerpt in Russian.
2. Find all the references to nature and its elements and circle them.
3. Find all the words and phrases in the dative case and underline them. Identify their nominative case forms.
4. Write a prose response from the perspective of a Swede about the founding of a Russian city so close to the Swedish border.

§ Зада́ние 11а

Write a composition or prepare a short oral presentation beginning with **Я удивля́юсь тому́, что...** (*I am surprised at the fact that...*).

§ Зада́ние 11б

Write a composition or prepare a short oral presentation beginning with **Я зави́дую тем лю́дям, кото́рые...** (*I envy those people who...*).

§ Зада́ние 11в

Write a composition or prepare an oral presentation beginning with **Мне ка́жется, что са́мая больша́я проблéма в Амéрике—_____, по слéдующим трём причи́нам. Во-пéрвых... Во-вторы́х... В-трéтьих...** (*I think that the biggest problem in America is _____ for the following three reasons. First... Second... Third...*).

§ Зада́ние 11г

Prepare a three-minute talk or composition about what you had to do every day when you were a schoolchild or what you need to do today. Remember to use imperfective verbs for recurring or frequent situations and perfective verbs for single events.

Numbers

Numbers are in the dative case if required by grammatical context.

1.	Мы разда́ли э́ти кни́ги всем трём студéнтам.	*We gave the books to all three students.*
2.	За́втра они́ расскáжут всю исто́рию четырём врачáм.	*Tomorrow they'll tell the whole story to the four doctors.*

In example 1, *all three students* is in the dative case because it is governed by the verb *to give*. In example 2, *four doctors* is in the dative case because it is governed by the verb *to tell*.

Review the dative case forms of the number nouns in **Табли́ца 16** in the Appendix.

You should memorize the dative case form of numbers 1 through 20, but you need only recognize the forms of the other numbers.

Russians use the preposition **к** and the dative case of the number noun or adjective to specify a deadline.

1.	Мы должны́ закóнчить э́ту рабóту к **двум** (часáм).	*We have to finish this job by two (o'clock).*

2. Мы полу́чим но́вые материа́лы к
   (ты́сяча девятьсо́т) **девяно́сто
   шесто́му го́ду.**

We'll get the new materials by '96.

3. Она́ защити́т диссерта́цию к
   пятна́дцатому ноября́.

*She'll defend her dissertation by the
fifteenth of November.*

Note that in compound numbers, such as 62 or 96, only the last digit of the adjective is
declined. The previous digits are written and pronounced as nouns. Memorize the
number adjectives and their dative case forms. Review the number adjectives in
Табли́ца 17 in the Appendix.

✳ Упражне́ние 11и

Provide the missing form of the number as required by grammatical context. Some of
the missing numbers are nouns, others are adjectives. Write out all numbers as words.

Мы пое́дем в Росси́ю на сле́дующей неде́ле. Когда́ мы бу́дем там, мы обяза́тельно
позвони́м (3) _____ друзья́м Фёдоровых, кото́рые живу́т в Москве́. Мы обеща́ли
всем (5) _____ Фёдоровым, что позвони́м их друзья́м к (7th) _____, потому́ что
их друзья́ уезжа́ют в Санкт-Петербу́рг 9-ого числа́. Фёдоровы хотя́т, чтобы мы
привезли́ с собо́й два экземпля́ра после́дних номеро́в журна́ла «Америка́нское
иску́сство» и подари́ли э́ти журна́лы (2) _____ из их друзе́й. (Third) _____ дру́гу,
ка́жется, не нра́вится иску́сство: мы должны́ привезти́ ему́ журна́л по спо́рту.
Нам на́до купи́ть журна́лы к (22nd) _____, потому́ что они́ бы́стро распродаю́тся
(*sell out*).

✳ Упражне́ние 11й

Write a paragraph describing when you have to complete homework assignments for
three different classes, using the dative construction to express deadlines. Use
зака́нчивать/зако́нчить зада́ние and **писа́ть/на- рабо́ту.**

§ Зада́ние 11д

Write a composition or prepare an oral presentation from the point of view of a famous politician setting out an agenda for your city, county, or state, or for the United
States or Russia. Use the dative case construction to express deadlines.

✳ Упражне́ние 11к

Continue your list of all the "connecting" words and phrases (such as *because, but, in
the first place, then,* and so forth) with those you can find in the texts of this unit. Next
to each connecting word or phrase, write out the clause or sentence in which they are
used. Keep this list in your notebook and add to it as you continue with this book.

✳   Упражнéние 11л

Add the verbs of this unit to your lists of first- and second-conjugation verbs, noting the stress pattern of each verb.

✳   Упражнéние 11м

Write out the dative case endings on the page in your notes dedicated to the dative case. Then write out some sentences with dative case constructions. Lastly, write up a list of all the verbs and the prepositions that take the dative case (as listed in this unit). Be sure to distinguish the verbs and the prepositions that *can* take the dative case from those verbs and prepositions that *must* take the dative case.

The Instrumental Case

Творительный падеж: *Кем? Чем?*

Дети в Москве.

Usage

The instrumental case (**твори́тельный паде́ж:** *кем? чем?*) is used to indicate a state of being, the means or instrument by which something is done, and with certain verbs and prepositions.

1. the means or instrument

    Я люблю́ писа́ть *кра́сным карандашо́м.*

    I like to write with a red pencil.

2. the agent in a passive construction

    Э́то бы́ло напи́сано *мои́ми друзья́ми.*

    This was written by my friends.

3. the manner in which something is done

    Она́ шла *бы́стрым ша́гом.*

    She was walking at a rapid pace.

    Всё бу́дет сде́лано *наилу́чшим о́бразом.*

    Everything will be done in the best possible way.

4. in certain time expressions

    Э́той зимо́й мы обяза́тельно пое́дем на юг.

    This winter we just have to go south.

    Я обы́чно чита́ю газе́ту *у́тром.*

    I usually read the paper in the morning.

    Мы уже́ рабо́таем над э́тим *часа́ми!*

    We've been working on this for hours already!

5. after certain verbs

    Я **ста́ну** *профе́ссором.*

    I will become a professor.

    Мать **рабо́тает** *фи́зиком.*

    My mother is a physicist.

    Я **счита́ю** его́ *тала́нтливым архите́ктором.*

    I consider him a talented architect.

    Она́ **оказа́лась** *худо́жником.*

    She turned out to be an artist.

    Тверь **ка́жется** *больши́м го́родом.*

    Tver seems to be a big city.

    О́ля сейча́с **занима́ется** *ру́сским языко́м.*

    Olia's doing her Russian homework now.

    Мы все **по́льзуемся** *э́тим словарём.*

    We all use this dictionary.

    Они́ все **интересу́ются** *ру́сской поли́тикой.*

    They are all interested in Russian politics.

    Лари́са Миха́йловна **руководи́т** *больши́м заво́дом.*

    Larisa Mikhailovna runs a large factory.

Я **горжу́сь** тобо́й.	*I am proud of you.*
Серге́ева **называ́ла** э́ту кни́гу *ужа́сной.*	*Sergeeva called this book terrible.*

6. after the verb **быть***

Она́ **была́** *хоро́шим врачо́м.*	*She was (had been) a good doctor.*
Они́ **бу́дут** *прекра́сными специали́стами.*	*They'll be great specialists.*
Он до́лжен быть *хоро́шим фото́графом.*	*He must be a good photographer.*

7. in certain constructions

Они́ ча́сто **смею́тся над** *на́ми.*	*They often laugh at us.*
Я сейча́с **рабо́таю над** *курсово́й рабо́той.*	*I'm working on my term paper now.*
Мы о́чень **(не)дово́льны** *ва́шей рабо́той.*	*We are very (un)satisfied with your work.*

8. after certain prepositions, "the instrumental six"

Мы **с** *сестро́й* живём вме́сте в общежи́тии.	*My sister and I live together in the dormitory.*
Я обы́чно сижу́ **ме́жду** *Оле́гом* и *Мари́ной.*	*I usually sit between Oleg and Marina.*
Карти́на Ре́пина виси́т **над** *две́рью.*	*The painting by Repin is hanging up over the door[way].*
Мы живём **за** *э́тими больши́ми дома́ми.*	*We live behind those big buildings.*
Мы оста́вили пусты́е буты́лки **под** *столо́м.*	*We left the empty bottles under the table.*
Я бу́ду стоя́ть **пе́ред** *ме́бельным магази́ном.*	*I'll be standing in front of the furniture store.*

9. in certain "connecting" phrases

по сравне́нию **с** *чем* / по сравне́нию **с** *тем, что...*	*in comparison with what / in comparison with the fact that . . .*
в связи́ **с** *чем* / в связи́ **с** *тем, что...*	*in connection with what / in connection with the fact that . . .*
в соотве́тствии **с** *чем* / в соотве́тствии **с** *тем, что...*	*in accordance with what / in accordance with the fact that*

---

* Usage of the instrumental in this context is not required except after the infinitive **быть**. Many Russians use the nominative case after the verb **быть** except when referring to professions and when **быть** is used in the infinitive. The instrumental case after **быть** is *never* used with nationalities or other qualities that are permanent and unchangeable: **Он был ру́сский**. *He was Russian (he's dead now).*

Comments on Constructions Requiring the Instrumental Case

1. Constructions that express the means or instrument frequently use the English preposition *with*. Note that the Russian construction features no preposition.
2. Review the instrumental case forms of the seasons: **зимóй, веснóй, лéтом, óсенью**.
3. Review the instrumental case forms of the times of day: **ýтром** (6:00–11:59), **днём** (12:00–17:59), **вéчером** (18:00–23:59), and **нóчью** (24:00–5:59). These forms are never used immediately after a specific clock time: The genitive case is used instead. **Онá придёт в 6 часóв утрá, и мы уéдем в Москвý в 10 часóв вéчера.** Memorize the time expressions **вчерá/сегóдня/зáвтра вéчером** (*yesterday/this/ tomorrow evening*), and **вчерá/сегóдня/зáвтра ýтром** (*yesterday/this/tomorrow morning*).
4. Note the Russian way of asking what someone does for a living: **Кем он/á рабóтает?**
5. The short-form adjective **довóлен/довóльна/довóльны** must agree in gender with the subject who is (or isn't) satisfied.
6. The English construction *Ivan and I* is translated in Russian as **Мы с Ивáном** with the instrumental case form of the other person (the one who is not *I*) after the preposition *with*. Note the lack of any conjunction meaning *and* in the Russian expression.
7. The Russian preposition **с(о)** is used with the instrumental case when it means *with*, but it is used with the genitive case when it means *off* or *from*.
8. The Russian preposition **за** is used with the instrumental case when it means *beyond* or *for* in the construction *to go somewhere for something or someone*, but it is used with the accusative case when it means *in exchange for*.
9. Both **за** and **под** + the accusative case are used for **кудá** constructions and are the only two of the "instrumental six" that can be used with the accusative case.

RUSSIAN

Saying

Быть мéжду мóлотом и наковáльней.

To be between the hammer and the anvil.
[To be between a rock and a hard place.]

ТЕКСТ 12a

This excerpt is from an article charging that representatives from one of Russia's leading broadcasting companies, Ostankino, "gave away" exclusive rights to Soviet-period television and radio archives to an American company. The authors note that some very prominent musicians signed a letter asking for a review of the situation.

Pre-reading Task

Why would Russians be angry about state television and radio archives being given over to an American company? What sort of objections would they raise? List the possible advantages and disadvantages of such a deal.

В январе́ 1992-го го́да Росси́йская госуда́рственная телерадио-веща́тельная[1] компа́ния «Оста́нкино» и америка́нская корпора́ция U.S.S.U. Arts Group, Inc. заключи́ли догово́р,[2] в соотве́тствии с кото́рым U.S.S.U. получи́ла семиле́тний эксклю́зив на испо́льзование[3] архи́ва а́удио- и видеоза́писей класси́ческих произведе́ний[4] РГТРК «Оста́нкино».

Со́бственно[5] сканда́л разгоре́лся[6] в са́мом нача́ле 1993-го го́да (то есть всего́-то[7] че́рез год по́сле подписа́ния догово́ра[8]!), когда́ в ру́ки журнали́стке газе́ты «Росси́я» Наде́жде Кожевнико́вой в ка́честве, как она́ сама́ написа́ла, «нового́днего пода́рка» случа́йно попа́ла[9] ко́пия догово́ра U.S.S.U.—«Оста́нкино»....Её гне́вный материа́л... трактова́л[10] подписа́ние и исполне́ние[11] э́того догово́ра, как ограбле́ние[12] «алма́зного фо́нда[13] росси́йской культу́ры».

За э́той статьёй после́довало весьма́ эмоциона́льное откры́тое[14] письмо́ на и́мя тогда́ ещё председа́теля Верхо́вного Сове́та Р. И. Хасбула́това, подпи́санное от и́мени Моско́вского сою́за музыка́нтов Генна́дием Рожде́ственским, Никола́ем Петро́вым, Ю́рием Башме́том, Эли́со Вирсала́дзе, Ве́рой Горноста́евой, Па́влом Ко́ганом, Михаи́лом Овчи́нниковым. Имена́, как ви́дите, коммента́риев не тре́бующие. В письме́ догово́р называ́лся «пира́тским», соста́вленным[15] «без консульта́ций с музыка́льной обще́ственностью,[16] Министе́рством культу́ры Росси́и, РАИС, а са́мое гла́вное—арти́стами-исполни́телями,[17] что само́ по себе́[18] уже́ явля́ется нарушенем[19] элемента́рных прав[20] челове́ка.»

[1] госуда́рственная... state television and radio broadcasting
[2] заключи́ли... concluded an agreement
[3] for the use
[4] класси́ческих... of classical works
[5] In fact
[6] broke out, burst into flames
[7] only
[8] че́рез... a year after the signing of the agreement
[9] случа́йно... accidentally fell into (the hands)
[10] Её... her furious report described
[11] the execution
[12] as robbery/theft of
[13] crown jewels (the алма́зный фонд is the State Collection of Jewels which Liza Minnelli visits in Unit 8).
[14] За... after this article there followed a highly open, public
[15] made up, compiled
[16] community, society
[17] musicians-performers
[18] что... that in and of itself
[19] a violation
[20] rights

Post-reading Tasks

1. Write a summary of the text in Russian in three sentences.
2. Identify the reason the underlined words and phrases are in the instrumental case using the numbered list of uses of the instrumental case.
3. The Russian word for *name* is used in two different contexts: Find these contexts and translate the word.
4. How does the author explain that the musicians who signed the letter are famous (and their names well known to Russian readers)?
5. The verb used by the author "describing" the agreement as *piratelike* is in the past tense. Write its infinitive and then conjugate the verb.

6. Identify all the English cognates and try to find Russian synonyms for them by consulting a dictionary.
7. What is the root of the Russian words *audio-* and *videorecordings*?
8. Write a response to this article either from the office of Khasbulatov, former chair of the Supreme Soviet, from the chair of the Ostankino Radio and Television Broadcasting Company, or from the chair of U.S.S.U. Arts Group, Inc.

PART 2
Singular and Plural Endings

In the instrumental case:

1. Masculine and neuter singular adjectives end in **-ым/-им**.
2. Feminine singular adjectives end in **-ой/-ей**. (Note: in poetry one often finds feminine singular adjectives in **-ою/-ею**.)
3. All masculine and neuter nouns end in **-ом/-ем** unless they are end stressed including

   - masculine nouns ending in **-ий** in the nominative, such as **Дми́трий**:

     Мы недово́льны Дми́трием.

   - neuter nouns ending in **-ие** in the nominative, such as **зда́ние**:

     Мы недово́льны э́тим зда́нием.

4. End-stressed soft-stem masculine and neuter nouns end in **-ём**.

   Exceptions to rules 3 and 4 are:

   - masculine nouns ending in **-а/-я** in the nominative, such as **па́па**, which take feminine endings, end in **-ой/-ей**:

     Мы ча́сто хо́дим в кино́ с па́пой.

5. feminine nouns ending in **-ь** in the nominative, such as **жизнь**, end in **-ью**:

   Они́ недово́льны э́той жи́знью.

6. All other feminine nouns, including those ending in **-ия**, end in **-ой/-ей**, except for those which are end stressed and soft stem.
7. All end-stressed soft-stem feminine nouns end in **-ёй**.
8. All plural adjectives end in **-ыми/-ими**.
9. All plural nouns end in **-ами/-ями**, except for

лю́ди	людьми́
до́чери	дочерьми́
де́ти	детьми́

ТЕКСТ 12б

In this poem by Tsvetaeva, the narrator seems to be happy that she isn't in love with a particular man and happy that the man isn't in love with her.

Pre-reading Task

Find as many expressions of love as you can in the poem and circle them. Then underline any images that are traditionally associated with romance and determine which of them are negated.

Мне нра́вится, что вы больны́[1] не мной.
Мне нра́вится, что я больна́ не ва́ми.
Что никогда́ тяжёлый шар земно́й[2]
Не уплывёт[3] под на́шими нога́ми.
Мне нра́вится, что мо́жно быть смешно́й,
Распу́щенной[4]—и не игра́ть слова́ми,
И не красне́ть удушливой волно́й,[5]
Слегка́ соприкосну́вшись рукава́ми.[6]

Мне нра́вится ещё, что вы при мне
Споко́йно обнима́ете другу́ю,[7]
Не про́чите[8] мне в а́довом огне́[9]
Горе́ть[10] за то, что я не вас целу́ю.[11]
Что и́мя не́жное[12] моё, мой не́жный, не
Упомина́ете[13] ни днём, ни но́чью—всу́е,[14]
Что никогда́ в церко́вной тишине́
Не пропою́т[15] над на́ми: аллилу́йя!

Спаси́бо вам и се́рдцем, и руко́й
За то, что вы меня́—не зна́я[16] са́ми!—
Так лю́бите: за мой ночно́й поко́й,[17]
За ре́дкость[18] встреч зака́тными часа́ми,[19]
За на́ши не гуля́нья[20] под луно́й,
За со́лнце,[21] не у нас над голова́ми,—
За то, что вы больны́—увы́![22]—не мной,
За то, что я больна́—увы́!—не ва́ми!

М. И. Цвета́ева, 1915

[1] *sick (with love)*
[2] *шар... the earth*
[3] *swim away*
[4] *relaxed*
[5] *красне́ть... to blush, in a stifling wave*
[6] *Слегка́... having lightly touched sleeves*
[7] *обнима́ете... embrace another (woman)*
[8] *intend*
[9] *а́довом... fires of hell*
[10] *to burn*
[11] *kiss*
[12] *tender*
[13] *mention, utter*
[14] *in vain*
[15] *sing, chant*
[16] *knowing*
[17] *tranquillity*
[18] *infrequency*
[19] *зака́тными... twilight hours*
[20] *strolls*
[21] *sun*
[22] *alas!*

Post-reading Tasks

1. Write a three-sentence summary of the poem in Russian.
2. Identify all expressions in the instrumental case and determine why they are in that case.

3. Look at your list of romantic images and expressions conveying a sense of love (which you compiled in the Pre-reading Task). Do you think the narrator really loves the person to whom the poem is addressed or not, as she claims? Why?

4. Write a prose response to this poem in Russian from the person to whom it is addressed.

RUSSIAN Saying

За двумя зайцами погонишься, ни одного не поймаешь.

If you chase after two hares, you won't catch even one.
[A bird in hand is worth two in the bush.]

※ Упражнéние 12а

Put the noun phrases in the instrumental case to answer the question **Кем (чем) вы недовóльны?**

1. э́тот большóй портфéль
2. дли́нная статья́
3. Бéлый дóм (в Вашингтóне и́ли в Москвé?)
4. э́та скýчная газéта
5. «Вечéрняя Москвá»
6. роди́тели
7. профéссор
8. Гали́на Матвéевна

※ Упражнéние 12б

Make your own chart for the case endings in the instrumental case, with singular and plural columns for the following nouns: **словáрь, гáлстук, дя́дя, рýчка, дочь, консерватóрия, ночь, письмó, пóле, здáние.** Add adjectives to modify these nouns in both columns. Compare your chart with the charts in the Appendix.

 Personal Pronouns

Review the declension of the personal pronouns in **Табли́ца 12** in the Appendix.

The personal pronouns in parentheses (**мнóю, тобóю, éю**) are often found in poetry (to make the meter fit better). You shouldn't use these forms, but be prepared to recognize them in poetry. (Can you find any examples of these forms in **Те́ксты 9а, 12в**?)

Remember that third-person personal pronouns (**им, ей, и́ми**) in the instrumental case acquire the letter **н** when preceded by a preposition (**с, под, над, ме́жду, за, перед**): **ним, ней, ни́ми**.

Упражне́ние 12в

Fill in the blanks with the correct form of the personal pronoun.

1. Мы поговори́ли с (они́) _____ вчера́, и они́ сказа́ли, что прие́дут за́втра.
2. Вы ра́зве недово́льны (он) _____?
3. Мы о́чень хоро́шие друзья́. Ме́жду (мы) _____ нет никаки́х пробле́м.
4. Пе́ред (вы) _____ виси́т карти́на Шага́ла, над карти́ной Канди́нского.
5. Где кни́га? Ви́дите вон там газе́ту? Кни́га лежи́т под (она́) _____.

PART 4 Last Names

Russian last names that end in **-ов/-ев** or **-ын/-ин** decline as adjectives in both genders, both singular and plural.

Аса́нов	Мы о́чень дово́льны Аса́новым.
Аса́нова	Мы о́чень дово́льны Аса́новой.
Аса́новы	Мы о́чень дово́льны Аса́новыми.
Солжени́цын	Мы о́чень дово́льны Солжени́цыным.
Солжени́цына	Мы о́чень дово́льны Солжени́цыной.
Солжени́цыны	Мы о́чень дово́льны Солжени́цыными.

Women's last names that end in a consonant do not decline at all.

female: А́ндрея Смит	Мы о́чень дово́льны А́ндреей Смит.
male: Андре́й Смит	Мы о́чень дово́льны Андре́ем Сми́том.

Упражне́ние 12г

Complete the sentence with the correct form of the names.

Мы о́чень недово́льны...

1. Михаи́л Горбачёв
2. Раи́са Горбачёва
3. Горбачёвы
4. Бори́с Е́льцин
5. Е́льцины

Numbers

Numbers are in the instrumental case if required by grammatical context.

1. Мы говори́ли с **семью́ но́выми инжене́рами**.

   We were talking with seven new engineers.

2. Мы наве́рно найдём э́ти бума́ги ме́жду **двумя́ кни́гами**.

   We'll probably find the papers between two books.

3. Она́ руководи́т **тремяста́ми нау́чными рабо́тниками**.

   She supervises three hundred scientific (scholarly) workers.

4. Я зайду́ ме́жду **четырьмя́ и пятью́** (**часа́ми**).

   I'll drop by between four and five (o'clock).

In example 1, *seven new engineers* is in the instrumental case because it is governed by the preposition *with*. In example 2, *two books* is in the instrumental case because it is governed by the preposition *between*. In example 3, *three hundred scientific (scholarly) workers* is in the instrumental case because it is the object of the verb *supervise*. In example 4, the numbers are governed by the preposition *between* and modify the implied noun *hours*.

Review the instrumental case forms of the number nouns in **Табли́ца 16** in the Appendix. Note that many of the instrumental case number nouns (50, 60, 200, 300) have *two* stresses.

You should memorize the instrumental case form of numbers 1 through 20, but you need only recognize the forms of the other numbers.

The following examples demonstrate the instrumental form of number adjectives.

5. Я поговорю́ с **шесты́м** кандида́том, а вы—с **тре́тьим**.

   I'll talk with the sixth candidate, and you with the third.

6. Она́ зако́нчила **пе́рвой**, а он— **вторы́м**.

   She finished first, and he—second.

7. Еле́на рабо́тает над **два́дцать восьмо́й зада́чей**.

   Elena is working on the twenty-eighth problem.

Note that in compound numbers, such as 62 or 96, only the last digit of the adjective is declined, as demonstrated in the seventh example sentence. The previous digits are written and pronounced as nouns. Memorize the number adjectives and their instrumental case forms for use in such constructions. Review the number adjectives in **Табли́ца 17** in the Appendix.

❊   Упражнéние 12д

Provide the missing form of the number as required by grammatical context. Some of the missing numbers are nouns, others are adjectives. Be careful to use appropriate endings. Write out all numbers as words.

Пáвел сме́ялся над (4) _____ студéнтками, котóрых он хотéл пригласи́ть на тáнцы. Он не знал, что пéрвая из них рабóтает с (2) _____ из мои́х друзéй, а трéтья руководи́т (227) _____ специали́стами на завóде. Он колебáлся (hesitated) мéжду (2nd) _____ дéвушкой и (4th) _____, наконéц реши́лся пригласи́ть меня́, но пóздно. Я ужé собирáюсь идти́ с (1) _____ пáрнем, с котóрым я познакóмилась на лéкции. Бéдный Пáвел!

𝄞   Задáние 12а

Prepare a presentation or composition about what or whom you are satisfied (or dissatisfied) with or proud of.

❊   Упражнéние 12е

Memorize this poem by Tiutchev:

> Умóм[1] Росси́ю не поня́ть,
> Арши́ном óбщим[2] не измéрить:[3]
> У ней[4] осóбенная стать[5]—
> В Росси́ю мóжно тóлько вéрить.

[1] *By means of the mind*
[2] *a standard measurement*
[3] *to measure*
[4] *archaic = у неё*
[5] *reason, nature, being*

❊   Упражнéние 12ё

Continue your list of all the "connecting" words and phrases (such as *because, but, in the first place, then,* and so forth) with those you can find in the texts of this unit. Next to each "connecting" word or phrase, write out the clause or sentence in which they are used. Keep this list in your notebook and add to it as you continue with this book.

❊   Упражнéние 12ж

Add the verbs of this unit to your lists of first- and second-conjugation verbs, noting the stress pattern of each verb as you do so.

❊   Упражнéние 12з

Write out the instrumental case endings on the page in your notes dedicated to the instrumental case. Then write out some example sentences with instrumental case constructions on that page. Lastly, write up a list of all the verbs and the prepositions that take the instrumental case (as listed in this unit). Be sure to distinguish the verbs and the prepositions that *can* take the instrumental case from those verbs and prepositions that *must* take the instrumental case.

UNIT 13

Review of All Cases

Повторе́ние всех падеже́й

—Сейча́с изме́рим пу́льс.

PART 1

Review of
Nouns and Adjectives

Units 7 to 12 present each of the six cases in turn; the endings for adjectives and nouns are presented separately for each case. It is productive to review groups of nouns and adjectives to grasp the larger picture of the declension system. Groups of nouns that decline in similar ways are called "paradigms." There are separate paradigms for masculine nouns with hard stems, with soft stems, and those ending in **-ий**; for feminine nouns ending in **-а**, **-я**, **-ия**, and **-ь**; and for neuter nouns ending in **-о**, **-е**, and **-ие**. There are also different classes of adjectives: those with hard stems, soft stems, stems ending in **-г**, **-к**, or **-х**, and separate classes for those with end stress or stem stress ending in **-ж**, **-ш**, **-щ**, **-ч**, or **-ц**. The tables in the Appendix depict the paradigms of the major declension patterns for Russian nouns and adjectives. Learning these paradigms will help you use the grammatical endings more automatically.

✳ Упражнéние 13а

Review **Таблúцы 1** to **7** in the Appendix and determine which cases provide for a distinction (different endings) between animate and inanimate nouns.

✳ Упражнéние 13б

Using the **Таблúцы** in the Appendix, determine which noun types the following nouns are and then create your own tables depicting their declension in both singular and plural forms: **стенá, компьютер, собáка, жирáф, письмó, кремль, дверь, лаборатóрия, здáние, журнáл, трамвáй, хúмик, словáрь, отéц, санатóрий, описáние, кýхня, газéта, лéкция, жизнь, лóшадь.**

✳ Упражнéние 13в

Review adjectival endings in **Таблúцы 8** to **11** in the Appendix and determine how many different endings there are for feminine adjectives. Then determine when masculine adjectives have the same endings as neuter adjectives. Lastly, come up with a list of three other adjectives for each adjectival type (column heading) and make up your own **Таблúцы**.

✳ Упражнéние 13г

Determine why some learners of Russian confuse instrumental singular and prepositional singular endings for adjectives and nouns.

 ТЕКСТ 13а

Read the poem by Akhmadulina about the duels in which Lermontov and Pushkin lost their lives.

Pre-reading Task

What do you think Akhmadulina's perspective on these duels might be? Make some predictions to see if you're right. Skim through the poem and determine the name of the man who killed Pushkin in 1837 and the name of the man who killed Lermontov in 1841.

Дуэ́ль

И сно́ва, как огни́ марте́нов,[1]
Огни́ грозы́ над голово́й[2]...
Так кто же победи́л:[3] Марты́нов
Иль Ле́рмонтов в дуэ́ли той?
Данте́с иль Пу́шкин? Кто там пе́рвый?
Кто вы́играл и встал с земли́?[4]
Кого́ доро́гой э́той бе́лой
На чёрних са́нках повезли́?[5]
Но как же так! По всем приме́там[6]
Друго́й там вы́играл, друго́й,
Не тот, кто на снегу́ примя́том
Лежа́л курча́вой голово́й![7]
Что де́лать, е́сли в схва́тке ди́кой[8]
Всегда́ дура́к был на виду́,[9]
Меж тем[10] как челове́к вели́кий,
Как ма́льчик, попада́л в беду́[11]...
Чем я уте́шу поражённых[12]
Ничто́жным превосхо́дством зла,[13]
Осме́янных и отчуждённых[14]
Поэ́тов, погиба́вших зря?[15]
Я так скажу́: на са́мом де́ле,
Давны́м-давно́, кото́рый год,
Забы́ли мы и прогляде́ли[16]
Что всё идёт наоборо́т:[17]
Марты́нов пал под той горо́ю,[18]
Он был нака́зан тяжело́,[19]
А во́ронье ночно́й поро́ю
Его́ терза́ло и несло́.[20]
А Ле́рмонтов зато́ снача́ла
Всё начина́л и гнал коня́,[21]
И же́нщина ему́ крича́ла:
«Люби́ меня́! Люби́ меня́!»
Данте́с лежа́л среди́ сугро́ба,[22]
Подня́ться не уме́л с земли́,[23]

[1] как... *like the fires of furnaces*
[2] Огни́... *like the fires of a storm over one's head*
[3] Так... *who triumphed, anyway?*
[4] Кто... *Who won and rose from the earth?*
[5] Кого́... *Who was carried away on the black sled on the white road?*
[6] По... *according to all signs*
[7] Не... *Not the one with the curly hair, lying on the crushed snow*
[8] в... *in a fierce struggle*
[9] Всегда́... *a fool always stood out*
[10] *at the same time*
[11] попада́л... *fell into harm*
[12] Чем... *How can I console those defeated*
[13] Ничто́жным... *by the meaningless superiority of evil*
[14] Осме́янных... *laughed at and alienated*
[15] Поэ́тов... *poets who perished in vain*
[16] Забы́ли... *We forgot the year and didn't notice*
[17] Что... *That everything is completely the opposite*
[18] Марты́нов... *Martynov fell at that mountain*
[19] Он... *He was punished severely*
[20] во́ронье... *a night raven tortured him and carried off his body*
[21] гнал... *raced horses*
[22] лежа́л... *was lying in the snowbank*
[23] Подня́ться... *could not get up from the ground*

35   А ми́мо ме́дленно, суро́во,[24]
     Не огляну́вшись,[25] лю́ди шли.
     Он у́мер и́ли жив оста́лся[26]—
     Никто́ того́ не различа́л,[27]
     А Пу́шкин пил вино́, смея́лся,
40   Друзе́й встреча́л, озорнича́л.[28]
     Стихи́ писа́л, не знал печа́ли,[29]
     Дела́ его́ прекра́сно шли,
     И поводи́ла всё плеча́ми
     И улыба́лась Натали́.[30]
45   Для их спасе́ния[31] наве́чно[32]
     Поря́док э́тот утвержде́н.[33]
     И торжеству́ющий неве́жда
     Приговоре́н и осужде́н.[34]

                          Б. А. Ахмаду́лина, 1962

[24] *severely*
[25] *Не... not looking back*
[26] *Он... Was he alive or dead*
[27] *Никто́... no one could tell*
[28] *made mischief*
[29] *grief*
[30] *поводи́ла... Natalie (Pushkin's wife) shrugged her shoulders and smiled through it all*
[31] *salvation*
[32] *for eternity*
[33] *Поря́док... this order is established*
[34] *И... and the victorious ignoramous is sentenced and convicted*

Post-reading Tasks

1. Write a two-sentence summary in Russian of the duels in which Lermontov and Pushkin died.
2. Write a summary of Akhmadulina's "rewriting of history."
3. Note the case of each underlined form and identify the reason.
4. Write a paragraph in Russian explaining why Akhmadulina's poem might have special meaning for a poet writing in the Soviet era.

✳   Упражне́ние 13д

Use the tables of the declension of nouns and adjectives in the Appendix to fill in the blanks.

1. Лю́да ча́сто е́здит в (Калу́га и Тверь) _____.
2. Там у́чатся студе́нты из (Мэрила́ндский университе́т) _____.
3. Вы когда́-нибудь бы́ли и́ли в (Калу́га и́ли Тверь) _____?
4. Там мно́го (интере́сные па́мятники) _____.
5. (Америка́нские студе́нты) _____ о́чень нра́вятся програ́ммы в (стари́нные города́) _____.

кото́рый, кто, and *что*

Кото́рый is a regular adjective in formation, but not in function. Adjectives modify nouns, but **кото́рый** is used instead to refer back to a noun in a preceding clause. The case of **кото́рый** is determined by the grammatical context of the clause in which it is used, but the gender and the number of **кото́рый** are determined by the antecedent to which it refers.

> **1.** Мы говори́ли о студе́нтах, **кото́рым** мы помога́ли про́шлым ле́том.
>
> *We were speaking about the students whom we helped last summer.*
>
> **2.** Мы говори́ли о его́ сестре́, **с кото́рой** мы познако́мились в сре́ду.
>
> *We were speaking about his sister whom we met on Wednesday.*

In example 1, the antecedent **студе́нтах** is plural, so the pronoun **кото́рый** must also be plural. The case of the pronoun is dative, because the verb **помога́ть** (*to help*) requires an object in the dative case.

In example 2, the antecedent **сестре́** is singular and feminine, so the pronoun **кото́рый** must also be singular and feminine. The case of the pronoun **кото́рый** is instrumental, as required by the preposition **с** when it means *with*.

❋ Упражне́ние 13е

Fill in the blanks with the appropriate form of the word **кото́рый**.

1. Вчера́ мы говори́ли с сосе́дями, о _____ я вам расска́зывала.
2. Они́ сказа́ли, что хорошо́ зна́ют Го́льдбергов, с _____ Та́ня хо́чет познако́миться.
3. Они́ предложи́ли пригласи́ть Та́ню на обе́д, на _____ приглася́т и Го́льдбергов.
4. Таки́м о́бразом, Та́ня смо́жет поговори́ть с ни́ми о пробле́ме, для _____ она́ давно́ и́щет реше́ния.

Use the pronouns **кто** or **что** to refer to antecedents that are pronouns.

> **3.** Мы положи́ли в чемода́н всё, **что** нам ну́жно.
>
> *We put everything that we need in the suitcase.*
>
> **4.** Все, **кто** был (бы́ли) в Оде́ссе, счита́ют э́тот го́род прекра́сным куро́ртом.
>
> *Everyone who has been in Odessa thinks that city is a wonderful resort.*

In example 3, **что** refers to an inanimate antecedent. In example 4, **кто** refers to an animate antecedent (*all the people*). The verb that agrees with **кто** may be singular or plural in this kind of construction. The declension of **кто/что** is provided in **Табли́ца 15** in the Appendix.

❋ Упражне́ние 13ё

Fill in the blanks with the appropriate form of the word **кото́рый**, **кто**, or **что**.

1. Андре́евы показа́ли нам фотогра́фии, _____ они́ сде́лали в Новосиби́рске.
2. Все, _____ был в Новосиби́рске, говоря́т, что э́то прекра́сный го́род.

3. Андре́евы сказа́ли, что они́ по́мнят абсолю́тно всё, о _____ говори́ла Тама́ра, их гид.

4. Тама́ра, с _____ они́ познако́мились в Петербу́рге в про́шлом году́, мно́го зна́ет об исто́рии архитекту́ры.

друг дру́га

The expression *each other/one another* is conveyed in Russian with some version of the words **друг дру́га**. Note how these words are used in the examples, which could describe a couple very much in love.

1. Они́ о́чень лю́бят друг дру́га.   *They love each other very much.*
2. Они́ ча́сто говоря́т друг о дру́ге.   *They often talk about each other.*
3. Они́ ча́сто ви́дятся друг с дру́гом.   *They often see each other.*
4. Они́ всё вре́мя помога́ют друг   *They always help each other.*
   дру́гу.

In each example, the *first* word **друг** is always in the nominative singular case and is followed by a preposition only if required by the construction, as in examples 2 and 3. The *second* word **дру́га** is never in the nominative case and is either governed by a verb (as in examples 1 and 4) or by the preposition that immediately precedes it (as in examples 2 and 3).

✳ Упражне́ние 13ж

Fill in the blanks with the appropriate form of the word **друг**.

1. То́ля и Со́ня ча́сто звоня́т друг _____.
2. Лари́са Петро́вна и Андре́й Васи́льевич ча́сто се́рдятся друг на _____.
3. Э́ти преподава́тели иногда́ смею́тся друг над _____.
4. Мы́ ча́сто быва́ем в гостя́х друг у _____.
5. Э́ти студе́нты и профессора́ о́чень уважа́ют друг _____.

𝄢 Зада́ние 13а

Write a paragraph about a couple or group of people who don't like one another. Use the expression *one another* as many times in as many different forms as you can. See who can come up with the greatest number of uses of this expression and the most expressive paragraph.

PART 3
Review of Last Names

For Russian last names ending in **-ов/-ев/-ёв** or **-ин/-ын**

1. Feminine last names are adjectival except for the nominative and accusative cases.
2. Masculine last names are adjectival in the instrumental.
3. Plural last names are adjectival except in the nominative case.
4. Russian last names ending in **-ский/-ская, -цкий/-цкая, -стóй/-стáя, -цкóй/-цкáя** are always adjectival.

For non-Russian last names:

5. Masculine names ending in a consonant decline regularly. Masculine names ending in a vowel do not decline.
6. Feminine names ending in the vowels **-а/-я** decline regularly. Feminine names ending in a consonant do not decline.

❋ Упражнéние 13з

Use the tables of the declension of nouns and adjectives in the Appendix to fill in the blanks.

1. Вчерá мы собирáлись у (Верони́ка Кузнецóва) _____.
2. Верá дóлго говори́ла с (Никола́й Трубецкóй и А́нджела Джóнс) _____.
3. Вы случа́йно не зна́ете (А́нна Сини́цына и Сти́вен Сми́т) _____?
4. Они́ весь вéчер говори́ли тóлько о (Па́вловы и Щерби́цкие) _____.
5. Ка́жется, что (Ди́ма Миха́йлов и Лéна Мака́рова) _____ óчень нра́вятся Кузнецóвы.

𝄞 Зада́ние 13б

Write a story with at least ten sentences about a meeting of two families, the **Прокóфьевы**, and an American family of any ethnic or racial background *except* Russian. Try to use the different last names in as many cases as you can to demonstrate your mastery of this grammatical topic. Be creative!

𝄞 Зада́ние 13в

Try to memorize your paragraph by writing it out several times, saying it out loud several times, and recording it so that you can listen to it several times.

PART 4
Possessive Modifiers Derived from Names

Russian provides for another way to express possession—with a modifier formed from a common Russian name or familial relationship.

1.	Это—**па́пина** маши́на.	*This is dad's car.*
2.	Ты не ви́дела **О́лину** кни́гу?	*Did you happen to see Olia's book?*
3.	**То́линому** дру́гу о́чень понра́вился э́тот фильм.	*Tolia's friend really liked that film.*
4.	Мы идём на та́нцы с **Па́шиными** друзья́ми.	*We're going to the dance with Pasha's friends.*

These special possessive forms are created from only the most common Russian names and familial relationships. They consist of the first syllable of the name or familial relationship together with the ending **-ин** and a grammatical ending corresponding in gender, number, and case with the noun it modifies. These possessives are declined like last names ending in **-ин/-ын** or **-ов/-ев/-ёв**. Review the rules for these last names.

✳   Упражне́ние 13и

Determine the antecedent with which the boldface special possessive form agrees in examples 1 through 4.

✳   Упражне́ние 13й

Fill in the blanks with the appropriate form of the possessive modifier.

1. Это—(Пе́тя) _____ га́лстук.
2. Нам о́чень понра́вился (Та́ня) _____ муж.
3. Вы не нашли́ (Бо́ря) _____ маши́ну?
4. Это, наве́рно, (Ла́ра) _____ де́ньги.
5. На ве́чере мы познако́мились с (ма́ма) _____ колле́гами.

PART 5
Personal Pronouns and *себя́*

Pronouns are words that take the place of nouns. Review the declension of the personal pronouns (**я, ты**, etc.), possessive modifiers (**мой, твой, свой**, etc.), and the pronoun *oneself* (**сам**) in **Табли́цы 12** to **14** in the Appendix.

The third-person personal pronouns add the letter **н** to the beginning of the pronoun when those pronouns are preceded by a preposition.

1. Я бу́ду у **него́**.
2. Мы ходи́ли к **ней** вчера́ ве́чером.
3. Ки́ра ещё на про́шлой неде́ле говори́ла с **ни́ми** об э́том.

I'll be at his place.
We went to see her yesterday evening.
Kira already talked with them about this last week.

❋ Упражне́ние 13к

Fill in the blanks with the appropriate form of the personal pronoun.

1. (Ты) _____ не зна́ешь, как (она́) _____ зову́т?
2. (Он) _____ ну́жно поговори́ть с (они́) _____ об э́том.
3. (Вы) _____ бы́ло интере́сно на ле́кции? Жаль, что (мы) _____ там не́ было.
4. Дире́ктор уже́ говори́л со (я) _____ о (он) _____.
5. Прошу́ (ты) _____ не говори́ть об э́том при (она́) _____.

себя

The reflexive pronoun **себя** is declined like **тебя**, except that it lacks a nominative case form. **Себя** is used in Russian to refer back to the subject of a nonreflexive verb (i.e., a verb that does *not* end in **-ся**). **Себя** can also be translated as *myself, himself, herself, yourself/yourselves,* and *themselves,* but it fulfills a different grammatical and lexical role than **сам** (Part 7).

1. Мы купи́ли **себе́** но́вую маши́ну.
2. Иногда́ я бою́сь самого́ **себя**!
3. Сего́дня он чу́вствует **себя** пло́хо.

We bought a new car for ourselves.
Sometimes I'm afraid of my very own self!
He feels bad today.

Себя is also used to distinguish the subject of a verb from the object of the same verb.

4. Га́ля попроси́ла до́чку купи́ть **ей** э́ту кни́гу.
5. Га́ля попроси́ла до́чку купи́ть **себе́** э́ту кни́гу.

Galia asked her daughter to buy her (Galia) that book.
Galia asked her daughter to buy herself (the daughter) that book.

As illustrated in examples 1 and 5, **себя** is often used with the verb **покупа́ть/купи́ть** to indicate that the object being purchased is specifically intended for the person who is purchasing it (i.e., not a gift for someone else). **Себя** is often used in set expressions with particular verbs.

чу́вствовать/почу́вствовать себя	*to feel (as in one's health)*
представля́ть/предста́вить себе́	*to imagine*
брать/взять с собо́й	*to bring along*
вести́ себя́ (хорошо́/пло́хо)	*to behave oneself (well, poorly)*

RUSSIAN

Saying

Кусáть себé лóкти.

To bite one's elbows.
[To cry over spilt milk.]

Упражнéние 13л

Fill in the blanks with the appropriate form of **себя́**.

1. Как ты _____ чýвствуешь сегóдня, Тáня?
2. О чёрт! Мы забы́ли взять с _____ докумéнты!
3. Я не могý представить _____ жи́зни без докумéнтов.
4. Ты ужáсно _____ ведёшь сегóдня, Ми́ша!

PART 6 Possessive Modifiers

The interrogative pronoun **чей** (**чья**, **чьё**, **чьи**), meaning *whose*, is declined for gender, number, and case and agrees with the noun it modifies.

—Чей э́то словáрь?	—*Whose dictionary is that?*
—Э́то словáрь Э́дика.	—*That's Edik's dictionary.*
—Чья э́то сýмка?	—*Whose bag is that?*
—Э́то сýмка Ки́ры.	—*That's Kira's bag.*

The answers to the questions with the interrogative *whose* often involve answers with the genitive case of the person named as the possessor of the item in question. In the preceding examples, the interrogative pronouns were always in the nominative case. Here is an example in which the interrogative is in another case.

—К чьемý дрýгу вы ходи́ли в гóсти вчерá вéчером?	—*Whose friend did you visit last night?*
—К дрýгу Ки́ры.	—*Kira's friend.*

Review the declension of the interrogative pronoun **чей** in **Табли́ца 13** in the Appendix.

✳ Упражне́ние 13м

Fill in the blanks below with the appropriate form of *whose*.

ОБРАЗЕ́Ц: _____ бра́та ты ви́дела в общежи́тии? →

Чьего́ бра́та ты ви́дела в общежи́тии?
Whose brother did you see in the dormitory?

1. Э́то—_____ маши́на?
   Э́то маши́на Мари́ны Па́вловны.
2. К _____ друзья́м вы идёте сего́дня вече́ром.
   К друзья́м Алёши Петро́ва.
3. О _____ де́ньгах вы говори́те?
   О де́ньгах Са́ши Кузнецо́вой.
4. В _____ рюкзаке́ ве́щи бы́ли на́йдены?
   В рюкзаке́ Лёни Петруше́нко.
5. С _____ детьми́ ты говори́ла на ве́чере?
   Я говори́ла с детьми́ А́нны Петро́вны.

RUSSIAN

Saying

На чьём возу́ сижу́, того́ и пе́сенку пою́.

I sing the song of the one on whose cart I sit.
[Don't bite the hand that feeds you.]

✳ Упражне́ние 13н

Use **Табли́ца 13** in the Appendix as a model to create a new chart for the declension of the adjective **тре́тий** (*third*), whose declension pattern is identical to that of **чей**. Then write a paragraph using the adjective **тре́тий** in as many different cases as you can.

The declension of the possessive modifiers (**чей/чья, мой/моя́, её/его́**, etc.) is similar to that of the adjectives, but differs in key ways.

The third-person personal pronouns have the same form as the possessive modifiers (**его́/её/их**), but function differently. The possessive modifiers do not take the letter **н-** when preceded by a preposition.

1. Мы ходи́ли в кино́ с **его́** сестро́й.	*We went to the movies with his sister.*
2. Они́ бу́дут жить у её бра́та.	*They will live with her brother.*

When the possessive modifier refers back to a third-person subject, noun, or pronoun in the same clause, the modifier **свой** must be used if a possessive modifier is required at all.

3. Ми́ша и Та́ня никогда́ ни убира́ют свою́ кварти́ру.	*Misha and Tania never clean their (own) apartment.*

If the possessive pronoun **их** were used, instead of **свою**, then the example would mean that Misha and Tania never clean up someone else's apartment. (In English these constructions are ambiguous.) Consider these example sentences.

4.	Óля лю́бит своего́ му́жа.	*Olia loves her (own) husband.*
5.	Óля лю́бит её му́жа.	*Olia loves her (some other woman's) husband.*
6.	Óля попроси́ла сестру́ убра́ть свою́ ко́мнату.	*Olia asked her sister to clean up her (the sister's) room.*
7.	Óля попроси́ла сестру́ убра́ть её ко́мнату.	*Olia asked her sister to clean up her (Olia's) room.*

These example sentences clearly illustrate the ambiguity of the English translations, as compared with the clarity of the Russian. In example 6, the possessive modifier **свой** refers back to the sister (the implied subject of the nearest verb, **убра́ть**), while in example 7, the possessive **её** refers back to Olia.

The question of when to use **свой** and when not to becomes a little trickier when your sentence has two clauses. If the two clauses have different subjects, you can't use **свой** to refer the second subject back to the first (as illustrated in example 8); if, however, the subject of the two clauses is in fact the same, you must use **свой** (example 9).

8.	Ма́ша сказа́ла, что её сестра́ сейча́с в Росто́ве-на-Дону́.	*Masha said that her (Masha's) sister is now in Rostov-on-the-Don.*
9.	А́лла ду́мает, что (она́/А́лла) расска́жет свое́й подру́ге об э́той пробле́ме за́втра ве́чером.	*Alla thinks that she (Alla) will tell her friend about this problem tomorrow evening.*

As the rule you've just been given suggests, **свой** in general doesn't modify anything in the nominative case; but there are exceptions to every rule. **Свой** can modify the grammatical subject of a sentence with the construction *to have*.

10.	У них есть своя́ кварти́ра. (Они́ не живу́т у роди́телей.)	*They have their own apartment. (They don't live with their parents.)*
11.	У дире́ктора был свой план. (А у меня́ есть и свой план!)	*The director had his own plan. (But I have my own plan!)*
12.	Анто́н—свой челове́к.	*Anton is our kind of guy.*

Remember that Russians do not use possessive modifiers to refer to immediate family members and body parts when the relationship between these people or parts and the subject is clear from the context. If any indication of this relationship is given, it is usually given by means of the construction **у кого́** (**у** + **роди́тельный паде́ж**) rather than with a modifier: **У меня́ боли́т рука́.** (*My hand hurts.*)

ТЕКСТ 136

Read this excerpt from Turgenev's novella *First Love*. Explain the case (and gender and number, if possible) of the underlined pronouns and identify antecedents whenever possible.

Pre-reading Task

Do you remember the summer when you were sixteen? Where did you live that summer and what did you do? Do you think you'll remember that summer thirty years from now? Why or why not?

Мне́ бы́ло тогда́ шестна́дцать лет. Де́ло происходи́ло ле́том 1833 го́да.
    Я жил в Москве́ у мои́х роди́телей. Они́ нанима́ли[1] да́чу о́коло Калу́жской заста́вы, про́тив Нескӳчного.[2] Я гото́вился в университе́т, но рабо́тал о́чень ма́ло и не торопя́сь.

5   Никто́ не стесня́л мое́й свобо́ды.[3] Я де́лал, что хоте́л, осо́бенно с тех пор, как я расста́лся[4] с после́дним мои́м гуверне́ром-францу́зом, кото́рый ника́к не мог привы́кнуть к мы́сли,[5] что он упа́л[6] «как бо́мба»...в Росси́ю.... Оте́ц обходи́лся со мно́й равноду́шно-ла́сково;[7] ма́тушка почти́ не обраща́ла на меня́ внима́ния,[8] хотя́ у ней,[9] кро́ме

10   меня́, не бы́ло дете́й.... Мой оте́ц, челове́к ещё молодо́й и о́чень краси́вый, жени́лся на ней по расчёту:[10] она́ была́ ста́рше его́ деся́тью года́ми....

    Я никогда́ не забу́ду пе́рвых неде́ль, проведённых мно́ю[11] на да́че. Пого́да стоя́ла чуде́сная; мы перее́хали из го́рода девя́того ма́я, в са́мый

15   Нико́лин день. Я гуля́л—то в саду́ на́шей да́чи, то по Нескӳчному, то за заста́вой; брал с собо́ю каку́ю-нибудь кни́гу...я всё ждал, робе́л[12] чего́-то и всему́ диви́лся[13] и весь был наготбве; фанта́зия игра́ла и носи́лась бы́стро вокру́г одни́х и тех же представле́ний,[14] как на заре́ стрижи́ вокру́г колоко́льни[15]....

И. С. Турге́нев, «Пе́рвая любо́вь», 1860

[1] *rented*
[2] *о́коло... near the Kaluga Gate, opposite Neskuchni garden (not far from Sparrow Hills)*
[3] *Никто́... No one hindered my freedom*
[4] *с... since the time I parted*
[5] *не... couldn't get used to the idea*
[6] *fell*
[7] *обходи́лся... treated me with affectionate indifference*
[8] *не... didn't pay me any attention*
[9] *archaic:* **у неё**
[10] *по... by plan (not for love)*
[11] *проведённых... spent by me*
[12] *was shy, timid, scared*
[13] *всему́... wondered at everything*
[14] *вокру́г... around one and the same ideas/notions*
[15] *как... like martins around the bell tower at twilight*

Post-reading Tasks

1. Write a summary of the text in Russian in three sentences.
2. What is the narrator's attitude toward his time spent at the dacha?
3. What is the meaning of the word **то** in the last paragraph (in which it is used three times in one sentence to describe how the narrator took strolls).
4. Continue the text by writing another paragraph or two or reminiscing about your own childhood memories in Russian.

RUSSIAN

Saying

Своя́ руба́шка бли́же к те́лу.

One's own shirt is closer to one's skin.
[Charity begins at home.]

❋   Упражнéние 13о

Fill in the blanks with the appropriate possessive modifier.

1. Нам óчень нрáвится Вадúм! Он _____ человéк.
2. Мы весь вéчер говорúли о Вадúме и о (his) _____ сестрé, котóрую зовýт Марúна.
3. Вадúм óчень мнóго расскáзывал о (his) _____ сестрé.
4. Вадúм сказáл, что (his) _____ сестрá рабóтает фúзиком в Москóвском наýчно-исслéдовательском (scholarly research) институтé.
5. Он сказáл, что у неё есть (her own) _____ лаборатóрия!

Saying

RUSSIAN

Быть не в своéй тарéлке.

To be not in one's own plate.
[To be out of sorts.]

Special Modifiers:
одúн, э́тот, тот, весь, сам

The special modifiers **одúн** (*one*), **э́то/э́тот/э́та** (*this*), **тот/та** (*that*), **весь/вся** (*all/ entire*), and **сам** (*self*) are declined as demonstrated in **Таблúца 14** in the Appendix.

Saying

RUSSIAN

Одúн за всех, все за однóго.

One for all and all for one.

Note that the plural form **все** is used to refer to *everyone*, while the singular form **всё** is used to refer to *everything*.

❋   Упражнéние 13п

Review the declension of the word **весь** in **Таблúца 14** in the Appendix and fill in the blanks below with the appropriate form of this word.

1. Мы сиде́ли и говори́ли _____ ночь.
2. Ты говори́ла со _____ студе́нтами в америка́нской гру́ппе?
3. Мы с Лёней хорошо́ поговори́ли обо _____.
4. _____ день шёл дождь: она вошла́ в ко́мнату и сказа́ла,—Я _____ мо́края!
5. Почему́ тут фами́лия «Андре́ев»? Ведь Миха́йлова—а́втор _____ статьи́!

✳ Упражне́ние 13p

In what way is the declension of **э́тот** similar to the declension of **оди́н**? In what way are these two declension patterns different? In what way is the declension pattern of **весь** similar to and different from the other declension patterns in **Табли́ца 14** in the Appendix?

The word **тот** is used in the Russian expressions **не тот** (*the wrong one*) and **тот же/ тот же са́мый** (*the same one*).

1. По оши́бке я взяла́ не ту кни́гу.	*I took the wrong book by mistake.*
2. Мы говори́ли не с тем челове́ком.	*We were talking with the wrong person.*
3. Они́, наве́рно, уви́дятся: они́ ча́сто обе́дают в том же рестора́не.	*They will probably see each other: They often eat in the same restaurant.*
4. Она́ была́ в той же са́мой ю́бке.	*She was wearing the very same skirt.*

The expression **тот же** (*the same one*) can also be expressed as **тако́й же**, when it means a similar but not identical one.

5. У нас така́я же маши́на.	*We have a similar car.*
6. Бро́нские живу́т в тако́й же кварти́ре.	*The Bronskys live in a similar apartment.*

✳ Упражне́ние 13c

Fill in the blanks as required by context.

1. Он был в (the very same suit) _____.
2. Они́ рабо́тают вме́сте с (the very same [Marina]) _____.
3. Мы ча́сто хо́дим в (the same movie theater) _____.
4. Он наде́л (the wrong necktie) _____.
5. Она́ занима́лась (the wrong problem: зада́ча) _____.

сам

The word **сам** is used to refer back to the subject or object of a verb and to emphasize the fame or significance of that subject or object. The English equivalents of many **сам** constructions include *myself, himself, herself, yourself,* or *themselves.*

7.	Она **сама** это сказала!		*She said it herself!*
8.	Мы говорили с **самим** директором об этом.		*We spoke with the director himself about this.*
9.	Мы были в гостях у **самой** Толстой!		*We were at the home of Tolstaia herself!*

In example 7, the word **сам** emphasizes the subject of the verb, while in examples 8 and 9 the word emphasizes the object of the preposition. Examples 7 and 8 emphasize the significance of a particular person in a particular context, while example 9 emphasizes her fame.

RUSSIAN

Saying

Сами с усами.

We're old enough to have a mustache, too!
[We weren't born yesterday.]

Study the declension of the word **сам** as shown in **Таблица 14** in the Appendix.

✳ Упражнéние 13т

Fill in the blanks with the appropriate form of the word **сам**.

1. Мы _____ помогаем своим профессорам.
2. Он _____ попросил нас это сделать.
3. Я поговорила с _____ Петровыми на эту тему.
4. Мы подарили эту книгу _____ Ельцину!
5. Вчера мы говорили о Хрущёвой, и как раз она _____ зашла в комнату.

𝄞 Задáние 13г

Write a paragraph about a famous person, using the word **сам** in as many different cases as you can.

𝄞 Задáние 13д

Memorize the paragraph you wrote in **Задáние 13а**. Write it out several times, practice saying it out loud several times. Record it on tape and listen to your recording several times.

❋ Упражне́ние 13у

Continue your list of all the "connecting" words and phrases (such as *because*, *but*, *in the first place*, *then*, and so forth) with those you can find in the texts of this unit. Next to each "connecting" word or phrase, write out the clause or sentence in which they are used. Keep this list in your notebook and add to it as you continue with this book.

❋ Упражне́ние 13ф

Add the verbs of this unit to your lists of first- and second-conjugation verbs, noting the stress pattern of each verb as you do so.

❋ Упражне́ние 13х

Review your notes for all the cases and make certain that they are accurate. Then add to them based on the information presented in this unit.

UNIT 14

Anytime, Sometime, Never, Whenever

Когда́-нибудь, когда́-то, никогда́, когда́ бы...ни

Тут на́до немедле́нно убра́ть!

Identifying Adverbial and Pronominal Expressions

You are probably already familiar with adverbial expressions such as **когда́/никогда́** (*when*/*never*), **где/нигде́** (*where*/*nowhere, in no place*), and **куда́/никуда́** (*where/ nowhere, to no place*). It is important to remember that the verb used with negative adverbial expressions **никогда́**, **нигде́**, and **никуда́** must also be negated.

1.	—Когда́ вы с Га́лей обы́чно хо́дите в кино́?	—*When do you and Galia usually go to the movies?*	
	—А мы́ **никогда́ не** хо́дим в кино́: мы бо́льше лю́бим теа́тр.	—*We never go to the movies: We like the theater better.*	

The adverbial expression in example 1 is governed by the same rules that govern pronominal expressions **ничего́/никого́**, **ничему́/никому́**, **ни о чём/ни о ко́м**, and **ниче́м/нике́м**.* These pronominal expressions provide negated objects (*what? whom?*) for verb constructions requiring the genitive, dative, prepositional, and instrumental cases, respectively.

2.	—Чего́ бои́тся А́нна?	—*What is Anna afraid of?*
	—А́нна о́чень сме́лая: она́ **ничего́ не** бои́тся.	—*Anna is very brave: She isn't afraid of anything.*
3.	—О чём говоря́т э́ти не́мцы?	—*What are those Germans talking about?*
	—Они́ **ни о чём не** говоря́т.	—*They're not talking about anything (in particular).*

Because the double negative is not allowed in English, the English equivalents of these pronominal expressions would be words like *anyone, anywhere,* and *anything.* Russian uses the specially negative particle **ни** together with the negative pronoun or adverbial expression. Example 3 illustrates how prepositions split the negative particle **ни** from the pronoun (**чём, ком, чем,** and **кем**).

Saying

Ничего́ не поде́лаешь.

There's nothing you can do.
[There's nothing to be done.]

---

* The word *pronominal* is derived from the word *pronoun.*

✿ Упражне́ние 14a

Reread examples 1 through 3 and circle every expression or preposition that requires a particular case for the interrogative or negative adverbial or pronominal expression. Identify the case used.

✿ Упражне́ние 14б

Fill in the blanks in this story about a "nowhere man" named Akakii. Use the appropriate form of the negative adverbial or pronominal expression and insert prepositions as necessary.

1. Ака́кий (no one) _____ не лю́бит, и никто́ не лю́бит его́.
2. Он то́же (no one) _____ не нра́вится.
3. Ну, (nothing) _____ не поде́лаешь!
4. Коне́чно, он (never) _____ не говори́т.
5. Поэ́тому, мо́жет быть, он (nowhere) _____ не хо́дит.

Pronominal Expressions Like *не́когда*

Review Part 5 of Unit 11, Special Impersonal Constructions: **есть когда́** and **не́когда**.

PART 2
Indefinite Particles

The two most commonly used indefinite particles are **-то** and **-нибудь**. They are usually translated as the English prefixes *some-* and *any-*.

1. —**Кто́-нибудь** звони́л, когда́ меня́ не́ было?
   —Да, **кто́-то** звони́л и сказа́л, что перезвони́т.

   —*Did anyone call while I was out?*
   —*Yes, someone called and said he would call back.*

2. —Ты **кого́-нибудь** из знако́мых ви́дела на ле́кции?
   —Да, я **кого́-то** ви́дела, но забы́ла кого́.

   —*Did you see anyone you know at the lecture?*
   —*Yes, I saw someone, but I forgot whom.*

3. —Ты ви́дел **каку́ю-нибудь** иностра́нку в институ́те?
   —Нет, я **никаку́ю** иностра́нку **не** ви́дел.

   —*Did you see some foreigner in the institute?*
   —*No, I didn't see any foreigner in the institute.*

4. —Расскáжет ли Антóн о **какóй-нибудь** жéнщине?	—*Will Anton tell about some woman?*
—Нет, навéрно он **ни о кóм не** расскáжет.	—*He probably won't talk about anyone at all.*

Before translating English indefinite expressions with the prefixes *some-* or *any-* into Russian, consider the rules governing **-то** and **-нибудь**. Some students of Russian try to translate these expressions by examining the English constructions and basing their choice of the Russian particle on the English prefix. This is not a productive strategy, because English is not nearly as systematic as Russian is with respect to these constructions.

When choosing between **-то** and **-нибудь**, use the following rules in the order they are presented.

1. If there is a negation in the sentence, you may not be able to use either **-то** or **-нибудь** even if the English uses *some-* or *any-* for the same expression; you may need to use a negative pronominal or adverbial expression (as described in Part 1).
2. If the particle is part of a question, use **-нибудь**.
3. If the particle is in a declarative sentence in any tense with a time expression conveying frequency (*always*, *frequently*, and so forth), use **-нибудь**.
4. If the particle is in a declarative sentence in the past tense, use **-то**.
5. If the particle is in a declarative sentence or question in the future tense or in an imperative, use **-нибудь**.

❀ Упражнéние 14в

Reread examples 1 through 4 and assign to them one of the five particle rules to explain the use of **-то** and **-нибудь**.

❀ Упражнéние 14г

Rewrite the examples to reflect your own life and circumstances. Use the names of friends or family members as subjects.

ТЕКСТ 14а

Read the excerpt from Pasternak's novel *Doctor Zhivago*, in which the narrator describes the childhood of Dr. Iurii Zhivago.

Pre-reading Task

When you reach your early thirties, what do you think you might remember about your childhood? What stands out most in your childhood memories now?

Пока́ жива́ была́ мать,[1] Юра не знал, что оте́ц давно́ бро́сил их, е́здит по ра́зным города́м Сиби́ри и заграни́цы,[2] ку́тит и распу́тничает, и что он давно́ просади́л и развея́л по ве́тру их миллио́нное состоя́ние.[3] Юре всегда́ говори́ли, что он то в Петербу́рге, то на како́й-нибудь я́рмарке,[4] ча́ще всего́ на Ирби́тской.

А пото́м у ма́тери, всегда́ боле́вшей,[5] откры́лась чахо́тка.[6] Она́ ста́ла е́здить лечи́ться[7] на юг Фра́нции и в Се́верную Ита́лию, куда́ Юра её два ра́за сопровожда́л.[8] Так в беспоря́дке и среди́ постоя́нных зага́док[9] прошла́ де́тская жизнь Юры, ча́сто на рука́х у чужи́х, кото́рые всё вре́мя меня́лись.[10] Он привы́к к э́тим переме́нам,[11] и в обстано́вке ве́чной нескла́дицы отсу́тствие отца́ не удивля́ло его́.[12]

Ма́леньким ма́льчиком он заста́л ещё то вре́мя,[13] когда́ и́менем, кото́рое он носи́л, называ́лось мно́жество саморазли́чнейших веще́й.[14] Была́ мануфакту́ра[15] Жива́го, банк Жива́го, дома́ Жива́го, спо́соб завя́зывания и зака́лывания га́лстука була́вкою Жива́го,[16] да́же како́й-то сла́дкий пиро́г кру́глой фо́рмы,[17]...под назва́нием Жива́го....

Б. Л. Пастерна́к, «До́ктор Жива́го», 1955

[1] Пока́... *While his mother was still alive*
[2] оте́ц... *his father had left them, was traveling in Siberia and abroad*
[3] развея́л... *had squandered their million-ruble estate*
[4] *fair*
[5] всегда́... *who had always been sickly*
[6] откры́лась... *came down with tuberculosis*
[7] е́здить... *to convalesce, be treated by doctors*
[8] *accompanied*
[9] в... *in chaos and among constant riddles, puzzles*
[10] на... *in the hands of strange people who kept changing all the time*
[11] Он... *He got used to these changes*
[12] в... *in the circumstances of this eternal incoherence the absence of his father didn't surprise him*
[13] Ма́леньким... *As a young lad he lived in that time*
[14] когда́... *when a multiplicity of things were called by his own last name*
[15] *textile mill*
[16] спо́соб... *a way of tying and fastening a necktie with a Zhivago tie pin*
[17] сла́дкий... *a sweet round pie, pastry*

Post-reading Tasks

1. Summarize the text in three to five sentences in Russian.
2. Find two indefinite particles. Assign to them one of the five particle rules to explain the use of **-то** and **-нибудь**.
3. Find the Russian word meaning *disorder* or *chaos* and break it down into its root and prefix.
4. Find the Russian words related to the concept *change* and determine what root they have in common.
5. Write a paragraph in Russian from the point of view of Iurii's mother, describing the events of Iurii's childhood.

✳ Упражне́ние 14д

Fill in the blanks with the correct particle, **-то** or **-нибудь**.

1. Кто́-_____ приходи́л, когда́ меня́ не́ было?
Да, приходи́л како́й-_____ челове́к, и сказа́л, что вернётся ве́чером.

2. Купи́ мне каку́ю-_____ интере́сную кни́гу, когда́ ты бу́дешь в Москве́.
А я ра́ньше всегда́ что́-_____ интере́сное покупа́ла тебе́, когда́ я была́ в Москве́.

3. Са́ша говори́л по телефо́ну о ко́м-_____, но я не узна́ла и́мя.

4. Та́ня говори́ла о чём-_____, когда́ меня́ не бы́ло?
   Нет, она́ ни о чём не говори́ла.

5. Андре́й всегда́ что-_____ интере́сное расска́зывает, когда́ возвраща́ется из Петербу́рга.

 Упражне́ние 14е

Review Unit 5 and look for indefinite particles in the explanations and examples. What correlation can you find, if any, between the imperfective aspect and the particle **-нибудь**?

PART 3 *whenever, wherever, no matter*

Russian uses a very simple construction to convey meanings equivalent to the English words *whenever, wherever,* or *no matter...* The construction uses the particle **бы**, the particle **ни**, and the past tense of the relevant verb.

1. С кем **бы** вы **ни говори́ли**, все говоря́т, что она́ прекра́сная.

   It doesn't matter whom you talk to: Everybody thinks she's great.

2. Где **бы** вы **ни иска́ли**, всё равно́ не найдёшь э́ту кни́гу.

   Wherever you look, you still won't find that book.

3. Чего́ **бы** э́то **ни сто́ило** (во что **бы** то **ни ста́ло**), нам придётся э́то сде́лать.

   No matter what it costs we have to do it.

 ТЕКСТ 14б

This poem is by Nabokov, a brilliantly bilingual writer who left Russia at the time of the revolution and then lived in both Europe and America. He became famous not just for his own creative writing but also for his expertise in butterflies, chess problems, translations, and literary criticism.

Pre-reading Task

Nabokov spent virtually all of his adult life in exile. What do you think he'll say in this poem about that moment in history when Russia's very existence might have been in jeopardy? Make some predictions and see if you're right.

Каки́м бы полотно́м бата́льным[1] ни явля́лась
сове́тская суса́льнейшая Русь,[2]
како́й бы жа́лостью[3] душа́ ни наполня́лась,[4]
     не поклоню́сь, не примирю́сь[5]
5   со все́ю ме́рзостью, жесто́костью и ску́кой[6]
немо́го ра́бства[7]—нет, о нет,
ещё я ду́хом жив,[8] ещё не сыт разлу́кой,[9]
     уво́льте,[10] я ещё поэ́т.

                              В. В. Набо́ков, 1944

[1] полотно́м... *battle scene (in a painting)*
[2] сове́тская... *tinselly Soviet Russia*
[3] *pity*
[4] *was filled*
[5] не... *will not bend, will not reconcile myself*
[6] со... *with all the filth, brutality and boredom*
[7] немо́го... *of silent servitude*
[8] ду́хом... *my spirit is still quick*
[9] не... *exile hungry*
[10] *count me out*

Post-reading Tasks

1. What is the poet's attitude toward his homeland, even in its time of peril?
2. What is the root of the Russian word meaning *to reconcile*?
3. Find the two "no matter" constructions and translate them.
4. What is the gender of the three nouns in the fifth line of the poem? What is their nominative case form?
5. What is the common root of the two Russian words meaning *spirit* or *soul*?
6. Write a paragraph-long response to the poet from the viewpoint of a communist fighting the Nazi occupation of Russia.

� Упражне́ние 14ё

Fill in the blanks.

1. (No matter to whom you [give]) _____ дава́ли свою́ кни́гу, она́ всё равно́ (no one, never) _____ не понра́вится.
2. (No matter what you talk about) _____ с ним, с ним всегда́ ску́чно!
3. (No matter how they avoid) _____ его́, им всё равно́ прихо́дится обща́ться с ним ча́сто.
4. (No matter how much you offer) _____ ей, она́ не прода́ст вам свою́ маши́ну «Корве́тт».
5. (Wherever you might enroll) _____ в аспиранту́ру, вам всё равно́ придётся заплати́ть за обуче́ние.

� Упражне́ние 14ж

Continue your list of all the "connecting" words and phrases (such as *because, but, in the first place, then,* and so forth) with those you can find in the texts of this unit. Next

to each "connecting" word or phrase, write out the clause or sentence in which they are used. Keep this list in your notebook and add to it as you continue with this book.

✳ Упражнéние 14з

Add the verbs of this unit to your lists of first- and second-conjugation verbs, noting the stress pattern of each verb as you do so.

UNIT 15

Short-form Adjectives

Прилага́тельные кра́ткой фо́рмы

Пе́рвое сентября́: пе́рвый класс,
пе́рвый день в шко́ле.

PART 1
Understanding Short-form Adjectives

Short-form adjectives, **прилага́тельные кра́ткой фо́рмы**, are adjectives used in predicative rather than attributive position. They generally convey the same meaning as their long-form counterparts, although there are some exceptions to this rule, as will be explained. Here are some examples of short- and long-form adjectives.

1. Э́та пе́сня о́чень **грустна́**!   *This song is very sad!*
2. Э́то о́чень **гру́стная** пе́сня!   *This is a very sad song!*
3. Таки́е кни́ги нам о́чень **нужны́**.   *Such books are very necessary for us.*
4. Други́е студе́нты по́льзуются   *Other students are using the books*
   ну́жными нам кни́гами.   *we need.*

Examples 1 and 3 feature short-form adjectives in predicative position, while examples 2 and 4 feature long-form adjectives in attributive position.

Attributive adjectives generally precede the nouns they modify (as in examples 2 and 4). Long-form attributive adjectives may be used in any case, as noted in the previous units. Predicate adjectives generally follow the nouns they modify (as in examples 1 and 3) and are always nominative because they are the subject complement of a verb meaning *to be*, most often **быть**, which has no present-tense form, as in examples 1 to 3. In other words, predicate adjectives can be thought of as one side of a statement of equality: *this song = sad* or *these books = necessary*.

RUSSIAN Saying

Не красна́ [краси́ва] изба́ угла́ми, а красна́ пирога́ми.

A peasant cabin is beautiful not for its corners, but because of its pies.
[One judges the beauty of a home not by how big it is, but by the hospitality of its hosts.]

Some adjectives are commonly used or even only used in their short form, such as **ну́жен/нужна́/ну́жно/нужны́**. Here is a list of some of the most commonly used short-form adjectives, many of which you probably already know. Note that the stress may shift in some of these words from the stem to the ending in the feminine only or in both feminine and plural.

MASCULINE	NEUTER*	FEMININE	PLURAL	MEANING
бо́лен	больно́	больна́	больны́	*sick*
винова́т	винова́то	винова́та	винова́ты	*guilty*

MASCULINE	NEUTER*	FEMININE	PLURAL	MEANING
гото́в	гото́во	гото́ва	гото́вы	*ready*
до́лжен	должно́	должна́	должны́	*must*
како́в	каково́	какова́	каковы́	*what kind of*
ну́жен	ну́жно	нужна́	нужны́	*needed*
похо́ж	похо́же	похо́жа	похо́жи	*similar to, resembles*
не/пра́в	не/пра́во	не/права́	не/пра́вы	*right (wrong)*
рад	ра́до	ра́да	ра́ды	*happy*
согла́сен	согла́сно	согла́сна	согла́сны	*in agreement*
серди́т	серди́то	серди́та	серди́ты	*angry*
тако́в	таково́	такова́	таковы́	*this kind of*

* For some of these adjectives, the neuter form is rarely used.

RUSSIAN

Saying

Такова́ жизнь.

That's life.

Long-form adjectives may be used as predicate or attributive adjectives. Short-form adjectives may be used only in the predicative position; they *cannot* be in the attributive position in modern Russian. Exceptions are found in such old idiomatic expressions as **среди́ бе́ла дня** (*in broad daylight*) and **лить крокоди́ловы слёзы** (*to cry crocodile [fake] tears*).

ТЕКСТ 15a

Read the opening of Gogol's novel *Dead Souls*. The narrator describes the main character, Chichikov, as he arrives at a hotel in a provincial Russian city.

Pre-reading Task

What do you think people might notice in someone arriving in a small American city in the late twentieth century? What do you think might be noticed in someone arriving in a small Russian city in the early nineteenth century?

В воро́та[1] гости́ницы губе́рнского го́рода NN[2] въе́хала дово́льно краси́вая рессо́рная небольша́я бри́чка,[3] в како́й е́здят холостяки́:[4] отставны́е подполко́вники, штабс-капита́ны, поме́щики, име́ющие о́коло со́тни душ крестья́н,[5]—сло́вом, все те, кото́рых называ́ют господа́ми

5

[1] *gates*
[2] губе́рнского... *provincial city NN*
[3] дово́льно... *a small, but rather attractive carriage on springs*
[4] в... *of the type used by bachelors*
[5] отставны́е... *retired lieutenant colonels, quarter captains, landed gentry with about a hundred serfs*

сре́дней руки́.[6] В бри́чке сиде́л господи́н, не краса́вец, но и не дурно́й нару́жности,[7] ни сли́шком толст,[8] ни сли́шком то́нок;[9] нельзя́ сказа́ть, чтобы стар, одна́ко ж и не так, чтобы сли́шком мо́лод. Въезд его́ не произвёл в го́роде соверше́нно никако́го шу́ма[10] и не́ был сопровождён ниче́м осо́бенным[11]...

Н. В. Го́голь, «Мёртвые ду́ши», 1842

[6] те́... *those called gentlemen of average means*
[7] не... *not bad looking either*
[8] *fat*
[9] *thin*
[10] не... *didn't make any "noise"*
[11] не... *was not accompanied by anything special*

Post-reading Tasks

1. What exactly do we find out about Chichikov's appearance?
2. Find all the negative particles and words that describe Chichikov by telling us what he is not.
3. Find all the short-form adjectives and identify their antecedents.
4. Assume the point of view of someone observing the arrival of Chichikov and write another description in Russian.

※ Упражне́ние 15a

Indicate whether the underlined adjectives are attributive or predicative by marking each sentence with the English letter **A** (for attributive) or **P** (for predicative). Note that long-form adjectives may be used in the predicative position, but that short-form adjectives can *only* be used in the predicative.

1. Э́та маши́на о́чень краси́ва.
This car is very beautiful.

2. Э́ти лю́ди о́чень бестолко́вые.
These people have no sense.

3. Э́то интере́сная кни́га.
This is a very interesting book.

4. Э́ти бестолко́вые лю́ди не понима́ют, в чём де́ло.
These people with no sense don't understand the point.

5. Э́тот костю́м мне вели́к.
This suit is too big for me.

PART 2 Meaning and Usage

Some short-form adjectives convey the meaning of a temporary condition, while their long-form counterparts suggest a permanent condition. An important example is the short form **бо́лен/больна́/больны́**, which means *sick*, and the long-form **больно́й/ больна́я/больны́е**, which means *sickly* (prone to illness, of poor health in general) or *patient* (in a hospital or clinic).

Saying

RUSSIAN

Сыт по го́рло.

To be filled up to the neck.
[To have it up to here.]

Some other short-form adjectives have a meaning that is also quite different from their long-form counterparts. The most important adjectives of this type are probably those used to describe the fit (or lack thereof) of clothing items.

MASCULINE	NEUTER	FEMININE	PLURAL	MEANING
мал	мало́	мала́	малы́	*too small*
вели́к	велико́	велика́	велики́	*too big*

The expression used to convey that an item of clothing is just the right size is **как раз**. Consider the following examples.

1. Э́та руба́шка ему́ **велика́**.   *This shirt is too big for him.*
2. Э́ти брю́ки мне **малы́**.   *These pants are too small for me.*
3. Э́то пла́тье мне **как раз**.   *This dress fits me just right.*

Saying

RUSSIAN

Ни жив, ни мёртв.

Neither alive nor dead.
[More dead than alive.]

---

§   Зада́ние 15a

Find an advertisement for some clothing in a newspaper or magazine and bring it into class. With a classmate, decide whether some of the clothing items depicted in the advertisement are too small, just right, or too big for the models wearing them.

PART 3 Formation

Short-form adjectives are created by dropping the adjectival case endings (**-ый**, **-ая**, **-ое**, and **-ые**, for example) and adding the feminine marker **-а** or **-я**, the neuter marker **-о** or **-е**, and the plural marker **-ы** or **-и**, depending on the spelling rule. Masculine short-form adjectives do not have markers: They have a **Ø** ending.

	LONG-FORM ADJECTIVE	SHORT-FORM ADJECTIVE
MASCULINE	краси́вый	краси́в
NEUTER	краси́вое	краси́во
FEMININE	краси́вая	краси́ва
PLURAL	краси́вые	краси́вы

EXCEPTIONS

1. Not every adjective has a short-form version. Generally speaking, adjectives ending in **-ский**, **-шний**, **-янный**, and **-анный** do not have a short form.
2. Two frequently used adjectives, **большо́й** and **ма́ленький**, have special short-form versions: **вели́к** and **мал**, respectively.
3. The adjective **хоро́ший** is linked with the short form **хоро́ш** (*good*), but also with the expression **хоро́ш собо́й** (*pretty, handsome*).
4. Stress shifts in these forms are irregular and unpredictable: They must be memorized.

RUSSIAN Saying

Старо́, как мир.

Old, like the world.
[As old as the hills.]

✳ Упражне́ние 156

Practice using some of the most common short-form adjectives by writing the correct ending (masculine, feminine, neuter, or plural) of the words. Refer to the chart in Part 1 of this unit for correct spellings of the endings.

1. Она́ не _____ в том, что она́ опозда́ла!
She's not at fault for being late!

2. Мы соверше́нно не _____ с ва́ми.
We disagree with you completely.

3. Я о́чень _____, что ты пришёл.
I'm so glad that you came.

4. Вы _____ выступа́ть?
Are you ready to make your presentation?

5. Он был не _____, что прие́хал без предупрежде́ния.
He was wrong to have come without warning.

RUSSIAN

Saying

Мир те́сен.

The world is crowded.
[It's a small world.]

ТЕКСТ 156

This text begins a book called **Бытие́**.

Pre-reading Task

Skim the text and see if you can recognize it.

---

1. В нача́ле сотвори́л Бог не́бо и зе́млю.
2. Земля́ же была́ безви́дна и пуста́, и тьма над бе́здною; и Дух Бо́жий носи́лся над водо́ю.
3. И сказа́л Бог: да бу́дет свет, и стал свет.
5 4. И уви́дел Бог свет, что он хоро́ш; и отдели́л Бог свет от тьмы.
   5. И назва́л Бог свет днём, а тьму но́чью. И был ве́чер, и бы́ло у́тро: день оди́н.

Post-reading Tasks

1. Compare the word order of the Russian version with that of an English version.
2. Find the short-form adjectives and identify their antecedents.
3. Write a summary of the text in two or three sentences.

✳ Упражнéние 15в

Examine the Russian proverbs and sayings in this unit and find as many short-form adjectives as you can. Identify the long-form adjective for each short form.

♪ Задáние 15б

Bring in a photograph of a large group of people (perhaps your family). With a class-mate, discuss who resembles whom in the picture and whether or not you and your classmate agree. Then discuss whether some of the people in the picture are wearing clothing that is either too large or too small for them.

RUSSIAN

Saying

Лёгок на подъём./Тяжёл на подъём.

Easy on the rise./Heavy on the rise.
[Quick on one's toes./Hard to get going.]

ТЕКСТ 15в

This poem by Gippius is entitled "Electricity" and was written in 1901.

Pre-reading Task

What would you expect to read about in a poem titled "Electricity" that was written when electricity first came into common use?

Электри́чество

Две ни́ти вмéсте сви́ты,[1]
Концы́ обнажены́.[2]
То 'да' и 'нет',—не сли́ты,[3]
Не сли́ты—сплетены́.[4]
Их тёмное сплетéнье[5]
И тéсно, и мертвó.[6]
Но ждёт их воскресéнье,[7]
И ждут они́ егó.
Концóв концы́ коснýтся—[8]
Други́е 'да' и 'нет',
И 'да' и 'нет' проснýтся,[9]
Сплетённые сольются,[10]
И смерть[11] их бýдет—Свет.[12]

З. Н. Ги́ппиус, 1901

5

10

[1] Две... wires, threads wound together
[2] bare
[3] не... not soldered together
[4] wound together, spliced
[5] splicing, connection
[6] И... both tight and dead
[7] resurrection
[8] touch one another
[9] wake up
[10] pour into one another, come together
[11] death
[12] Light

Post-reading Tasks

1. If the poem is not about electricity, what is it about?
2. Write a summary of the poem in two or three sentences.
3. What are the *yes* and the *no* referred to in the poem?
4. Find all the short-form adjectives and identify the nouns they modify.
5. Imagine seeing a light bulb go on for the first time and write a paragraph about that experience, or imagine being in love and compare meeting your loved one to a physical force of nature.

Saying

Блажён, кто смолоду был молод,
Блажён, кто вовремя созрел.
А. С. Пушкин

Blessed are they who enjoy youth when they're young,
Blessed are they who mature at the right time.

✳ Упражнёние 15г

Continue your list of all the "connecting" words and phrases (such as *because*, *but*, *in the first place*, *then*, and so forth) with those you can find in the texts of this unit. Next to each "connecting" word or phrase, write out the clause or sentence in which they are used. Keep this list in your notebook and add to it as you continue with this book.

✳ Упражнёние 15д

Add the verbs of this unit to your lists of first- and second-conjugation verbs, noting the stress pattern of each verb as you do so.

✳ Упражнёние 15е

Write out some of the more common short-form adjectives presented in this unit and write sentences to illustrate each adjective.

Comparative and Superlative Adjectives and Adverbs

Сравни́тельная и превосхо́дная сте́пень прилага́тельных и наре́чий

Приве́т!

PART 1

Comprehension of Comparatives and Superlatives

Adjectives and adverbs have three degrees of comparison, as shown in **Таблица 16a**.

Таблица 16a

	ADJECTIVE Имя прилагательное	MEANING	ADVERB Наречие	MEANING
POSITIVE DEGREE Положительная степень	сильный, сильная, сильное, сильные	*strong*	сильно	*strongly*
COMPARATIVE DEGREE Сравнительная степень	сильнее	*stronger*	сильнее	*more strongly*
SUPERLATIVE DEGREE Превосходная степень	самый сильный, самая сильная, самое сильное, самые сильные	*strongest*	*very rarely used*	

The positive degree of an adjective or adverb is used when there is no comparison. The comparative degree is used when one or more people or objects are compared with another individual group. The superlative degree is used to express the superiority of one or more people or objects to all others. In the following English examples, the underlined words are in the comparative form.

1. Ann and Fred need to buy a new car; Fred is a smart shopper, but Ann is a <u>smarter</u> shopper.
2. Ann knows that Porsches are <u>faster</u> than Volvos.
3. But Ann also knows that Volvos are said to be <u>safer</u> than Porsches.
4. Fred wants a Porsche <u>much more</u> than he wants a Volvo.

In most of the examples, the underlined comparative forms are adjectives. In example 4, however, the comparative is an adverb: *much more* modifies (describes) how Fred wants a Porsche. In addition, the words *much more* in example 4 are comparative adverbs, because they modify the verb; this two-word combination (*much more*) is a compound comparative. Compound comparatives can be contrasted with simple comparatives, which consist of only one word, such as *smarter*, *faster*, or *safer*.

The object of a comparative or superlative expression is the thing that is compared. In example 1, the object is *shopper*, while in example 2 the object is *Volvos*.

In the following examples, the underlined words are in the superlative form.

5. The saleswoman at the Ford dealership told Ann and Fred that the Taurus is the <u>most popular</u> car in America.

6. She also told them that the Escort, however, was the <u>least expensive</u> car in the Ford line.
7. After Fred and Ann took both cars out for a test drive, Fred said that he thought that the Taurus was the <u>best</u> American car he had driven in years.

Compound superlative forms are found in examples 5 and 6, while a simple superlative form is found in sentence 7.

Comparative and superlative forms of adjectives and adverbs are also used in expressions such as **чем бо́льше, тем лу́чше** (*the bigger, the better*) and **всё лу́чше и лу́чше** (*better and better* [*every day*]).

PART 2
Simple and Compound Comparatives

Russian comparatives can be both simple and compound, just as in English.

Compound Comparative Adjectives and Adverbs

Some Russian adjectives and adverbs have *only* a compound form for the comparative; they have no simple forms. (In English, for example, we say *more expensive*, never *expensiver*.) Adjectives of this type are more than three syllables (with some exceptions), have no short form, feature the suffix **-ов-**, *or* end in **к, г, х, д,** or **т** before the final adjectival ending. Adverbs ending in **-ский** are also of this type. In order to make comparatives with these adjectives and adverbs, you must use either **бо́лее** or **ме́нее** together with the given adjective or adverb.

1. Э́тот сувени́р о́чень ру́сский, но тот сувени́р ещё **бо́лее ру́сский**.
   This souvenir is very Russian, but that souvenir is even more Russian.

2. Фаши́сты ва́рварски напа́ли на э́тот го́род, но ещё **бо́лее ва́рварски** напа́ли на тот го́род.
   The fascists barbarically attacked this city, but even more barbarically attacked that city.

In addition, when any Russian adjective is in attributive position, a compound form must be used.

3. Они́ купи́ли **ме́нее дорогу́ю** маши́ну, чем мы.
   They bought a less expensive car than we did.

4. **Бо́лее дороги́е** маши́ны продаю́тся в друго́м ме́сте.
   (The) More expensive cars are sold in a different place.

✳   Упражне́ние 16a

Fill in the blanks as required, using a compound comparative (with either the word **бо́лее** or **ме́нее**). Make certain that the adjective agrees with the noun it modifies.

1. Гончаро́вская чита́ет (more interesting) _____ кни́ги, чем чита́ет Ми́ша.
2. Эти инжене́ры занима́ются (a more complicated) _____ пробле́мой, чем занима́ются инжене́ры на́шей гру́ппы.
3. Они́ помога́ют (poorer) _____ лю́дям, чем мы помога́ем.
4. Наро́ды се́верной Сиби́ри живу́т в (colder) _____ райо́нах, чем живу́т исла́ндцы.
5. Мы ре́дко хо́дим в (more expensive) _____ рестора́ны, кото́рые нахо́дятся в це́нтре го́рода.

Simple Comparative Adjectives and Adverbs

In most instances, simple comparative adjectives and adverbs have the same form, for example: **лу́чше** is derived both from the adjective **хоро́ший/хоро́шая/хоро́шее** and from the adverb **хорошо́**.

5. Она́ пи́шет лу́чше его́.   *She writes better than he [does].*
6. Этот рестора́н лу́чше того́   *This restaurant is better than that*
   [рестора́на].   *[one].*

Many of the most commonly used Russian adjectives and adverbs have simple forms for the comparative. These simple forms *must* be used whenever the comparative expressions are predicative (i.e., they are separated from the noun they modify by a form of the verb *to be* and serve to complete the sentence). Simple comparative forms typically end in **-ee**, although sometimes, in many common words, the ending is **-e** preceded by a consonantal mutation similar to those observed in the verb conjugations described in Units 2 and 3. Simple comparative forms with **-ee** have the same stress as the positive degree adjective if the adjective is four or more syllables; adjectives three syllables or fewer shift the stress onto the ending (with some exceptions: **краси́вый→ краси́вее**, **спосо́бный→спосо́бнее**).

7. В Му́рманске **холодне́е**, чем в   *In Murmansk it's colder than in*
   Москве́.   *Moscow.*
8. «Война́ и мир» **интере́снее**, чем   *War and Peace is more interesting*
   «А́нна Каре́нина», с то́чки   *than Anna Karenina from the*
   зре́ния филосо́фии исто́рии   *point of view of Tolstoy's*
   Толсто́го.   *philosophy of history.*
9. О́зеро Байка́л **глу́бже** о́зера   *Lake Baikal is deeper than Lake*
   Онта́рио.   *Ontario.*

The formation of simple comparative forms with mutations such as the one in example 10 will be discussed later.

Note that when two items are compared with a predicative comparative adjective, the object of comparison is expressed either in the genitive case or in the nominative case after the word **чем**.

10. Со́ня бе́гает **быстре́е** Пе́ти. (Со́ня   *Sonia runs more quickly than Petia.*
бе́гает **быстре́е**, чем Пе́тя.)

Six commonly used adjectives have special comparative forms for the predicative adjective and the comparative adverb. In the attributive position, these adjectives do not use **бо́лее** or **ме́нее**, but rather a second simple comparative.

	PREDICATIVE COMPARATIVE OR COMPARATIVE ADVERB	ATTRIBUTIVE COMPARATIVE
большо́й	бо́льше	бо́льший
ма́ленький	ме́ньше	ме́ньший
хоро́ший	лу́чше	лу́чший
плохо́й	ху́же	ху́дший
ста́рый	ста́рше	ста́рший
молодо́й	моло́же	мла́дший

The special comparative forms for these adjectives are similar, in some ways, to the special English comparative forms for *good* and *bad*: *better* and *worse*. Note the use of the adjectives **ста́рший** and **мла́дший** to describe one's older or younger siblings or children.

11. Э́то моя́ **ста́ршая** сестра́, Ка́тя.   *This is my older sister, Katia.*
12. Я ненави́жу их **мла́дшего** сы́на: *I hate their younger (youngest) son:*
он ужа́сный эгои́ст.   *He's a terrible egotist.*

❇ Упражне́ние 166

Fill in the blanks as required, using one of the predicative or attributive comparatives listed in the chart above.

1. Вчера́ мы познако́мились с его́ (older) _____ бра́том.
2. Петербу́рг ([is] smaller) _____ Москвы́ по террито́рии и по чи́сленности населе́ния.
3. За́втра мы встре́тимся с её (younger) _____ сестро́й на собра́нии.
4. В рестора́не «Пра́га» гото́вят (better) _____, чем в рестора́не «Пеки́н».
5. Они́ занима́ются в (best) _____ библиоте́ке в го́роде.

Comparative expressions sometimes feature the words **так/как** and **сто́ль(ко)/ско́ль(ко)** to convey a sense of *as x*, but these expressions don't show comparative forms per se. The words **гора́здо** and **намно́го** are used synonymously with comparative forms (simple and compound) to express the idea *much x-er*, while the prefix **по-** is attached to comparatives to convey the idea *a little bit x-er*: **полу́чше**. The expressions *the x-er, the better* (the greater the degree of x, the better), *x-er and x-er* (with each passing period of time, the greater the degree of x), and *as x as possible* are conveyed with comparatives.

13.	Та́ня **так** же умна́, **как** Пе́тя.	*Tania is just as smart as Petia.*
14.	Со́ня **столь** же симпати́чная, **сколь** же и у́мная.	*Sonia is just as nice as she is smart.*
15.	Па́ша **намно́го спосо́бнее** (гора́здо спосо́бнее) Пе́ти.	*Pasha is much more talented than Petia.*
16.	Со́ня пришла́ **попо́зже** Па́ши.	*Sonia came a little bit later than Pasha.*
17.	**Чем** ра́ньше, **тем** лу́чше.	*The earlier, the better.*
18.	Приходи́те, пожа́луйста, **как мо́жно ра́ньше.**	*Please come as early as possible.*
19.	Вре́мя прохо́дит **всё быстре́е (и быстре́е).**	*Time goes by faster and faster.*

RUSSIAN

Saying

Ти́ше е́дешь, да́льше бу́дешь.

Go calmly, get farther.
[Slow and steady wins the race.]

ТЕКСТ 16a

Read the excerpt from Babel's story "Awakening," which is about a young Jewish boy in Odessa in the early twentieth century. His family tries to compel him to take violin lessons, but all he wants to do is read and write literature and learn to swim. In this excerpt, the boy (the narrator) describes how he decided one day not to go to his music teacher, Zagurskii, and what happened next.

Pre-reading Task

What kinds of ideas do you expect to find in a story about the conflict in a boy's soul between what he wants for himself and what his parents want for him?

Я шёл по Нѐжинской у́лице, мне бы поверну́ть[1] на Дворя́нскую, чтобы попа́сть к Загу́рскому,[2] вме́сто э́того я подня́лся вверх по Тира́спольской и очути́лся в порту́.[3] Поло́женные мне три часа́ пролете́ли в Практи́ческой га́вани.[4] Так начало́сь освобожде́ние.[5] Приёмная[6] Загу́рского бо́льше не уви́дела меня́. Дела́ поважне́е за́няли все мои́ по́мыслы.[7] С однока́шником мои́м Нѐмановым мы пова́дились на парохо́д «Ке́нсингтон» к ста́рому одному́ матро́су[8] по и́мени ми́стер Троттибэ́рн. Нѐманов был на́ год моло́же меня́, он с восьми́ лет занима́лся са́мой замыслова́той торго́влей[9] в ми́ре. Он был ге́ний в торго́вых дела́х и испо́лнил[10] всё, что обеща́л. Тепе́рь он миллионе́р в Нью-Йо́рке, дире́ктор General Motors Co., компа́нии столь же могу́щественной,[11] как и Форд. Нѐманов таска́л[12] меня́ с собо́й потому́, что я повинова́лся ему́ мо́лча.[13] Он покупа́л у ми́стера Троттибэ́рна тру́бки, провози́мые контраба́ндой.[14] Э́ти тру́бки точи́л[15] в Линко́льне брат ста́рого матро́са....

Тяжёлые во́лны у да́мбы отдаля́ли меня́ всё бо́льше от на́шего до́ма, пропа́хшего лу́ком и евре́йской судьбо́й[16]...

И. Э. Ба́бель, «Пробужде́ние», 1931

1 to turn
2 попа́сть... to get to Zagur-skii's (the violin teacher)
3 я... I went up Tiraspol'skaia St. and wound up at the port
4 Поло́женные... the three hours I had (for the violin les-son) flew by at the harbor
5 liberation
6 Waiting room
7 Дела́... More important af-fairs occupied all my thoughts
8 got into the habit of going to the steamship Kensington to an old sailor
9 са́мой... the most intricate trade, commerce
10 fulfilled
11 powerful, great
12 dragged, took, pulled
13 я... I obeyed, listened to him silently
14 тру́бки... pipes smuggled in as contraband
15 made (sharpened)
16 Тяжёлые... The heavy waves at the dam separated me more and more, took me far-ther and farther away... which smelled of onion and Jewish destiny

Post-reading Tasks

1. Write a two-sentence summary of the text in Russian.
2. Identify all the comparative adjectives and adverbs. Then underline the compara-tive forms, note whether they are compound or simple, and circle all the objects of comparison.
3. Write a continuation of this story or a paragraph from the point of view of either the violin teacher or the boy's parents.

The Formation of Simple Comparative Adjectives and Adverbs

Most simple comparatives are regularly formed: Simply remove the adjectival or ad-verbial ending and add **-ee**.

ADJECTIVE	ADVERB	COMPARATIVE ADJECTIVE OR ADVERB	MEANING
интере́сный	интере́сно	интере́снее	*more interesting, more interestingly*
краси́вый	краси́во	краси́вее	*more beautiful, more beautifully*
сла́бый	сла́бо	слабе́е	*weaker, more weakly*

ADJECTIVE	ADVERB	COMPARATIVE ADJECTIVE OR ADVERB	MEANING
стра́шный	стра́шно	страшне́е	*more terrible, more terribly*
тёплый	тепло́	тепле́е	*warmer, more warmly*

Remember that for the most part, adjectives of four or more syllables will not show a stress shift in the simple comparative, while those of three or fewer syllables shift the stress onto the ending (exceptions to this rule include **краси́вый** and **спосо́бный** as noted previously).

✳ Упражне́ние 16в

Review the typical mutations in first- and second-conjugation verbs presented in Unit 2. Make a list of these mutations.

In these simple comparative forms we observe the following shifts: **г** and **д**→**ж**; **т** and **к**→**ч**; **ст**→**щ**; and **х**→**ш**.

Табли́ца 16б

POSITIVE DEGREE ADJECTIVE/ADVERB	SIMPLE COMPARATIVE DEGREE FORM
мя́гкий	мя́гче (*softer, more softly*)
твёрдый	твёрже (*harder, more hardly*)
чи́стый, чи́сто	чи́ще (*cleaner, more cleanly*)
дешёвый, дёшево	деше́вле (*cheaper, more cheaply*)
дорого́й, до́рого	доро́же (*more expensive/ly*)
далёкий, далеко́	да́льше (*farther*)
бли́зкий, бли́зко	бли́же (*nearer*)
широ́кий, широко́	ши́ре (*broader, wider*)
у́зкий	у́же (*narrower*)
коро́ткий, ко́ротко	коро́че (*shorter, more shortly*)
высо́кий, высоко́	вы́ше (*taller, higher*)
ни́зкий, ни́зко	ни́же (*shorter, lower*)
ти́хий, ти́хо	ти́ше (*quieter, more quietly*)
до́лго	до́льше (*longer*)
ре́дкий, ре́дко	ре́же (*more infrequent/ly*)
ча́стый, ча́сто	ча́ще (*more frequent/ly*)
я́ркий, я́рко	я́рче (*more bright/ly*)
бога́тый	бога́че (*wealthier*)
стро́гий, стро́го	стро́же (*more strict/ly*)
гро́мкий, гро́мко	гро́мче (*louder*)
молодо́й	моло́же (*younger*)
ста́рый	ста́рше (*older* [for people]) старе́е (*older* [for things])
лёгкий, легко́	ле́гче (*easier, more easily*)

POSITIVE DEGREE ADJECTIVE/ADVERB	SIMPLE COMPARATIVE DEGREE FORM
просто́й, про́сто	про́ще (*simpler, more simply*)
по́здний, по́здно	по́зже, поздне́е (*later*)
глубо́кий, глубоко́	глу́бже (*deeper, more profoundly*)
ро́бкий, ро́бко	ро́бче (*more shy, more timidly*)
ра́нний, ра́но	ра́ньше (*earlier*)
сла́дкий	сла́ще (*sweeter*)

✳ **Упражне́ние 16г**

Fill in the blanks as required, using a simple comparative form. Some of the comparatives are regular (**-ee**), but some will be irregular, so consult the list of irregular simple comparatives in **Табли́ца 16б** and review comparative constructions illustrated in examples 13 through 22 above.

1. Ири́на Алексе́евна (is much smarter) _____ Петра́ Влади́мировича.
2. Ра́зве Рокфе́ллеры (wealthier) _____ Мэ́ллонов?!
3. Чем (faster) _____, тем (better) _____.
4. Говори́те, пожа́луйста, как мо́жно (louder) _____.
5. Петро́вы хо́дят к нам всё (more and more often) _____.
6. Акце́нт э́тих япо́нцев (stronger) _____, чем акце́нт тех америка́нцев.

✳ **Упражне́ние 16д**

Read the dialogue between Lee Iacocca and Boris Yeltsin and note the underlined expressions. Substitute the numbered expressions for the underlined expressions to create another version of the dialogue.

Ли Аяко́ка (бы́вший президе́нт компа́нии «Кра́йслер») говори́т с Бори́сом Е́льциным и объясня́ет, почему́ ру́сские должны́ покупа́ть америка́нские маши́ны, а не япо́нские.

А. По сравне́нию с япо́нскими маши́нами, америка́нские маши́ны «Додж», «Пли́мут», «Кра́йслер», «Джип»—о́чень <u>краси́вые</u>.
Е. Да, они́ намно́го (гора́здо, значи́тельно) <u>краси́вее</u> япо́нских маши́н.
А. Да, с ка́ждым го́дом на́ши маши́ны всё <u>краси́вее</u>.
Е. Ну, мы хоти́м маши́ны <u>как мо́жно краси́вее</u>. В Москве́ говоря́т: <u>чем краси́вее, тем лу́чше</u>!

1. е́здят бы́стро
2. ти́хие
3. кре́сла (*seats*) мя́гкие
4. о́чень чи́стые

⌘ **Зада́ние 16а**

Continue the discussion among Yeltsin and American and Japanese auto manufacturers, comparing the relative merits and disadvantages of the cars made in each country.

Зада́ние 166

Prepare a three-minute talk in which you share your own feelings about comparing American and Japanese cars or any two types of things.

Saying

Ста́рый друг лу́чше но́вых двух.

One old friend is better than two new ones.
[Make new friends but keep the old.]

 ТЕКСТ 166

This untitled poem is by Gorbanevskaia, a twentieth-century poet who became famous as a dissident writer when she protested the Soviet invasion of Czechoslovakia in 1968. Her poem refers to articles 70 and 72 of the Soviet constitution, which established a broad and ambiguously defined category of political acts ("anti-Soviet activities") as criminal.

Pre-reading Task

What do you know about the dissident movement in the 1960s and 1970s? How do you think some of the dissidents might have felt during this period, when few would have imagined that the Soviet Union was doomed to collapse before the end of the century?

Я не суме́ю объясни́ть,[1] почему́
бе́лые но́чи не беле́й рукава́
ночно́й руба́шки,[2] занесённой в тюрьму́[3]
статья́ми се́мьдесят и се́мьдесят два.[4]
5   Я не суме́ю объясни́ться,[5] почём[6]
се́рые кле́тки[7] пла́тят за ночле́г,[8]
заночева́в на щите́[9] и под ключо́м
и ежеча́сно пуска́ясь в побе́г.[10]
Я не пущу́сь[11] ничего́ объясня́ть
10   ни изнутри́,[12] ни, что про́ще, извне́.[13]
Руба́шку снять и на ре́шке распя́ть,[14]
спино́ю го́лою к цеме́нтной стене́.[15]

Н. Е. Горбане́вская, 1980

[1] не... *will not be able, not know how to explain*
[2] бе́лые... *white nights (of Petersburg at summer solstice) are not whiter than the sleeves of a night shirt*
[3] занесённой... *brought to prison*
[4] статья́ми... *by articles 70 and 72*
[5] *to explain to myself*
[6] *how much*
[7] се́рые... *gray cells*
[8] *for a night's sleep*
[9] заночева́в... *having spent the night on a board*
[10] ежеча́сно... *hourly setting off for, embarking on escape*
[11] Я... *I won't set out*
[12] *from the inside*
[13] *from the outside*
[14] Руба́шку... *to take off one's shirt and to crucify on heads (or tails)*
[15] спино́ю... *naked back to the cement wall*

Post-reading Tasks

1. What do you think the poem is about?
2. Find the comparative forms and identify them.
3. Find all the words related to the word *explain* and identify how they are different from one another.
4. Write a response to the poem from the perspective of a prisoner or someone writing to a friend or loved one who is in a difficult situation.

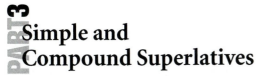

Simple and Compound Superlatives

Superlative adjectives are often compound in form, using the word **са́мый**.

1.	Вчера́ я чита́ла **са́мую** интере́сную кни́гу.	*Yesterday I read the most interesting book.*

Sometimes simple superlatives may be formed using the suffix **-ейший** or **-айший** for certain adjectives to convey the meaning *one of the x-est* or *a most x*.

2.	У меня́ нет ни **мале́йшего** сомне́ния.	*I haven't the slightest doubt.*
3.	Где здесь **ближа́йшая** ста́нция метро́?	*Where is the nearest metro station?*
4.	Она́ **умне́йший** и **миле́йший** челове́к.	*She is one of the smartest and kindest people.*

Another way that simple superlatives are formed involves the prefix **наи-**, which is most commonly used in the expression «**наилу́чшие пожела́ния**» (*best wishes*).

5.	Переда́йте ва́шим роди́телям на́ши **наилу́чшие** пожела́ния!	*Please give your parents our best wishes!*

Not every adjective can form these simple superlatives. Learn to recognize and understand the simple superlatives and memorize the expression in example 5, but use the compound superlative, with **са́мый**.

❋ Упражне́ние 16e

Reread the text in **Текст 16a**. Find a superlative adjective and identify the case in which it is used.

✳   Упражне́ние 16ё

Fill in the blanks as required with a compound superlative (**са́мый** + adjective), checking to make sure that your adjectives agree in case and gender or number with the nouns they modify.

1. Гончаро́вская всегда́ чита́ет (the most interesting) _____ кни́ги.
2. Э́ти инжене́ры занима́ются (the most complicated) _____ пробле́мой.
3. Они́ помога́ют (the poorest) _____ лю́дям в Челя́бинске.
4. Наро́ды се́верной Сиби́ри живу́т в (the coldest) _____ райо́нах Росси́и.
5. (The most expensive) _____ рестора́ны нахо́дятся в це́нтре го́рода.
6. Петро́вы живу́т недалеко́ от (the oldest) _____ це́ркви в го́роде.

✳   Упражне́ние 16ж

Fill in the blanks as required, using a simple superlative adjective (with the suffix **-айший** or **-ейший**). Make certain that the adjective agrees with the noun it modifies.

1. Верони́ка Петро́вна чита́ет (a most interesting) _____ кни́гу.
2. Как ты мо́жешь обижа́ться на (a most kind) _____ челове́ка?!
3. Мы сейча́с недалеко́ от (nearest) _____ ста́нции метро́: пройдёмте туда́ пешко́м.
4. Любо́вь Васи́льевна ([is] a most intelligent, smart) _____ челове́к.
5. В Москве́ име́ются ([some] of the most beautiful) _____ зда́ния в Росси́и.

✳   Упражне́ние 16з

Continue your list of all the "connecting" words and phrases (such as *because, but, in the first place, then,* and so forth) with those you can find in the texts of this unit. Next to each "connecting" word or phrase, write out the clause or sentence in which they are used. Keep this list in your notebook and add to it as you continue with this book.

✳   Упражне́ние 16и

Add the verbs of this unit to your lists of first- and second-conjugation verbs, noting the stress pattern of each verb as you do so.

♪   Зада́ние 16в

Write out the simple comparative forms of the most commonly used adjectives and adverbs and write a paragraph or a short monologue in which you to try to use as many of them as you can.

Time Expressions

Выраже́ния вре́мени

Ма́льчики игра́ют в хокке́й в но́вом райо́не.

PART 1 Clock Time and Dates

The expression of clock time and dates is idiosyncratic in both English and Russian. Consider, for example, that in English we say *on the 23d of April* but omit the definite article in *on April 23d*. These rules may seem arbitrary, but they establish conventions for the expression of time.

Clock Time

The English expression *What time is it?* can be rendered in Russian in two ways: **Ско́лько сейча́с вре́мени?** or **Кото́рый сейча́с час?** The English expression *At what time...?* can be rendered in Russian in three ways: **Когда́?**, **Во ско́лько?**, or **В кото́ром часу́?** Expressions of clock time (*it's 3:00*) or the clock time at which something happened or will happen (*at 3:00*) are classified according to the minutes of the hour on the clock.

1. on the hour

Ско́лько сейча́с вре́мени?	Во ско́лько?
What time is it?	*At what time?*
Сейча́с час.	В час.
It's 1:00.	*At 1:00.*
Сейча́с пять часо́в.	В пять часо́в.
It's 5:00.	*At 5:00.*

2. between the hour and the half hour

Ско́лько сейча́с вре́мени?	Во ско́лько?
What time is it?	*At what time?*
Сейча́с пять мину́т пе́рвого.	В пять мину́т пе́рвого.
It's 12:05.	*At 12:05.*

   It is important to note that whereas English tells time between the hour and the half hour by referring to the hour just past, Russian refers to the hour in the process of passing. Therefore, the English expression *five minutes past two (2:05)* translates into Russian as **пять мину́т тре́тьего** (*five minutes of the third hour*).

3. on the half hour

Ско́лько сейча́с вре́мени?	Во ско́лько?
What time is it?	*At what time?*

Сейча́с полови́на второ́го.	В полови́не второ́го.
It's 1:30.	*At 1:30.*

Russian tells time on the half hour by referring to the hour in the process of passing. Therefore, the English expression *half past two* (2:30) translates into Russian as **полови́на тре́тьего** (*half of the third hour*).

4. between the half hour and the hour

Ско́лько сейча́с вре́мени?	Во ско́лько?
What time is it?	*At what time?*
Сейча́с без пяти́ [мину́т]* пя́ть.	Без пяти́ [мину́т]* пя́ть.
It's 4:55.	*At 4:55.*

For times between the half hour and the hour, we use the same construction to answer the question "at what time" and "what time is it?"

Сейча́с без двадцати́ [мину́т]* час.	*It's now 12:40.*
Мы пришли́ без пятна́дцати [мину́т]* де́сять.	*We came at 9:45.*

In these constructions, use the genitive case for the number of minutes and the nominative case for the hour.

5. Deadlines and *From . . . to . . .*

In Russian we convey the sense that something must be completed by a certain time with the preposition **к** and the dative case of the time expression that follows.

Э́то на́до зако́нчить **к** . . .
    ча́су (1:00)
    пятна́дцати мину́там второ́го (1:15)
    полови́не тре́тьего (2:30)
    четырём часа́м (4:00)
    без пятна́дцати час (12:45)

From . . . to . . . is expressed by the preposition **с** followed by the genitive case of the first time expression and then **до** followed by the genitive case of the second time expression. When this construction refers to times from the half hour to the hour a double preposition must be used (**с без че́тверти три до без десяти́ четы́ре** [*from 2:45 to 3:50*]).

Э́тот магази́н откры́т . . .
    с ча́су до двух (1:00–2:00)
    с трёх [часо́в] до пятна́дцати мину́т шесто́го (3:00–5:15)
    с двена́дцати [часо́в] до без пяти́ два (12:00–1:55)
    с без двадцати́ четы́ре до полови́ны седьмо́го (3:40–6:30)

---

* The word **мину́т** is not usually said, but only implied and is therefore in brackets.

✳ Упражнёние 17а

Answer the question **Скóлько сейчáс врёмени?** with the following time expressions. Write out numbers as words in Russian and practice saying them several times.

1.	1:05	**4.**	4:20	**7.**	7:35	**10.**	9:50
2.	2:10	**5.**	5:25	**8.**	7:40	**11.**	10:55
3.	3:15	**6.**	6:30	**9.**	8:45	**12.**	11:58

✳ Упражнёние 17б

Answer the question **Когдá начинáется лёкция?** with the following time expressions. Write out numbers as words in Russian and practice saying them several times.

1.	2:05	**4.**	5:20	**7.**	8:35	**10.**	11:50
2.	3:10	**5.**	6:25	**8.**	9:40	**11.**	12:55
3.	4:15	**6.**	7:30	**9.**	10:45	**12.**	1:58

✳ Упражнёние 17в

Answer the question **Когдá (К какóму чáсу?) надо сдáть** (*submit*) **рабóту?** with the following time expressions. Write out numbers as words in Russian and practice saying them several times.

1.	3:05	**4.**	6:20	**7.**	9:35	**10.**	12:50
2.	4:10	**5.**	7:25	**8.**	10:40	**11.**	1:55
3.	5:15	**6.**	8:30	**9.**	11:45	**12.**	2:58

✳ Упражнёние 17г

Answer the question **Когдá э́тот магази́н закрывáется на обéд?** with the following time expressions. Write out numbers as words in Russian and practice saying them several times.

1.	4:05–5:00	**4.**	7:20–8:15	**7.**	9:35–10:05	**10.**	12:50–1:20
2.	5:10–6:10	**5.**	8:25–9:40	**8.**	10:40–11:50	**11.**	1:55–2:25
3.	6:15–7:30	**6.**	9:30–10:45	**9.**	11:45–12:25	**12.**	2:58–4:00

ТЕКСТ 17а

Read the opening of L. N. Tolstoy's story "Woodcutting." The narrator is establishing the setting of his tale about people and events during the Crimean War.

Pre-reading Task

Imagine that you are fighting a war. You have been assigned an important and dangerous mission for the next day and are going to bed for the night. How might you sleep? How might you feel upon being awakened?

В середи́не зимы́ 185. го́да дивизио́н на́шей батаре́и стоя́л в отря́де в Большо́й Чечне́.[1] Ве́чером четы́рнадцатого февраля́, узна́в,[2] что взвод,[3] кото́рым я кома́ндовал, за отсу́тствием офице́ра,[4] назна́чен в за́втрашней коло́нне на ру́бку ле́са,[5] и с ве́чера же получи́в и переда́в ну́жные приказа́ния,[6] я ра́ньше обыкнове́нного отпра́вился в свою́ пала́тку[7] и, не име́я дурно́й привы́чки нагрева́ть её горя́чими угля́ми,[8] не раздева́ясь лёг на свою́ постро́енную на ко́лышках посте́ль,[9] надви́нул на глаза́ папа́ху,[10] заку́тался в шу́бу и засну́л тем осо́бенным кре́пким и тяжёлым сном,[11] кото́рым спи́тся в мину́ты трево́ги и беспоко́йства пе́ред опа́сностью.[12] Ожида́ние де́ла наза́втра привело́ меня́ в э́то состоя́ние.[13]

В три часа́ утра́, когда́ ещё бы́ло соверше́нно темно́,[14] с меня́ сдёрнули обогре́тый тулу́п,[15] и багро́вый ого́нь све́чки неприя́тно порази́л мои́ за́спанные глаза́.[16]

Л. Н. Толсто́й, «Ру́бка ле́са», 1855

[1] В... *in the middle of winter in 185x (the author does not specify the year) a division of our battery was in a detachment in Grand Chechnia*
[2] *having found out*
[3] *the regiment*
[4] за... *due to the absence of an officer*
[5] назна́чен... *was assigned to tomorrow's column for chopping wood*
[6] получи́в... *having received and given the necessary orders*
[7] отпра́вился... *headed for my tent*
[8] не... *not having the bad habit of heating it with hot coals*
[9] не... *without undressing lay down on my bed built on pegs*
[10] надви́нул... *covered my eyes with my fur hat*
[11] заку́тался... *buried myself in my coat and fell into that special deep and heavy sleep*
[12] кото́рым... *which one sleeps in times of anxiousness*
[13] Ожида́ние... *The expectation of the matter for tomorrow brought me to this state*
[14] когда́... *while it was still completely dark*
[15] с... *my warm coat was pulled off me*
[16] багро́вый... *the crimson fire of a candle unpleasantly surprised my sleepy eyes*

Post-reading Tasks

1. What is the infinitive of the Russian verb meaning *to command*? How is this verb conjugated? What case does it take?
2. What is the root of the Russian word meaning *habit*? Do you know any other words with this root? What are the roots of the Russian words meaning *to heat up* and *warmed up*? Do you know any other words with these roots?
3. Write a summary in Russian of the text in three sentences.
4. Find all the time expressions and translate them into English.
5. Assume the point of view of the narrator or the person who woke him up and continue the story in Russian.

Dates

The question *What is today's date?* is conveyed in Russian as

Како́е сего́дня число́?

The answer to this question uses the neuter form of the ordinal (number) adjective.

Сего́дня седьмо́е [число́].
Сего́дня два́дцать второ́е [число́].

The ordinal (number) adjective may be followed by a specification of the month in the genitive case.

> Сегóдня девя́тое сентября́.
> Сегóдня двенáдцатое ию́ня.

All of the months except March through August are end-stressed (the months at either "end" of the year): **января́, февраля́, мáрта, апрéля, мáя, ию́ня, ию́ля, áвгуста, сентября́, октября́, ноября́, декабря́.**

Notice that the names of the months are not capitalized in Russian unless they are the first word of a sentence. Compare the expressions for the months with those for the days of the week.

> Какóй сегóдня день недéли?
> Сегóдня—понедéльник.

Упражнéние 17д

Practice asking and answering the following questions.

1. Какóе сегóдня числó?
2. Какóе бы́ло вчерá числó?
3. Какóе зáвтра бу́дет числó?

When Russians ask when (on what date) something occurred or will occur, they use the question **Когдá?** or **Какóго числá?** Unlike the English expression *On what date?*, the Russian does not take a preposition but uses the genitive case.

Какóе сегóдня числó? *What's the date today?*	Когдá э́то случи́лось? Какóго числá э́то случи́лось? *On what date did it happen?*
Сегóдня трéтье мáрта. *Today's the third of March.*	Э́то случи́лось трéтьего мáрта. *It happened on the third of March.*

The constructions that answer this question vary widely. Memorize the examples in the following exercise to use whenever you need to explain when something happened or will happen.

Упражнéние 17е

Practice reading the following questions and answers out loud. Note that Roman numerals are used to indicate the months of the year.

Когдá роди́лся Пéтя? (3.I.75)

1. трéтьего января́ [ты́сяча девятьсóт] сéмьдесят пя́того гóда
2. в январé [ты́сяча девятьсóт] сéмьдесят пя́того гóда
3. зимóй [ты́сяча девятьсóт] сéмьдесят пя́того гóда
4. в [ты́сяча девятьсóт] сéмьдесят пя́том году́

Когда́ родила́сь Со́ня? (6.X.80)

5. шесто́го октября́ [ты́сяча девятьсо́т] восьмидеся́того го́да

6. в октябре́ [ты́сяча девятьсо́т] восьмидеся́того го́да

7. о́сенью [ты́сяча девятьсо́т] восьмидеся́того го́да

8. в [ты́сяча девятьсо́т] восьмидеся́том году́

Когда́ Ва́ся око́нчит университе́т? (12.VI.2001)

9. двена́дцатого ию́ня две ты́сячи пе́рвого го́да

10. в ию́не две ты́сячи пе́рвого го́да

11. весно́й две ты́сячи пе́рвого го́да

12. в две ты́сячи пе́рвом году́

Когда́ они́ поже́нятся? (4.VIII.2000)

13. четвёртого а́вгуста двухты́сячного го́да

14. в а́вгусте двухты́сячного го́да

15. ле́том двухты́сячного го́да

16. в двухты́сячном году́

ТЕКСТ 176

Read the excerpt from Turgenev's novel *Fathers and Children* (sometimes translated as *Fathers and Sons*), which describes the lives of Arkadii Kirsanov's mother, father, and grandparents.

Pre-reading Task

What do you think you might find in a brief biography of an aristocratic Russian family in the first half of the 19th century on the eve of the emancipation of the serfs?

...В 1835 году́ Никола́й Петро́вич вы́шел из университе́та кандида́том, и в том же году́ генера́л Кирса́нов [его́ оте́ц], уво́ленный в отста́вку за неуда́чный смотр,[1] прие́хал в Петербу́рг с жено́ю на житьё. Он на́нял бы́ло[2] дом у Таври́ческого са́да и записа́лся в англи́йский клуб, но внеза́пно у́мер от уда́ра.[3] Агафокле́я Кузьми́нишна [его́ жена́] ско́ро за ним после́довала:[4] она́ не могла́ привы́кнуть к глухо́й столи́чной жи́зни;[5] тоска́ отставно́го существова́нья её загры́зла.[6] Ме́жду тем Никола́й Петро́вич успе́л, ещё при жи́зни роди́телей и к нема́лому их огорче́нию,[7] влюби́ться в до́чку чино́вника Преполове́нского, бы́вшего хозя́ина его́ кварти́ры,[8] милови́дную и, как говори́тся, разви́тую деви́цу:[9] она́ в журна́лах чита́ла серьёзные статьи́ в отде́ле «Нау́к». Он жени́лся на ней, как то́лько мину́л срок тра́ура,[10] и, поки́нув министе́рство уде́лов,[11] куда́ по проте́кции[12] оте́ц его́ записа́л, блаже́нствовал со свое́ю Ма́шей сперва́ на да́че о́коло Лесно́го институ́та, пото́м в

[1] уво́ленный... *retired for an unsuccessful inspection*
[2] на́нял... *was going to rent*
[3] внеза́пно... *suddenly died from a stroke*
[4] *followed*
[5] глухо́й... *hollow life in the capital*
[6] тоска́... *boredom of retired life ate away at her*
[7] к... *to their great disappointment*
[8] влюби́ться... *to fall in love with the daughter of a bureaucrat who was the landlord of his apartment*
[9] милови́дную... *attractive and developed (intellectual) maiden*
[10] как... *as soon as the mourning period passed*
[11] поки́нув... *leaving the Ministry of princely estates*
[12] по... *through connections*

городе, в ма́ленькой и хоро́шенькой кварти́ре, с чи́стою ле́стницей и холоднова́тою гости́ной, наконе́ц—в дере́вне, где он посели́лся[13] оконча́тельно и где у него́ в ско́ром вре́мени роди́лся сын Арка́дий. Супру́ги жи́ли о́чень хорошо́ и ти́хо: они́ почти́ никогда́ не расстава́лись,[14] чита́ли вме́сте, игра́ли в четы́ре руки́ на фортепья́но, пе́ли дуэ́ты; она́ сажа́ла цветы́ и наблюда́ла за пти́чным дворо́м,[15] он и́зредка е́здил на охо́ту и занима́лся хозя́йством,[16] а Арка́дий рос да рос[17]—то́же хорошо́ и ти́хо. Де́сять лет прошло́ как сон.[18] В 47-м году́ жена́ Кирса́нова сконча́лась.[19] Он едва́ вы́нес э́тот уда́р,[20] поседе́л[21] в не́сколько неде́ль; собра́лся бы́ло за грани́цу,[22] чтобы хотя́ немно́го рассе́яться[23]...но тут наста́л 48-о́й год.[24] Он понево́ле[25] верну́лся в дере́вню и по́сле дово́льно продолжи́тельного безде́йствия заня́лся хозя́йственными преобразова́ниями.[26] В 55-м году́ он повёз сы́на в университе́т; про́жил с ним три зимы́ в Петербу́рге, почти́ никуда́ не выходя́ и стара́ясь заводи́ть знако́мства[27] с молоды́ми това́рищами Арка́дия. На после́днюю зи́му он прие́хать не мог,—и вот мы ви́дим его́ в ма́е ме́сяце 1859 го́да, уже́ совсе́м седо́го, пу́хленького и немно́го сго́рбленного:[28] он ждёт сы́на, получи́вшего, как не́когда он сам,[29] зва́ние кандида́та.

И. С. Турге́нев, «Отцы́ и де́ти», 1862

[13] settled
[14] separated (almost never did things separately)
[15] сажа́ла... planted flowers and took care of the birdhouse
[16] е́здил... went hunting and managed household affairs
[17] рос... kept getting bigger
[18] dream
[19] died
[20] Он... He barely survived this blow
[21] turned gray
[22] собра́лся... was planning to go abroad
[23] чтобы... to try to forget a little
[24] наста́л... 1848 began (a year of revolutions in Europe)
[25] involuntarily
[26] заня́лся... began to take care of transformations of the estate
[27] заводи́ть... strike up acquaintance
[28] совсе́м... completely grey, somewhat chubby, and somewhat hunched over
[29] как... as he once did

Post-reading Tasks

1. Write a five-sentence summary in Russian of this biography of Arkadii's father and mother.
2. How does the narrator express the idea *was going to...*? (The construction is used twice.)
3. Find all the time expressions and translate them into English.
4. What is the root of the Russian word meaning *died* (used in reference to Arkadii's mother)? Do you know any other words with the same root? What other words in the text have the same root? What do they mean?
5. In what contexts is the word **записа́ться** used?
6. Write a paragraph in Russian from Arkadii's point of view as he approaches his reunion with his father or from the narrator's point of view as he describes the meeting of father and son (thus continuing the story).

✳ Упражне́ние 17ё

Analyze the answers in **Упражне́ние 17e** and determine which answers use the prepositional case (and for which part of the answer), the instrumental case (for which part of the answer), and the genitive case (for the entire answer). Note the answers that use prepositions.

§   Зада́ние 17а

Practice asking and answering when your family members and classmates were born and when you and your classmates will finish school (**око́нчить университе́т и́ли получи́ть дипло́м**).

§   Зада́ние 17б

Make up sentences for each of the most important dates in your life and the lives of the people who are closest to you: birthdays (**день рожде́ния**), anniversaries (**годовщи́на сва́дьбы**), and other important occasions.

✳   Упражне́ние 17ж

Practice your knowledge of Russian, American, and world history by asking your classmates the following questions.

1.   Когда́ была́ револю́ция, в кото́рой пришли́ к вла́сти большевики́?
2.   Когда́ Алекса́ндр II освободи́л крепостны́х (serfs)?
3.   Когда́ Не́льсон Манде́ла освободи́лся из тюрьмы́?
4.   Когда́ Япо́ния напа́ла на Аме́рику?
5.   Когда́ была́ америка́нская револю́ция?
6.   Когда́ была́ америка́нская гражда́нская война́?
7.   Когда́ америка́нки получи́ли пра́во голосова́ть?
8.   Когда́ уби́ли Ма́ртина Лю́тера Ки́нга?

As it does with clock times, Russian conveys the sense that something must be completed by a certain time with the preposition **к** and the dative case of the time expression that follows.

> Э́то на́до зако́нчить к...
>   ве́черу
>   среде́
>   два́дцать пе́рвому ноября́

The construction **с** and the genitive case with **до** and the genitive case conveys the idea from a particular date up to but not including another specified date. Thus, if you tell the hotel clerk that you want a room **с пя́того апре́ля до семна́дцатого апре́ля**, it means that you will check out on the 17th by checkout time. However, if you want to stay through the end of the day on the 17th (keeping your luggage in the room, having a place to shower later in the day, and so forth), then you need to use the expression **с** and the genitive case and **по** and the accusative case: **с пя́того апре́ля по семна́дцатое апре́ля**.

§   Зада́ние 17в

Practice asking and answering by what date you and your classmates will finish various projects (such as term papers) for various classes: **Когда́ тебе́ на́до сда́ть курсову́ю рабо́ту** (*term paper*), **курсово́й прое́кт** (*course project*), **дипло́мную рабо́ту** (*senior thesis*)?

§   Зада́ние 17г

Practice asking and answering from what date until what date you and your classmates will be in some other city after the end of the school year (**по́сле оконча́ния уче́бного го́да**) or after graduation (**по́сле оконча́ния университе́та**).

✳   Упражне́ние 17з

Make hotel reservations using the following dialogue. Fill in different dates each time you practice.

> —Слу́шаю вас.
> —До́брый день. Я хочу́ заказа́ть но́мер в ва́шей гости́нице.
> —Пожа́луйста. Когда́ вам ну́жен но́мер?
> —С тре́тьего ноября́ по трина́дцатое ноября́.
> —На ско́лько челове́к?
> —На одного́.
> —Хорошо́. Ва́ша фами́лия?
> —Моя́ фами́лия _____.
> —Ваш но́мер зака́зан. Вы должны́ бу́дете офо́рмить докуме́нты здесь в гости́нице к шести́ часа́м тре́тьего ноября́, а то отдади́м ваш но́мер друго́му челове́ку.
> —Хорошо́, я по́нял (я поняла́). Спаси́бо.

PART 2
At a Particular Time*

The rules surrounding the expression of a particular time in Russian, like the rules for equivalent expressions in English, are idiosyncratic. For instance, in English, we use a preposition in the expression *in the evening*, but not in the expressions *last night* or *last week*. In Russian, some expressions require prepositions, while others do not. There is no direct relationship to the English rules on using a preposition for one or another expression.

---

* Excluding dates.

1. Я приду́ в полови́не восьмо́го
    утра́.

2. Я приду́ за́втра у́тром (днём,
    ве́чером, но́чью).

3. Я приду́ во вто́рник.

4. Я приду́ на сле́дующей неде́ле.

5. Я прие́ду в сле́дующем ме́сяце.

6. Я прие́ду сле́дующей о́сенью.

7. Я прие́ду в сле́дующем году́.

I'll come at 7:30 a.m.

*I'll come tomorrow morning
    (afternoon, evening, night).*

I'll come on Tuesday.

I'll come next week.

I'll come next month.

I'll come next fall.

I'll come next year.

In addition, there are three ways to express repetition.

8. Она́ захо́дит к нам по пя́тницам
    (по утра́м/вечера́м).

9. Она́ захо́дит к нам ка́ждую
    неде́лю (ка́ждое у́тро/ка́ждый
    ме́сяц).

10. Она́ захо́дит к нам раз в неде́лю
    (раз в день/два ра́за в ме́сяц).

*She drops by (to visit us) on Fridays
    (in the mornings/in the evenings).*

*She drops by (to visit us) every week
    (every morning/every month).*

*She drops by (to visit us) every week
    (once a day/twice a month).*

✳ Упражне́ние 17и

Determine which of the time expressions require a preposition and which do not.
Which expressions use the prepositional case, the accusative, the genitive, the instrumental, or the dative?

PART 3 Time Expressions of Duration

Time expressions of duration usually use the accusative case of the time period in
question; if the time expression involves a number of minutes, hours, days, weeks,
months, or years, the number is in the accusative case (inanimate), and the case of the
time period itself is governed by the number (genitive singular for numbers 2 through
4 and 22 through 24, genitive plural for numbers 5 through 20, 25 through 30, and so
forth). Remember that for 1, 21, 31, etc., the noun following the number is always in
the same case as the number, which means that here it will be in the accusative. Note
that most Russian time expressions of duration do not require a preposition, whereas
the equivalent English expressions often do require one.

1. Мы бу́дем здесь ещё одну́ мину́ту
    (две мину́ты/пять мину́т).

2. Мы учи́лись в Новосиби́рске
    ме́сяц (два ме́сяца/пять
    ме́сяцев).

*We'll be here for another minute
    (two minutes/five minutes).*

*We studied in Novosibirsk for a
    month (two months/five months).*

3. Она́ сиди́т и чита́ет весь день (всё   *She's been sitting and reading all day*
   у́тро/весь ве́чер/всю ночь/всю   *(all morning/all evening/all night/*
   неде́лю).   *all week).*

❋   Упражне́ние 17й

In example 3, the Russian word for *all* is used to indicate duration. In which of the time expressions is the time period feminine? How can you tell?

❋   Упражне́ние 17к

It is possible to omit the number one in time expressions. In which examples is this number omitted? Note that the number one is considered a modifier, and the time expression that follows it is in the accusative case (the number and time expression agree in gender, number, and case). In all other instances, the case of the time expression is governed by the number that precedes it.

§   Зада́ние 17д

Choose an important event in your life and rewrite five examples to describe the various relationships of time to that event.

❋   Упражне́ние 17л

When the number and the time expression are inverted (**го́да три**), it indicates an approximate time period. Rewrite examples 1 through 4 to give an approximate time.

RUSSIAN

Saying

У́тро ве́чера мудрене́е.

The morning is wiser than the evening.
[Let's sleep on it.]

Note that in all the examples, the expression of duration is used with an imperfective verb. This is always the rule except when you want to emphasize the achievement of a particular result within a particular time frame. In that case, use the perfective verb with the preposition **за** and the time expression in the accusative case.

4. Я прочита́ла э́тот рома́н за   *I read this novel (got it read) in a*
   неде́лю.   *week's time.*

§ Зада́ние 17е

Prepare a three-minute talk in Russian explaining how long it took you to complete part or all of your homework, to decide what courses to take this semester, to decide what foreign language(s) to study, or to finish some other task you faced last year.

RUSSIAN

Saying

Гото́вь са́ни ле́том, а теле́гу зимо́й.

Prepare the sled in the summer, and the cart in the winter.
[A stitch in time saves nine.]

---

§ Зада́ние 17ё

Prepare a three-minute talk in Russian explaining how long it will take you to do each step in the research and writing of a term paper or other large project, to make the necessary arrangements for a trip you're planning, or to complete some other task you face next year.

PART 4 Relating Events to Time

There are many ways that an event can be related to time.

1. We can specify the event as taking place during a certain time period.
2. We can specify the event as taking place after a certain time period has elapsed.
3. We can specify the event as taking place a certain time before or after another event.
4. We can specify that the consequences of the event remain in effect for a certain time.

We have already discussed how to express duration (1) in Part 3 of this unit.

If the event takes place after a specified time has elapsed (2), we can express this idea in Russian with the preposition **че́рез** and the accusative case of the time period.

1. Они́ верну́тся че́рез два часа́.   *They'll return in two hours (two hours from now).*

It is important to distinguish these constructions from similar ones using the preposition **в**, which refer to clock time: **Я верну́сь в три часа́** (*I'll return at 3:00*).

If we want to relate a particular event in time to another event (3), we use the expression **че́рез...по́сле** (**того́, как...**) or **за....до** (**того́, как**).

2. Я верну́сь че́рез час по́сле того́, как ко́нчится фильм. (Я верну́сь че́рез час по́сле фи́льма.)

I'll return an hour after the film is over (an hour after the film).

3. Они́ верну́тся за два часа́ до того́, как начнётся ле́кция. (Они́ верну́тся за два часа́ до ле́кции.)

They'll return two hours before the lecture begins (two hours before the lecture).

An event can be said to have consequences that remain in effect for a specified time (4). In this case, we use the preposition **на** and the accusative case of the time period.

4. Она́ пое́дет в Москву́ на две неде́ли.

She's going to Moscow for two weeks.

5. Я запо́мню э́то на всю жизнь!

I'll remember this for my whole life!

The expressions **пока́ не** + *verb* and **до тех пор, как** are used to convey the meaning of *until another event takes place* and **до сих пор** is used to convey the meaning *until the present.*

6. Де́ти бу́дут продолжа́ть пла́кать, пока́ не придёт мать.

The children will continue crying until their mother returns.

7. Де́ти бу́дут продолжа́ть пла́кать до тех пор, как придёт мать.

The children will continue crying until their mother returns.

8. Де́ти пла́чут до сих пор.

The children have been crying until now (are still crying).

The expression **с тех пор, как** is used to convey the meaning *since.*

9. Ко́ля бо́льше не боле́л с тех пор, как на́чал принима́ть витами́ны.

Kolia hasn't been sick since he started taking vitamins.

 Упражне́ние 17м

Translate the following sentences into English.

1. Она́ два дня писа́ла э́то письмо́.
2. Он пое́дет в Росси́ю че́рез неде́лю.
3. Мы наконе́ц получи́ли кни́ги че́рез два ме́сяца по́сле того́, как мы их заказа́ли.
4. Мо́жет быть, за́втра профе́ссор нас отпу́стит за 15 мину́т до конца́ заня́тий.
5. Ва́ся прие́дет к нам в го́сти на всё ле́то.
6. Петро́вы приду́т по́сле ле́кции.
7. Валенти́на отпра́вит нам материа́лы по́сле того́, как она́ вернётся из Росто́ва-на-Дону́.
8. Ди́ма не переста́нет говори́ть о Ле́не, пока́ не придёт Лю́да.

9. Ди́ма говори́т о Ле́не с тех пор, как он с ней познако́мился.

10. Мы не мо́жем говори́ть об э́том прое́кте до тех пор, как вернётся Ни́на Серге́евна.

 ТЕКСТ 17в

This poem is by the Russian poet Fet.

Pre-reading Task

What do you think of when you think of the spring?

Это у́тро, ра́дость[1] э́та,
Э́та мощь[2] и дня и све́та,[3]
   Э́тот си́ний свод,[4]
Э́тот крик и верени́цы,[5]
Э́ти ста́и,[6] э́ти пти́цы,
   Э́тот го́вор вод,[7]
Э́ти и́вы и берёзы,[8]
Э́ти ка́пли—э́ти слёзы,[9]
   Э́тот пух—не лист,[10]
Э́ти го́ры, э́ти до́лы,[11]
Э́ти мо́шки, э́ти пчёлы,[12]
   Э́тот зык и свист,[13]
Э́ти зо́ри без затме́нья,[14]
Э́тот вздох[15] ночно́й селе́нья,[16]
   Э́та ночь без сна́[17]
Э́та мгла и жар посте́ли,[18]
Э́та дробь и э́ти тре́ли,[19]
   Это всё весна́.

А. А. Фет, 1881(?)

1 *joy*
2 *power*
3 *light*
4 си́ний... *blue heavens*
5 Э́тот... *cry and lines, rows*
6 *flocks*
7 го́вор... *murmur of the waters*
8 и́вы... *willows and birch trees*
9 Э́ти... *these drops and these tears*
10 пух... *feathers, fluff; not a leaf*
11 Э́ти... *these mountains and these valleys*
12 Э́ти... *these moths and these bees*
13 зык... *loudness and whistle*
14 зо́ри... *dawns without darkness*
15 *sigh*
16 *settling in*
17 без... *without sleep*
18 мгла... *gloom, darkness and the heat, fire of the bed*
19 Э́та... *that flutter and those trills, warbles*

Post-reading Tasks

1. Do you agree with Fet's description of spring?
2. What might the narrator mean when he refers to "dawns without darkness"?
3. Find all the time expressions in the poem.
4. What is the adjective derived from the Russian word for *night*? What is its English equivalent?
5. Write a description in Russian of another season of the year or time of day.

✳   Упражнéние 17н

Write out examples of the five time expressions you find most challenging and use them in sentences. Then combine the sentences into a paragraph using some of the "connecting" words or phrases from your list.

✳   Упражнéние 17о

Continue your list of "connecting" words and phrases (such as *because, but, in the first place, then,* and so forth) with those you can find in the texts of this unit. Next to each "connecting" word or phrase, write out the clause or sentence in which they are used. Keep this list in your notebook and add to it as you continue with this book.

✳   Упражнéние 17п

Add the verbs of this unit to your lists of first- and second-conjugation verbs, noting the stress pattern of each verb as you do so.

UNIT 18

The Conditional, *whether* Constructions and Reported Speech

Сослага́тельное наклоне́ние и ко́свенная речь

Молоды́е ребя́та игра́ют в
баскетбо́л.

PART 1

whether
Constructions

It is common in English for the word *if* to be used synonymously with the word *whether*, as in the following examples.

1. I don't know if she's going to come over this evening.
2. They're sure to ask me if I'll get it done by Thursday.

If you replace the word *if* with the word *whether* in these sentences, you'll see that there is no difference in meaning.

In the following sentences, however, *if* is not synonymous with *whether*.

3. If she comes over this evening, I'll try to ask her about this.
4. They're sure to have a great time if they speak English well.

In examples 3 and 4, *if* is so different in meaning from *whether* that it would be impossible to replace *if* with *whether* and retain the same meaning.

In Russian the particle **ли** (*whether*) and the word **éсли** (*if*) are distinctly different and cannot overlap in meaning as the English words do in examples 1 and 2; **ли** is used to introduce an indirect question (*whether*), while **éсли** is used to introduce a condition. Observe how **ли** is used in the following sentences.

1. Ты не знáешь, говоря́т ли они́ по-англи́йски?
    Do you know whether they speak English?
2. Ты не знáешь, говори́ли ли они́ по-англи́йски?
    Do you know whether they were speaking in English?
3. Ты не знáешь, бу́дут ли они́ говори́ть по-англи́йски?
    Do you know whether they will be speaking in English?

RUSSIAN | Saying

То ли ещё бу́дет.

It just can't get any worse.

The particle **ли** is also used in writing to convey meaning that would otherwise be made by intonation in speech. For instance, the question «**Он читáл э́ту газéту вчерá?**» could have several meanings depending on how the speaker raises or lowers the pitch of her voice.

1. Was it he who read this newspaper yesterday?
2. Did he read this newspaper yesterday, or just leaf through it?
3. Did he read this newspaper yesterday, or some other newspaper?

4. Did he read this newspaper yesterday, or a magazine?
5. Did he read this newspaper yesterday or the day before yesterday?

Because there is no way to convey the precise meaning of a question when it is written down, Russians use the particle **ли**, placing it immediately after the word being questioned. In most instances, the particle **ли** is placed directly after the verb. Sometimes, however, the particle **ли** is placed after another word if meaning requires it. Now consider five sentences in Russian with the particle **ли**.

> Он ли читáл э́ту газéту вчерá?
>
> Читáл ли он э́ту газéту вчерá?
>
> Э́ту ли газéту читáл он вчерá?
>
> Газéту ли читáл он вчерá?
>
> Вчерá ли читáл он э́ту газéту?

In these examples, the word in question is the first word in the sentence and **ли** is the second word. However, **ли** need not necessarily be the second word if the item being questioned includes a preposition.

> В Москву́ ли éдут Петрóвы?

✳ Упражнéние 18а

Read the Russian sentences. Then write a sentence stating that you don't know whether or not the underlined item is true. Use the particle **ли** in each sentence.

ОБРАЗÉЦ: Вéра сейчáс читáет <u>э́тот журнáл</u>, но тот ужé прочитáла. →

Я не знáю, э́тот ли журнáл читáет Вéра.

1. Пéтя и Вáся <u>говоря́т</u> по-япóнски, но плóхо пи́шут.
2. Пéтя и Вáся говоря́т хорошó <u>по-япóнски</u>, но плóхо по-немéцки.
3. <u>Áня</u> былá на рабóте в семь.
4. Áня <u>былá</u> на рабóте в семь.
5. Áня былá на рабóте <u>в семь</u>.

✳ Упражнéние 18б

Read the Russian sentences and then write a question that asks about the underlined item in each sentence. Use the particle **ли** in each question.

ОБРАЗÉЦ: Вéра сейчáс читáет <u>э́тот журнáл</u>, но тот ужé прочитáла. →

Э́тот ли журнáл читáет Вéра?

1. Лáра и О́ля <u>говоря́т</u> по-францу́зски, но плóхо пи́шут.
2. Лáра и О́ля говоря́т <u>по-францу́зски</u>, но плóхо по-немéцки.
3. Ви́тя <u>сказáл</u>, что он придёт в семь часóв.
4. <u>Ви́тя</u> сказáл, что придёт в семь часóв.
5. Ви́тя, навéрно, <u>скáжет</u>, что придёт в семь часóв.

PART 2
Conditional for Possible Events

The Russian word **éсли** (*if*) is reserved for conditional constructions.

1. If it rains, the picnic will be cancelled.
2. If it had rained, the picnic would have been cancelled.

Example 1 may be called "conditional and possible," because the condition described might actually come to pass. Example 2 may be called "conditional and contrary to fact," because the condition described did not come to pass. These two conditional constructions feature different grammatical patterns in Russian and are therefore presented separately here.

Although conditional and possible sentences like example 1 generally refer to a future possibility, English expresses the condition in the present tense; Russian, however, is more logical and puts both condition and result in the future tense. Compare the English and the Russian in the following sentences.

1. Éсли он **позвони́т**, я его **приглашу́** в теа́тр.

   *If he **calls** I **will** invite him to the theater.*

2. Я на них **рассержу́сь**, éсли они́ опя́ть **опозда́ют**.

   *I **will** get angry at them if they **are** late again.*

Éсли can also be used with an infinitive to convey the question as to whether or not to undertake a course of action:

3. Éсли **пригласи́ть** Макси́ма, то придётся пригласи́ть и Ко́стю.

   If Maxim is invited, then it will be necessary to invite Kostia as well.

✳ Упражне́ние 18в

Reread the Russian examples with their English translations. Identify the tense and aspect of each Russian verb.

✳ Упражне́ние 18г

Review the formation of future-tense imperfective and perfective verbs by translating these sentences.

1. I will be reading for three hours tonight.
2. I will read this newspaper tonight.
3. He will be cooking for two hours tonight.
4. He will cook dinner tonight.

ТЕКСТ 18а

Read the excerpt from Chekhov's play *The Cherry Orchard*. Lopakhin, a merchant, is trying to warn Liubov' Andreevna Ranevskaia, an impoverished aristocrat, that she and her family (including her brother, Gaev) are in dire financial straits. If they don't split up the cherry orchard into small parcels to rent out to vacationers, Lopakhin says, they risk losing not only the cherry orchard, but also the entire estate.

Pre-reading Task

How might Lopakhin and Ranevskaia view the sale of the cherry orchard, given their respective class affiliations?

ЛОПА́ХИН. ...Вам уже́ изве́стно, вишнёвый сад[1] ваш продаётся за долги́,[2] на два́дцать второе а́вгуста назна́чены торги́,[3] но вы не беспоко́йтесь, моя́ дорога́я, спи́те себе́ споко́йно,[4] вы́ход есть[5].... Вот мой прое́кт. Прошу́ внима́ния![6] Ва́ше име́ние[7] нахо́дится то́лько в двадцати́ верста́х[8] от го́рода, во́зле прошла́ желе́зная доро́га,[9] и е́сли вишнёвый сад и зе́млю по реке́ разби́ть на да́чные уча́стки и отдава́ть пото́м в аре́нду под да́чи,[10] то вы бу́дете име́ть са́мое ма́лое[11] два́дцать пять ты́сяч в год дохо́да.[12]

ГА́ЕВ. Извини́те, кака́я чепуха́[13]!

ЛЮБО́ВЬ АНДРЕ́ЕВНА. Я вас не совсе́м понима́ю, Ермола́й Алексе́ич.

ЛОПА́ХИН. Вы бу́дете брать с да́чников[14] са́мое ма́лое по два́дцать пять рубле́й в год за десяти́ну,[15] и е́сли тепе́рь же объя́вите,[16] то, я руча́юсь чем уго́дно,[17] у вас до о́сени не оста́нется ни одного́ свобо́дного клочка́, всё разберу́т.[18] Одни́м сло́вом, поздравля́ю, вы спасены́.[19] Местоположе́ние чуде́сное, река́ глубо́кая. То́лько коне́чно, ну́жно поубра́ть, почи́стить[20].... наприме́р, ска́жем, снести́ все ста́рые постро́йки,[21] вот э́тот дом, кото́рый уже́ никуда́ не годи́тся,[22] вы́рубить[23] ста́рый вишнёвый сад...

ЛЮБО́ВЬ АНДРЕ́ЕВНА. Вы́рубить? Ми́лый мой, прости́те, вы ничего́ не понима́ете. Е́сли во всей губе́рнии[24] есть что́-нибудь интере́сное, да́же замеча́тельное, так это то́лько наш вишнёвый сад.

ЛОПА́ХИН. Замеча́тельного в э́том саду́ то́лько то, что он о́чень большо́й. Ви́шня роди́тся раз в два го́да,[25] да и ту дева́ть не́куда,[26] никто́ не покупа́ет.

ГА́ЕВ. И в «Энциклопеди́ческом словаре́» упомина́ется[27] про э́тот сад.

[1] вишнёвый... *cherry orchard*
[2] за... *for debts (to pay off debts)*
[3] на... *sale is scheduled for August 22*
[4] вы... *don't worry my dear, sleep calmly*
[5] вы́ход... *there's a solution, a way out*
[6] Прошу́... *Attention please!*
[7] Ва́ше... *Your estate*
[8] в... *twenty versts (verst = 3,500 feet)*
[9] во́зле... *the railroad has been built nearby*
[10] е́сли... *if the cherry orchard and the land near the river is split up into dacha plots and then rented out for dachas*
[11] са́мое... *at least*
[12] *income*
[13] кака́я... *what nonsense!*
[14] с... *from those renting dachas*
[15] за... *for a desiatina (desiatina = 2.7 acres)*
[16] *announce*
[17] я... *I swear by anything you want*
[18] до... *by the fall there won't be a free plot of land left, they'll take it all*
[19] вы... *you're saved*
[20] *to clean up*
[21] снести́... *tear down all the old buildings*
[22] кото́рый... *which isn't fit anymore*
[23] *cut down*
[24] во... *in the entire province*
[25] Ви́шня... *Cherries are produced only once every two years*
[26] ту... *there's nothing that can be done with them*
[27] *is mentioned*

30   **ЛОПА́ХИН.** (*взгляну́в на часы́*). Е́сли ничего́ не приду́маем[28] и ни к чему́ не придём,[29] то два́дцать второ́го а́вгуста и вишнёвый сад и всё име́ние бу́дут продава́ть с аукцио́на. Реша́йтесь же! Друго́го вы́хода нет, кляну́сь вам.[30] Нет и нет.

[28] *think up*
[29] к... *come to some decision*
[30] кляну́сь... *I swear to you*

А. П. Че́хов, «Вишнёвый сад», 1903

Post-reading Tasks

1. Write a four-sentence summary in Russian of the text.
2. Find the conditional constructions that are possible (not contrary to fact). Circle these constructions and identify the tense and aspect of the verb used.
3. Write in Russian another scene to follow or precede this one in which the same characters interact.
4. Write a letter in Russian from Lopakhin's point of view, urging the sale of the cherry orchard.

RUSSIAN

Saying

Была́ бы спина́, найдётся и вина́.

First find the person to accuse, then think up (find) the accusation.
[Shoot first, ask questions later.]

 Упражне́ние 18д

Provide an appropriate conclusion to the following conditional and possible sentences. Pay attention to tense and aspect.

ОБРАЗЕ́Ц: Е́сли они́ приду́т ра́но,... →

Е́сли они́ приду́т ра́но, мы смо́жем вме́сте поу́жинать сего́дня ве́чером.
If they come early, we can have dinner together tonight.

1. Е́сли сего́дня бу́дет хоро́шая переда́ча по телеви́зору,...
2. Е́сли за́втра ко мне прие́дет ста́рый друг,...
3. Е́сли профе́ссор не зада́ст нам дома́шнего зада́ния,...
4. Е́сли в магази́не не бу́дет хоро́шего сы́ра,...
5. Е́сли в магази́не бу́дет больша́я распрода́жа (*sale*),...

Зада́ние 18а

Write a paragraph beginning with one of the sentences in the preceding exercise.

ТЕКСТ 18б

This poem by Pushkin describes a strategy for dealing with life's ups and downs.

Pre-reading Task

Think about your own strategy for dealing with life's setbacks. Then read the poem and see if you agree with Pushkin's approach.

Éсли жизнь тебя обма́нет,[1]
Не печа́лься, не серди́сь![2]
В день уны́ния смири́сь:[3]
День весе́лья, верь, наста́нет.[4]
Се́рдце в бу́дущем[5] живёт;
Настоя́щее уны́ло:[6]
Всё мгнове́нно, всё пройдёт;[7]
Что пройдёт, то бу́дет ми́ло.[8]

А. С. Пу́шкин, 1825

[1] Éсли... *If life should deceive you*
[2] Не... *Don't be sad, don't be angry*
[3] В... *Reconcile yourself in the day of despair*
[4] День... *The day of joy, believe it, will come*
[5] Се́рдце... *The heart in the future*
[6] Настоя́щее... *The present is cheerless*
[7] Всё... *Everything is fleeting, everything passes*
[8] Что... *That which passes will be fine*

Post-reading Tasks

1. Write a one- or two-sentence summary in Russian of Pushkin's philosophy.
2. Do you agree or disagree with his philosophy? Write a paragraph in Russian explaining why.
3. Find all the imperatives in the poem and identify the infinitives from which they are derived.
4. Find the conditional construction and identify whether it is contrary to fact. Then determine the tense of the verb used.
5. Assume the point of view of someone who disagrees with Pushkin's philosophy and write a paragraph in Russian explaining why.

Упражне́ние 18е

Translate the following sentences into Russian.

1. If Sasha calls, tell him I'm at the library.
2. If the weather is good tomorrow, let's go to the park.
3. If we can buy good tickets, let's go to the theater on Tuesday.
4. If Anna can't have dinner with us, let's have dinner with Alla.

PART 3

Conditional for Contrary-to-Fact Events

Conditional constructions that are contrary to fact or unreal have a different grammatical pattern: They require the conditional particle **бы**. This particle requires the past-tense form of each verb that is conditional and contrary to fact, or unreal: The past-tense form of the verb does not carry any inherent tense meaning in these constructions.

1.	Éсли бы я вы́играла в лотере́ю, я бы поплыла́ на тропи́ческий о́стров.	*If I were to win the lottery, I would sail to a tropical island (unlikely, since I don't buy tickets).*
2.	Éсли бы я вы́играла в лотере́ю, я бы поплыла́ на тропи́ческий о́стров.	*If I had won the lottery, I would have sailed to a tropical island (I did buy tickets and could, in theory, have won).*

In English it is clear that example 1 sets up a conditional construction involving an event in the future deemed extremely unlikely, whereas example 2 refers to an event that could have happened in the past but did not. In Russian, however, these distinctions are made only by context: There is no grammatical difference between the two sentences in Russian.

The conditional particle **бы** may be placed in several different positions in the conditional sentence.

3.	Éсли **бы** вчера́ была́ хоро́шая пого́да, мы **бы** пошли́ на пикни́к.	*If the weather had been good yesterday, we would have gone on the (a) picnic.*
4.	Éсли вчера́ была́ **бы** хоро́шая пого́да, мы пошли́ **бы** на пикни́к.	

Examples 3 and 4 are synonymous in meaning, despite the different placement of **бы**. In general, place the conditional particle **бы** directly after the word **éсли**, directly after the subject, or directly before or after the verb.

ТЕКСТ 18в

Read the excerpt from Chekhov's play *Three Sisters*. Irina is depressed and Ol'ga, her sister, advises her to get married.

Pre-reading Task

Why do women get married today? What might be some reasons that women would or would not get married in the nineteenth century?

ÓЛЬГА. Ми́лая, говорю́ тебе́ как сестра́, как друг, е́сли хо́чешь моего́ сове́та,[1] выходи́ за баро́на[2]!

Ири́на ти́хо пла́чет.

Ведь ты его́ уважа́ешь, высоко́ це́нишь[3]... Он, пра́вда, некраси́вый, но он тако́й поря́дочный,[4] чи́стый...Ведь за́муж выхо́дят не из любви́,[5] а для того́, чтобы испо́лнить свой долг.[6] Я по кра́йней ме́ре[7] так ду́маю, и я бы вы́шла без любви́. Кто бы ни посва́тал,[8] всё равно́ бы пошла́,[9] лишь бы[10] поря́дочный челове́к. Да́же за старика́ бы пошла́...

ИРИ́НА. Я всё ждала́, пересели́мся в Москву́,[11] там мне встре́тится мой настоя́щий,[12] я мечта́ла о нём,[13] люби́ла...Но оказа́лось, всё вздор,[14] всё вздор...

ÓЛЬГА. (*обнима́ет*[15] *сестру́*). Ми́лая моя́, прекра́сная сестра́, я всё понима́ю; когда́ баро́н Никола́й Льво́вич оста́вил вое́нную слу́жбу и пришёл к нам в пиджаке́,[16] то показа́лся мне таки́м некраси́вым, что я да́же заплака́ла[17]...Он спра́шивает: «Что[18] вы пла́чете?» Как я ему́ скажу́![19] Но е́сли бы Бог привёл ему́ жени́ться на тебе́,[20] то я была́ бы сча́стлива.[21] Тут ведь друго́е, совсе́м друго́е.[22]

А. П. Че́хов, «Три сестры́», 1901

[1] моего́... *my advice*
[2] выходи́... *get married to the baron*
[3] Ведь... *After all you respect him, think highly of him*
[4] *decent (morally)*
[5] за́муж... *women get married not for love*
[6] чтобы... *to fulfill their obligation*
[7] по... *at least*
[8] *whoever (regardless of who-ever) proposed*
[9] *get married*
[10] лишь... *as long as (it was)*
[11] Я... *I was always waiting for us to move to Moscow*
[12] там... *there I would meet my true love*
[13] я... *I dreamed about him*
[14] оказа́лось... *it turned out it was all rubbish*
[15] *embraces, hugs*
[16] оста́вил... *retired from military service and came to us in a jacket (not a uniform)*
[17] я... *I burst out in tears*
[18] **Почему́**
[19] Как... *How could I tell him!*
[20] е́сли... *If God brought him here to marry you*
[21] *happy*
[22] друго́е... *something else, something entirely different*

Post-reading Tasks

1. Write a three-sentence summary of the passage.
2. Find all the conditional constructions that are contrary to fact.
3. What is the root of the Russian word meaning *obligation*? Do you know any other words with this root?
4. Assume the point of view of one of the sisters and continue the argument, or recast the argument in the late twentieth century.

Saying

Чем бы дитя́ ни те́шилось, лишь бы не пла́кало.

No matter what the child amuses itself with, as long as it doesn't cry.
[No matter what the price.]

✳   Упражнéние 18ё

Rewrite the following sentences to make them contrary to fact.

ОБРАЗÉЦ: Éсли завтра бýдет хорóшая погóда, мы пойдём на пикнúк. ⎫ →
             If the weather is good tomorrow, we'll go on a picnic. ⎭

             Éсли бы былá хорóшая погóда, мы бы пошлú на пикнúк.
             If the weather had been good, we would have gone on a picnic.

1. Éсли бýдет идтú дождь, отмéнится пикнúк.
    If it rains, the picnic will be cancelled.

2. Мы пойдём в поxóд на лы́жах, éсли зáвтра бýдет хорóшая погóда.
    We'll go skiing if the weather is good tomorrow.

3. Éсли он позвонúт, я егó приглашý в теáтр.
    If he calls I'll invite him to the theater.

4. Я на них рассержýсь, éсли онú опя́ть опоздáют.
    I'll get angry at them if they are late again.

5. Éсли э́тот профéссор окáжется óчень стрóгим, мы смóжем послýшать курс у какóго-нибудь другóго профéссора.
    If this professor turns out to be strict, we will be able to take the course from some other professor.

✳   Упражнéние 18ж

Provide an appropriate conclusion to the following conditional and contrary-to-fact sentences. Taking into account the aspect of your completed sentence, consider how you might translate it into English.

ОБРАЗÉЦ: Éсли бы онú пришлú рáно,... →

             Éсли бы онú пришлú рáно, мы смоглú бы вмéсте поýжинать.
             If they had come early, we could have had dinner together.

1. Éсли бы сегóдня былá хорóшая передáча по телевúзору ...
2. Éсли бы вчерá ко мне приéхал стáрый друг, ...
3. Éсли бы профéссор не зáдал нам домáшнего задáния ...
4. Éсли бы в магазúне нé было хорóшего сы́ра,...
5. Éсли бы в магазúне былá большáя распродáжа (*sale*),...

    ТЕКСТ 18г

This is an untitled poem by Akhmatova.

Pre-reading Task

How can you count yourself a strong or wealthy person?

Éсли б все, кто по́мощи душе́вной[1]
У меня́ проси́л на э́том све́те,
Все юро́дивые и немы́е,[2]
Бро́шенные[3] жёны и кале́ки,[4]
5   Ка́торжники и самоуби́йцы[5]
Мне присла́ли б по одно́й копе́йке,[6]—
Ста́ла б я бога́че всех в Еги́пте,[7]
Как гова́ривал Кузьми́н поко́йный.[8]
Но они́ не сла́ли мне копе́йки,
10 А со мной свое́й дели́лись си́лой.[9]
И я ста́ла всех сильне́й на све́те,
Так что да́же э́то мне не тру́дно.

А. А. Ахма́това, 1960

[1] по́мощи... *spiritual help, emotional support*
[2] юро́дивые... *holy fools and mute people*
[3] *abandoned*
[4] *cripples*
[5] *people in forced labor and suicides*
[6] Мне... *would have sent me one kopeck each*
[7] бога́че... *wealthier than all the people in (ancient) Egypt*
[8] Как... *As the late Kuzmin would say (M. A. Kuzmin, Russian poet, 1875–1936)*
[9] со... *shared their strength with me*

Post-reading Tasks

1. Write a two-sentence summary of the poem in Russian.
2. What is the root of the Russian word meaning *spiritual*? Do you know any other words with the same root?
3. What is the root of the two Russian words meaning *to send*? Do you know any other words with the same root?
5. Write a paragraph explaining what you think the word **э́то** stands for in the last line of the poem.
6. Compare the conditional constructions in **Те́ксты 18а, 18б, 18в**, and **18г** and determine which constructions are contrary to fact and which are not. Note in **Текст 18г** that **б** is used instead of the full form **бы** for metric reasons. Identify the tense of the verbs in each conditional construction.

♪ Зада́ние 18б

Prepare a three-minute talk or a hundred-word composition describing what you would do if you had a lot of money: **Éсли бы у меня́ бы́ло о́чень мно́го де́нег...**

PART 4 Translating *would* and Reported Speech

In Parts 2 and 3 of this unit we saw how conditional constructions that are possible and those that are contrary to fact or unreal require the conditional particle **бы**. The English equivalents of the contrary-to-fact and unreal constructions require the word *would.* You'll find that all the examples in Part 3 include the word *could* or *would* in the English translation, while those in Part 2 do not.

However, not every use of the word *would* in English requires a Russian conditional construction!

The English *would* is often used in sentences in indirect or "reported" speech. The reporting of English speech requires a transformation of the tenses used in the actual speech. Consider the following dialogue.

SALLY: What time does the movie start?
STEVE: It starts at 8:00.
SALLY: Okay, I'll meet you at 7:00 at the restaurant next door to the theater.

Now imagine that Sally wants to tell her friend Sue about the conversation she had with Steve. Sally would "report" her own "speech" and Steve's "speech" to Sue. In the process, she'd change some of the verb tenses in English. In the following dialogue, every verb tense changed in the reported speech is underlined.

SALLY: I asked Steve what time the movie started and he told me that it started at 8:00. I said that I would meet him at 7:00 at the restaurant next to the theater.

The grammatical transformations of the English verb as it is moved from actual speech to reported speech are somewhat complicated for foreigners to learn; native English speakers often take these transformations for granted.

Зада́ние 18в

Write out a dialogue in English between you and a friend that actually occurred and then rewrite it as a paragraph of reported, or indirect, speech. Circle all the tense transformations of the verbs from the dialogue to the reported speech.

In Russian, speech is reported just as it was originally spoken: There are no grammatical transformations. The verb tense in reported speech is the same tense used in the original speech. Consider the following Russian dialogue and reported speech.

СТЁПА. Когда́ начина́ется фильм?
 СО́НЯ. В 8 часо́в.
СТЁПА. Ла́дно, встре́тимся в 7 в рестора́не ря́дом с кино́.

Now imagine that Stepa wants to tell his friend Sasha about the conversation he had with Sonia. Note the tense of the underlined verbs.

СТЁПА. Я спроси́л Со́ню, когда́ начина́ется фильм. Она́ отве́тила, что он начина́ется в 8 часо́в. Я предложи́л ей встре́титься в 7 в рестора́не ря́дом с кино́.

The underlined verbs have the same tense and aspect as the corresponding verbs in the dialogue.

Now let's look more closely at some transformations from dialogue to reported speech. In the following examples, direct speech (actual dialogue) is represented in quotation marks («»).

1. «Они́ обяза́тельно посмо́трят э́тот фильм сего́дня»,—сказа́ла Ве́ра.

   "They will definitely watch this film tonight," said Vera.

   Вчера́ Ве́ра сказа́ла, что они́ обяза́тельно посмо́трят э́тот фильм сего́дня.

   Yesterday Vera said that they would definitely watch the film tonight.

2. «Они́ обяза́тельно посмо́трят э́тот фильм сего́дня»,— наве́рно ска́жет Ве́ра.

   Vera will probably say, "They will definitely watch this film tonight."

   Завтра́ Ве́ра наве́рно ска́жет, что они́ обяза́тельно посмо́трят э́тот фильм сего́дня.

   Tomorrow Vera will probably say that they would definitely watch the film tonight.

In each example pair, the Russian reported speech "preserves" the tense of the verbs used in the direct speech (actual dialogue), while the English uses different tenses for reported speech.

Imperative forms in Russian direct speech are transformed according to one of two patterns, depending on the verb used to report the speech.

3. «А́нна, переда́йте, пожа́луйста, ру́чку,»—сказа́л То́ля.

   "Anna, please pass me the pen," said Tolia.

4. То́ля сказа́л А́нне, чтобы она́ ему́ передала́ ру́чку.

   Tolia asked Anna to pass him the pen.

5. То́ля попроси́л А́нну переда́ть ру́чку.

   Tolia asked Anna to pass the pen.

Examples 3, 4, and 5 are synonymous. When transforming direct speech with an imperative into indirect speech, use either **сказа́ть** with a **что́бы** clause, as in example 4, or **попроси́ть** with an infinitive, as in example 5. Review the use of **что́бы** in Unit 6.

ТЕКСТ 18д

Read the excerpt from Kozhevnikov's short story "Two Notebooks." The story consists of entries from the diaries of two Leningrad teenagers. Galia writes about a conversation with a boy (Vsevolod) who loves her and another conversation with her friend Marina (Marinka). In that conversation, Marina tells Galia not to pine for another boy, Misha (Mishka). She also tells Galia about her relationship with her own boyfriend, Sasha, who is the father of the child she's carrying.

Pre-reading Task

What do you think are some of the most important criteria for choosing friends and boyfriends or girlfriends? What do you think two teenagers might think are some of the most important criteria?

Я сказа́ла Все́володу, что́бы он не ходи́л ко мне, не звони́л. Не могу́ его́ ви́деть.

...Ко мне заходи́ла Мари́нка. Она́ сказа́ла, что все мои́ страда́ния[1] по Ми́шке—ерунда́.[2] Вот она́ поняла́, что не лю́бит Са́шку, а ведь живёт с ним. Она́ от него́ ничего́ не получа́ет, не чу́вствует себя́ же́нщиной, то́лько бо́льно[3] всегда́, но идёт на э́то ра́ди[4] Са́шки—он к ней о́чень привя́зан.[5] У них бу́дет ребёнок, и роди́тели разреши́ли им жить.[6] Сейча́с они́ хо́дят в исполко́м,[7] что́бы вы́бить Мари́нке разреше́ние на брак.[8] Она́ сказа́ла, что зря я отказа́ла[9] Все́володу, а тем бо́лее бро́сила[10] То́лю. Он сейча́с из-за меня́ пьёт.[11]

Я расска́зывала Мари́нке, как люблю́ Ми́шу. Она́ до́лго не соглаша́лась, что мо́жно, как я, сиде́ть уни́женной[12] и ждать. Пото́м сказа́ла, что вообще́-то кто его́ зна́ет.[13] А когда́ уходи́ла, сказа́ла, хоть я и ду́ра,[14] а она́ мне зави́дует.[15]

П. Кожéвников, «Две тетра́ди», 1980

[1] sufferings
[2] nonsense
[3] painful
[4] for the sake of
[5] он... he's very attached to her
[6] роди́тели... parents have allowed them to live (together)
[7] city executive committee
[8] вы́бить... to get permission for Marina to be married (she's only sixteen years old)
[9] зря... in vain rejected
[10] тем... even worse abandoned, left
[11] Он... he's taken to drink because of me
[12] humiliated
[13] кто... but who knows?
[14] хоть... although I'm a fool
[15] envies

Post-reading Tasks

1. Write a summary of the passage in five sentences in Russian.
2. What is the root of the Russian word meaning *attached*? Do you know any other words with this root?
3. What is the root of the Russian word meaning *permit*? Do you know any other words with this root?
4. Reread the text and use it as a basis for creating two Russian dialogues, one between Galia and Vsevolod, the other between Galia and Marina.
5. Write a letter in Russian from one of the characters mentioned in the text to another character, and continue the melodrama.

✳ Упражне́ние 18з

Read the first act of a "play in four acts" and rewrite it as reported speech.

I. *Понеде́льник, 7:00*

то́ля. Здоро́во, О́ля. Ты не слы́шала о том, что случи́лось с Ма́шей и Па́шей?
о́ля. Приве́т, То́ля. Расскажи́, что с ни́ми!?
то́ля. Па́ша влюби́лся в Ма́шу. Я ду́маю, что за́втра он ей ска́жет, что он её лю́бит.
о́ля. Ну, интере́сно! Посмо́трим!

✳ Упражне́ние 18и

Reread **Текст 18a**. Rewrite the dialogue as reported speech.

✵   Упражнéние 18й

Reread **Текст 18в**. Rewrite the dialogue as reported speech.

✵   Упражнéние 18к

Continue your list of all the "connecting" words and phrases (such as *because, but, in the first place, then*, and so forth) with those you can find in the texts of this unit. Next to each "connecting" word or phrase, write out the clause or sentence in which they are used. Keep this list in your notebook and add to it as you continue with this book.

✵   Упражнéние 18л

Add the verbs of this unit to your lists of first- and second-conjugation verbs, noting the stress pattern of each verb as you do so.

UNIT 19

Passive
Participles

Страда́тельные прича́стия

Алёша — худо́жник.

PART 1
Identifying Participles: Recognizing Meaning

Participles are adjectives formed from verbs; sometimes they are called *verbal adjectives*. Consider the English participles *torn* ("These pants are torn.") and *written* ("This well-written argument demonstrates that we need to fund this program."). In Russian, you'll always be able to identify the verbal stem of any participle, which will help you determine the lexical meaning of the word. For example, the participle **напи́сан** has something to do with writing; the participle **рассказа́вший** has something to do with saying, telling. Once you learn how to determine the grammatical information conveyed by the form of the participle, you will understand how that form combines with the lexical meaning and figure out the meaning of that participle in its context. The goal is to combine your understanding of the meaning of the verb with an understanding of the meaning of the grammatical form.

✳ Упражне́ние 19a

Review the endings for adjectives for each of the six cases before you proceed with this unit. Write out a chart in your notes for the singular (masculine, feminine, and neuter) and plural endings for the adjectives *new* and *good*. Note how the spelling rules affect the spelling of the adjective *good*.

✳ Упражне́ние 19б

Identify the lexical meaning of the participle for each underlined and numbered form. Don't worry about the grammar for now: Just focus on meaning. Use context to determine from what verb (infinitive) the participle is derived.

Вот кни́ги, (1) забы́тые Андре́ем сего́дня ве́чером. Андре́й мно́го ку́рит и всегда́ всё забыва́ет. Я счита́ю, что все (2) куря́щие—лю́ди неаккура́тные. Э́ти кни́ги бы́ли (3) ку́плены в кни́жном магази́не «Дру́жба наро́дов». В э́том магази́не, (4) находя́щемся на Тверско́й у́лице, продаю́тся кни́ги из мно́гих стран. Э́то мой (5) люби́мый кни́жный магази́н во всей Москве́. Бе́дный Андре́й! Он наве́рно ду́мает, что его́ кни́ги (6) поте́ряны. Я за́втра возьму́ его́ кни́ги с собо́й на заня́тия и там их ему́ отда́м.

PART 2
Present Passive Participles

The present passive participle might be a long and intimidating term, but the grammatical form it identifies is a simple one to use. The present passive participle is an adjective formed from a verb. For example the present passive participle of the verb

to read is *is, are (being) read* or, as we more often say, *readable*, as in *this is definitely readable*. The key here is that these forms carry the inherent meaning of present tense and that the people or things the present passive participles modify are passive in the construction in which they appear.

Russian present passive participles can be formed only from transitive verbs, that is, those verbs that take an accusative case direct object (without a preposition). For instance, **называть** (*to call, to name*), **уважать** (*to respect*), **любить** (*to love*), **выносить** (*to carry out or to bear, to endure*), and **забывать** (*to forget*) are all verbs of this type (because we can say, *to name something, to respect whom, to forget something*, and so forth). These verbs have present passive participles, as you will see.

Many Russian verbs, such as **писать**, **брать**, **шить**, and **мыть**, do not have present passive participles. Rather than give you a complete list of which verbs have these forms and which do not, it would be better at this point for you to learn several of the forms, recognize what key features they share, and be ready to encounter similar forms. You are not expected to form present passive participles from either "old" or "new" verbs in your vocabulary, because so few verbs have them. Instead, memorize the eleven present passive participles listed below.

The key feature of the present passive participle is the letter **-м-** and a regular adjectival ending (short or long form).*

PARTICIPLE	MEANING
любимый (любить)	*beloved or favorite*
(так) называемый (называть)	*(so) called*
(много-) уважаемый (уважать)	*(very) respected (used in salutations in letters)*
невыносимый (выносить)	*unbearable*
незабываемый (забывать)	*unforgettable*
неотвратимый (отвратить)	*inevitable*
необъяснимый (объяснить)	*inexplicable*
непоправимый (поправить)	*irreparable*
рекомендуемый (рекомендовать)	*recommended*
независимый (зависеть)	*independent*

Note that present passive participles, like all other participles, have regular adjectival endings that decline for gender and number, as well as for case, when in the long form.

1. Почему ты избегаешь своих **любимых** друзей?

    Why are you avoiding your best friends?

2. Я не люблю читать работы так **называемого** отца социализма Карла Маркса.

    I don't like to read the works of the so-called father of socialism Karl Marx.

3. **Уважаемые** Сергей Ильич и Анна Михайловна! Здравствуйте!

    Respected Sergei Il'ich and Anna Mikhailovna! Greetings!

---

* For a review of short-form adjectives, see Unit 15.

4. Росси́я—одно́ из госуда́рств в Содру́жестве **незави́симых** госуда́рств.	*Russia is one of the states in the Commonwealth of Independent States.*

✳ Упражне́ние 19в

Write sentences containing each of the present passive participles listed in the chart on page 240. Try to combine them into a paragraph or letter.

 ТЕКСТ 19a

The following text by Pushkin is probably the single most memorized poem in all of Russian literature.

Pre-reading Task

The poem begins with the words *I loved you once* (*I used to love you*). How do you think it will end?

> Я вас люби́л: любо́вь ещё, быть мо́жет,
> В душе́ мое́й уга́сла[1] не совсе́м;
> Но пусть она́ вас бо́льше не трево́жит;[2]
> Я не хочу́ печа́лить[3] вас ниче́м.
> Я вас люби́л безмо́лвно, безнаде́жно,[4]
> То ро́бкостью, то ре́вностью томи́м;[5]
> Я вас люби́л так и́скренно, так не́жно,[6]
> Как дай вам Бог люби́мой быть други́м.[7]
>
> А. С. Пу́шкин, 1829

5

[1] В... *in my soul has not been extinguished*
[2] вас... *trouble you no more*
[3] *sadden*
[4] безмо́лвно... *silently, hopelessly*
[5] То... *exhausted, tormented first by timidness, then by jealousy*
[6] *so sincerely, so tenderly*
[7] Как... *May God grant you to be thus loved by someone else*

Post-reading Tasks

1. Write a two- to three-sentence summary of the poem in Russian.
2. What are the roots of the Russian verbs meaning *trouble* and *sadden*? Do you know the Russian nouns for *trouble* and *sadness*? Look them up in a dictionary.
3. What is the root of the Russian word meaning *hopelessly*? Do you know another word with this root?
4. Find two present passive participles in the poem. Define them and identify the infinitives from which they are derived. Identify any instrumental case agent (passive subject) used with either of the participles.
5. Assume the point of view of the woman to whom this poem was written and write a letter in Russian to respond.

✳ Упражне́ние 19г

Translate the following sentences into Russian.

1. Tolstoy is my favorite writer and *Anna Karenina* is my favorite novel. I often read [works of] my favorite writer.
2. She thinks that the climate in Irkutsk is unbearable.
3. The architecture in St. Petersburg is unforgettable.
4. His behavior (**поведе́ние**) is inexplicable.
5. Here is a list (**спи́сок**) of the recommended books.

✳ Упражне́ние 19д

Write three sentences in Russian using the expression **так называ́емый** (*so called*). Remember that your use of the term is ironic.

✳ Упражне́ние 19е

Write salutations using the term **уважа́емый/-ая/-ые** in formal letters to the following people: Raisa Maksimovna, Vitalii Viktorovich, and Dmitrii Pavlovich and Aleksandra Sergeevna (husband and wife).

ᕐ Зада́ние 19а

Prepare a short presentation or write a short composition on one of the following topics.

1. Э́то бы́ло неотврати́мо...
2. Он сде́лал непоправи́мую оши́бку...
3. Э́то бы́ло непостижи́мо...

PART 3

Identifying and Understanding Past Passive Participles

The past passive participle is an adjective formed from a verb. For example, the past passive participle of the verb *to do* is *done*, as in *That job is already done* in the sense that it has been *completed*. Whereas the present passive participle conveys the meaning that a condition is continuing in the present, the past passive participle indicates that an event has been completed. The key here is that past passive participles carry the inherent meaning of past tense and that the people or things the past passive participles modify are passive in the construction in which they appear.

Russian past passive participles, like present passive participles, can be formed only from transitive verbs (i.e., those verbs that take an accusative case direct object (without a preposition). For instance, **написа́ть, откры́ть, закры́ть, постро́ить, забы́ть, сде́лать, нача́ть, ко́нчить,** and **купи́ть** are all verbs of this type and have past passive participles: things can be *written* (**напи́санный**), *opened* (**откры́тый**), *closed* (**закры́тый**), *built* (**постро́енный**), *forgotten* (**забы́тый**), *made* (**сде́ланный**), *begun* (**на́чатый**), *finished* (**ко́нченный**), and *purchased* (**ку́пленный**).

Past passive participles are generally formed only from perfective verbs, because they convey the meaning of an event that has been completed in its entirety.

The key feature of the past passive participle is the letter **-н-** or **-т-** followed by an adjectival ending (short or long form). Sometimes the stress of the past passive participle differs from the stress of the verb's infinitive or conjugated forms; this will be explained later. In addition, first-conjugation verbs that undergo consonantal mutation (such as **написа́ть, с→ш: напи́шет**) do *not* show the mutation in the past passive participle (**напи́санный**), while second-conjugation verbs that undergo this kind of mutation (such as **пригласи́ть, с→ш: приглашу́; почи́стить, ст→щ: почи́щу**) *do* show the mutation (**приглашённый, почи́щенный**).

Note that past passive participles formed from verbs with the **-йти-** stem, such as **пройти́** and **найти́** have **-ден-** in the past passive participle: **найти́→на́йденный: Я прочита́ла кни́гу, на́йденную Са́шей.** (*I read the book that had been found by Sasha.*)

The past passive participles, like all other participles, have regular adjectival endings. The short-form endings decline only for gender or number (**напи́сан, напи́сана, напи́сано, напи́саны**), while the long-form endings decline for gender, number, and case.

One of the most important past passive participles for Americans is the participle *united*, **соединённый: Соединённые Шта́ты Аме́рики (США).** A slightly different verb is used for the participle *united* in the name of the United Nations: **Организа́ция Объединённых На́ций (ООН).**

Saying

Это заколдо́ванный круг!

It's a bewitched circle.
[It's a vicious circle!]

Short-form past passive participles may be used with a tense indicator—a form of **был/-а́/-о/-и** or **бу́дет/бу́дут**—when the participles are acting as subject complements. Sometimes the past passive participle is used with a logical subject in the instrumental case; the logical subject in the instrumental case is the "agent" responsible for the action. Instrumental case agents are italicized and past passive participles are boldfaced in the following examples.

1. У Ма́ши собира́ются друзья́. Я зна́ю, что среди́ **приглашённых** бу́дут и Серге́евы. — *Masha's having some friends over. I know that the Sergeevs will be among those invited.*
2. Здесь сейча́с нет газе́ты, **ку́пленной** вчера́ *мои́м бра́том*. — *The newspaper bought yesterday by my brother isn't here.*
3. Мы не нашли́ никаки́х оши́бок в пи́сьмах, **напи́санных** *на́шими студе́нтами*. — *We didn't find any mistakes in the letters written by our students.*
4. Мы говори́ли об исто́рии, **расска́занной** нам *О́лей*. — *We were talking about the story that Olia had told us (told to us by Olia).*

Упражне́ние 19ё

For each emphasized participle in examples 1 through 4, identify the antecedent with which the participle agrees. Identify the case, number, and gender of each emphasized participle. Where possible, rewrite sentences in more colloquial Russian using **кото́рый** clauses.

Упражне́ние 19ж

For each emphasized participle in examples 1 through 4, identify the agent, if there is one, in the instrumental case. Then provide the nominative case form.

RUSSIAN

Saying

Ска́зано—сде́лано.

If it's said, it's done.
[It's as good as done.]

Упражне́ние 19з

Translate the following sentences into English.

1. —Магази́н ещё откры́т?
   —Нет, магази́н уже́ давно́ закры́т!
2. —Ва́ша дома́шняя рабо́та уже́ сде́лана?
   —Коне́чно, она́ уже́ давно́ сде́лана.

3. —Вчера́ я прочита́ла о́чень интере́сную статью́, напи́санную америка́нским
учёным.

—Когда́ была́ напи́сана э́та статья́?

—Она́ была́ напи́сана в про́шлом году́.

Saying

Ломи́ться в откры́тую дверь.

To break down an already open door.
[To reinvent the wheel.]

Зада́ние 19б

Write a paragraph including one of the preceding examples.

ТЕКСТ 19б

Read the poem by Pushkin about a dried flower found in a book.

Pre-reading Task

What could a dried flower tucked away in an old book symbolize?

Цвето́к засо́хший, безуха́нный,[1]
Забы́тый в кни́ге ви́жу я;
И вот уже́ мечто́ю стра́нной[2]
Душа́ напо́лнилась моя́:[3]

5 Где цвёл[4]? когда́? како́й весно́ю?
И до́лго ль[5] цвёл? И со́рван[6] кем,
Чужо́й, знако́мой ли руко́ю?
И поло́жен[7] сюда́ заче́м?
На па́мять[8] не́жного ль свида́нья,[9]

10 И́ли разлу́ки роково́й,[10]
Иль одино́кого гуля́нья[11]
В тиши́ поле́й, в тени́ лесно́й?[12]
И жив ли тот,[13] и та жива́ ли?
И ны́нче[14] где их уголо́к[15]?

15 И́ли уже́ они́ увя́ли,[16]
Как сей[17] неве́домый[18] цвето́к?

А. С. Пу́шкин, 1828

---

[1] засо́хший... *dried, without fragrance*
[2] мечто́ю... *a strange dream*
[3] Душа́... *my soul has been filled up*
[4] *did it bloom*
[5] **ли**
[6] *plucked*
[7] *laid down, placed*
[8] На... *In memory*
[9] не́жного... *tender rendezvous*
[10] разлу́ки... *fateful parting of the ways*
[11] одино́кого... *lonely stroll*
[12] В... *in the quiet of the fields, in the shadow of the forest*
[13] И... *And is the one (m.) still living*
[14] **тепе́рь**
[15] *place*
[16] *faded*
[17] **э́тот**
[18] *unknown*

Post-reading Tasks

1. Write a three-sentence summary in Russian of the narrator's feelings upon finding the flower.
2. Find all the words that are somehow altered in order to make the meter of the poem right.
3. Find three passive participles and determine their infinitives. Translate the clauses or sentences in which they occur.
4. Write a story in Russian from the point of view of the person who put the dried flower in the book.

PART 4
Formation of Past Passive Participles

Past passive participles are common in both written and spoken Russian, and you should learn how to form them. Past passive participles are formed from the infinitive in several different ways depending on the type of infinitive. Memorize the example verbs in each section.

Past Passive Participles for Verbs Like *вы́лить, забы́ть, запере́ть, обману́ть,* and *взять*

These verbs take an ending in **-тый**.

1. verbs with monosyllabic infinitives (not counting the addition of a prefix) ending in **-ить**, such as **вы́лить** and **приши́ть**
2. verbs with monosyllabic (excluding prefixes) infinitives ending in **-ыть**, such as **помы́ть** and **забы́ть**
3. verbs with monosyllabic (excluding prefixes) infinitives ending in **-еть**, such as **наде́ть**, and with infinitives in **-ереть**, such as **запере́ть**
4. verbs with infinitives ending in **-уть**, such as **дотяну́ть** and **обману́ть**
5. verbs with infinitives ending in **-ать** or **-ять** in which the conjugated forms have inserted **-м-** or **-н-**, such as **взять** and **снять**

For verbs of these types, remove the infinitive ending, and add **-т** + the appropriate adjectival ending (according to case, number, and gender). All of these form past passive participles with the ending **-тый**; note that infinitives ending in **-ереть** often shift the stress, dropping the second vowel of the stem: **вы́литый, по́литый, помы́тый, забы́тый, наде́тый, за́пертый, дотя́нутый, обма́нутый, взя́тый, сня́тый**.

Past Passive Participles for Verbs Like *написа́ть, прочита́ть,* and *прода́ть*

These verbs take an ending in **-анный**.

All other verbs with infinitives ending in **-ать** or **-ять**, such as **де́лать** and **потеря́ть**, in which the conjugated forms do *not* have an inserted **-м-** or **-н-**, such as **взять** and **снять**, form past passive participles with the ending **-анный/-я́нный**: **сде́ланный, прочи́танный, поте́рянный, напи́санный, расска́занный, прослу́шанный, про́данный**.

Remove the infinitive ending, add **-анн** + appropriate adjectival ending, and shift the stress back one syllable if possible. (Exception: Verbs with the stress on the first syllable after the prefix and verbs with infinitives ending in **-овать/-евать** do not have such stress shifts.)

Past Passive Participles for Verbs Like *принести́, реши́ть,* and *купи́ть*

These verbs take an ending in **-енный/-ённый**.

Verbs whose infinitives end in **-ти** (**принести́, завести́,** and **найти́**) and polysyllabic verbs whose infinitives end in **-ить** (**реши́ть, бро́сить, встре́тить, купи́ть,** and **постро́ить**), and **укра́сть** form past passive participles with the ending **-енный/-ённый**. These participles have a mutation if one occurs in the **я** form: **принесённый, заведённый, на́йденный, решённый, бро́шенный, встре́ченный, ку́пленный, постро́енный, укра́денный**.

Remove the ending (**-у/-ю**) from the first-person singular (**я**) form and add **-енн** or **-ённ** + appropriate adjectival ending. (Memorize which verbs require **-енн** and which require **-ённ**.)

Past Passive Participles for Verbs Like *бере́чь*

Verbs whose infinitives end in **-чь**, such as **сбере́чь**, form past passive participles with the ending **-ённый**: **сбережённый**. For other past passive participles ending in **-енный/-ённый**, remove the ending (**-ёшь**) from the second-person singular (**ты**) form and add **ённ** + appropriate adjectival ending.

✳ Упражне́ние 19и

Review first- and second-conjugation prototypical verbs in Units 2 and 3 and determine the type of past passive participle ending the verbs will take.

✳   Упражне́ние 19й

Form the past passive participle from each of the following verbs.

1. прочита́ть
2. откры́ть
3. почи́стить
4. влюби́ть
5. рассказа́ть

6. подержа́ть
7. фотокопи́ровать
8. испе́чь
9. вы́нести
10. стере́ть

ТЕКСТ 19в

Read the excerpt from the story "Sleepwalker in the Fog" by contemporary Russian writer Tolstaia. The narrator describes a man in midlife crisis (Denisov) who longs to be remembered after his death.

Pre-reading Task

What do you think someone in a midlife crisis might worry about? What do you think might be the connection between a midlife crisis and the title of Tolstaia's story?

До полови́ны про́йдена земна́я жизнь,[1] впереди́ втора́я полови́на, ху́дшая. Вот так прошелести́т Дени́сов по земле́ и уйдёт,[2] и никто́-то его́ не помя́нет[3]! Ка́ждый день помира́ют Петро́вы и Ивано́вы,[4] их просты́е фами́лии высека́ют на мра́море.[5] Почему́ бы и Дени́сову не задержа́ться на како́й-нибудь доске́,[6] почему́ не укра́сить свои́м про́филем Оре́хово-Бори́сово[7]? «В э́том до́ме прожива́ю я...» Вот он же́нится на Ло́ре и помрёт[8]—она́ же не реши́тся обрати́ться туда́, где э́то реша́ют, увекове́чивать,[9] нет ли... «Това́рищи, увекове́чьте моего́ четвёртого му́жа, а? Ну, това́рищи...» «Хо-хо-хо...» Ну в са́мом де́ле, кто он тако́й? Ничего́ не сочини́л, не пропе́л, не вы́стрелил.[10] Ничего́ но́вого не откры́л и и́менем свои́м не назва́л.[11] Да ведь и то сказа́ть, всё уже́ откры́то, перечи́слено[12] и поимено́вано,[13] всё, и живо́е и мёртвое,[14] от тарака́нов[15] до коме́т, от сы́рной пле́сени[16] до спира́льных рукаво́в зау́мных тума́нностей.[17] Вон како́й-нибудь ви́рус—дрянь,[18] дешёвка,[19] от него́ и ку́рица не чихнёт,[20] так нет, уже́ по́йман[21], на́зван, усыновлён па́рочкой[22] учёных не́мцев—смотри́ сего́дняшнюю газе́ту. Призаду́маешься—как они́ его́ де́лят на двои́х[23]?

Т. В. Толста́я, «Сомна́мбула в тума́не», 1989

[1] До... *life on earth is half over*
[2] Вот... *That's how Denisov will stroll the earth and leave*
[3] *remember, recall*
[4] Ка́ждый... *Every day Petrovs and Ivanovs die*
[5] их... *their simple names are carved in marble*
[6] Почему́... *Why shouldn't Denisov's name remain on some stone?*
[7] почему́... *why shouldn't the Orekhovo-Borisovo neighborhood be decorated with his profile?*
[8] *die*
[9] *memorialize, immortalize*
[10] Ничего́... *He didn't create anything, sing anything, shoot anything*
[11] и́менем... *didn't name anything after himself*
[12] *counted*
[13] *named*
[14] *alive and dead*
[15] *cockroaches*
[16] сы́рной... *cheese mold*
[17] спира́льных... *spiralling branches of the abstruse mists*
[18] *garbage*
[19] *something cheap*
[20] от... *from which even a chicken wouldn't sneeze*
[21] *caught*
[22] усыновлён... *adopted by a pair*
[23] как... *how will they split it up?*

Post-reading Tasks

1. Summarize the text in three sentences in Russian.
2. Find five past passive participles by looking for adjectives with **-н-** or **-т-**. Use a dictionary, if necessary, to determine from what infinitive they are derived. Identify the case they are in and what they mean in the given context.
3. What are the roots for the Russian words meaning *listed* and *named*? What other words do you know with those roots?
4. Write an epitaph for Denisov or write a paragraph from the perspective of Lora (his fiancée) about what she would do when he dies.

RUSSIAN

Saying

Вот где соба́ка зары́та!

Here's where the dog is buried!
(Here's the point, the most important idea!)

Упражне́ние 19к

Continue your list of all the "connecting" words and phrases (such as *because*, *but*, *in the first place*, *then*, and so forth) with those you can find in the texts of this unit. Next to each "connecting" word or phrase, write out the clause or sentence in which they are used. Keep this list in your notebook and add to it as you continue with this book.

Упражне́ние 19л

Add the verbs of this unit to your lists of first- and second-conjugation verbs, noting the stress pattern of each verb as you do so.

Упражне́ние 19м

Write out the present and past passive participle forms for three different verbs for each of the prototypes presented in Units 2 and 3.

Active Participles
Действи́тельные прича́стия

Они́ охраня́ют ве́чный ого́нь.

PART 1
Identifying and Understanding Present Active Participles

Like the passive participle, the present active participle* is an adjective formed from a verb. The main point is that these forms carry the inherent meaning of the present tense and that the things or people the present active participles modify are active in the construction in which they appear. For example, the present active participle of the verb *to read* is *reading, reads* or (*the one/s*) *which/who is/are reading*. Present active participles either replace a **который** clause or serve as substantives (that is, act as nouns themselves).

1.	Вот челове́к, **говоря́щий** по-францу́зски.	*There's a person who speaks French.*
2.	В на́шем институ́те о́чень нужны́ **говоря́щие** по-францу́зски.	*Our institute really needs some speakers of French.*

Example 1 can be reworded without a participle as follows: **Вот челове́к, кото́рый говори́т по-францу́зски.** In example 2, the participle is a substantive modifying the implied word *people*.

The key identifying feature of the present active participle is the letter **-щ-**, which must occur in every form of the present active participle; for example, **говоря́щий** (*one who speaks*), **слу́жащий** (*one who serves or works, an employee*), **выдаю́щийся** (*one who is outstanding*), **уча́щийся** (*one who studies, a student at any educational level*). Note that reflexive verbs (verbs ending in **-ся**) can form present active participles, and their reflexive endings will always be **-ся** in every form of the present active participle, even when this ending is preceded by a vowel.

3.	Вчера́ мы поговори́ли с но́вой студе́нткой, **говоря́щей** по-ру́сски.	*Yesterday we had a chat with the new student, who speaks Russian.*

The present active participle in example 3 introduces a participial clause set off by commas: Note that the words *people, person* and *who* are omitted in the Russian construction.

4.	Мы говори́ли о **жела́ющих** пое́хать в Чика́го.	*We were talking about the people who want to go to Chicago.*

The present active participle in example 4 is used as a substantive: Note that the words *people who* are omitted in the Russian construction.

---

* Sometimes called verbal adjectives.

Упражне́ние 20a

Identify the case and gender of the boldfaced participles in examples 1 through 4. Then identify the word the participle modifies. (Note: The participle may modify an implied noun.) Rewrite the examples using **кото́рый**, **все/кто**, or **те/кто** clauses to eliminate the participles.

Saying

RUSSIAN

Утопа́ющий за соло́минку хвата́ется.

A drowning man will grasp for a straw.

 Упражне́ние 20б

Translate the following sentences into English.

1. Мы уви́димся на сле́дующей неде́ле.
2. Ско́лько в ва́шем университе́те уча́щихся?
3. На э́том заво́де о́чень нужны́ говоря́щие по-англи́йски.
4. Пу́шкин, Ле́рмонтов, Го́голь—выдаю́щиеся ру́сские писа́тели пе́рвой полови́ны девятна́дцатого ве́ка.
5. Ка́тя—бу́дущий фи́зик. Хотя́ ей то́лько 15 лет, уже́ ви́дно, что она́ о́чень спосо́бная.
6. Э́тот курс—специа́льно для боя́щихся лета́ть.

ТЕКСТ 20a

Read the excerpt from Gogol's short story "Nevskii Prospect." The narrator is gushing with enthusiasm as he describes the different people (especially their feet and shoes) who walk upon Nevsky Prospect, the most important thoroughfare in St. Petersburg.

Pre-reading Task

Nevsky Prospect is St. Petersburg's most important street. You may have already read about it elsewhere or earlier in this book in Unit 7 in the excerpt from Belyi's novel, *Petersburg*. Take a moment to write down three or four ideas or images you have associated with this street.

...Всемогу́щий[1] Не́вский проспе́кт! Еди́нственное развлече́ние бе́дного на гуля́нье Петербу́рга![2] Как чи́сто подметены́ его́ тротуа́ры,[3] и, Бо́же, ско́лько ног оста́вило на нём следы́ свои́[4]! И неуклю́жий гря́зный сапо́г[5] отставно́го

[1] *All-powerful*
[2] Еди́нственное... *The only entertainment for a poor person in Petersburg*
[3] Как... *How well swept are its sidewalks*
[4] ско́лько... *how many feet have left their traces on it!*
[5] неуклю́жий... *the clumsy filthy boot*

5   солда́та, под тя́жестью кото́рого, ка́жется, тре́скается[6] са́мый
гранит, и миниатю́рный, лёгкий, как дым, башмачо́к[7]
моло́денькой да́мы, обора́чивающей свою́ голо́вку к
блестя́щим[8] о́кнам магази́на, как подсо́лнечник[9] к со́лнцу, и
гремя́щая са́бля испо́лненного надёжд пра́порщика,[10]
10   проводя́щая по нём ре́зкую цара́пину,[11]—всё вымеща́ет на
нём могу́щество си́лы и́ли могу́щество сла́бости.[12] Кака́я
бы́страя соверша́ется на нём фантасмаго́рия в тече́ние
одного́ то́лько дня![13]

Н. В. Го́голь, «Не́вский проспе́кт», 1834

[6] *cracks*
[7] *sandal, light shoe*
[8] *sparkling, glistening*
[9] *sunflower*
[10] гремя́щая... *ensign full of hopes crashing his saber*
[11] ре́зкую... *sharp scratch*
[12] вымеща́ет... *vents, wreaks on it the power of force or power of weakness*
[13] Кака́я... *What rapid phantasmagoria unfolds on it in the course of only a single day!*

Post-reading Tasks

1. Write a five-sentence summary of the text.
2. Compare the depiction of Petersburg and Nevsky Prospect in this text to the depiction of these places in **Текст 7б**.
3. Find several present active participles in the text. Identify the infinitive for each one and identify the noun with which the participle agrees in gender and number.
4. Determine if there are any passive participles. Identify the infinitive for each one and the noun with which the participle agrees in gender and number.
5. Write a description of your own main street (in the city where your school is located or in your hometown), using Gogol's excerpt as a model.

Saying

Из ря́да вон выходя́щий.

Standing out from the row.
[*It's outstanding.*]

PART 2
Formation of
Present Active Participles

The formation of present active participles is easy. Study the following steps and examples. Note that these participles are derived from imperfective verbs only, because they carry the inherent meaning of the present tense.

STEPS		EXAMPLES	
1.	Use the third-person plural (**они́**) form of the verb	сле́дуют (*they follow*)	у́чатся (*they study*)
2.	Drop the final **-т**.	сле́дую-	уча-... ся
3.	Add **-щ.-**	сле́дующ-	учащ-... ся
4.	Add the regular adjectival ending, declined for case, gender and number.	сле́дующий (-ая/-ее/-ие)	уча́щийся
5.	Check the stress: It may be as in the infinitive or the third-person plural form of the verb.	сле́дующий (*the following one*)	уча́щийся (*one who studies, a student at any level*)

- Note the difference in stress between the infinitive **учи́ться** and the third-person plural form **у́чатся** and that the stress in this participle is the same as that in the infinitive. This is not always the case; for example, **служи́ть** (*to work, to be employed*), but **слу́жащий**.
- Note that participles derived from reflexive verbs continue to have the reflexive particle **-ся** in all declension endings (never **-сь**); for example, **уча́щаяся**, **уча́щиеся**, **уча́щуюся**, even though according to the rules of conjugation you would expect **-сь** to follow vowels.
- There is no present active particle from the verb **хоте́ть**; to create the form *is wanting or wants*, use **жела́ть** (**жела́ющий**). Similarly, there is no present active particle for the verb **ждать**; to create the form *is waiting or expecting*, use **ожида́ть** (**ожида́ющий**).

The key feature of the present active participle is the letter **-щ-** and a regular adjectival ending declined for case, gender, and number (in long form only).

Present active participles may replace **кото́рый** clauses and may be used as adjectives modifying nouns (in which case they will precede the nouns they modify). Present active participles may also be used as substantives (modifying the implied words *person* or *people*). Here are some commonly used present active participles.

PARTICIPLE (INFINITIVE)	MEANING OF PARTICIPLE
бу́дущий (быть)	*future*
говоря́щий (говори́ть)	*speaks, is speaking*
жела́ющий (жела́ть)	*wants, desires*
начина́ющий (начина́ть)	*begins, is beginning*
приезжа́ющий (приезжа́ть)	*arrives, is arriving*
продолжа́ющий (продолжа́ть)	*continues, is continuing*
сле́дующий (сле́довать)	*following, next*
слу́жащий (служи́ть)	*serves*
уезжа́ющий (уезжа́ть)	*departs, is departing*
уча́щийся (учи́ться)	*studies, is studying*
выдаю́щийся (выдава́ться)	*outstanding*
ожида́ющий (ожида́ть)	*waits, is waiting*

PARTICIPLE (INFINITIVE)	MEANING OF PARTICIPLE
трéбующий (трéбовать)	*demands, is demanding*
находя́щийся (находи́ться)	*is located*
иду́щий (идти́)	*is going*
пью́щий/непью́щий (пить)	*drinks, is drinking/is a teetotaler*
куря́щий (кури́ть)	*smokes, is smoking*
блестя́щий (блестéть)	*sparkling, glistening*
гремя́щий (гремéть)	*thundering, crashing*
потряса́ющий (потряса́ть)	*shocking, stunning*
веду́щий (вести́)	*leading (most important)*
соотвéтствующий (соотвéтствовать)	*corresponds, corresponding*

✳ Упражнéние 20в

In the following sentences, create present active participles from the infinitives. Remember to make certain that the participle agrees in gender, case, and number with the noun it modifies or the antecedent to which it refers. Then rewrite the sentences in more colloquial Russian, using **котóрый**, **все/кто**, and **те/кто** clauses.

1. Лю́ди, (сидéть) _____ на стрóгой диéте, ча́сто жа́луются, что им хóчется есть.
2. (Учи́ться) _____ в э́том институ́те стано́вятся врача́ми и мéдиками.
3. У мои́х друзéй, (жить) _____ в Нóвгороде, родила́сь дóчка.
4. Скóлько здесь (жела́ть) _____ пойти́ в кинó сегóдня вéчером? Идёт интерéсный фильм!
5. Преподава́тель сказа́л, что емý нра́вится рабóтать с (начина́ть) _____.

𝄞 Зада́ние 20а

Pick one of the sentences in the preceding exercise and use it as the beginning of a short presentation. Try to use as many different present active participles as you can. Refer to the list of commonly used present active participles.

 ТЕКСТ 20б

Lermontov's poem, "The Dream," is set in far-off Dagestan and in St. Petersburg.

Pre-reading Task

What might a poem with this title and these two settings have to do with one another and with the title?

Сон

В полдне́вный жар в доли́не Дагеста́на[1]
С свинцо́м в груди́[2] лежа́л недви́жим[3] я;
Глубо́кая ещё дыми́лась ра́на,[4]
По ка́пле кровь точи́лася моя́.[5]

5   Лежа́л оди́н я на песке́[6] доли́ны;
Усту́пы скал тесни́лися круго́м,[7]
И со́лнце жгло их жёлтые верши́ны[8]
И жгло меня́—но спал я мёртвым сном.[9]

И сни́лся мне[10] сия́ющий огня́ми
10   Вече́рний пир в роди́мой стороне́.[11]
Меж ю́ных жён, увенчанных цвета́ми,[12]
Шёл разгово́р весёлый обо мне.

Но, в разгово́р весёлый не вступа́я,[13]
Сиде́ла там заду́мчиво[14] одна́,
15   И в гру́стный сон[15] душа́ её млада́я
Бог зна́ет чем была́ погружена́;[16]

И сни́лась ей доли́на Дагеста́на:
Знако́мый труп[17] лежа́л в доли́не той;
В его́ груди́, дымя́сь, черне́ла ра́на,[18]
20   И кровь лила́сь хладе́ющей струёй.[19]

М. Ю. Ле́рмонтов, 1841

[1] В... *In the midday sun in a valley in Dagestan*
[2] С... *With a bullet in my chest*
[3] *unmoving*
[4] Глубо́кая... *My deep wound still steamed*
[5] По... *my blood wasted away drop by drop*
[6] на... *on the sands*
[7] Усту́пы... *the sides of the cliffs crowded in around me*
[8] со́лнце... *the sun burned their yellow peaks*
[9] спал... *I slept a sleep of death*
[10] сни́лся... *I saw in my dream*
[11] Вече́рний... *an evening feast in my home land*
[12] Меж... *Among young women, decked with flowers*
[13] в... *without entering into the merry conversation*
[14] *engrossed in thought*
[15] в... *Into a sad revery*
[16] Бог... *God only knows with what her soul was carried away*
[17] Знако́мый... *familiar corpse*
[18] черне́ла... *the wound grew black*
[19] кровь... *the blood poured out in a stream that was growing cold*

Post-reading Tasks

1. Write a two- or three-sentence summary of the text in Russian.
2. What are the roots of the Russian words meaning *familiar, midday, engrossed in thought*? Do you know any other words with these roots?
3. Find the active participles and identify the infinitives from which they are derived.
4. Find the passive participles (both past and present passive) and identify their infinitives.
5. Write a short story in Russian that retells this story, but cast it in another time or place, for example, Chechnia or Bosnia in the 1990s.

Identifying and Understanding Past Active Participles

The past active participle is also an adjective formed from a verb. For example, the past active participle of the verb *to do* is *did*, or *was, were doing*. The past active participle **сде́лавший**, formed from the perfective verb **сде́лать**, means *did*, while the past active participle **де́лавший**, formed from the imperfective verb **де́лать**, means *was, were doing*. Note the aspectual differences in the meaning of the following pairs of participles.

сказа́вший	*said*
говори́вший	*was saying, used to talk or say*
научи́вшийся	*learned (to do something)*
учи́вшийся	*studied*

The most important point here is that these forms carry the inherent meaning of past tense and that the things or people the participles modify are active in the constructions in which they appear. The key identifying feature of the past active participle is the letter **-ш-**, which occurs in all forms of the past active participle.

Past active participles may replace **кото́рый** clauses and may serve as substantives (though less frequently than present active participles).

1. Ско́лько бы́ло **пожела́вших** пойти́ в кино́ вчера́ ве́чером?   *How many people wanted to go to the movies last night?*

In this example, the participle stands for the implied word *people*.

Also note that reflexive verbs (verbs ending in **-ся**) can form past active participles, and their reflexive ending is always **-ся** in every form of the past active participle, even when this ending is preceded by a vowel, such as **верну́вшиеся**.

2. Вчера́ ве́чером мы поговори́ли с на́шими **бы́вшими** профессора́ми, **прие́хавшими** из Москвы́.   *Yesterday evening we chatted with our former professors, who had returned from Moscow.*

3. Студе́нты, **верну́вшиеся** во вто́рник из Ирку́тска, уста́ли, но бы́ли о́чень ра́ды нас ви́деть.   *The students who had returned on Tuesday from Irkutsk were tired, but were very glad to see us.*

4. Мы ви́дели же́нщину, **говори́вшую** с Алёшей.   *We saw the woman who was talking with Alesha.*

5. Мы ви́дели же́нщину, **сказа́вшую** Алёше, что она́ ушла́ от му́жа.   *We saw the woman who told Alesha that she had left her husband.*

❇ Упражне́ние 20г

Identify the antecedent, case, gender, and number of each boldfaced participle in examples 1 through 5. Where possible, rewrite the sentences in more colloquial Russian using **кото́рый** clauses.

❇ Упражне́ние 20д

Translate the following sentences into English.

1. Вчера́ мы поговори́ли с инжене́рами, прие́хавшими из Владивосто́ка.
2. Уста́вший от дли́нного разгово́ра инжене́р сказа́л, что его́ рабо́та ещё не напи́сана.
3. Э́тот же инжене́р, сказа́вший, что он о́чень уста́л, пошёл к себе́ в ко́мнату и лёг спать.
4. Инжене́р, уше́дший к себе́ в ко́мнату, хорошо́ говори́т по-англи́йски. Жаль, что он не оста́лся вме́сте с на́ми.
5. Лари́са Па́вловна, сама́ уе́хавшая из Владивосто́ка, сказа́ла, что верну́вшаяся в э́тот го́род эмигра́нтка о́чень дово́льна но́вой жи́знью там.

§ Зада́ние 20б

Continue the story begun in the preceding exercise (or create your own story) using as many past active participles as you can.

❇ Упражне́ние 20е

Many place names in the former Soviet Union have been changed as part of a campaign to restore historical names and remove those names honoring Communist heroes and mythology no longer in favor. Use the partial list of such name changes to create sentences following the model. Then try to find as many of the streets as you can on the maps of Moscow and St. Petersburg (found after the Prefaces).

ОБРАЗЕ́Ц: Охо́тный ряд—Проспе́кт Ма́ркса →

Охо́тный ряд? Э́то бы́вший проспе́кт Ма́ркса.
Hunter's Row? That's the former Marx Prospect.

МОСКВА́		САНКТ-ПЕТЕРБУ́РГ	
ТРАДИЦИО́ННОЕ НАЗВА́НИЕ	СОВЕ́ТСКОЕ НАЗВА́НИЕ	ТРАДИЦИО́ННОЕ НАЗВА́НИЕ	СОВЕ́ТСКОЕ НАЗВА́НИЕ
Тверска́я у́лица	у́лица Го́рького	Горо́ховая у́лица	у́лица Дзержи́нского
Театра́льная пло́щадь	Пло́щадь Свердло́ва	Больша́я Коню́шенная у́лица	у́лица Желя́бова

МОСКВА		САНКТ-ПЕТЕРБУ́РГ	
ТРАДИЦИО́ННОЕ НАЗВА́НИЕ	СОВЕ́ТСКОЕ НАЗВА́НИЕ	ТРАДИЦИО́ННОЕ НАЗВА́НИЕ	СОВЕ́ТСКОЕ НАЗВА́НИЕ
Лубя́нская пло́щадь	пло́щадь Дзержи́нского	Каменно-остро́вский проспе́кт	Ки́ровский проспе́кт
Мане́жная пло́щадь	Пло́щадь Пятидесяти-ле́тия октября́	Тро́ицкая пло́щадь	пло́щадь Револю́ции
Патриа́ршие пруды́	Пионе́рские пруды́	Ко́нногварде́йский бульва́р	бульва́р Профсою́зов
Но́вый Арба́т	Кали́нинский проспе́кт	Благове́щенская пло́щадь	пло́щадь Труда́

✳ Упражне́ние 20ё

Practice using these place names and the past active participle **бы́вший** (*former*) in the prepositional case construction shown in the model. Remember that the word **пло́щадь** is feminine (**на пло́щади**).

ОБРАЗЕ́Ц: Э́тот магази́н нахо́дится на... →

Э́тот магази́н нахо́дится на Охо́тном ряду́, то есть на **бы́вшем** проспе́кте Ма́ркса.
This store is on Hunter's Row, that is, on the former Marx Prospect.

𝄞 Зада́ние 20в

Prepare a short presentation or composition explaining where to buy a number of items for a party in either St. Petersburg or Moscow. Give the location of the different stores using both old and new place names.

✳ Упражне́ние 20ж

Now use this list of some of the major cities and places in Russia and the former Soviet Union whose names have changed to create sentences following the models (see the maps after the Prefaces).

ТРАДИЦИО́ННОЕ НАЗВА́НИЕ	СОВЕ́ТСКОЕ НАЗВА́НИЕ
Ни́жний Но́вгород	Го́рький
Тверь	Кали́нин
Екатеринбу́рг	Свердло́вск
Санкт-Петербу́рг	Ленингра́д

ТРАДИЦИО́ННОЕ НАЗВА́НИЕ	СОВЕ́ТСКОЕ НАЗВА́НИЕ
Содру́жество незави́симых госуда́рств; Росси́йская Федера́ция (РФ)	Сове́тский Сою́з; Росси́йская Сове́тская Федерати́вная Социалисти́ческая Респу́блика (РСФСР)
Сама́ра	Ку́йбышев

ОБРАЗЕ́Ц: Тверь—Кали́нин →
Тверь? Это **бы́вший** Кали́нин.

ОБРАЗЕ́Ц: Они́ родили́сь... →
Они́ родили́сь в Твери́, то есть в **бы́вшем** Кали́нине.

§ Зада́ние 20г

Prepare a biography of a fictitious man or woman who lived in many of the places listed in the preceding exercise. Be sure to include both old and new names for each place you mention.

ТЕКСТ 20в

Read the excerpt from L. N. Tolstoy's novel *War and Peace*. Fifteen-year-old Petia Rostov is going to see the tsar at a public rally in the Kremlin not long before the fall of Moscow to Napoleon.

Pre-reading Task

What do you think would take place at a public rally for the tsar on the eve of Napoleon's invasion of Russia?

Пе́тя отёр[1] рука́ми пот,[2] покрыва́вший его́ лицо́, и попра́вил размочи́вшиеся[3] от по́та воротнички́,[4] кото́рые он так хорошо́, как у больши́х,[5] устро́ил[6] до́ма.

5 Пе́тя чу́вствовал, что он име́ет непрезента́бельный вид, и боя́лся, что е́жели таки́м он предста́вится камерге́рам,[7] то его́ не допу́стят до госуда́ря.[8] Но опра́виться и перейти́ в друго́е ме́сто не́ было никако́й возмо́жности от тесноты́.[9] Оди́н из проезжа́вших

10 генера́лов был знако́мый Росто́вых. Пе́тя хоте́л проси́ть его́ по́мощи, но счёл,[10] что э́то бы́ло бы проти́вно му́жеству.[11] Когда́ все экипа́жи[12] прое́хали, толпа́ хлы́нула[13] и вы́несла и Пе́тю на пло́щадь, кото́рая была́ вся занята́ наро́дом.[14] Не то́лько по

[1] *wiped away*
[2] *sweat*
[3] **размочи́ться** *(to become wet)*
[4] *collars*
[5] как... *like the grownups do it*
[6] *had set up*
[7] е́жели... *if he were to present himself looking like this to the gentlemen in attendance*
[8] то... *they would never let him see the emperor*
[9] опра́виться... *Because of the crowd there was no possibility of straightening himself up there or of going to another place*
[10] *believed*
[11] проти́вно... *wouldn't have been manly*
[12] *carriages*
[13] толпа́... *crowd gushed forth*
[14] пло́щадь... *the square, which was full of people*

15 пло́щади, но на отко́сах, на кры́шах, везде́[15] был наро́д.
Только что Пе́тя очути́лся на пло́щади, он я́вственно
услыха́л[16] наполня́вшие[17] весь Кремль зву́ки
колоколо́в[18] и ра́достного наро́дного го́вора.[19]

Одно́ вре́мя на пло́щади бы́ло просто́рнее,[20] но
20 вдруг все го́ловы откры́лись, всё бро́силось ещё куда́-
то вперёд.[21] Пе́тю сдави́ли так,[22] что он не мог
дыша́ть,[23] и всё закрича́ло: «Ура́! урра́! ура́!» Пе́тя
поднима́лся на цы́почки, толка́лся, щипа́лся, но ничего́
не мог ви́деть, кро́ме наро́да вокру́г себя́.[24]

25 ...в э́то вре́мя толпа́ заколеба́лась наза́д[25] (спе́реди
полице́йские отта́лкивали[26] надви́нувшихся[27] сли́шком
бли́зко к ше́ствию;[28] госуда́рь проходи́л из дворца́ в
Успе́нский собо́р), и Пе́тя неожи́данно получи́л в бок
тако́й уда́р по рёбрам[29] и так был прида́влен,[30] что
30 вдруг в глаза́х его́ всё помути́лось[31] и он потеря́л
созна́ние.[32] Когда́ он пришёл в себя́,[33] како́е-то
духо́вное лицо́,[34] с пучко́м седе́вших[35] воло́с наза́ди,[36] в
потёртой си́ней ря́се,[37] вероя́тно, дьячо́к,[38] одно́й руко́й
держа́л его́ под мы́шку,[39] друго́й охраня́л[40] от
35 напира́вшей[41] толпы́.

Л. Н. Толсто́й, «Война́ и мир», 1869

[15] на... *on the slopes (next to the square), on the rooftops; everywhere*
[16] То́лько... *As soon as Petia got to the square, he clearly heard*
[17] **наполня́ть** *(to fill up)*
[18] зву́ки... *sounds of bells*
[19] ра́достного... *joyful speech of the people (language used by common people)*
[20] *more spacious*
[21] всё... *everything rushed forward somewhere*
[22] Пе́тю... *Petia was squeezed or crushed*
[23] *breathe*
[24] поднима́лся... *stood on his tiptoes, pushed, shoved, but he couldn't see anything but the people around him*
[25] в... *at that time the crowd swept backward*
[26] спе́реди... *in front (from the front) the police pushed back*
[27] **надви́нуться** *(to approach, to move forward on)*
[28] сли́шком... *too close to the procession (of the tsar)*
[29] уда́р... *a blow to the ribs*
[30] *crushed*
[31] всё... *everything became dark*
[32] потеря́л... *lost consciousness*
[33] Когда́... *When he came to*
[34] како́е-то... *some kind of cleric (clergyman)*
[35] **седе́ть** *(to gray)*
[36] *gathered up in the back*
[37] потёртой... *worn out blue cassock (worn by Russian Orthodox clerics)*
[38] *sexton*
[39] держа́л... *held him under his arm*
[40] *was protecting (him)*
[41] **напира́ть** *(to press [forward])*

Post-reading Tasks

1. Write a three-sentence summary of the text in Russian.
2. Find five past active participles by looking for adjectives with **-ш-**. Use a dictionary, if necessary, to determine from what infinitive they are derived. Then identify their case and what they mean in context.
3. Look for any passive participles and determine their infinitives and the nouns they modify.
4. Write a description in Russian of a young person in trouble in a crowd in America today (at a sporting event or a rock concert). Use Tolstoy's excerpt as a model.

PART 4
Formation of
Past Active Participles

The formation of past active participles is relatively simple. Study the following steps and examples. Note that these participles are derived from both perfective and imperfective verbs according to the aspectual meaning required by context.

Verbs with Infinitives Ending in *-ть*

	STEPS		EXAMPLES
		писа́ть	написа́ть
1.	Drop the infinitive ending.	писа́-	написа́-
2.	Add -вш-.	писа́вш-	написа́вш-
3.	Add the regular ending, declined for case, gender, and number.	писа́вший (-ая/-ее/-ие) (*was writing*)	написа́вший (*wrote*)

Verbs Without *-л-* in Masculine Past Tense: *нести́, умере́ть, везти́*

	STEPS		EXAMPLES
1.	Take the masculine past-tense form.	нёс	у́мер
2.	Add -ш-.	нёсш-	у́мерш-
3.	Add the appropriate adjectival ending for case, gender, and number	нёсшая (*was carrying*)	уме́ршие (*died, dead*)

Verbs with *-сти* Stems That Have *-л-* in Masculine Past Tense: *вести́, цвести́*

	STEPS		EXAMPLES
1.	Take the infinitive and remove the -сти.	вести́ ве-	цвести́ цве-
2.	Add -дш- or -тш- (memorize which verb takes which infix).	ве́дш-	цве́тш-
3.	Add the appropriate adjectival ending for case, gender, and number.	ве́дший (*was leading*)	цве́тший (*bloomed*)

Exception: **идти́** and all prefixed forms of this verb (**прийти́, уйти́,** and so forth) take a past active participle in **ше́дший: прише́дший, уше́дший**.

- The key feature of all these forms is -ш-. When you see this letter in participial form, you know that the participle is a past active participle.
- As was the case with present active participles, past active participles derived from reflexive verbs retain the reflexive particle -ся ending in all forms, even in those in which you might otherwise expect -сь to follow vowels; for instance, **верну́вшиеся, удиви́вшаяся**.

Past active participles are also sometimes used as adjectives modifying nouns (in which case they precede the nouns they modify) or as substantives (implicitly modifying the word *person* or *people*). They may begin a participial clause separated from the main clause by commas. Here are some commonly used past active participles.

PARTICIPLE	MEANING
бы́вший (быть)	*former, previous*
верну́вшийся (верну́ться)	*returned*
говори́вший (говори́ть)	*was talking*
отда́вший (отда́ть)	*gave away*
приня́вший (приня́ть)	*received, took*
прие́хавший (прие́хать)	*arrived*
проше́дший (пройти́)	*went by, past*
сказа́вший (сказа́ть)	*said*
сумасше́дший (с ума́ сойти́)	*crazy, insane*
уше́дший (уйти́)	*went away*

✳ Упражне́ние 20з

Provide the correct past active participle with the appropriate ending, given the context. Rewrite the sentences into more colloquial Russian using **кото́рый** clauses.

1. Я сказа́ла подру́ге, (позвони́ть) _____ мне по телефо́ну, что О́ля тут.
2. Я наде́юсь, что меха́ник смо́жет почини́ть маши́ну, (слома́ться) _____ взера́.
3. Я не зна́ю челове́ка, (откры́ть) _____ две́рь.
4. А́ня хорошо́ знако́ма с профе́ссором, (прочита́ть) _____ ле́кцию о Толсто́м.
5. Па́вел не узна́л своего́ дру́га, (верну́ться) _____ в Петербу́рг.

§ Зада́ние 20д

Use one of the sentences in the preceding exercise to begin a story. Try to use as many past active participles as possible.

PART 5
Review of Passive and Active Participles

	PRESENT	PAST
PASSIVE	-м- люби́мый уважа́емый невыноси́мый незабыва́емый	-т-, -н- ска́занный откры́тый напи́санный забы́тый
ACTIVE	-щ- говоря́щий жела́ющий подходя́щий уча́щийся	-ш- сказа́вший откры́вший верну́вшийся прише́дший

❉   Упражнéние 20и

Insert the past active, present active, or past passive participle as required by context. Look for clues for tense or time to determine whether to use the past or present active participle. Rewrite the sentences into more colloquial Russian using **котóрый** clauses.

1. В университéте я говорúла с профéссором, недáвно (приéхать) _____ из Росси́и.
2. Мы недáвно получúли письмó от сестры́, (жить) _____ в Петербýрге.
3. Вы не знáете студéнта, (сидéть) _____ в пéрвом рядý?
4. Мы говорúли о мáльчике, мéдленно (идтú) _____ по ýлице.
5. Óля хорошó знáет журналúста, (написáть) _____ на прóшлой недéле интерéсную статью́ о Самáре.

❉   Упражнéние 20й

Provide the correct participle (past active, present active, past passive, present passive) with the appropriate ending, given the context and the English cues. Where possible, rewrite the sentences in more colloquial Russian using **котóрый** clauses.

1. Нáши друзья́, Пóли и Бил, (who returned) _____ недáвно из Еврóпы, подарúли нам э́ти красúвые сувенúры.
2. Онú бы́ли в нéкоторых (former) _____ социалистúческих странáх: в Болгáрии, в Пóльше, в Чéхии. Мы бы́ли у них вчерá вéчером, и онú мнóго расскáзывали о своём путешéствии по центрáльной Еврóпе.
3. Пóли, (who had given away) _____ в Пóльше все свой пластúнки и кассéты, котóрые онá взялá с собóй из Амéрики, сказáла, что онá купúла хорóшие пóльские пластúнки и что ей óчень нрáвится пóльская мýзыка.
4. Бил сказáл, что егó женá (crazy) _____, потомý что он не лю́бит пóльскую мýзыку.
5. Егó (favorite) _____ музыкáльная традúция—америкáнский джаз.
6. Бил сказáл, что их (next) _____ поéздка бýдет в Нóвый Орлеáн, где онú смóгут слýшать хорóший джаз.
7. Карл, недáвно (who left) _____ из э́того гóрода, сказáл, что там действúтельно хорóший джаз.
8. Пóли сказáла, что ей не хóчется éхать в (so called) _____ «столúцу джáза».
9. Онá говорúла о (ones who want, desire) _____ поéхать вмéсте с ней в (next/future) _____ годý в Парúж.
10. «К сожалéнию», сказáла Пóли, «агéнтство путешéствий сейчáс (closed) _____, а то я бы немéдленно позвонúла!»

❉   Упражнéние 20к

Translate the following sentences and identify the type of participle, using the preceding summary chart if you find it helpful. Note that some sentences may have more than one participle! Where possible, rewrite sentences in more colloquial Russian using **кото́рый** clauses.

1. Ско́лько бы́ло в ва́шей гру́ппе жела́ющих пойти́ в кино́?
2. Фёдоров о́чень изве́стный писа́тель: он оди́н из мои́х са́мых люби́мых писа́телей.
3. Я не зна́ю же́нщину, закры́вшую окно́, разби́тое вчера́ Са́шей.
4. Ру́сская грамма́тика соверше́нно невыноси́мая!
5. Но́вый уче́бник, напи́санный на́шим профе́ссором, не понра́вился студе́нтам, верну́вшимся из Росси́и.

✳ Упражне́ние 20л

Review two texts in any earlier unit in this book and find as many passive and active participles as you can. For each participle you find, identify its infinitive and the noun it modifies. Then translate the clause or sentence in which the participle occurs.

✳ Упражне́ние 20м

Continue your list of all the "connecting" words and phrases (such as *because*, *but*, *in the first place*, *then*, and so forth) with those you can find in the texts of this unit. Next to each "connecting" word or phrase, write out the clause or sentence in which they are used. Keep this list in your notebook and add to it as you continue with this book.

✳ Упражне́ние 20н

Add the verbs of this unit to your lists of first- and second-conjugation verbs, noting the stress pattern of each verb as you do so.

Verbal Adverbs

Дееприча́стия

Как хорошо́, когда́ име́ется
компью́тер!

Identifying and Understanding Verbal Adverbs

Whereas participles (verbal adjectives) are adjectives derived from verbs, verbal adverbs are adverbs derived from verbs.* Verbal adverbs come in two types, imperfective and perfective, and have different meanings accordingly. For example, the verbal adverb of the imperfective verb *to do* is *while doing*. The verbal adverb of the perfective verb *to do* is *having done*.

These forms are rarely used in colloquial speech, but are fairly frequent in writing and in formal speeches. Not all verbs have verbal adverbs.† Note that examples 4 and 7 convey the same idea as examples 1 and 6 respectively, but *without* a verbal adverb.

1.	Она́ пи́шет свою́ рабо́ту, **слу́шая** ра́дио.	*She writes her work while listening to the radio.*
2.	Она́ бу́дет писа́ть свою́ рабо́ту, **слу́шая** ра́дио.	*She will write her work while listening to the radio.*
3.	Она́ писа́ла свою́ рабо́ту, **слу́шая** ра́дио.	*She was writing her work while listening to the radio.*
4.	Когда́ она́ пи́шет свою́ рабо́ту, она́ слу́шает ра́дио.	*While she writes her work she listens to the radio.*
5.	**Посмотре́в** переда́чу, она́ напи́шет свою́ рабо́ту.	*Having watched the program, she will write her work.*
6.	**Посмотре́в** переда́чу, она́ написа́ла свою́ рабо́ту.	*Having watched the program, she wrote out (completed) her work.*
7.	По́сле того́, как она́ посмотре́ла переда́чу, она́ написа́ла свою́ рабо́ту.	*After she watched the program, she wrote out (completed) her work.*

Note that in examples 1 through 3, imperfective verbal adverbs describe one action given as a background to another. The background action went on, goes on, or will go on simultaneously with the main action (described by the principal verb, *to write* or *to think*). Simultaneity is also conveyed *without* a participle in example 4. In examples 5 and 6, perfective verbal adverbs describe one event that will have taken place or has already taken place before another event (described by the principal verb, *to write*). Sequentiality is also expressed *without* a participle in example 7. Imperfective verbal adverbs are used when events are simultaneous, while perfective verbal adverbs are used when events are consecutive to one another ("first A, then B"). The background action described by an imperfective verbal adverb can also be "interrupted" by the main action (described by the principal verb).

---

* Some instructors call these gerunds.

† Some verbs that don't have verbal adverbs include **мочь**, **смотре́ть**, and **хоте́ть**; see pages 271–72.

Moreover, in all the examples the subject of the principal verb is also the implied subject of the verbal adverb. This rule governs the use of verbal adverbs. In order to determine the implied subject of a given verbal adverb, look for the principal verb in the main clause and identify the grammatical (nominative case) subject with which it agrees: This must also be the logical subject for the verbal adverb.

When negated, verbal adverbs mean *without x-ing* or *without having x-ed*, as in the following examples.

Кири́лл вы́бежал из ко́мнаты, не прости́вшись со свои́ми друзья́ми.	*Kirill ran out of the room without saying goodbye to his friends.*
Ири́на ка́ждый день уходи́ла с рабо́ты, не проща́ясь ни с Лю́сей, ни с Вади́мом.	*Irina would leave work every day without saying goodbye to either Liusia or Vadim.*

This construction is used in a very important Russian phrase, **не говоря́ уж о/б (ком/чём)**, meaning *not to mention.*

Ки́ра Воронцо́ва и Ди́ма Беля́ев о́чень спосо́бные архите́кторы, не говоря́ уж о Гали́не Росси́нской.	*Kira Vorontsova and Dima Beliaev are very talented architects, not to mention Galina Rossinskaia.*

The key identifying feature of the imperfective verbal adverb is the ending **-а/-я**. (But note that this imperfective verbal adverb ending is also used for perfective verbal adverbs for verbs ending in **-ти**.) The key identifying feature of the perfective verbal adverb is more variable than the imperfective, but it is usually **-в**, but sometimes **-ши**. Reflexive verbs may form verbal adverbs; the reflexive ending for verbal adverbs is always **-сь** (which helps distinguish reflexive verbal adverbs from reflexive participles). Thus, imperfective reflexive verbal adverbs end in **-ась** or **-ясь**, while perfective verbal adverbs end in **-вшись**.

The formation of perfective verbal adverbs from verbs whose infinitives end in **-ти** is somewhat exceptional and will be described in greater detail in Part 2.

Saying

RUSSIAN

Начина́я де́ло, о конце́ помышля́й.

When beginning something, think how you'll finish it.
[Don't start something you can't finish.]

✳ Упражне́ние 21а

Read the following sentences and circle every verbal adverb. Note whether each verbal adverb is reflexive or not and whether it is imperfective or perfective. Then translate the sentences into English. Last, rewrite the sentences in Russian without using verbal adverbs.

Вася е́дет в Петербу́рг, потому́ что его́ ба́бушка в больни́це

1. Чита́я письмо́, Ва́ся вре́мя от вре́мени пла́чет (*cries*): в письме́ напи́сано, что его́ ба́бушку положи́ли в больни́цу.
2. Прочита́в письмо́, он реши́л сра́зу же пое́хать в Петербу́рг.
3. Идя́ на вокза́л за биле́том, он бу́дет ду́мать то́лько о Петербу́рге.
4. Придя́ на вокза́л, он сра́зу ку́пит биле́т, ся́дет на по́езд и уе́дет.
5. Прие́хав в Петербу́рг, он позвони́т свое́й тёте и узна́ет, как сейча́с ба́бушка.

Saying

Не зна́я бро́ду, не су́йся в во́ду.

If you don't know the ford, don't jump into the water.
[Look before you leap.]

ТЕКСТ 21a

Read the excerpt from Pushkin's novella *The Queen of Spades*. Lizaveta Ivanovna is a poor unhappy woman who takes care of a distant relation, a bitter old countess. In this excerpt, Lizaveta first notices young Hermann outside her window.

Pre-reading Task

What do you expect Lizaveta to think when she sees Hermann outside her window? What do you think Hermann will do? What would you think if you saw an attractive young man or woman lingering outside your window?

...одна́жды Лизаве́та Ива́новна, си́дя под око́шком за пя́льцами,[1] неча́янно взгляну́ла[2] на у́лицу и уви́дела молодо́го инжене́ра, стоя́щего неподви́жно[3] и устреми́вшего глаза́[4] к её око́шку. Она́ опусти́ла[5] го́лову и сно́ва заняла́сь рабо́той; че́рез пять мину́т взгляну́ла опя́ть—молодо́й офице́р стоя́л на том же ме́сте. Не име́я привы́чки[6] коке́тничать с прохо́жими офице́рами, она́ переста́ла гляде́ть[7] на у́лицу и ши́ла о́коло двух часо́в, не приподнима́я головы́. По́дали обе́дать.[8] Она́ вста́ла, начала́ убира́ть свои́ пя́льцы и, взгляну́в неча́янно на у́лицу, опя́ть уви́дела офице́ра. Э́то показа́лось ей дово́льно стра́нным. По́сле обе́да она́ подошла́ к око́шку с чу́вством не́которого беспоко́йства,[9] но уже́ офице́ра не́ было,—и она́ про него́[10] забы́ла.

Дня че́рез два,[11] выходя́ с графи́ней[12] сади́ться в каре́ту,[13] она́ опя́ть

[1] *lace frame*
[2] *неча́янно... accidentally (not on purpose) glanced*
[3] *motionlessly*
[4] *устреми́вшего... staring*
[5] *lowered*
[6] *Не... Not having the habit*
[7] *to glance*
[8] *По́дали... dinner was served*
[9] *с... with a feeling of some anxiety*
[10] **о нём**
[11] *Дня... about two days later*
[12] *countess*
[13] *carriage*

его уви́дела. Он стоя́л у са́мого подъе́зда, закры́в лицо́ бобро́вым воротнико́м:[14] чёрные глаза́ его́ сверка́ли[15] из-под шля́пы. Лизаве́та Ива́новна испуга́лась,[16] сама́ не зна́я чего, и се́ла в каре́ту с тре́петом неизъясни́мым.[17]

Возврати́сь[18] домо́й, она́ подбежа́ла к око́шку,—офице́р стоя́л на пре́жнем[19] ме́сте, устреми́в на неё глаза́: она́ отошла́, му́чась[20] любопы́тством[21] и волну́емая[22] чу́вством, для неё соверше́нно но́вым.

А. С. Пу́шкин, «Пи́ковая да́ма», 1833

[14] бобро́вым... *beaver fur collar*
[15] *sparkled*
[16] *was frightened*
[17] тре́петом... *inexplicable trepidation*
[18] **верну́вшись**
[19] *former*
[20] **му́читься** = *to torment oneself*
[21] *curiosity*
[22] *worried*

Post-reading Tasks

1. Write a three-sentence summary of the passage.
2. Circle every verbal adverb. Note whether the verbal adverb is reflexive and whether it is imperfective or perfective. Then translate the sentences with the verbal adverbs into English.
3. Find the Russian words meaning *glance* or *gaze* and identify their roots. Do you know any other words with these roots?
4. Find all the participles and identify whether they are active or passive, past or present.
5. Continue the story, explaining what might happen next.

Formation of Verbal Adverbs

The formation of imperfective and perfective verbal adverbs is not complicated.

Imperfective Verbal Adverbs: Key Feature *-я/-а*

STEPS			EXAMPLES	
1. Start with the **они́** form.	де́лают	говоря́т	у́чатся	
2. Delete the last two letters.	де́ла-	говор-	уч-...ся	
3. Add **-я** (or **-а**, if necessary, due to spelling rules).	де́лая	говоря́	уча́сь	
	(while doing)	*(while speaking)*	*(while studying)*	

- Stress in these forms is identical to the stress in the infinitive except for the following verbal adverbs, whose stress is irregular: **лёжа** (**лежа́ть**), **си́дя** (**сиде́ть**), **сто́я** (**стоя́ть**), **мо́лча** (**молча́ть**), and **гля́дя** (**гляде́ть**).

- Verbal adverbs formed from reflexive verbs always have the reflexive particle in the -сь form (which distinguishes them from participles).
- Verbs like **дава́ть** add -я or -ясь to the infinitive stem: **дава́я, узнава́я, устава́я**.

Perfective Verbal Adverbs for Infinitives Ending in *-ти*

	STEPS	EXAMPLES	
1.	Start with the **они́** form.	приду́т	уведу́т
2.	Delete the **они́** ending.	прид-	увед-
3.	Add -я.	придя́	уведя́
		(*having arrived*)	(*having led away*)

Note carefully the difference in aspect between these two forms.

идя́ (imperfective): while going

придя́ (perfective): having arrived

Perfective Verbal Adverbs for All Other Perfective Verbs: *-в, -вшись*

	STEPS	EXAMPLES	
1.	Start with the infinitive.	посмотре́ть	верну́ться
2.	Delete the infinitive ending.	посмотре́-	верну́-...ся
3.	If not reflexive, add -в; if reflexive, add -вшись.	посмотре́в	верну́вшись
		(*having watched*)	(*having returned*)

- There exist some archaic perfective verbal adverbs that end in -вши.
- Stress in the perfective verbal adverb is identical to the stress in the infinitive.

Two Irregular Verbal Adverbs

Two commonly used verbs have irregularly formed verbal adverbs; these forms should simply be memorized.

е́хать   е́дучи

быть   бу́дучи

Verbs with No Verbal Adverb Forms

Some commonly used verbs have no verbal adverb forms, but it is possible to use verbal adverbs formed from other verbs similar in meaning.*

---

* This list is derived from one in F. M. Borras and R. F. Christian, *Russian Syntax: Aspects of Modern Russian Syntax and Vocabulary* (Oxford: Oxford University Press, 1987, 2d edition), p. 207.

VERBS WITHOUT VERBAL ADVERBS	VERBS WITH RELATED MEANINGS	VERBAL ADVERB
хоте́ть (*to want*)	жела́ть	жела́я
слать (*to send*)	посыла́ть	посыла́я
ждать (*to wait*)	ожида́ть	ожида́я
петь (*to sing*)	распева́ть	распева́я
пить (*to drink*)	выпива́ть	выпива́я
писа́ть (*to write*)	запи́сывать	запи́сывая
смотре́ть (*to look*)	гляде́ть	гля́дя

Verbs whose infinitives end in **-чь** have no verbal adverb. Verbal adverbs have no inherent tense meaning in and of themselves, but rather are linked to the principal or main verb of the clause in which they appear.

Упражне́ние 21б

Transform the following sentences by replacing the underlined verbal adverb with another construction, such as one with a **когда́** or **кото́рый** clause or one with conjunctions such as **а**, **но**, or **и**.

ОБРАЗЕ́Ц: Ма́ша писа́ла письмо́, слу́шая ра́дио. →
Когда́ Ма́ша писа́ла письмо́, она́ слу́шала ра́дио.

1. Я всегда́ за́втракаю, чита́я газе́ту.
2. Опа́здывая, Анто́н всегда́ интере́сно опра́вдывается.
3. Мы ча́сто говори́ли о Са́ше, возвраща́ясь домо́й.
4. Ожида́я авто́бус, мы говори́ли с ребёнком, игра́вшим в па́рке, пе́ред кото́рым была́ остано́вка.
5. Верну́вшись домо́й, я сра́зу се́ла на дива́н и включи́ла телеви́зор, что́бы узна́ть после́дние но́вости.

Упражне́ние 21в

Fill in the blanks with a verbal adverb formed from the verb in parentheses.

1. (Пое́хать) _____ в Москву́ на це́лый семе́стр, вы, наве́рно, познако́митесь с о́чень интере́сными людьми́.
2. (Выходи́ть) _____ из кварти́ры, мы вдру́г услы́шали телефо́н—э́то звони́ла Га́ля.
3. (Учи́ться) _____ в э́том университе́те, вы, наве́рно, бу́дете жить в э́том общежи́тии.
4. (Научи́ться) _____ води́ть маши́ну, вы, наве́рно, бу́дете счита́ть, что не смо́жете предста́вить себе́ жи́зни без автомоби́ля.
5. (Написа́ть) _____ ма́тери письмо́, он пошёл в библиоте́ку.

ТЕКСТ 216

In this poem by Akhmatova, the narrator describes losing her lover.

Pre-reading Task

What do you expect to find in a scene in which lovers part?

Сжа́ла[1] ру́ки под тёмной вуа́лью[2]...

«Отчего́ ты сего́дня бледна́[3]?»

—Оттого́, что я те́рпкой печа́лью[4]

Напои́ла его́ допьяна́.[5]

5   Как забу́ду? Он вы́шел, шата́ясь,[6]

Искриви́лся мучи́тельно рот[7]...

Я сбежа́ла, пери́л не каса́ясь,[8]

Я бежа́ла за ним до воро́т.[9]

Задыха́ясь, я кри́кнула:[10] «Шу́тка[11]

10   Всё, что бы́ло. Уйдёшь, я умру́».

Улыбну́лся споко́йно и жу́тко[12]

И сказа́л мне: «Не стой на ветру́».[13]

А. А. Ахма́това, 1911

[1] *squeezed*
[2] *тёмной... dark veil*
[3] *pale*
[4] *те́рпкой... with bitter sadness*
[5] *Напои́ла... made him drunk*
[6] *reeling, stumbling*
[7] *Искриви́лся... his mouth twisted in pain*
[8] *сбежа́ла... ran down, not touching the banister*
[9] *бежа́ла... ran after him up to the gate*
[10] *Задыха́ясь... gasping for air, out of breath, I shouted*
[11] *Joke*
[12] *Улыбну́лся... smiled calmly and terribly*
[13] *Не... don't stand there in the wind (bad weather)*

Post-reading Tasks

1. Write a summary of the poem in two or three sentences.
2. Find all the verbal adverbs in the poem. Translate them and identify the infinitives from which they are derived.
3. Does the man still love the narrator? Why do you think so?
4. Write a paragraph or two from the point of view of the man in this poem.

�֍ Упражне́ние 21г

Continue your list of all the "connecting" words and phrases (such as *because, but, in the first place, then,* and so forth) with those you can find in the texts of this unit. Next to each "connecting" word or phrase, write out the clause or sentence in which they are used. Keep this list in your notebook and add to it as you continue with this book.

Verbs of Position and Placement

Глаго́лы пози́ции и размеще́ния

—Ско́ро бу́дем обе́дать.

PART 1 Understanding Verbs of Position and Placement

Russian verbs of position and placement are very systematic. Russian uses different verbs to express the vertical and horizontal placement of objects and the vertical and horizontal position of objects that have been placed.

1. Вчера́ мы **положи́ли** газе́ты на стол. Газе́ты сейча́с **лежа́т** на столе́. Мы ча́сто **кладём** газе́ты на э́тот стол. За́втра мы **поло́жим** газе́ты на стол.

    Yesterday we put the newspapers on the table. The newspapers are now on the table. We often put the newspapers on this table. Tomorrow we will put the newspapers on the table.

2. Вчера́ мы **поста́вили** пусты́е буты́лки под стол. Пусты́е буты́лки сейча́с **стоя́т** под столо́м. Мы ча́сто **ста́вим** пусты́е буты́лки под э́тот стол. За́втра мы **поста́вим** пусты́е буты́лки под стол.

    Yesterday we put the empty bottles under the table. The empty bottles are now under the table. We often put the empty bottles under the table. Tomorrow we'll put the empty bottles under the table.

3. Вчера́ мы **пове́сили** тря́пку на крючо́к в ку́хне. Тря́пка сейча́с **виси́т** на крючке́ в ку́хне. Мы ча́сто **ве́шаем** тря́пку на крючо́к в ку́хне. За́втра мы опя́ть **пове́сим** тря́пку на крючо́к в ку́хне.

    Yesterday we hung up the rag on a hook in the kitchen. The rag is now hanging on a hook in the kitchen. We often hang the rag up on a hook in the kitchen. Tomorrow we'll hang the rag up on a hook in the kitchen again.

Examples 1 through 3 illustrate transitive and intransitive verbs of placement and position used generally with inanimate objects (newspapers, bottles, a rag). Examples 4 through 7 illustrate transitive and intransitive verbs of placement and position used generally with people.

4. Он пришёл домо́й и **лёг** спать на дива́н. Он обы́чно прихо́дит домо́й и **ложи́тся** спать на дива́н. Он сейча́с **лежи́т** и спит на дива́не. За́втра он **придёт** домо́й и сра́зу **ля́жет** спать на дива́н.

    He came home and lay down to sleep on the couch. He usually comes home and lies down to sleep on the couch. Right now he's lying on the couch and sleeping. Tomorrow he'll come home and immediately lie down to sleep on the couch.

5. Она́ пришла́ домо́й и сра́зу **се́ла** за стол. Она́ обы́чно прихо́дит домо́й и **сади́тся** за стол. Она́ сейча́с **сиди́т** за столо́м. За́втра она́ придёт домо́й и сра́зу **ся́дет** за стол.

    She came home and immediately sat down at the table. She usually comes home and sits down at the table. She is sitting at the table right now. Tomorrow she'll come home and sit down at the table right away.

6. Роди́тели пришли́ домо́й и сра́зу **положи́ли** дете́й спать. Они́ обы́чно прихо́дят домо́й и **кладу́т** дете́й спать. Они́ сейча́с **кладу́т** дете́й спать. За́втра они́ приду́т домо́й и **поло́жат** дете́й спать.

    The parents came home and immediately put their children to bed. They usually come home and put their children to bed. They are putting the children to bed right now. Tomorrow they'll come home and put the children to bed.

7. Мы пришли́ в рестора́н, и нас **посади́ли** за большо́й стол. Нас ча́сто **сажа́ют** за э́тот стол. Нас сейча́с **сажа́ют** за э́тот стол. За́втра нас **поса́дят** за э́тот стол.

    We got to the restaurant and were seated at a big table. We are often seated at this table (asked to sit down at this table). We are now being shown to that table (seated at this table). Tomorrow they will seat us at this table.

❋ Упражне́ние 22a

Review the preceding examples and group the boldfaced verbs according to type of motion, aspect, and case government (movement in a direction versus location).

PART 2
Conjugation of Verbs of Position

Four intransitive verbs of position, which cannot take a direct object, are conjugated in the following chart. In each case, the perfective verb is formed by adding the prefix **по-** to the imperfective verb. The resulting perfective verb means *to be hanging, sitting, lying,* or *standing* for a limited period of time. These perfective verbs are not used as frequently as their imperfective counterparts.

		висе́ть/по- (*to be hanging*)	сиде́ть/по- (*to be sitting*)	лежа́ть/по- (*to be lying*)	стоя́ть/по- (*to be standing*)
PRESENT/ FUTURE	я ты они́	вишу́ виси́шь вися́т	сижу́ сиди́шь сидя́т	лежу́ лежи́шь лежа́т	стою́ стои́шь стоя́т

The verb **висе́ть** (*to be hanging*) is generally used only in the third-person forms (to refer, for example, to clothing on a hanger or a painting in a museum). However, it is also used in first- and second-person forms in the following idiomatic expressions.

RUSSIAN

Sayings

Висе́ть на волоске́

To be hanging by a thread.

Висе́ть в во́здухе.

To be hanging in the air.

Висе́ть на телефо́не.

To be hanging (talking for a long time) on the phone.

When the verb *to be hanging* is not used idiomatically and refers to a person it means *hanging from a gallows.*

The imperatives for these verbs are generally used to ask someone to continue doing what they are already doing. For instance, if you enter a room where people are seated and they begin to rise to greet you, you can say «Сиди́те, пожа́луйста!»

Also note that **сиде́ть** can only be used with something that has knees (that is, a person or animal), while **висе́ть**, **лежа́ть**, and **стоя́ть** may be used with people, animals, or inanimate objects.

✳ Упражне́ние 226

Use the verbs in the preceding chart to fill in the blanks with the correct form of the verb required by context.

1. В галере́е (is hanging) _____ но́вая карти́на Канди́нского!
2. Твои́ ве́щи (were hanging) _____ в гардеро́бе, но тепе́рь их там нет.
3. Све́та (is sitting) _____ за столо́м вме́сте с Та́ней.
4. Мы (were sitting for a while) _____, поговори́ли и пото́м пошли́ домо́й.
5. Мы (were reclining, lying down for a while) _____ на пля́же, поговори́ли о пого́де, пото́м пошли́ домо́й.
6. Они́ (are lying down) _____ на полу́ и смо́трят телеви́зор в большо́й ко́мнате.
7. Мы уже́ (were standing) _____ в о́череди 30 мину́т, когда́ откры́лся магази́н.
8. Они́ (are standing) _____ на углу́ Тверско́й и ждут нас сейча́с.

§ Зада́ние 22а

Find a picture of a room showing furniture, other objects, and people and bring it to class. Prepare a description of the room, stating the location of the room's contents and using the verbs from the chart. In class, put all your pictures on one table. Describe your picture to a classmate so that she or he can pick it out of all the pictures brought to class.

PART 3 Conjugation of Transitive Verbs of Placement

Four pairs of verbs of placement are conjugated in the following charts. Note that all these verbs take accusative case direct objects: The things hung or placed are in the accusative case. The places where these objects are hung or placed are also in the accusative case. Note, however, that these verbs are used with locational adverbs (see Unit 10 in the *Workbook*).

		ве́шать, IMPF. (*to hang something*)	класть, IMPF. (*to place horizontally*)	сажа́ть,* IMPF. (*to seat someone, to plant something*)	ста́вить, IMPF. (*to place vertically*)
PRESENT	я	ве́шаю	кладу́	сажа́ю	ста́влю
	ты	ве́шаешь	кладёшь	сажа́ешь	ста́вишь
	они́	ве́шают	кладу́т	сажа́ют	ста́вят
		пове́сить, PF. (*to hang something*)	положи́ть, PF. (*to place horizontally*)	посади́ть,* PF. (*to seat someone, to plant something*)	поста́вить, PF. (*to place vertically*)
FUTURE	я	пове́шу	положу́	посажу́	поста́влю
	ты	пове́сишь	поло́жишь	поса́дишь	поста́вишь
	они́	пове́сят	поло́жат	поса́дят	поста́вят

* These verbs may also mean "to imprison."

RUSSIAN Saying

Па́льца в рот (кому́?) не клади́.

Don't dare put your finger in that person's mouth.
[Don't trifle with that person.]

✳ Упражнéние 22в

Use the verbs in the preceding chart to fill in the blanks with the correct form of the verb required by context.

1. Кудá студéнты (hang) _____ свои пальтó?
2. Тáня (is now hanging) _____ свою юбку в шкаф.
3. Свéта (will hang) _____ эту картину тудá.
4. Я боюсь, что егó (will hang) _____!
5. Олéг (is putting) _____ на стол дéньги, котóрые он сегóдня получил.
6. Мы всегдá (put) _____ свёклу в этот суп.
7. Мы ужé (put, *past*) _____ все нáши кáрты на стол.
8. Они (will put) _____ этот журнáл сюдá, тогдá мы егó и возьмём.
9. Я всегдá (put) _____ книги на эту пóлку.
10. Они (are putting) _____ бутылки винá на этот стóл.
11. Мы ужé (put, *past*) _____ бутылки под стол.
12. Они (will put) _____ стóл тудá, а шкаф мы (will put) _____ тудá.
13. Кудá нас (are they seating) _____?
14. Такúх престýпников обычно (are imprisoned) _____ на дéсять лет.
15. Я (will seat) _____ тебя за тот мáленький стол.
16. (Seat) _____ всех детéй вмéсте, пожáлуйста, за один стол!

ТЕКСТ 22а

This excerpt is from a letter a Russian exchange student in America wrote to a friend back in Russia. The exchange student is describing his efficiency apartment.

Pre-reading Task

What are some of the characteristics of an American efficiency apartment? Make a list of three or four important characteristics and then see if the letter writer mentions them.

Я сейчáс снимáю[1] квартиру, котóрая по-здéшнему называется "efficiency" или "studio." Тóчного эквивалéнта этому понятию по-рýсски нет—это чтó-то врóде[2] мáленькой однокóмнатной квартиры, в котóрой кýхня практически не отделенá[3] от кóмнаты. Срáзу при вхóде[4]—спрáва у меня
5   вéшалка, а слéва—дверь в туалéт и душ. Затéм—<u>стоит плитá</u>, рáковина[5] и <u>висят</u> кухóнные шкафы. Здесь же <u>стоит</u> обéденный стол.

Дáльше начинáется сóбственно жилáя зóна. Чтóбы хоть кáк-то отгородить[6] её от кýхни, я постáвил поперёк[7] кóмнаты дивáн, на <u>котóром сижý или лежý</u>, когдá смотрю телевизор. Дивáн, кстáти, расклáдной, что
10   удóбно[8]—когдá ко мне в прóшлом мéсяце приезжáл брат, я мог <u>положить</u> егó спать нормáльно, а не на <u>полý</u>. Рабóтаю я за <u>письменным столóм</u>,

---

[1] rent
[2] like, along the lines of
[3] separated
[4] при... at the entrance
[5] sink
[6] хоть... at least in some way separate
[7] across
[8] кстáти... by the way, is foldout, which is comfortable

кото́рый стои́т в углу́ о́коло окна́, а ря́дом моя́ посте́ль. Украше́ний осо́бых[9] у меня́ никаки́х нет, кро́ме плака́тов 20-х годо́в, кото́рые я пове́сил над дива́ном. Вот и вся карти́на мое́й берло́ги.[10] Коне́чно, тесновато́,[11] но жить мо́жно. Хотя́, когда́ собира́ется мно́го наро́да, быва́ет не́куда[12] посади́ть госте́й. Ну да ничего́—мо́гут и постоя́ть. Э́то тем бо́лее не стра́шно, что сейча́с я зава́лен рабо́той и мне не до госте́й.[13]

В о́бщем, е́сли прие́дешь ле́том, сам уви́дишь, как мне здесь живётся, а я зака́нчиваю писа́ть и ложу́сь спать—за́втра дли́нный день и на́до ра́но встава́ть.

[9] Украше́ний... *any particular decorations*
[10] *den, lair*
[11] *a little crowded, tight*
[12] *there's nowhere to*
[13] зава́лен... *buried in work and I'm in no mood for visitors, I have no time for visitors, I'm not up to visitors*

Post-reading Tasks

1. Draw a picture of the writer's apartment. Then fill in any missing bits of information by using your imagination about where those things should be.
2. How does the narrator express the concept of *the language here* when he says that his apartment is called an efficiency *here*.
3. How does the writer say there is no precise equivalent of this concept in Russian?
4. Find the two different ways used to convey the meaning *to separate* or *be separated from*.
5. What is the Russian word for *kitchen cupboards*?
6. What is the root of the Russian word meaning *foldout* in the expression *foldout couch*?
7. Determine whether the underlined verbs are used in **где** or **куда́** constructions. Identify their subjects and direct objects, if any.
8. Identify the case of every word that has a double underline and determine the reason for the case used.
9. Write two or three paragraphs describing your efficiency apartment (if you have one), your room in a dormitory, or one or two rooms in your apartment or home.

Sayings

(По-)ста́вить вопро́с ребро́м.

To place the question edgewise.
[Not to mince words.]

(По-)ста́вить крест.

To place a cross.
[To kiss something good-bye.]

(По-)ста́вить кого́-нибудь на своё ме́сто.

To put someone in his/her place.

Зада́ние 22б

Prepare a short presentation or composition in which you describe where you usually put certain objects in your room and where you put them when people visit.

ТЕКСТ 22б

This text is Okudzhava's poem, "The Little Paper Soldier."

Pre-reading Task

What do you think a poem about a paper soldier might be about?

Бума́жный солда́тик

Оди́н солда́т на све́те жил
краси́вый и отва́жный,[1]
но он игру́шкой де́тской был:
ведь[2] был солда́т бума́жный.

Он переде́лать[3] мир хоте́л,
чтоб был счастли́вым ка́ждый,[4]
а сам на ни́точке висе́л:[5]
ведь был солда́т бума́жный.

Он был бы рад—в ого́нь и в дым,[6]
за вас поги́бнуть два́жды,[7]
но потеша́лись вы над ним:[8]
ведь был солда́т бума́жный.

Не доверя́ли вы ему́
свои́х секре́тов ва́жных,
а почему́?
А потому́,
что был солда́т бума́жный.

В ого́нь? Ну что ж, иди́! Идёшь?
И он шагну́л[9] одна́жды,
и там сгоре́л он ни за грош:[10]
ведь был солда́т бума́жный.

Б. Ш. Окуджа́ва, 1960

---

[1] Оди́н... *Once there was a handsome and brave soldier*
[2] *after all*
[3] *remake*
[4] *the implied noun here is* **челове́к**
[5] сам... *he himself was hanging on a thread*
[6] Он... *He would have been happy to go into fire or smoke*
[7] за... *to perish twice for you*
[8] потеша́лись... *you made fun of him (would make fun of him, used to make fun of him)*
[9] *took a step*
[10] *burned up for nothing, for no good reason (not for even a cent)*

Post-reading Tasks

1. What are the prefix and the root of the Russian word meaning *to remake*?
2. What are the words used to express the ideas *once* and *twice* in the third and fifth stanzas? What do you think would be the analogous term for *thrice*?
3. Write a summary of the poem in two sentences.
4. Explain the usage of the Russian verb meaning *to hang* in the second stanza.
5. Write a paragraph explaining what the paper soldier might symbolize.

PART 4
Conjugation and Usage of Intransitive Verbs of Placement

Certain verbs of placement describe how we position other people (such as putting children to bed or seating someone at a table) or things. Other verbs of placement describe how people position themselves: to take a seat, to lie down, or to get up from being seated or from lying down. The conjugation of these verbs is presented here.

		сади́ться (*impf.*) (*to take a seat*)	ложи́ться (*impf.*) (*to lie down*)	встава́ть (*impf.*) (*to get up*)
PRESENT	я	сажу́сь	ложу́сь	встаю́
	ты	сади́шься	ложи́шься	встаёшь
	они́	садя́тся	ложа́тся	встаю́т
		сесть (*pf.*) (*to take a seat*)	лечь (*pf.*) (*to lie down*)	встать (*pf.*) (*to get up*)
FUTURE	я	ся́ду	ля́гу	вста́ну
	ты	ся́дешь	ля́жешь	вста́нешь
	они́	ся́дут	ля́гут	вста́нут

Note that the imperative of **лечь** is irregular: **ляг(те)!**

 Упражне́ние 22г

Review the rules in Unit 6 governing aspect in the imperative and determine the aspect generally used in polite "invitations," such as *Sit down, please!*

✳ Упражне́ние 22д

Use the verbs in the preceding chart to fill in the blanks with the correct form of the verb required by context.

1. Не (take a seat!) _____ туда́. Это ме́сто уже́ за́нято.
2. Студе́нты обы́чно (take seats) _____ сза́ди.
3. Мы уже́ (took seats) _____ за стол и на́чали обе́дать, когда́ пришёл Вади́м.
4. Они́ (will take seats) _____ туда́ и поговоря́т с э́тими инжене́рами.
5. Де́ти обы́чно (lie down) _____ спать в де́вять часо́в.
6. (Don't lie down) _____ туда́! Там ещё лежи́т моё мо́крое полоте́нце.
7. Мы уже́ (lay down, went to bed) _____ спать, когда́ позвони́ла Га́ля.
8. Они́ (will go to bed) _____ спать че́рез час.
9. Де́ти обы́чно (get up) _____ в во́семь часо́в.
10. Не (get up) _____, пожа́луйста! Я не хочу́ вам меша́ть!
11. Я сейча́с (will get up) _____, пойду́ на ку́хню и пригото́влю ко́фе.
12. Они́ (will get up) _____ ра́но за́втра у́тром, потому́ что их самолёт вылета́ет в 8 утра́.

RUSSIAN | **Saying**

Не в свои́ са́ни не сади́сь.

Don't get into someone else's sled.
[Don't bite off more than you can chew.]

✳ Упражне́ние 22е

Translate the sentences in **Упражне́ние 22д** into English.

♫ Зада́ние 22в

Describe the usual seating arrangements when you have dinner with your friends or family and how those seating arrangements were altered (on purpose or by accident) at some important occasion.

✳ Упражне́ние 22ё

Continue your list of all the "connecting" words and phrases (such as *because*, *but*, *in the first place*, *then*, and so forth) with those you can find in the texts of this unit. Next to each "connecting" word or phrase, write out the clause or sentence in which they are used. Keep this list in your notebook and add to it as you continue with this book.

✻   Упражне́ние 22ж

Add the verbs of this unit to your lists of first- and second-conjugation verbs, noting the stress pattern of each verb as you do so.

§   Зада́ние 22г

Look again at the photograph on the first page of this unit and describe the position of the people and objects and their impending movement.

UNIT 23

Unprefixed Verbs of Motion

Глаго́лы движе́ния без приста́вок

На Кижа́х.

PART 1

Understanding Multidirectional Verbs of Motion

Russian verbs of motion may seem difficult to American learners, but the system of verbs of motion is actually logical. As verbs of motion are presented in this and the following units, you'll see how sensible the system is. Part 1 of this unit presents only certain verbs, the unprefixed, multidirectional* intransitive verbs of motion: **ходи́ть** (*to walk*), **бе́гать** (*to run*), **е́здить** (*to ride*), **пла́вать** (*to swim, sail*), and **лета́ть** (*to fly*), all of which are imperfective.

1.	Вчера́ мы **ходи́ли** в кино́.	*Yesterday we went to the movies.*
2.	В про́шлом году́ мы **е́здили** в Тверь.	*Last year we went to Tver'.*
3.	Ко́стя обы́чно **хо́дит** на рабо́ту, а Ко́ля **е́здит** на автобусе.	*Kostia usually walks to work (and back), while Kolia goes on the bus.*
4.	По сре́дам Ве́ра **пла́вает**, а по четверга́м—**бе́гает**.	*On Wednesdays Vera swims, and on Thursdays she runs.*
5.	Све́та получи́ла права́ **лета́ть**: тепе́рь она́ бу́дет ча́сто **лета́ть**.	*Sveta got her flying license: Now she's going to fly frequently.*
6.	Самолёты ча́сто **лета́ют** ме́жду Москво́й и Петербу́ргом.	*Planes frequently fly between Moscow and Petersburg.*

These examples illustrate some of the uses of the multidirectional verbs. They are called multidirectional because they inherently lack the meaning of motion in a single direction. In examples 1 and 2, the past-tense forms indicate that the movement in each case was a round trip, *to the movies and back, to Tver' and back.* The present-tense forms in example 3 also convey this meaning of round-trip, while the present-tense form in example 4 indicates that Vera swims and runs for physical exercise, rather than as a means for getting to a particular destination. Example 5 features a future tense expression that also provides no particular destination: Sveta will be flying a lot, sometimes to a particular destination (perhaps a different destination for each trip), and sometimes, perhaps, just for fun, without any particular destination (returning to the same airport from which she took off on any given trip). Example 6 focuses on the frequent trips in two different directions (from Moscow to Petersburg and from Petersburg to Moscow). In each of the examples, only multidirectional verbs could have been used.

Had unidirectional verbs (**идти́, бежа́ть, е́хать, плыть,** and **лете́ть**) been used, the examples would have conveyed very different meanings.

---

* These verbs are also called *indeterminate* in some textbooks and grammar references. The two words are roughly synonymous.

UNIDIRECTIONAL VERBS

1. Yesterday *when we were on our way* to the movies, we happened to see Vadim.
2. Last year *while we were on our way* to Petersburg we met Anna Matveeva, a sculptor from Tver'.
3. Kostia usually *walks* to work, but he *takes the bus* home from work.
4. Look! Vera *is swimming* toward the instructor.
5. We'll see how well Sveta handles the controls when she *will be flying* to Kaluga.
6. Do you see that plane? I think it's *flying* to Helsinki.

Had perfective verbs (**пойти́**, **побежа́ть**, **пое́хать**, **поплы́ть**, and **полете́ть**) been used, the sentences would have also conveyed very different meanings.

PERFECTIVE VERBS

1. Yesterday we *went* to the movies and then we *went* to a café and came home at 2:00 A.M.
2. We *went* to Petersburg last year, stayed there three weeks, and then *went* to Petrozavodsk.
3. Kostia *will go* to work at 8:00 A.M. tomorrow.
4. Look! Vera *will swim* toward the instructor.
5. Sveta *will fly* to Irkutsk next month.
6. Do you see that plane? I think it *will fly* to Helsinki tonight.

The use of these verbs will be discussed later in this unit. For now, we're going to focus our attention on the multidirectional verbs **ходи́ть**, **бе́гать**, **е́здить**, **пла́вать**, and **лета́ть**.

PART 2
Conjugation of Multidirectional Verbs of Motion

Review the conjugation of imperfective multidirectional verbs of motion in the following chart.

IMPERFECTIVE: MULTIDIRECTIONAL VERBS OF MOTION						
		ходи́ть (*to walk*)	**бе́гать** (*to run*)	**е́здить** (*to ride*)	**пла́вать** (*to swim, sail*)	**лета́ть** (*to fly*)
PRESENT	я	хожу́	бе́гаю	е́зжу	пла́ваю	лета́ю
	ты	хо́дишь	бе́гаешь	е́здишь	пла́ваешь	лета́ешь
	они́	хо́дят	бе́гают	е́здят	пла́вают	лета́ют

RUSSIAN

Saying

В чужой монастырь со своим уставом не ходят.

Don't go to someone else's monastery with your own charter.
[When in Rome, do as the Romans.]

※   Упражнение 23а

Use the verbs in the preceding chart to fill in the blanks with the correct form of the verb required by context. For future tense, use the correct form of **буду**, **будешь**, **будет**, and so on.

1. Куда (goes) _____ Соня по четвергам?
2. Толе только десять месяцев, но он уже (walks) _____!
3. Я не люблю автобус и поэтому (walk) _____ на работу.
4. По субботам Таня и Костя (go) _____ на танцы (*a dance*).
5. Вчера мы (went) _____ в театр.
6. Я не играю в футбол, но я (run) _____ три раза в неделю.
7. Лёне только 11 месяцев, но она уже не только ходит, но ещё и (runs) _____!

RUSSIAN

Saying

Мурашки бегают по спине.

Shivers run up one's back.
[To have goose bumps.]

8. Бассейн будет закрыт на следующей неделе, и поэтому мы (will run) _____, а не плавать.
9. Раньше я ходила на работу, но теперь я (ride) _____ на автобусе.
10. Бабушка и дедушка живут в Петербурге, и поэтому мы часто (go) _____ туда.
11. Ты часто (go) _____ в Америку в командировку?
12. Летом Ивановы (went) _____ на Чёрное море отдыхать.

RUSSIAN

Saying

В Тулу со своим самоваром не ездят.

It's like bringing one's own samovar to Tula (famous for its samovars).
[It's like bringing coals to Newcastle (famous for its coal).]

13. Ра́ньше я бе́гала, но пото́м у меня́ заболе́ло коле́но (*my knee got hurt*). Поэ́тому я тепе́рь (swim) _____ три ра́за в неде́лю.

14. Когда́ мы бы́ли на ю́ге, мы ка́ждый день бра́ли па́русную ло́дку на прока́т (*rented a sailboat*) и (sailed around) _____ часа́ два.

15. Андре́й Васи́льевич не лю́бит лета́ть и поэ́тому в Аме́рику он (sails) _____, а не лета́ет.

16. На́шей до́чери то́лько 2 го́да, но она́ уже́ хорошо́ (swims) _____.

17. Я не люблю́ е́здить на по́езде, и поэ́тому я (fly) _____ ме́жду Москво́й и Петербу́ргом: э́то быстре́е и удо́бнее.

18. Э́тот ребёнок так бы́стро бе́гает, что мо́жно поду́мать, что он ещё и (flies) _____!

19. Пти́цы ча́сто (fly around) _____ по э́тому запове́днику (*nature preserve*).

20. Ра́я перее́хала (*moved*) в Хаба́ровск, и тепе́рь мы ча́сто (will fly) _____ туда́.

21. Э́тот солове́й слома́л себе́ крыло́ (*broke its wing*), но как то́лько попра́вится (*heals, gets better*), он опя́ть (will fly) _____.

PART 3
Usage of Multidirectional Verbs of Motion

There are six different uses for unprefixed multidirectional verbs of motion.

- Past-tense multidirectional verbs are used for

  a. a single round trip or
  b. repeated round trips.

1.	Вчера́ мы **ходи́ли** к Татья́не Никола́евне.	*Yesterday we went to see Tat'iana Nikolaevna.*
2.	Ка́ждый год мы **е́здили** в Росси́ю, но в про́шлом году́ мы никуда́ не **е́здили**.	*Every year we went to Russia, but last year we didn't go anywhere.*

In example 1, the speakers use the multidirectional verb in the past tense to indicate that they are no longer at the home of Tat'iana Nikolaevna, while in example 2, the speakers refer to a number of round-trips in the past.

- Present-tense multidirectional verbs are used for

  c. repeated trips or round-trips or
  d. a single trip in several directions.

3.	Мы ча́сто **хо́дим** к Татья́не Никола́евне.	*We often go to see Tat'iana Nikolaevna.*
4.	Ко́сти сейча́с нет—он **хо́дит** по вся́ким дела́м.	*Kostia's not here right now: He's out running various errands.*

In example 3, the speakers explain that they make repeated trips to see Tat'iana Nikolaevna (each trip is, presumably, a round-trip, since they don't live with her). In example 4, the speaker explains that Kostia is taking care of a number of different errands. The multidirectional verb of motion conveys the idea that Kostia's errands will take him to more than one particular destination.

- Future-tense multidirectional verbs are used for

    e. repeated trips.

    5. Мария перее́хала в Минск, и тепе́рь мы **бу́дем** ча́сто **е́здить** туда́.   *Maria has moved to Minsk, and now we'll be going there often.*

In example 5, the speakers explain that they will be making frequent or regular trips to Minsk.

- In all tenses, multidirectional verbs of motion are used to express

    f. movement itself, the ability to move or movement for the sake of some kind of fun.

    6. На́шему сы́ну то́лько что испо́лнилось де́сять ме́сяцев, но он уже́ **хо́дит**.   *Our son just turned ten months old, but he's already walking.*

    7. За́втра мы **бу́дем** весь день **е́здить** по го́роду на на́шей но́вой маши́не.   *Tomorrow we'll spend the whole day driving around town in our new car.*

    8. Вчера́ Со́ня три часа́ **пла́вала** на па́русной ло́дке.   *Sonia spent three hours sailing [on a sailboat] yesterday.*

✳ Упражне́ние 23б

Reread the sentences in **Упражне́ние 23а** and assign to each multidirectional verb of motion a letter a through f corresponding to one of the six different uses of these verbs.

✳ Упражне́ние 23в

Answer the following questions using the verb **ходи́ть** or **е́здить**.

    ОБРАЗЕ́Ц: Где ты была́ вчера́? (Анто́н) →

                  Вчера́ я ходи́ла к Анто́ну.

1. Где он был на про́шлой неде́ле? (Калу́га)
2. Где они́ бы́ли в сре́ду? (друзья́)
3. Где ты был сего́дня у́тром? (врач)
4. Где она́ была́ в четве́рг ве́чером? (кино́)
5. Где вы бы́ли в семь часо́в ве́чера? (теа́тр)

§   Зада́ние 23a

Prepare a short presentation or composition about where you (or someone you know) frequently or usually go at certain times of the day or certain days of the week.

PART 4
Choosing the Appropriate Verb of Motion: On Foot or by Vehicle?

Multidirectional verbs of motion express the ideas of movement on foot (at a normal pace or running), movement in water (whether by vehicle or not), and movement in air (whether by vehicle or not). There is a strict set of rules governing the verb to use in any given situation that calls for a verb of motion. These rules apply to multidirectional verbs of motion as well as to other types of verbs of motion. The rules provide multidirectional verbs as examples that you should be able to understand. Later in this unit and in the following units you will practice the same rules with other types of verbs of motion as they are presented.

1.   To describe the movement of people or animals, use

   a.   **ходи́ть** (movement on foot) unless
   b.   the motion is in the air or in the water;
   c.   the motion is to a city, country, continent, or other clearly distant destination;
   d.   the motion involves an idiomatic expression that requires another verb; or
   e.   the speaker wants to emphasize running (at a swift pace).

   In addition, to emphasize that the movement is on foot, use **ходи́ть** with the expression **пешко́м** (*on foot*).

2.   If any one of the conditions b through e is relevant, use **е́здить** (movement by vehicle) to describe the movement of people or animals, unless

   f.   the speaker wants to emphasize that motion was in the air or water;
   g.   the motion is, was, or will be undertaken by an animal;
   h.   the motion involves an idiomatic expression that requires another verb; or
   i.   the speaker wants to emphasize running.

3.   If any one of the conditions f through i is relevant, use the following verbs as required by context.

   Use **пла́вать** (movement in water) to describe the movement of people or animals, if the speaker

   j.   wants to emphasize that motion is, was, or will be by a person in the water or in a boat; or
   k.   the motion is, was, or will be undertaken by an animal (fish, dolphin, and so on).

Use **летáть** (movement in air) to describe the movement of people or animals, if the speaker

l. wants to emphasize that motion is, was, or will be undertaken by a person in a plane or helicopter; or

m. the motion is, was, or will be undertaken by an animal (bird, insect, and so on).

Use **бéгать** (running movement) to describe the movement of people or animals, if the speaker

n. wants to emphasize running (at a swift pace) on land.

4. To describe the movement of vehicles, use

o. **ходи́ть** (movement by foot) for ground vehicles of mass transportation on a regular schedule such as buses or trains;

p. **éздить** (movement by vehicle) for private automobiles and taxis;

q. **плáвать** (movement in water) for boats of any kind; and

r. **летáть** (movement in air) for planes and helicopters.

As you can see, the contexts for using **плáвать**, **летáть**, and **бéгать** are restricted; the context for using **éздить** is somewhat restricted. In order to better understand the restrictions on these verbs, consider the following examples.

1. Э́ти инженéры из Владивостóка чáсто **éздят** на конферéнции в Амéрику.

    These engineers from Vladivostok often go to conferences in America.

2. Бори́с Валенти́нович бои́тся летáть и поэ́тому он тóлько **плáвает** в Амéрику.

    Boris Valentinovich is afraid of flying, so he only sails to America.

3. На прóшлой недéле мы **летáли** во Влади́мир на ли́чном самолёте Светлáны Андрéевны.

    Last week we flew to Vladimir in Svetlana Andreevna's own (personal) plane.

In example 1, the verb **éздить** is used because there is no emphasis on the fact that the trip was most likely by plane (although possibly by ship), but certainly not by land (from Vladivostok). It is assumed that the transportation is not by train or car, but the mode of transportation is not emphasized. In example 2, the verb **плáвать** is used because Boris Valentinovich does not fly. The speaker emphasizes that Boris's preferred mode of transportation to America is by ship. In example 3, the speaker emphasizes that the trip was by plane (although most people traveling from Moscow to Vladimir probably go by automobile, bus, or train), because she or he wants to emphasize that the trip was made in the plane of an acquaintance.

Saying

Волко́в боя́ться, в лес не ходи́ть.

If you're afraid of the wolves, don't go to the forest.
[If you can't stand the heat, stay out of the kitchen.]

❋   Упражне́ние 23г

Review the rules a through r to determine which apply to the following sentences.

1. Пассажи́ры, кото́рые ча́сто лета́ют на самолётах э́той авиакомпа́нии, получа́ют беспла́тные биле́ты.
2. Еле́на Вади́мовна лю́бит пла́вать на па́русной ло́дке.
3. Мы ча́сто хо́дим в го́сти к Фёдоровым.
4. Самолёты лета́ют сли́шком бли́зко к на́шему до́му.
5. Вчера́ мы ходи́ли к сосе́дям, кото́рые живу́т на второ́м этаже́ на́шего до́ма.

❋   Упражне́ние 23д

Fill in the blanks with a verb of motion in the correct form.

1. Поезда́ регуля́рно (go) _____ ме́жду Москво́й и Петербу́ргом.
2. У Же́ни есть аква́риум, в кото́ром (swim) _____ тропи́ческие ры́бки.
3. Ты ча́сто (go) _____ в Аме́рику в командиро́вку?
4. Вчера́ мы (went) _____ в музе́й.
5. На про́шлой неде́ле она́ (went) _____ в го́сти к Петро́вым, кото́рые живу́т в Но́вгороде.

𝄞   Зада́ние 23б

Prepare a short composition about where some famous person, real or fictitious, frequently or usually goes at certain times of the day or certain days of the week. Read your presentation or composition and let your classmates guess the identity of the famous person based only on his or her itinerary.

PART 5
Unidirectional Verbs of Motion

So far this unit has presented one type of verb of motion, multidirectional verbs of motion. Like multidirectional verbs, unidirectional* verbs are also imperfective verbs:

---
* Some people refer to these as *determinate* verbs.

идти́, бежа́ть, е́хать, плыть, and **лете́ть**. These verbs are used in very few situations, especially compared with their multidirectional mates. Review the conjugation of the imperfective unidirectional verbs of motion in the following chart.

		идти́ (*to walk*)	**бежа́ть** (*to run*)	**е́хать** (*to ride*)	**плыть** (*to swim, sail*)	**лете́ть** (*to fly*)
PRESENT	я ты они́	иду́ идёшь иду́т	бегу́ бежи́шь бегу́т	е́ду е́дешь е́дут	плыву́ плывёшь плыву́т	лечу́ лети́шь летя́т

Упражне́ние 23е

Use the charts for the conjugation of multidirectional and unidirectional verbs of motion to answer the following questions.

1. Which multidirectional verb is linked by meaning to which unidirectional verb?
2. Which, if any, multidirectional and unidirectional verbs have similar conjugation patterns?
3. Which unidirectional verbs are completely irregular in their conjugation?

Упражне́ние 23ё

Which verbs of motion have rhyming forms?

RUSSIAN

Saying

На охо́ту е́хать—соба́к корми́ть.

Feed the dogs right before the hunt.
[Don't be foolish. Plan ahead.]

Упражне́ние 23ж

Use the verbs in the preceding chart to fill in the blanks with the correct form of the verb required by context. For future tense, use the correct form of **бу́ду**, **бу́дешь**, **бу́дет**, and so on.

1. Вот (goes) _____ Вади́м! Вади́м, подожди́ нас!
2. Я обы́чно (walk) _____ на рабо́ту, но е́ду домо́й на авто́бусе.
3. Когда́ мы (were going) _____ в кино́, мы уви́дели Та́ню.
4. Кино́ нахо́дится далеко́. Пешко́м мы (will be going) _____ два часа́. Дава́йте пое́дем на метро́.
5. Извини́те, ребя́та, но я о́чень опа́здываю—я (am running) _____!

6. Та́ня всё вре́мя спеши́т. Куда́ она́ сейча́с (is running) _____, я спра́шиваю.

7. Мы уви́дели Анто́на, когда́ он (was running) _____ в апте́ку за лека́рствами для ба́бушки.

8. Когда́ ты (will ride) _____ ми́мо теа́тра, пожа́луйста, посмотри́, како́й спекта́кль бу́дет идти́ в четве́рг.

9. На про́шлой неде́ле мы (rode) _____ на рабо́ту на авто́бусе, но домо́й шли пешко́м.

10. Вот (go, ride) _____ Тама́ра Васи́льевна на своём но́вом мотици́кле!

11. Мы с ни́ми познако́мились на корабле́, когда́ мы все (were sailing) _____ в Ри́гу.

12. Вон, ви́дишь как (is flying) _____ э́тот самолёт? Я ду́маю, что он (is flying) _____ в Сиби́рь.

13. Когда́ я в после́дний раз (was flying) _____ в Росси́ю, я до́лго говори́ла с пассажи́ром, сиде́вшим ря́дом, и мы ста́ли друзья́ми.

14. Когда́ вы (will be flying) _____ на на́шем самолёте сего́дня, мы вам пока́жем фильм «До́ма оди́н».

Saying

Плыть по тече́нию.

Swim/sail with the current.
[To go with the flow.]

PART 6
Usage of Unidirectional Verbs of Motion

The unidirectional verbs **идти́**, **бежа́ть**, **е́хать**, **плыть**, and **лете́ть** can be used only in very restricted contexts.

1. Past-tense unidirectional verbs are used

    a. to indicate one trip in one direction in progress at the time of speech (when the speaker says something like *There went…* or *When X was going…*); or

    b. to refer to repeated trips in one direction, often to one particular part of a trip (the trip there or the trip back) or "leg" of a trip in several stages, especially to convey how much time elapses during a part of the trip.

2. Present-tense unidirectional verbs are used

    c. to indicate one trip in one direction in progress at the time of speech (when the speaker says something like *There goes...* or *When X is going...*) or a trip that is about to take place (*She is going to Petersburg tomorrow...*); or

    d. to refer to repeated trips in one direction, more often than not to one particular part of a trip (the trip there or the trip back) or "leg" of a trip in several stages, especially to convey how much time elapses during a part of the trip.

3. Future-tense unidirectional verbs are used

    e. to indicate one trip in one direction in progress at the time of speech (when the speaker says something like *There will go...* or *When X will be going...*); or

    f. to refer to repeated trips in one direction, more often than not to one particular part of a trip (the trip there or the trip back) or "leg" of a trip in several stages, especially to convey how much time elapses during a part of the trip.

※ Упражне́ние 23з

Reread the sentences in **Упражне́ние 23ж** and assign to each sentence a letter a through f corresponding to the six different uses of unidirectional verbs of motion.

※ Упражне́ние 23и

Review rules a through r in Part 4 of this unit that explain verbs of motion (walking, running, riding, swimming, and flying). In that explanation, only multidirectional verbs are provided as examples. Add the corresponding unidirectional verbs (for example **ходи́ть→идти́**) at each point on the list. Then read the following sentences and assign a rule that explains the choice of the underlined verb.

1. Пассажи́ры, кото́рые <u>летя́т</u> сего́дня в Москву́, должны́ сейча́с пройти́ на поса́дку.
2. Еле́на Вади́мовна сейча́с <u>плывёт</u> к пля́жу.
3. Мы сейча́с <u>идём</u> в го́сти к Фёдоровым.
4. Э́тот самолёт <u>лети́т</u> сли́шком бли́зко к на́шему до́му.
5. Они́ <u>иду́т</u> к сосе́дям, кото́рые живу́т на второ́м этаже́ на́шего до́ма.

ТЕКСТ 23а

This excerpt opens Paustovskii's story, "Lenka from the Little Lake."

Pre-reading Task

The introduction describes how the narrator and his party were trying to follow an old map to a country lake. The map is very old, and although the people who live in the area are eager to help, the narrator's party can't seem to find what they're looking for. Imagine yourself in a similar situation. How might you feel? Make some predictions about the emotional tone of the text and see if you're right.

Мы шли по ка́рте, соста́вленной[1] в семидеся́тых года́х про́шлого ве́ка.[2] В углу́ ка́рты была́ сде́лана припи́ска[3] о том, что ка́рта соста́влена «на основа́нии расспро́сов ме́стных жи́телей».[4] На́дпись э́та, несмотря́ на её открове́нность, не ра́довала нас.[5]

5   Мы то́же занима́лись расспро́сами ме́стных жи́телей, но их отве́ты почти́ всегда́ бы́ли нето́чны.[6]

«Ме́стные жи́тели» до́лго и горячо́ крича́ли, переру́гивались и упомина́ли мно́го приме́т.[7] Их объясне́ния вы́глядели приме́рно так:[8] «Как дойдёте до кана́вы,[9] бери́те кру́то вкось к

10   ле́су,[10] а там иди́те и иди́те на край доро́ги по горе́лым опу́шкам к са́мой барсу́чьей я́ме,[11] за я́мой на́до бы вам угоди́ть пря́мо на холми́ще,[12] его́ отту́да чуть-чуть вида́ть,[13] а за холми́щем доро́га, мо́жно сказа́ть, совсе́м проста́я[14]—по ко́чкам до са́мого о́зера.[15] Так и дойдёте».

15   Мы то́чно сле́довали э́тим приме́там,[16] но никогда́ не доходи́ли.

Сейча́с мы шли по ка́рте, но всё же заблуди́лись в сухи́х боло́тах, заро́сших ме́лким ле́сом.[17]

К. Г. Паусто́вский, «Лёнка с ма́лого о́зера», 1937

[1] *drawn up*
[2] *про́шлого... last century*
[3] *note*
[4] *на... on the basis of information from local residents*
[5] *несмотря́... despite its open admission, didn't make us happy*
[6] *imprecise, inaccurate*
[7] *переру́гивались... shouted at one another and mentioned many landmarks*
[8] *Их... Their instructions sounded about like this:*
[9] *Как... When you get to the ditch*
[10] *бери́те... make a sharp turn across to the forest*
[11] *а... then go on and on to the end of the road across the burnt clearings until you get to the badger's hole*
[12] *за... from the hole make straight for the hill*
[13] *его́... it's just barely visible in the distance*
[14] *а... and beyond it the path is clear*
[15] *до... to the lake itself*
[16] *Мы... we followed the landmarks*
[17] *всё... got lost anyway in dry swamps overgrown with a sparse wood*

Post-reading Tasks

1. Write a summary of the text in two or three sentences.
2. Find all the unprefixed verbs of motion and identify the contexts in which they are used. Translate the clauses in which the verbs occur.
3. What is the root of the Russian word meaning *mentioned*? Do you know any other words with this root?
4. Find all the words that seem colloquial, rather than standard, in the speech of the local residents. How do these words seem to depart from standard Russian?
5. Assume the point of view of a local resident and write a short passage describing your amusement at the city folk looking for the lake but unable to find it, or continue the passage from the narrator's point of view.

✳ Упражне́ние 23й

Fill in the blanks with a unidirectional verb of motion in the correct form.

1. Вот (comes) _____ авто́бус: (run) _____ скоре́е!
2. Когда́ Же́ня (was going) _____ в кни́жный магази́н, он заме́тил, что в теа́тре идёт но́вый спекта́кль.
3. Когда́ То́ля (was swimming) _____ к бе́регу, Со́ня спря́тала всю его́ оде́жду.

4. Когда́ ты (will be riding) _____ ми́мо кино́, посмотри́, како́й фильм бу́дет идти́ в четве́рг.

5. Они́ уже́ (were riding) _____ в музе́й, когда́ по́няли, что музе́й закры́т по вто́рникам.

PART 7
Conjugation of Perfective Verbs of Motion Without Spatial Prefixes

The perfective verbs of motion that are "mates" for the multidirectional and unidirectional verbs we've studied so far are **пойти́**, **побежа́ть**, **пое́хать**, **поплы́ть**, and **полете́ть**. Like all perfective verbs, these verbs have no present-tense forms. Conjugated forms are in the future tense. Review the conjugation of the perfective verbs in the following chart.

		пойти́ (*to walk*)	побежа́ть (*to run*)	пое́хать (*to ride*)	поплы́ть (*to swim, sail*)	полете́ть (*to fly*)
FUTURE	я	пойду́	побегу́	пое́ду	поплыву́	полечу́
	ты	пойдёшь	побежи́шь	пое́дешь	поплывёшь	полети́шь
	они́	пойду́т	побегу́т	пое́дут	поплыву́т	полетя́т

�֍ Упражне́ние 23к

Use the charts for the conjugation of multidirectional, unidirectional, and perfective verbs of motion and answer the following questions.

1. Which multidirectional and unidirectional verbs are linked by meaning to which perfective verb?

2. Which, if any, multidirectional, unidirectional, and perfective verbs have similar conjugation patterns?

3. Which perfective verbs, if any, are completely irregular in their conjugation?

�֍ Упражне́ние 23л

Use the verbs in the preceding chart to fill in the blanks with the correct form of the verb required by context.

1. Че́рез час Вади́м (will go) _____ в магази́н за хле́бом. Тебе́ чтó-нибудь ну́жно?

2. Ты не (will go) _____ с на́ми в кино́ сего́дня ве́чером?

3. Ле́ны сейча́с нет, она́ уже́ (left) _____ на рабо́ту.

4. Где же Пе́тя и Та́ня? Они́ (left) _____ в магази́н.

5. А́ня, ты всё вре́мя опа́здываешь и спеши́шь! Куда́ ты сейча́с (will run off) _____?

6. То́ля (ran off) _____ на остано́вку авто́буса, сел и уе́хал!

7. Когда́ ты (will go) _____ в Петербу́рг, купи́ мне откры́тки с ви́дом Зи́мнего дворца́.

8. Снача́ла мы (went) _____ на Кра́сную пло́щадь, а пото́м мы верну́лись в гости́ницу.

9. Тама́ра Васи́льевна (will go, ride) _____ пе́рвой в командиро́вку в Аме́рику, а пото́м (will go, ride) _____ Пётр Евге́ньевич.

10. Арка́ша хорошо́ пла́вает. Сейча́с он (will swim) _____ к ма́ленькой ло́дке.

11. Они́ (will sail) _____ в Ри́гу на корабле́, потому́ что так деше́вле, чем на други́х ви́дах тра́нспорта.

12. Петро́вы (sailed) _____ в Хе́льсинки на корабле́, но верну́тся в Петербу́рг на по́езде.

13. Тру́дно ве́рить, что на сле́дующей неде́ле мы (will fly) _____ в Ирку́тск.

14. Снача́ла я (will fly) _____ в Росси́ю, а пото́м пое́ду на по́езде на Украи́ну.

15. Мы (flew) _____ в Москву́, бы́ли там не́сколько дней, пото́м пое́хали на по́езде в Петербу́рг, провели́ там не́сколько дней, а пото́м (flew) _____ в Я́лту.

PART 8
Usage of Perfective Verbs of Motion Without Spatial Prefixes

The perfective verbs of motion—**пойти́, побежа́ть, пое́хать, поплы́ть,** and **полете́ть**—can be used only in restricted contexts.

1. Past-tense perfective verbs are used

   a. to indicate one trip in one direction, with the result of that trip still in effect (unless another verb follows which reveals additional information).

2. Future-tense perfective verbs are used

   b. to indicate one trip in one direction, often with emphasis on the act of departure itself.

�֍   Упражне́ние 23м

Reread the sentences in **Упражне́ние 23л** and assign to each sentence the letter a or b corresponding to the two uses of perfective verbs of motion.

✳   Упражне́ние 23н

Review rules a through r in Part 4 of this unit that explain verbs of motion (walking, running, riding, swimming, and flying). Then read the following sentences and assign a rule that explains the choice of the underlined verb.

1. Пассажи́ры, кото́рые полетя́т на сле́дующей неде́ле в Аме́рику, должны́ офо́рмить свою́ ви́зу.

   2. Еле́на Вади́мовна сейча́с <u>поплывёт</u> к пля́жу.
   3. Ве́чером мы <u>пойдём</u> в го́сти к Фёдоровым.
   4. Я ду́маю, что э́тот самолёт <u>полети́т</u> сли́шком бли́зко к на́шему до́му.
   5. Они́ <u>пошли́</u> к сосе́дям, кото́рые живу́т на второ́м этаже́ на́шего до́ма, и верну́лись домо́й о́чень по́здно.

❋   Упражне́ние 23о

Fill in the blanks with a perfective verb of motion in the correct form.

   1. Еле́на Васи́льевна уже́ (left) _____ на рабо́ту.
   2. Же́ня (ran off) _____ в кни́жный магази́н, когда́ он услы́шал, что появи́лось но́вое изда́ние Пастерна́ка.
   3. Когда́ То́ля (swam off) _____ к друго́му бе́регу, Со́ня спря́тала всю его́ оде́жду.
   4. Когда́ ты (will go) _____ в кино́, посмотри́, како́й фильм бу́дет идти́ в четве́рг.
   5. Они́ уже́ (left for) _____ в музе́й, когда́ по́няли, что му́зей закры́т по вто́рникам.

§   Зада́ние 23в

Prepare a short presentation or composition about where you will go tomorrow or on your next vacation, including several different destinations (in succession).

§   Зада́ние 23г

Prepare a short presentation or composition about where some famous person, real or fictitious, will go tomorrow or next week, including several different destinations (in succession). Read your presentation or composition and let your classmates guess the identity of the famous person based only on his or her itinerary.

§   Зада́ние 23д

Look again at the photograph for Unit 24 and prepare a presentation or short composition describing the comings and goings of people in this location.

PART 9
Summary of Verbs of Motion Without Spatial Prefixes

You have now practiced using multidirectional and unidirectional unprefixed verbs of motion in various tenses as well as perfective verbs of motion in both the past and the future. You have reviewed the rules governing the selection of different verbs. The following chart summarizes the situations or contexts in which multidirectional, unidirectional, and perfective verbs of motion are used.

	IMPERFECTIVE		PERFECTIVE
	MULTIDIRECTIONAL	**UNIDIRECTIONAL**	
SAMPLE VERBS	ходи́ть е́здить бе́гать пла́вать лета́ть	идти́ е́хать бежа́ть плыть лете́ть	пойти́ пое́хать побежа́ть поплы́ть полете́ть

PAST	one round-trip
	
	repeated trips
		one trip in one direction
		   in progress
		
		repeated trips in one direction
			an action begun once, still
			   in progress or result still
			   in effect

PRESENT	repeated trips
	round-trips or a trip in
	   several directions
		repeated trips in one direction
		one-time action in one
		   direction in progress
			no present tense

FUTURE	repeated trips
	
	round-trips or a trip in several
	   directions
		one trip in one direction,
		   emphasis on duration
		   of trip
		repeated trips in one
		   direction
			one concrete single
			   trip, with emphasis
			   on the act of departure

ALL TENSES	movement without direction (walking around or running around for pleasure)		

✳ Упражне́ние 23п

Refer to the preceding chart and the rules for selecting a verb of motion by foot, by vehicle, in the air, and so forth in Part 4 of this unit. Fill in the blanks with the correct form of the verb.

1. Я вчера́ (went) _____ в кино́.
2. Где де́ти? [Их здесь нет.] Они́ уже́ (left for) _____ в парк.
3. Ки́ра обы́чно (goes) _____ в шко́лу на трамва́е, а домо́й она́ (goes) _____ пешко́м.
4. У Оле́га боле́ли но́ги и он до́лго не (walked) _____.
5. Ле́том Ми́ша ча́сто (goes) _____ на пляж.

Idiomatic Expressions with Verbs of Motion Without Spatial Prefixes

Many idiomatic expressions use verbs of motion, and you're probably familiar with several of them already, some of which concern the weather. Here are a few of these expressions that use the verbs presented in this unit.

Бо́же мой, как вре́мя лети́т!	*My, how time flies!*
Ти́хо! Здесь иду́т заня́тия!	*Be quiet! Classes are in session here!*
В кинотеа́тре на на́шей у́лице иде́т но́вый америка́нский фильм.	*The movie theater on our street is showing a new American film.*
Ско́ро пойде́т дождь/снег.	*Soon it's going to rain/snow.*

 Упражне́ние 23p

Refer to the preceding examples and translate the following sentences into English.

1. What's being shown in the movie theater this week?
2. It's going to snow tomorrow.
3. It snowed all day on Wednesday.
4. It is going to snow this evening.
5. Do you know if it's supposed to rain on Saturday?
6. Quiet! An exam is going on here.

 ТЕКСТ 23б

This excerpt is from Nekrasov's poem "On the Eve of a Bright Holiday."

Pre-reading Task

What do you see in a small American town near the town church on the morning of Easter Sunday? What do you think Nekrasov might have seen in a Russian village right before the midnight mass that precedes Orthodox Easter?

Накану́не све́тлого пра́здника

1

Я е́хал к Росто́ву
Высо́ким холмо́м,[1]
Лесо́к малоро́слый[2]
Тяну́лся на нём;[3]
Берёза, оси́на,

[1] Высо́ким... *Along a high hill*
[2] Лесо́к... *Young forest*
[3] Тяну́лся... *Stretched out on it*

5

Да ель, да сосна;[4]
А сле́ва—доли́на,
Как ска́терть ровна́.[5]
Пестре́л деревня́ми,
Доро́гами дол,[6]
Он всё понижа́лся
И к о́зеру шёл.[7]
Ни о́зера, де́ти,
Забы́ть не могу́,
Ни це́ркви на са́мом
его́ берегу́:[8]
Тут чу́до-карти́ну[9]
Я ви́дел тогда́!
Её вспомина́ю
Охо́тно[10] всегда́...

2

Начну́ по поря́дку:[11]
Я е́хал весно́й,
В Страстну́ю суббо́ту,
Пред са́мой Свято́й.[12]
Домо́й поспеша́я
С тяжёлых рабо́т[13]
С утра́ мне встреча́лся
Рабо́чий наро́д;
Скуча́я смерте́льно
Реша́л я вопро́с:[14]
Кто пло́тник, кто сле́сарь,
Маля́р, водово́з?[15]
Нетру́дное де́ло!
Иду́т кузнецы́[16]—
Кто их не узна́ет?
Они́ молодцы́
И петь и руга́ться,[17]
Да день не тако́й!
Идёт кривоно́гий
Гуля́ка-портно́й:[18]
В одно́м сертучи́шке,
Фура́жка как блин,[19]—
Гармо́ния, тру́бка,
Утю́г и арши́н![20]...

4 Берёза... Birch, aspen, spruce and pine
5 А... To the left a valley as flat as a tablecloth
6 Пестре́л... my valley was mottled with villages and roads
7 Он... It (the valley) declined lower and lower and went to the lake
8 Ни... Nor the church on its shore
9 wonderful tableau (picture, image)
10 Willingly, happily
11 Начну́... I'll begin at the beginning
12 В... On Holy Saturday, the day before Easter
13 Домо́й... hurrying home from difficult work
14 Скуча́я... Bored to death, I tried to determine
15 Кто... Who's a carpenter, metalworker, painter, water carrier?
16 blacksmiths
17 петь... singing and swearing
18 кривоно́гий... bowlegged reveling tailor
19 сертучи́шке... peasant shirt and a cap like a pancake
20 Гармо́ния... Accordion, pipe, iron, and measuring stick

At this point the narrator describes other working people he observes and wishes them the best as they make their way home to celebrate Easter (the most important religious holiday in the Russian Orthodox calendar).

3

45   Стемнéло.[21] Болтáя
с мои́м ямщико́м,[22]
Я éхал всё тем же
Высо́ким холмо́м;
Взгляну́л на доли́ну,
50   Что к о́зеру шла,
И ви́жу—доли́на
Моя́ ожила́:[23]
На ка́ждой тропи́нке,
Веду́щей к селу́[24]
55   Толпы́ появи́лись;[25]
Вечéрнюю мглу
Огни́ озари́ли:[26]
Куда́-то идёт
С пучка́ми горя́щей
60   Соло́мы наро́д.[27]
Куда́? Я поду́мать
О том не успéл,[28]
Как ко́локол гро́мко
Отвéт прогудéл[29]!
65   У о́зера я́рко
Горéли костры́,[30]—
Туда́ направля́лись
Наря́дны, пестры́,
При свéте горя́щей
70   Соло́мы,—толпы́...[31]
У Бо́жьего хра́ма
Сходи́лись тропы́,[32]—
Наро́дная ма́сса
Сдвига́лась, росла́.[33]
75   Чудéсная, дéти,
Карти́на была́!..

Н. А. Некра́сов, 1873

[21] *It became dark*
[22] Болтáя... *Chatting with my driver*
[23] доли́на... *the valley came alive*
[24] На... *On every path leading to the village*
[25] Толпы́... *Crowds appeared*
[26] Огни́... *Fires lit up the evening gloom*
[27] С... *the people are going somewhere with bundles of burning straw*
[28] не... *didn't have time*
[29] ко́локол... *The church bell loudly rang the answer*
[30] У... *fires were burning at the lake*
[31] Туда́... *the crowds, all dressed up and colorful, were heading there under the light of the burning straw*
[32] У... *The paths came together at God's temple*
[33] Наро́дная... *The mass of people moved and grew*

Post-reading Tasks

1. What structure or building is located on the lakeshore?
2. Write a three-sentence summary of the poem.
3. What are the roots of the Russian word meaning *young* in the expression *young forest*? What other words with those roots do you know?
4. How does the narrator express the word *and* in the sixth line? Is this standard Russian? What style might this word represent?
5. What is the root of the Russian word meaning *it got dark*? What are the tense and aspect of this verb?
6. Why did the valley become alive?
7. What gave the answer about where everyone was going?
8. Find all the unprefixed verbs of motion and determine the context in which they are used.
9. Find a synonym for the verb **шли** in the poem.
10. Imagine that you are flying in a helicopter and looking down at people going to a big event, such as a worship service, wedding, funeral, or ball game. Write a description of the scene from this perspective using as many unprefixed verbs of motion as possible.

PART 11

Verbs of Motion with the Temporal Prefixes *с(ъ)-* and *по-*

The multidirectional verbs **ходи́ть**, **е́здить**, **бе́гать**, **лета́ть**, and **пла́вать** can be used with the prefix **по-** to mean *to walk around for a while* (**походи́ть**), *to ride around for a while* (**пое́здить**), *to run around for a while* (**побе́гать**), *to fly around for a while* (**полета́ть**), and *to swim around for a while* (**попла́вать**).

Мы походи́ли по па́рку и пото́м пошли́ домо́й.	We walked around the park for a while and then went home.
Мы пое́здим по го́роду и пото́м пое́дем в рестора́н.	We'll drive around the city for a while and then go to a restaurant.
Бе́лки побе́гали ме́жду тремя́ дере́вьями и пото́м убежа́ли от нас.	The squirrels ran around for a while between three trees and then ran away from us.
Пти́чки полета́ли над на́шим балко́ном и пото́м се́ли на балко́н.	The little birds flew around for a while above our balcony and then landed on the balcony.
Мы то́лько что обе́дали: снача́ла немно́го отдохнём а пото́м попла́ваем.	We just had lunch: We'll rest for a while and then go swimming for a while.

This usage of these verbs is fairly restricted. Russians often use the word **погуля́ть** instead of **походи́ть, поката́ться** instead of **пое́здить**.

These verbs can also take the temporal prefix **с(ъ)-** to mean *to make a quick round-trip*: **сходи́ть** (**схожу́, схо́дишь, схо́дят**), **сбе́гать** (**сбе́гаю, сбе́гаешь, сбе́гают**), **съе́здить** (**съе́зжу, съе́здишь, съе́здят**).

У нас ко́нчилось молоко́: я сбе́гаю за ним в магази́н.	*We ran out of milk: I'll run down to the store for it.*
Ва́ня! Сходи́, пожа́луйста, за по́чтой!	*Vania! Please go (make a quick trip) to get the mail.*
За́втра я должна́ съе́здить в Петербу́рг, но смогу́ встре́титься послеза́втра.	*Tomorrow I have to make a quick trip to St. Petersburg, but I can meet the day after tomorrow.*

✳ Упражне́ние 23c

Fill in the blanks as required by context.

1. Я хочу́ снача́ла (go for a run, run for a while) _____, а пото́м приму́ душ.
2. Как нет ча́я?! А́ня то́лько что (made a trip) _____ в магази́н за ча́ем!
3. Кири́лл Анато́льевич! Вам ну́жно (walk for a while) _____, а то вы всё вре́мя то́лько сиди́те и лежи́те!
4. Мы (make a trip) _____ в Яросла́вль за Ни́ной, а пото́м все смо́гут вме́сте встреча́ть Но́вый год здесь у нас!
5. Ребя́та ещё (swam for a while) _____, а пото́м пошли́ обе́дать.

✳ Упражне́ние 23т

Continue your list of all the "connecting" words and phrases (such as *because, but, in the first place, then,* and so forth) with those you can find in the texts of this unit. Next to each "connecting" word or phrase, write out the clause or sentence in which they are used. Keep this list in your notebook and add to it as you continue with this book.

✳ Упражне́ние 23у

Add the verbs of this unit to your lists of first- and second-conjugation verbs, noting the stress pattern of each verb as you do so.

Coming and Going: Verbs of Motion with Spatial Prefixes

Глаго́лы движе́ния с приста́вками

На Не́вском проспе́кте.

Understanding Imperfective and Perfective Verbs of Motion with Spatial Prefixes

PART 1

Prefixes with spatial meanings (*to, from, in, out, toward, away from,* and so forth) can be attached to multidirectional verbs of motion (such as **ходи́ть, бе́гать, е́здить, пла́вать,** and **лета́ть**) to form imperfective prefixed verbs of motion conveying frequent movement in one direction or a single round-trip.

1. Ма́ша обы́чно **ухо́дит** на рабо́ту в 8 часо́в и **прихо́дит** домо́й в 6 часо́в.

   Masha usually leaves for work at 8:00 and comes home at 6:00.

2. Когда́ тебя́ не́ было, **заходи́л** То́ля. Он сказа́л, что за́втра бу́дет экза́мен по фи́зике.

   While you were out Tolia dropped by (but didn't stay). He said that there would be a physics test tomorrow.

Example 1 illustrates the use of the imperfective prefixed verb of motion conveying frequent movement in one direction (each verb in that sentence expresses motion in one direction). Example 2 expresses the idea of the single round-trip (Tolia dropped by, left a message, and then left).

When the same spatial prefixes are attached to unidirectional verbs of motion (such as **идти́, бежа́ть, е́хать, плыть,** and **лете́ть**), perfective prefixed verbs of motion are created. These verbs express a single movement in one direction, with the result of that movement still in effect (until otherwise explicitly stated), as illustrated in examples 3 and 4.

3. Ма́ша уже́ **ушла́** на рабо́ту и **придёт** домо́й то́лько в 6 часо́в.

   Masha has already left for work and will come home only at 6:00 (she's not home anymore).

4. Когда́ тебя́ не́ было, **зашёл** То́ля: он хо́чет поговори́ть с тобо́й об экза́мене по фи́зике.

   While you were out Tolia dropped by: He wants to talk with you about the physics test (he's still here now).

RUSSIAN

Saying

Выходи́ть/Вы́йти сухи́м из воды́.

To come out dry from the water.
[To get off scot free.]

Example 3 illustrates the use of the perfective prefixed verb of motion conveying a single movement in one direction (each verb in that sentence expresses motion in one direction). Example 4 expresses the idea of a single movement whose result is still in effect (Tolia dropped by and is still there).

ТЕКСТ 24a

Read the excerpt from the screenplay of the film *The Irony of Fate*, directed by E. Riazanov and E. Braginskii (1979).

Background: This film tells the story of Zhenia Lukashin, an unlucky Moscow doctor who lives in one of Moscow's "new regions," where all the buildings look alike. Lukashin goes with his friends to the bath on New Year's Eve to celebrate the passing of the old year. The men get drunk and forget which one of them was supposed to go to Leningrad. By mistake, Lukashin winds up on the plane for Leningrad. Too drunk to realize that he's arrived in Leningrad, he gets in a taxi and gives the driver his address. There happens to be an identical address in Leningrad and, owing to the wonders of a planned economy, Lukashin's key fits the door of the Leningrad apartment. This excerpt begins when the real occupant of the Leningrad apartment, a schoolteacher named Nadia, discovers a strange man sleeping on her bed. She tries to wake him up, but can't, until she pours some cold water on his head.

Pre-reading Task

How would you react if you found a stranger in your home as you were set to prepare for a very important date? Make three predictions of what you expect Nadia to do when she finds Zhenia Lukashin in her bed.

ЛУКÁШИН. (*блажéнно*)[1] Ой, как хорошó!.. Ой, поплы́ли! (*Просыпáется.*)[2] Вы что? С умá сошли́![3] Выметáйтесь отсю́да![4]

НÁДЯ. (*поражена́*)[5] Это неслы́ханно[6]! Что вы здесь дéлаете?

ЛУКÁШИН. Я... Мы... Мы тут спим! (*Постепéнно оцéнивая происходя́щее.*)[7] Кто вы такáя? Что вам здесь ну́жно?

НÁДЯ. Как вы сюдá вошли́? Что вы здесь разлегли́сь?[8] Ну-ка, выкáтывайтесь[9] немéдленно!

ЛУКÁШИН. Ну, э́то уж нахáльство[10]! Мáло того, что[11] вы ворвали́сь ко мне в кварти́ру,[12] вы ведёте себя́[13] как банди́тка!

НÁДЯ. К вам в кварти́ру?

ЛУКÁШИН. Да, представьте себé, я живу́ здесь ужé семь лет!

НÁДЯ. А где, по-вáшему, живу́ я? (*В изнеможéнии опускáется на стул.*)[14]

ЛУКÁШИН. Этого я не знáю. Пожáлуйста, уйди́те отсю́да, и как мóжно скорéе. Сейчáс придёт моя́ невéста,[15] и я совсéм не хочу́, чтобы онá застáла[16] меня́ с какóй-то жéнщиной!

[1] *blissfully*
[2] *wakes up*
[3] С... *gone crazy (idiom)*
[4] Выметáйтесь... *Get out of here!*
[5] *astonished*
[6] *unheard of*
[7] Постепéнно... *Gradually evaluating what's going on*
[8] Что... *Why have you stretched yourself out here?*
[9] *Get out of here*
[10] *impudence*
[11] Мáло... *It isn't enough that*
[12] вы... *you've broken into my apartment*
[13] вы... *you're behaving yourself*
[14] В... *in exhaustion, lowers herself onto a chair*
[15] *fiancée*
[16] *caught*

НА́ДЯ. Объясни́те[17] мне наконе́ц, почему́ ва́ша неве́ста бу́дет иска́ть вас у меня́ до́ма?

ЛУКА́ШИН. Мне не до шу́ток.[18] Кото́рый час?

НА́ДЯ. Ско́ро оди́ннадцать! Ко мне должны́ прийти́ с мину́ты на мину́ту.[19] И ва́ше прису́тствие здесь необяза́тельно.[20]

ЛУКА́ШИН. Но почему́ ва́ши го́сти приду́т ко мне встреча́ть Но́вый год? И как вы сюда́ забрали́сь?[21]

НА́ДЯ. Послу́шайте, вы хоть что́-нибудь сообража́ете[22]? Вы где нахо́дитесь, по-ва́шему[23]?

ЛУКА́ШИН. У себя́ до́ма! 3-я у́лица Строи́телей, 25, кварти́ра 3!

НА́ДЯ. Нет, э́то я живу́: 3-я у́лица Строи́телей, 25, кварти́ра 3!

After a brief discussion about the furnishings in the apartment, which are also identical to the furnishings in Lukashin's Moscow apartment, Nadia and Zhenia figure out what has actually happened.

ЛУКА́ШИН. *(жа́лобно)*[24] Где я?

НА́ДЯ. *(е́дко)*[25] 3-я у́лица Строи́телей, 25, кварти́ра 3!

ЛУКА́ШИН. Но че́стное сло́во,[26] э́то мой дома́шний а́дрес! Хотя́ мне ка́жется, я всё-таки в чужо́й кварти́ре[27]!

НА́ДЯ. Наконе́ц-то! Тепе́рь вы мо́жете уйти́ со споко́йной душо́й.[28]

ЛУКА́ШИН. Но куда́ же я пойду́, когда́ я до́ма! Я жду Га́лю, она́ придёт по э́тому а́дресу. Я здесь пропи́сан.[29] *(Протя́гивает ру́ку, ле́зет в карма́н пиджака́, достаёт отту́да па́спорт и чита́ет.)*[30] Вот...го́род Москва́, 119-е отделе́ние мили́ции.[31] Пропи́сан постоя́нно по 3-й у́лице Строи́телей, 25, кварти́ра 3.

НА́ДЯ. Зна́чит, вы ду́маете, что вы в Москве́!

ЛУКА́ШИН. *(в отве́т смеётся)* А где я, по-ва́шему?

На́дя усмеха́ется,[32] ле́зет в су́мку, достаёт отту́да па́спорт и протя́гивает Лука́шину.

(Чита́ет вслух.)[33] Го́род Ленингра́д, 306-е отделе́ние мили́ции, пропи́сан постоя́нно: 3-я у́лица Строи́телей, 25... *(Возвраща́ет па́спорт.)* Вы что же...намека́ете,[34] что я нахожу́сь в Ленингра́де?

На́дя торжеству́юще молчи́т.[35]

(Засмея́лся и то́тчас сдержа́л смех.)[36] Но как я мог попа́сть[37] в Ленингра́д? Я ведь пошёл в ба́ню[38]...

НА́ДЯ. С лёгким па́ром![39]

ЛУКА́ШИН. Спаси́бо!

---

17 *explain*
18 *Мне... I'm in no mood for jokes*
19 *с... any minute now*
20 *ва́ше... your presence is not required*
21 *И как... And how did you get in here anyhow?*
22 *вы... do you understand anything at all?*
23 *in your opinion*

24 *pitifully*
25 *caustically*
26 *че́стное... honestly*
27 *в... in someone else's apartment*
28 *споко́йной... tranquil soul (without reservations)*
29 *registered**
30 *Протя́гивает... He sticks his arm (out from under the blanket), sticks it into the pocket of his jacket and gets his passport out of there and reads it.*
31 *отделе́ние... militia precinct (region in a city)*
32 *grins*
33 *Чита́ет... reads out loud*
34 *hint*
35 *торжеству́юще... is triumphantly silent*
36 *Засмея́лся... He burst out laughing and immediately restrained himself*
37 *wind up in*
38 *bathhouse, sauna*
39 *С... Hope you had a nice sauna! (a formulaic afterbath greeting)*

---

* Soviet-era regulations required individuals to be registered at a particular address. As of this date, this regulation still exists in Russian law.

> 50   **НА́ДЯ.**   А тепе́рь уже́ хва́тит![40] Уходи́те!
>
> **ЛУКА́ШИН.**   Но е́сли я действи́тельно в Ленингра́де...како́й у́жас, а?..
> Куда́ же мне <u>пойти́</u>?.. Посто́йте...мы <u>пое́хали</u> на аэродро́м...да, да...
> <u>пое́хали</u>, я по́мню, мы <u>провожа́ли</u> Па́вла.[41] Всё я́сно...нет, неуже́ли я
> <u>улете́л</u> вме́сто него́?
>
> Э. Браги́нский и Э. Ряза́нов, 1979–1983

[40] А... *Okay, that's enough now!*
[41] мы... *we were seeing off Pavel*

Post-reading Tasks

1. Identify the aspect and tense of the underlined verbs of motion and explain if they are used to convey frequent motion in a single direction, one round-trip, or one trip in a single direction.
2. Watch this scene in the film (if it is available to your instructor) a couple of times. Then turn off the sound, watch it again, and read the lines along with the action. Then perform the scene yourselves without the video.
3. Prepare a continuation of this scene. What will Zhenia and Nadia do next?

PART 2
Spatial Prefixes: Meaning and Usage

The first and perhaps most important feature of the prefixed verbs of motion are the spatial prefixes themselves. Here are charts showing some of the most important spatial prefixes, their meaning, verbs, prepositions most commonly used with the verbs, and examples. The charts of prefixes and the examples are grouped according to meaning.

PREFIX	MEANING	EXAMPLE VERBS	PREPOSITIONS
при-	coming to	приходи́ть, прийти́	в, на (куда́?)
у-	going away, leaving	убега́ть, убежа́ть	из, с, от (отку́да?)

1. Ка́тя обы́чно **прихо́дит** домой с рабо́ты в час.

   Katia usually comes home from work at 1:00.

2. Ти́хо, а то они́ **убегу́т** от нас!

   Quiet, or else they'll run away from us!

PREFIX	MEANING	EXAMPLE VERBS	PREPOSITIONS
в-	into an enclosed space	входи́ть, войти́	в (куда́?)
вы-	out of an enclosed space	выбега́ть, вы́бежать	из (отку́да?)

3. Еле́на Васи́льевна **вошла́** в лаборато́рию и се́ла за стол.
4. Он ча́сто **выбега́ет** из свое́й ко́мнаты, как то́лько слы́шит телеви́зор в гости́ной.

Elena Vasil'evna entered the laboratory and sat down at the table.
He usually runs out of his room as soon as he hears the television in the living room.

Saying

Сло́во не воробе́й, вы́летит—не пойма́ешь!

A word is not a sparrow: Once it flies out (of your mouth), you can't catch it!
[Think before you speak!]

PREFIX	MEANING	EXAMPLE VERBS	PREPOSITIONS
под-	toward	подъезжа́ть, подъе́хать	к (кому́? чему́?)
от-	away from	отходи́ть, отойти́	от (чего́?)
до-	up to (but not including)	доплыва́ть, доплы́ть	до (чего́?)

5. **Подъе́хало** такси́. Оле́г сел в него́ и уе́хал в аэропо́рт.
6. Ди́ма осторо́жно **отхо́дит** от злой соба́ки.
7. О́ля и Па́ша **доплы́ли** до друго́го бе́рега и пото́м приплы́ли обра́тно.

A taxi drove up. Oleg got in it and drove off to the airport.
Dima is carefully backing up (walking away) from the mean dog.
Olia and Pasha sailed to the other shore and then sailed back.

PREFIX	MEANING	EXAMPLE VERBS	PREPOSITIONS
за-[1]*	tangent from main direction	заезжа́ть, зае́хать	в, на (куда́?) к (кому́)? за (кем? чем?)
за-[2]	behind or beyond	заходи́ть, зайти́	за (что?)
об-[1]*	movement encircling, going completely around	обходи́ть, обойти́	вокру́г (чего́?)
об-[2]	passing	объезжа́ть, объе́хать	Ø†
об-[3]	several stops (the "rounds")	обходи́ть, обойти́	Ø†

* The prefixes **за-** and **об-** have been numbered to differentiate between meanings.
† This prefix can be used without a preposition with a direct object in the accusative case.

8. Когда́ мы е́дем в Петербу́рг, мы всегда́ **заезжа́ем** в Но́вгород к Тама́ре Никола́евне.

Whenever we go to Petersburg, we always make a stop in Novgorod (slightly out of the way) to see Tamara Nikolaevna.

9. Де́ти игра́ли в пря́тки, и О́ля **зашла́** за кио́ск и там спря́талась.

The children were playing hide-and-seek and Olia went behind the newspaper stand and hid.

10. Мы е́хали по скоростно́й доро́ге и **объезжа́ли** большо́й грузови́к, когда́ в пе́рвый раз услы́шали э́тот стра́нный зву́к.

We were driving on a highway and were passing a big truck when we first heard this strange sound.

11. По четверга́м Татья́на Евге́ньевна **обхо́дит** все кни́жные магази́ны на Не́вском проспе́кте.

On Thursdays Tat'iana Evgen'evna regularly makes the rounds of all the bookstores on Nevsky Prospect.

PREFIX	MEANING	EXAMPLE VERBS	PREPOSITIONS
про-	through, across (emphasizing space crossed)	пролета́ть, пролете́ть	Ø, че́рез (что?), ми́мо (чего?)
пере-	through, across (emphasizing to the other side)	перебега́ть, перебежа́ть	Ø, че́рез (что?)

12. Наш самолёт сейча́с **пролета́ет** над Атланти́ческим океа́ном.

Our plane is now crossing the Atlantic Ocean.

13. Дава́йте сейча́с **перебежи́м** у́лицу, пока́ ещё нет движе́ния.

Let's cross the street now while there's still no traffic.

RUSSIAN Saying

Жизнь прожи́ть—не по́ле перейти́.

To live one's life is not as simple as crossing a meadow.
[Life is not a bowl of cherries.]

PREFIX	MEANING	EXAMPLE VERBS	PREPOSITIONS
с-[1]*	down	сходи́ть, сойти́	с (чего?), в, на (куда́?) из, с, от (отку́да?)
вз-(вс-)...в-	up	всходи́ть, взойти́ въежа́ть, въе́хать	на (что?) (куда́?)

* The prefix **с-** has been numbered to differentiate between meanings: see the chart on the next page.

The prefix **в-** is used with the following verbs: **éхать**, **нести́**, **вести́**, and **везти́** (among others). The prefix **вз-** or **вс-** is used with **ходи́ть** and **лета́ть**.

14.	(В авто́бусе) —Вы сейча́с не **схо́дите?**	*(In a bus) —Are you getting off now?*
	—Да, сейча́с **сойду́.**	*—Yes, I'm going to get off.*
15.	Мы **сошли́** с авто́буса и сра́зу уви́дели на́ших друзе́й.	*We got off the bus and saw our friends right away.*
16.	Мы **взошли́** на пя́тый эта́ж и нашли́ Андре́еву.	*We went up to the fifth floor and found Andreeva.*

PREFIX	MEANING	EXAMPLE VERBS	PREPOSITIONS
с-[2]	coming together from different points of origin	съезжа́ться, съе́хаться	куда́? (отку́да?)
раз-	going to different destinations from a single origin	разбега́ться, разбежа́ться	по (каки́м места́м?)

The prefix **раз-** changes to **рас-** when it is combined with **ходи́ть**: **расходи́ть(ся)**.

17.	На э́ту конфере́нцию **съезжа́ются** делега́ции из 50 ра́зных стран.	*Delegations from 50 different countries are coming to this conference.*
18.	Ле́нка разби́ла окно́, и все де́ти **разбежа́лись** по дома́м.	*Lenka broke a window and all the children ran off to their (respective) homes.*

✳ Упражне́ние 24а

For each example, identify the aspect and tense of the boldfaced prefixed verbs of motion. In addition, for imperfective verbs, determine whether the verb refers to (a) a single round-trip (for which the subject is no longer at the destination), (b) a single trip in progress, or (c) a frequent trip.

✳ Упражне́ние 24б

Look at the diagrams and assign to each a particular prefix. Compare your prefix assignments with your classmates. After you reach a consensus, redraw the diagrams on a separate piece of paper. Every prefix except one has a drawing. Make your own drawing for the missing prefix, number 18.

1.   **2.**   **3.**

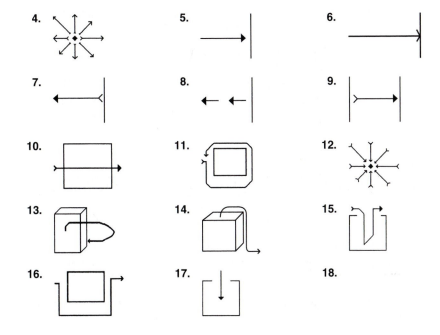

�֍ Упражне́ние 24в

Fill in the blanks with a prefix from the charts. Before you choose a prefix, be sure to look at the whole sentence and especially at any prepositional phrases, remembering that certain prepositions correspond to certain prefixes. Once you've found a prefix that seems right, go back to the charts and check that that prefix is possible given the grammatical context.

1. Та́ня обы́чно _____хо́дит домо́й с рабо́ты в 6 часо́в.
2. Го́льдман? Он эмигри́ровал, уже́ давно _____е́хал в Аме́рику!
3. Мы _____ъе́хали в гара́ж и поста́вили маши́ну.
4. _____ъе́хались все дя́ди, тёти, двою́родные бра́тья и сёстры из всей Аме́рики на ба́бушкин день рожде́ния.
5. Я сейча́с _____ойду́ к профе́ссору и спрошу́ его́ об э́том.
6. Мы обяза́тельно _____йдём к вам, когда́ мы бу́дем в Москве́.

Formation of Imperfective Verbs of Motion with Spatial Prefixes

PART 3

As you may have noticed in the examples and the sentences in **Упражне́ние 24в**, there are some irregularities in the formation of the imperfective prefixed verbs of motion.

Imperfective Verb Stems

Imperfective prefixed verbs of motion are formed from the combination of a spatial prefix and a multidirectional verb of motion (such as **ходи́ть**, **бе́гать**, **е́здить**, **пла́вать**, and **лета́ть**). Some of the multidirectional verbs of motion, however, use special forms when combined with a spatial prefix. **Ходи́ть** and **лета́ть** can be combined with spatial prefixes just as they are, but the verbs **бе́гать**, **е́здить**, and **пла́вать** use special forms when combined with prefixes—**-бега́ть**, **-езжа́ть**, **-плыва́ть**—as in the following chart.

MULTIDIRECTIONAL VERB AND CONJUGATION	+ PREFIX	= PREFIXED IMPERFECTIVE VERB AND CONJUGATION
бе́гать бе́гаю бе́гаешь бе́гают	в-	**вбега́ть** вбега́ю вбега́ешь вбега́ют
е́здить е́зжу е́здишь е́здят	при-	**приезжа́ть** приезжа́ю приезжа́ешь приезжа́ют
пла́вать пла́ваю пла́ваешь пла́вают	до-	**доплыва́ть** доплыва́ю доплыва́ешь доплыва́ют

The changes in the imperfective verb stems shown in the preceding chart are not specific to the prefixes **в-**, **при-**, **до-**, but rather typical of the transformation of the verb stem regardless of the prefix. In other words, attaching any prefix to these three verbs (**бе́гать**, **е́здить**, and **пла́вать**) results in the creation of new prefixed verbs **-бега́ть**, **-езжа́ть**, and **-плыва́ть**. (The dash in these forms indicates that the stems cannot stand alone without a prefix.)

Verbs That Require ъ

Imperfective verb stems beginning with a vowel (such as **-езжа́ть**) require the addition of the hard sign following prefixes ending with a consonant (such as **под-**, **раз-**, **с-**, and **от-**). Consider these infinitives: **подъезжа́ть**, **разъезжа́ться**, **съезжа́ться**, and **отъезжа́ть**. The hard sign is retained in all the conjugated forms of these infinitives.

Typical Conjugation Patterns

The following chart shows the conjugation patterns of several verbs of motion with one prefix, illustrating the conjugation patterns typical for all the verbs. Note that the hard sign is included in all the forms of **съезжа́ть** because its stem begins with a vowel, but its prefix ends in a consonant.

IMPERFECTIVE VERBS OF MOTION—PREFIXED						
		сходи́ть (*to walk down, off*)	**сбега́ть** (*to run down, off*)	**съезжа́ть** (*to ride down, off*)	**сплыва́ть** (*to swim, sail down, off*)	**слета́ть** (*to fly down, off*)
PRESENT	я	схожу́	сбега́ю	съезжа́ю	сплыва́ю	слета́ю
	ты	схо́дишь	сбега́ешь	съезжа́ешь	сплыва́ешь	слета́ешь
	они́	схо́дят	сбега́ют	съезжа́ют	сплыва́ют	слета́ют

�֎ Упражне́ние 24г

Using the preceding chart as a model, conjugate the following verbs, indicating the stress in each form: **подходи́ть, подбега́ть, заезжа́ть, залета́ть, приходи́ть, приплыва́ть, отъезжа́ть,** and **отбега́ть.** Compare your chart with the preceding chart.

�֎ Упражне́ние 24д

Fill in the blanks with a present-tense form of a prefixed imperfective verb of motion, as required by context and the English cues provided in parentheses.

Как я добира́юсь до университе́та

Я (exit) _____ и́з дому и (cross) _____ че́рез у́лицу. Я иду́ к остано́вке авто́буса и иногда́ (не ка́ждый день) (stop in) _____ в бу́лочную недалеко́ от остано́вки, там я покупа́ю ко́фе и пиро́жное. Я съеда́ю (*eat up*) пиро́жное и выпива́ю ко́фе до прихо́да авто́буса. Я (enter) _____ в авто́бус и (ride through, across) _____ три остано́вки. По́сле пе́рвой остано́вки авто́бус захо́дит на скоростну́ю доро́гу, и мы о́чень бы́стро (arrive) _____ в университе́тский городо́к. Че́рез две остано́вки я (get down) _____ с авто́буса, (walk around) _____ па́мятник Пу́шкину и (cross) _____ у́лицу. В э́то вре́мя я обы́чно (come, arrive) _____ к вы́воду (*conclusion*), что ужа́сно опа́здываю. Поэ́тому я (run across) _____ че́рез пло́щадь, повора́чиваю (*turn*) напра́во на Университе́тский проспе́кт, иду́ пря́мо и пото́м (run into, stop into) _____ в библиоте́ку за кни́гами, кото́рые нужны́ в э́тот день, и (fly into) _____ в зда́ние, в кото́ром нахо́дится на́ша лаборато́рия. Ле́том я так поте́ю (*sweat*) по доро́ге, что меня́ спра́шивают сотру́дники, отку́да я (arrive by swimming) _____ в университе́т, когда́ побли́зости нет никаки́х озёр.

Упражнéние 24е

Rewrite the paragraph in **Упражнéние 24д** so that the narrator describes how she or he used to go to the university campus in the past. Assume that the narrator is describing how she or he *generally* made the trip on a daily basis over an extended period of time. Use the imperfective past!

Упражнéние 24ё

Rewrite the paragraph in **Упражнéние 24д** so that the narrator describes how she or he will go to the university campus in the future. Assume that the narrator is describing how she or he will *generally* make the trip on a daily basis over an extended period of time. Use the imperfective future!

Задáние 24а

Using the paragraph in **Упражнéние 24д** as a model, write a paragraph explaining how you usually get to school from your home. Use as many verbs of motion and prefixes as you can. Keep your narration in the present tense, using imperfective verbs to explain what you do on a typical day. You may want to use the verb **поворáчивать (поворáчиваю, поворáчиваешь...кудá?)**, meaning *to turn*, with the expressions **налéво** (*to the left*) and **напрáво** (*to the right*) or the expression **идтú прямо** (*to go straight*). Try memorizing the paragraph by writing it out, reading it out loud, and recording it and listening to your recording several times.

Задáние 24б

Pick a starting point familiar to most students at your school and select a secret destination on your campus or in the city or town where your school is located. Prepare a three-minute presentation explaining how to get to your secret destination without mentioning the name of the destination itself. Your classmates follow along, drawing a map or using a campus map, and try to figure out where you are taking them. Keep your narration in the present tense, using imperfective verbs to explain how someone would usually go from the starting point to the destination. You may want to use expressions provided in **Задáние 24а**. Use as many prefixed imperfective verbs of motion as you can.

PART 4 Formation of Perfective Verbs of Motion with Spatial Prefixes

In Part 3 you read about the formation of prefixed imperfective verbs of motion and learned about stem changes for the verbs **бéгать** (**-бегáть**), **éздить** (**-езжáть**), and пла́вать (-плыва́ть). As you may have noticed in the examples and texts, there are also some irregularities in the formation of the perfective prefixed verbs of motion.

Perfective Verb Stems

Perfective prefixed verbs of motion are formed from the combination of a spatial prefix (described in Part 2 of this unit) and a unidirectional verb of motion (such as **идти́**, **бежа́ть**, **éхать**, **плыть**, and **лете́ть**). Most of these verbs have no special forms for combination with a spatial prefix. Only one of the verbs has a slight irregularity: **идти́**.

The verb **идти́** uses the stem **-йти́** when it is combined with any spatial prefix *except* **при-** to make a perfective verb of motion. Moreover, this stem requires the addition of the vowel **o** before all spatial prefixes ending in a consonant (such as **в-**, **под-**, **от-**, **об-**, **с-**, and **раз-**).

UNIDIRECTIONAL VERB AND CONJUGATION	+ PREFIX	= PREFIXED PERFECTIVE VERB AND CONJUGATION
идти́: иду́, идёшь, идёт, идём, идёте, иду́т, иди́! шёл, шла́, шли́	в-	войти́: войду́, войдёшь, войдёт, войдём, войдёте, войду́т, войди́! вошёл, вошла́, вошли́

Because the verb **прийти́** is an exception to this rule, you should memorize its conjugation: **прийти́, приду́, придёшь, придёт, придём, придёте, приду́т, приди́!*** **пришёл, пришла́, пришли́.**

Verbs That Require ъ

Perfective verb stems beginning with a vowel (such as **-éхать**) require the addition of the hard sign following prefixes ending with a consonant (such as **под-**, **раз-**, **с-**, and **от-**). Consider these infinitives: **подъéхать, разъéхаться, съéхаться,** and **отъéхать.** The hard sign is retained in all the conjugated forms of these infinitives.

Stress in Perfective Verbs with the Prefix *вы-*

The stress in *all* perfective verbs of motion with the prefix **вы-** falls on the prefix in *every* form of the verb: **вы́йти, вы́йду, вы́йдешь, вы́йдет, вы́йдем, вы́йдете, вы́йдут, вы́йди! вы́шел, вы́шла, вы́шли; вы́бежать, вы́бегу, вы́бежишь, вы́бежит, вы́бежим, вы́бежите, вы́бегут, вы́беги!, вы́бежал, вы́бежала, вы́бежали.**

---

* This form is rarely used. In general, imperatives that are invitations are imperfective, so Russians usually say **приходи́(те)!** or **иди́(те) сюда́!**

Typical Conjugation Patterns

The following chart shows the conjugation patterns of one prefixed verb of motion for each stem (**-йти́**, **-бежа́ть**, **-е́хать**, **-плыть**, and **-лете́ть**), illustrating the conjugation patterns typical for all the verbs. Note the vowel **о** in **отойти́** and the hard sign included in all the forms of **отъе́хать**.

PERFECTIVE VERBS OF MOTION—PREFIXED						
		отойти́ *(to walk away)*	**отбежа́ть** *(to run away)*	**отъе́хать** *(to ride away)*	**отплы́ть** *(to swim, sail away)*	**отлете́ть** *(to fly away)*
FUTURE	я	отойду́	отбегу́	отъе́ду	отплыву́	отлечу́
	ты	отойдёшь	отбежи́шь	отъе́дешь	отплывёшь	отлети́шь
	они́	отойду́т	отбегу́т	отъе́дут	отплыву́т	отлетя́т

❋ Упражне́ние 24ж

Using the preceding chart as a model, conjugate the following verbs, indicating the stress in each form: **подойти́**, **подбежа́ть**, **зае́хать**, **залете́ть**, **вы́йти**, **вы́ехать**, **приплы́ть**, **прие́хать**, **уйти́**, and **уплы́ть**.

❋ Упражне́ние 24з

Review the rules in Unit 21, Part 4 for selecting verbs of motion (on foot, by vehicle, running, in water, in air). Then fill in the blanks with a future-tense form of a prefixed perfective verb of motion, as required by context and the English cues provided in parentheses.

Как я пое́ду в университе́т за́втра у́тром

Я (exit) _____ и́з дому и (cross) _____ че́рез у́лицу. Я пойду́ к остано́вке авто́буса и (stop in) _____ в бу́лочную недалеко́ от остано́вки, там я куплю́ ко́фе и пиро́жное. Я съем (*eat up*) пиро́жное и вы́пью ко́фе до прихо́да авто́буса. Я (enter) _____ в авто́бус и (ride through, across) _____ три остано́вки. По́сле пе́рвой остано́вки авто́бус зайдёт на скоростну́ю доро́гу, и мы о́чень бы́стро (arrive) _____ в университе́тский городо́к. Че́рез две остано́вки я (get down) _____ с авто́буса, (walk around) _____ па́мятник Пу́шкину и (cross) _____ у́лицу. В э́то вре́мя я, наве́рно, (come, arrive) _____ к вы́воду (*conclusion*), что ужа́сно опа́здываю. Поэ́тому я (run across) _____ че́рез пло́щадь, поверну́ [turn] напра́во на Университе́тский проспе́кт, пойду́ пря́мо и пото́м (run into, stop into) _____ в библиоте́ку за кни́гами, кото́рые бу́дут нужны́, и (fly into) _____ в зда́ние, в кото́ром нахо́дится на́ша лаборато́рия. Я наве́рно так вспоте́ю (*sweat*) по доро́ге, что меня́ спро́сят сотру́дники, отку́да я (arrive by swimming) _____ в университе́т, когда́ побли́зости нет никаки́х озёр.

Упражнёние 24и

Rewrite the paragraph in **Упражнёние 24з** so that the narrator describes how she or he went to the university yesterday. Assume that the narrator is describing how she or he made the trip *once*. End the paragraph with the following sentence: **Я цёлый день рабо́тал/а и пото́м пое́хал/а домо́й.** Use the perfective past!

 Упражнёние 24й

Rewrite the paragraph in **Упражнёние 24з** so that it describes how two friends will go to the university tomorrow.

 ТЕКСТ 24б

The symbolist poet Blok wrote this poem soon after a major naval battle the Russians lost in the Russo-Japanese War of 1905.

Pre-reading Task

How do you think Russians might have felt after the loss of so many sailors and ships in this war with the Japanese? How did you feel when you heard of American casualties in the Gulf War or in Somalia?

> Дёвушка пёла в церко́вном хо́ре[1]
> О всех уста́лых в чужо́м краю́,[2]
> О всех корабля́х,[3] уше́дших в мо́ре,
> О всех забы́вших ра́дость[4] свою́.
> 5 Так пел её го́лос,[5] летя́щий в ку́пол,[6]
> И луч сия́л на бе́лом плече́,[7]
> И ка́ждый из мра́ка[8] смотре́л и слу́шал,
> Как бе́лое пла́тье пе́ло в луче́.
> И всем каза́лось, что ра́дость бу́дет,[9]
> 10 Что в ти́хой за́води все корабли́,[10]
> Что на чужби́не уста́лые лю́ди
> Све́тлую жизнь себе́ обрели́.[11]
> И го́лос был сла́док, и луч был то́нок,[12]
> И то́лько высо́ко,[13] у Ца́рских Врат,[14]
> 15 Прича́стный та́йнам,[15]—пла́кал ребёнок
> О том, что никто́ не придёт наза́д.
>
>   А. А. Блок, 1905

[1] пёла... *sang in a church choir*
[2] уста́лых... *tired people in a foreign land*
[3] *ships*
[4] *joy*
[5] *voice*
[6] в... *up to the cupola*
[7] луч... *ray of sunlight was shining on her white shoulder*
[8] из... *from the gloom*
[9] что... *that there would be joy*
[10] в... *all the ships are in a quiet harbor*
[11] на... *all the tired people in a foreign land had found a bright life for themselves*
[12] го́лос... *the voice was sweet and the ray of light was fine*
[13] *up high*
[14] у... *at the Holy Gates (of the church)*
[15] Прича́стный... *in communion with the holy mysteries*

Post-reading Tasks

1. Write a three-sentence summary of the poem.
2. Find the three verbs of motion (hint: two are active participles) and explain their meaning in the poem.
3. Find all the participles and identify their use.
4. Find all the Russian words meaning *foreign land*. What is the root of the Russian word for *foreign*? What is the opposite root?
5. Assume the point of view of someone else in the church and write a paragraph in which the girl's voice takes on an entirely different meaning.

Упражнéние 24к

Rewrite the paragraph in **Упражнéние 24з** so that it describes how two friends went to the university yesterday. End the paragraph with the following sentence: **Мы цéлый день рабóтали и потóм поéхали домóй.** Use the perfective past!

Задáние 24в

Using the paragraph in **Упражнéние 24з** as a model, write a paragraph explaining how you will go from school to your home (or somewhere else) at the end of the day today. Use as many verbs of motion and prefixes as you can. Keep your narration in the future tense, using perfective verbs to explain what you will do this afternoon or this evening. You may want to use the verb **повернýть** (**повернý, повернёшь...кудá?**), meaning *to turn*, with the expressions **налéво** (*to the left*) and **напрáво** (*to the right*) or the expression **пойтú прямо** (*to go straight*). Try memorizing the paragraph, writing it out and repeating it out loud several times. Try taping the paragraph and listening to your own voice to help you memorize it.

Задáние 24г

Pick a starting point familiar to many students at your school and select a secret destination on your campus or in the city or town where your school is located. Prepare a three-minute presentation explaining how to get to your secret destination without mentioning the name of the destination itself. Your classmates follow along, drawing a map or using a campus map, and try to figure out where you are taking them. Keep your narration in the future tense, using perfective verbs to explain how someone would make a single trip from the starting point to the destination. You may want to use expressions provided in **Задáние 24б**. Use as many prefixed perfective verbs of motion as you can.

PART 5 Idiomatic Expressions with Prefixed Verbs of Motion with Spatial Prefixes

Many prefixed verbs of motion are part of fixed expressions that are idiomatic or figurative in meaning. Here is a list of some of the most commonly used expressions.

входи́ть/войти́ в си́лу, в де́йствие, в систе́му	*to go into effect*
выходи́ть/вы́йти за́муж за кого?	*to get married (said of a woman only)*
доходи́ть/дойти́ до того́, что	*to get to the point when*
обходи́ться/обойти́сь (без чего)	*to get by (without something)*
переезжа́ть/перее́хать куда?	*to move (from one home to another)*
переходи́ть/перейти́ все преде́лы	*to cross all boundaries*
прибега́ть/прибе́гнуть к чему?	*to resort to something*
приходи́ть/прийти́ в го́лову (кому?)	*to come to mind to someone*
приходи́ть/прийти́ в себя́	*to come to oneself*
пробега́ть/пробежа́ть чем по чему? (па́льцами по кла́вишам, глаза́ми по страни́це)	*to run one's fingers over the keyboard, one's eyes over the page*
прохо́дит/пройдёт вре́мя	*time goes (will go) by*
проходи́ть/пройти́ что? (материа́л)	*to cover something (to cover some material) or to go through something (endure something)*
сходи́ть/сойти́ с ума́	*to go crazy, to lose one's mind*

❋ Упражне́ние 24л

Translate the following sentences into Russian using the idiomatic expressions in the preceding list.

1. We moved frequently (from one home to another) when I was little.
2. We just moved into a new apartment.
3. We haven't covered this material yet.
4. Maybe we can get by without a test.
5. This will go into effect tomorrow.
6. Lena got married to Vadim last week.
7. It's gotten to the point when we've gone crazy.
8. Now you've crossed all the boundaries!
9. It came to my mind to invite the Pavlovs.
10. A minute will go by and she'll come to herself.

RUSSIAN

Saying

Слы́шно, как му́ха пролети́т.

You could hear a fly flying past.
[You could hear a pin drop.]

※   Упражне́ние 24м

Continue your list of all the "connecting" words and phrases (such as *because*, *but*, *in the first place*, *then*, and so forth) with those you can find in the texts of this unit. Next to each "connecting" word or phrase, write out the clause or sentence in which they are used. Keep this list in your notebook and add to it as you continue with this book.

※   Упражне́ние 24н

Add the verbs of this unit to your lists of first- and second-conjugation verbs, noting the stress pattern of each verb as you do so.

※   Упражне́ние 24о

Make a list of the prepositions and cases that can be used with prefixes for the prefixed verbs of motion.

Bringing and Taking: Transitive Verbs of Motion

Перехо́дные глаго́лы движе́ния

Но́вый магази́н оде́жы в Москве́.

PART 1 Understanding Unprefixed Transitive Verbs of Motion

The preceding units presented unprefixed and prefixed intransitive verbs of motion. Those verbs of motion cannot take a direct object; they describe the movement of the subject to a destination (or from a point of origin), but cannot be used to describe a subject's movement of a direct object to a destination. In order to describe bringing and taking of people and things (by foot or by vehicle), we need to use the transitive verbs of motion, which also may be imperfective or perfective, prefixed or unprefixed.

Multidirectional Transitive Verbs of Motion—Unprefixed

The following chart shows the conjugation of three of the most commonly used transitive multidirectional verbs of motion: **носи́ть**, **води́ть**, and **вози́ть**.

IMPERFECTIVE: MULTIDIRECTIONAL TRANSITIVE VERBS OF MOTION WITHOUT SPATIAL PREFIXES				
		носи́ть *(to carry on foot)*	**води́ть** *(to lead by foot)*	**вози́ть** *(to transport by vehicle)*
PRESENT	я	ношу́	вожу́	вожу́
	ты	но́сишь	во́дишь	во́зишь
	они́	но́сят	во́дят	во́зят

✳ Упражне́ние 25а

Compare these verbs and their conjugation patterns with the conjugation patterns of the intransitive multidirectional verbs presented in Unit 24. Is there a verb in that group (**ходи́ть**, **бе́гать**, **е́здить**, **пла́вать**, or **лета́ть**) that has a similar conjugation pattern to these verbs?

There are six different uses for unprefixed multidirectional verbs of motion.

- Past-tense transitive multidirectional verbs are used for

    a. a single round-trip or
    b. repeated round-trips.

    1. Вчера́ мы **носи́ли** но́вые кни́ги к Татья́не Никола́евне.

    Yesterday we brought the new books to Tat'iana Nikolaevna (and we took the books away with us when we left).

2. Ка́ждый год мы **во́зим** ученико́в в Росси́ю, но в про́шлом году́ мы их **вози́ли** на Украи́ну.

Every year we take the schoolchildren to Russia, but last year we took them to the Ukraine.

In example 1, the speakers use the multidirectional verb in the past tense to indicate that they brought the new books to Tat'iana Nikolaevna, but left and took the books with them (a single round-trip in the past); the books are no longer at the home of Tat'iana Nikolaevna. In example 2, the speakers refer to a number of round-trips in the past.

- Present-tense multidirectional verbs are used for

  c. repeated trips or round-trips
  d. a single trip in several directions.

3. Мы ча́сто **во́дим** друзе́й к Татья́не Никола́евне.

We often bring our friends to see Tat'iana Nikolaevna.

4. Ко́сти сейча́с нет—он **во́зит** Джéссику по Москве́.

Kostia's not here right now: He's driving Jessica around Moscow.

In example 3, the speakers explain that they make repeated trips to bring friends to see Tat'iana Nikolaevna (each trip is, presumably, a round-trip, since they don't live with her). In example 4, the speaker explains that Kostia is out driving Jessica around Moscow, presumably showing her the sights or helping her run some errands. The multidirectional verb of motion is used to convey the idea that Kostia is driving Jessica to more than one destination.

- Future-tense multidirectional verbs are used for

  e. repeated trips.

5. Откры́лся но́вый спорти́вный клуб недалеко́ от на́шего до́ма: тепе́рь мы **бу́дем** ча́сто **води́ть** дете́й туда́.

A new sports club has opened near our house: Now we'll be bringing our children there frequently.

In example 5, the speakers explain that they will be making frequent or regular trips to the new club.

- In all tenses, multidirectional verbs of motion are used to express

  f. movement itself, the ability to move or movement for the sake of some kind of fun.

6. На́шей до́чери то́лько что испо́лнилось 13 ме́сяцев, но она́ уже́ **но́сит** ма́ленькие ве́щи в рука́х и не роня́ет их.

Our daughter just turned 13 months old, but she's already carrying small things in her hands without dropping them.

7. За́втра мы **бу́дем води́ть** госте́й
   из Испа́нии по го́роду.

   *Tomorrow we'll take our guests from
   Spain around town (on foot).*

8. Ра́ньше Гёна **вози́л** пассажи́ров в
   аэропо́рт, а тепе́рь он продаёт
   биле́ты в ка́ссе Аэрофло́та.

   *Gena used to drive passengers to the
   airport (and back), but now he
   sells tickets at the Aeroflot agency.*

- In addition, **носи́ть** and **води́ть** have two special idiomatic uses referring to
  movement itself.

  g. носи́ть оде́жду (сви́тер, руба́шку, брю́ки, ю́бку)
     to wear clothing (generally)

9. Она́ обы́чно **но́сит ю́бку**, но
   сего́дня она́ в джи́нсах.

   *She usually wears a skirt, but today
   she's wearing jeans.*

   h. води́ть маши́ну (хорошо́/пло́хо)
      to be driving a car, to be able to drive a car, to be a good or bad driver

10. Тама́ра Никола́евна хорошо́
    во́дит маши́ну: с ней за рулём
    я не бою́сь!

    *Tamara Nikolaevna is a good driver:
    When she's behind the wheel I'm
    not afraid!*

RUSSIAN

Saying

Води́ть кого́-нибудь за́ нос.

To lead someone around by the nose.
[To pull the wool over someone's eyes.]

✳ Упражне́ние 25б

Review the rules a through h to determine which one applies to each of the following
sentences.

1. На самолётах э́той авиакомпа́нии во́зят пассажи́ров, кото́рые хотя́т покупа́ть
   са́мые дешёвые биле́ты.
2. Мы ча́сто но́сим свою́ рабо́ту к Фёдоровым.
3. Вчера́ мы води́ли Тама́ру к сосе́дям, кото́рые живу́т на второ́м этаже́ на́шего
   до́ма.
4. В про́шлом году́ я вози́ла свои́ фотогра́фии к своему́ бра́ту в Москву́.
5. Зака́зные авто́бусы регуля́рно во́зят тури́стов по на́шей у́лице.
6. Э́тот грузови́к во́зит бо́льше маши́н, чем тот грузови́к.
7. Э́ти студе́нты почему́-то ча́сто но́сят га́лстуки.
8. Я ча́сто вожу́ ученико́в в э́ту библиоте́ку занима́ться.
9. Мари́не то́лько 16 лет, но она́ уже́ хорошо́ во́дит маши́ну.
10. Ки́ра сего́дня во́дит Сти́вена по го́роду.

✳ Упражнéние 25в

Use the preceding chart to fill in the blanks with the correct present-tense form of the verb. Then define the context of each sentence, using the rules a through h.

1. Мúша всегдá (wears) _____ гáлстук на занятия.
2. Этот автóбус ýтром (takes) _____ школьников в шкóлу, а днём—домóй.
3. Мы (take) _____ дóчку на урóки игры на скрúпке два рáза в недéлю.
4. Сергéй óпытный экскурсовóд и чáсто (takes) _____ турúстов по Кремлю́.
5. На рабóте я весь день (take, carry) _____ бумáги к рáзным директорáм.

Unidirectional* Transitive Verbs of Motion—Unprefixed

The unidirectional transitive verbs of motion are all conjugated in a similar way. The following chart sums up their conjugation patterns.

IMPERFECTIVE: UNIDIRECTIONAL TRANSITIVE VERBS OF MOTION WITHOUT SPATIAL PREFIXES				
		нестú *(to carry on foot)*	**вестú** *(to lead by foot)*	**везтú** *(to transport by vehicle)*
PRESENT	я	несý	ведý	везý
	ты	несёшь	ведёшь	везёшь
	онú	несýт	ведýт	везýт

✳ Упражнéние 25г

Review the conjugation of the unidirectional intransitive verbs of motion presented in Unit 24. Is there a verb in that group (**идтú**, **бежáть**, **éхать**, **плыть**, or **летéть**) whose conjugation is similar to the conjugation of the verbs in the preceding chart?

The unidirectional verbs **нестú**, **вестú**, and **везтú** can be used only in very restricted contexts.

- Past-tense transitive unidirectional verbs are used

   a. to indicate one trip in one direction in progress at the time of speech (when the speaker says something like *There goes X carrying...* or *When X was leading...*); or

   b. to refer to repeated trips in one direction, more often than not to one particular part of a trip (the trip there or the trip back) or "leg" of a trip in several stages, especially to convey how much time elapses during a part of the trip.

   11. Ларúса Николáевна **неслá** нам   *Larisa Nikolaevna was bringing us*
   газéту, когдá онá упáла.   *the newspaper when she fell.*

---

* Some people refer to these as *determinate* verbs.

12. Ра́ньше Вади́м Петро́вич обы́чно **вёл** дете́й в шко́лу, а его́ жена́ их **вела́** домо́й.

Vadim Petrovich used to take the children to school, and his wife used to bring them home.

- Present-tense transitive unidirectional verbs are used

  c. to indicate one trip in one direction in progress at the time of speech (when the speaker says something like *There goes...* or *When X is taking...*) or a trip that is about to take place (*She is taking Vadim to Petersburg tomorrow...*); or

  d. to refer to repeated trips in one direction, more often than not to one particular part of a trip (the trip there or the trip back) or "leg" of a trip in several stages, especially to convey how much time elapses during a part of the trip.

13. Лари́са Никола́евна **несёт** нам газе́ту. Спаси́бо!

Larisa Nikolaevna is bringing the newspaper to us. Thanks!

14. Вади́м Петро́вич обы́чно **ведёт** дете́й в шко́лу, а его́ жена́ их **ведёт** домо́й.

Vadim Petrovich usually takes the children to school, while his wife brings them home.

- Future-tense transitive unidirectional verbs are used

  e. to indicate one trip in one direction in progress at the time of speech (when the speaker says something like *There X will be taking...* or *When X will be taking...*); or

  f. to refer to repeated trips in one direction, more often than not to one particular part of a trip (the trip there or the trip back) or "leg" of a trip in several stages, especially to convey how much time elapses during a part of the trip.

15. Когда́ ты **бу́дешь везти́** америка́нцев ми́мо кни́жного магази́на, посмотри́, не поступи́ла ли там в прода́жу после́дняя кни́га Ахмаду́линой.

When you take the Americans past the bookstore, take a look to see if Akhmadulina's latest book hasn't become available.

16. На бу́дущей неде́ле Никола́й Абра́мович **бу́дет вести́** дете́й в шко́лу, а его́ жена́ **бу́дет** их **вести́** домо́й.

Next week Nikolai Abramovich will take the children to school, but his wife will bring them home.

RUSSIAN Saying

И у́хом не ведёт.

Without wiggling an ear.
[Without batting an eyelash.]

✳ Упражнéние 25д

Use the verbs in the preceding chart to fill in the blanks with the correct form of the verb required by context. For future tense, use the correct form of **бýду, бýдешь, бýдет**, and so on. Then determine which of the rules a through f applies to each sentence.

1. Вот Кóля (is carrying) _____ цветы́, навéрно, какóй-нибудь дéвушке!
2. Я обы́чно (take) _____ мла́дшего бра́та в шкóлу, когда́ я идý на рабóту.
3. Когда́ мы (were taking) _____ на́ших друзéй в аэропóрт, у нас слома́лась маши́на.
4. Кинó нахóдится далекó. Пешкóм мы (will be taking) _____ вас два часа́. Мы вас лýчше повезём на метрó.
5. У Вéры слома́лась маши́на. На бýдущей недéле она́ (will take) _____ проéкты на метрó.

Perfective Transitive Verbs of Motion Without Spatial Prefixes

The perfective transitive verbs of motion without spatial prefixes are completely regular in their formation, as shown in the following chart.

PERFECTIVE: TRANSITIVE VERBS OF MOTION WITHOUT SPATIAL PREFIXES				
		понести́ *(to carry on foot)*	повести́ *(to lead by foot)*	повезти́ *(to transport by vehicle)*
FUTURE	я	понесý	поведý	повезý
	ты	понесёшь	поведёшь	повезёшь
	они́	понесýт	поведýт	повезýт

✳ Упражнéние 25е

Use the verbs in the preceding chart to fill in the blanks with the correct form of the verb required by context. Then determine which rule, a or b, applies to each sentence.

1. Ты не (will take) _____ с собóй буты́лку кра́сного вина́ на пикни́к?
2. Лéны сейча́с нет—она́ ужé (went to take) _____ рабóту к дирéктору.
3. Где же Пéтя и Та́ня? Они́ (went to take) _____ бракóванный ча́йник в магази́н.
4. Па́ша, вы с сы́ном всё врéмя опа́здываете и спеши́те! Куда́ ты сейча́с (will take him off to) _____?
5. Óля (took) _____ дóчку на останóвку автóбуса, где они́ должны́ встрéтить америка́нского студéнта.
6. Когда́ ты (will take) _____ Антóна в Петербýрг, купи́ мне откры́тки с ви́дом Зи́мнего дворца́.
7. Снача́ла мы (took) _____ тури́стов на Кра́сную плóщадь, а потóм мы все вернýлись в гости́ницу.

8. Тама́ра Васи́льевна (will take) _____ му́жа с собо́й в командиро́вку в Воро́неж
   и Сама́ру.

9. Где же Са́ша? Она́ уже́ (left to take) _____ подру́гу на заня́тия.

The transitive perfective verbs of motion **понести́**, **повести́**, and **повезти́** can be used
only in very restricted contexts.

- Past-tense transitive perfective verbs are used

  a. to indicate one trip in one direction, with the result of that trip still in effect
     (unless another verb follows which reveals additional information).

- Future-tense transitive perfective verbs are used

  b. to indicate one trip in one direction, often with emphasis on the act of depar-
     ture itself.

PART 2
Understanding Prefixed Transitive Verbs of Motion

The prefixed transitive verbs of motion are formed by combining a spatial prefix with a
multidirectional verb of motion (such as **носи́ть**, **води́ть**, and **вози́ть**) or a unidirectional verb of motion (such as **нести́**, **вести́**, and **везти́**). When these verbs are combined with the spatial prefixes they undergo no stem changes whatsoever (unlike the
intransitive verbs of motion presented in the preceding units).

Imperfective Prefixed Transitive Verbs of Motion

The conjugation patterns of the transitive prefixed verbs of motion are shown in the
following chart.

IMPERFECTIVE: TRANSITIVE VERBS OF MOTION WITH SPATIAL PREFIXES		приноси́ть *(to carry on foot)*	приводи́ть *(to lead by foot)*	привози́ть *(to transport by vehicle)*
PRESENT	я	приношу́	привожу́	привожу́
	ты	прино́сишь	приво́дишь	привозишь
	они́	прино́сят	приво́дят	привозят

 Упражне́ние 25ё

Using the preceding chart as a model, conjugate the following verbs, indicating their
stress in each form: **подноси́ть**, **выводи́ть**, and **увози́ть**.

Saying

Своди́ть/Свести́ концы́ с конца́ми.

To bring ends together.
[To make ends meet.]

The rules governing the usage of the imperfective prefixed transitive verbs of motion are the same as those governing the imperfective prefixed intransitive verbs of motion. Specifically, such verbs are used

1. to convey frequent trips in one direction (in the past, present, or future tenses)

   У Ивано́вых слома́лась маши́на: на бу́дущей неде́ле Пе́тя бу́дет **подвози́ть** их на рабо́ту, а Та́ня бу́дет **привози́ть** их домо́й.

   The Ivanovs' car broke down: Next week Petia will take them (the Ivanovs) to work, and Tania will bring them home.

2. to convey the single leg of a single trip or motion (in the past, present, or future tenses)

   У Ивано́вых слома́лась маши́на: Пе́тя сейча́с **подвози́т** Ле́ну Ивано́ву на рабо́ту.

   The Ivanovs' car broke down: Petia is taking Lena Ivanova to work.

3. to convey the single leg of a frequent trip (in the past, present, or future tenses)

   У Ивано́вых слома́лась маши́на: на бу́дущей неде́ле Пе́тя бу́дет **подвози́ть** их на Не́вский проспе́кт, а отту́да они́ бу́дут добира́ться до рабо́ты са́ми.

   The Ivanovs' car broke down: Next week Petia will take them as far as Nevsky Prospect, and from there they'll get to work on their own.

Saying

Из избы́ со́ра не выноси́.

Don't carry garbage out of the house.
[Don't wash your dirty linen in public.]

It's important to remember that the prefix **от-** means *to drop off* (as well as *away from*) for imperfective transitive verbs of motion: **относи́ть** (*to take and drop off something*), **отводи́ть** (*to take and drop off someone*), **отвози́ть** (*to take and drop something or someone off by vehicle*).

Perfective Transitive Verbs of Motion—Prefixed

The perfective transitive verbs of motion with spatial prefixes also undergo no stem transformations whatsoever (unlike the intransitive verbs of motion). The following chart shows their conjugation patterns.

PERFECTIVE: TRANSITIVE VERBS OF MOTION WITH SPATIAL PREFIXES				
		принести (*to bring,* *carry on foot*)	**привести** (*to bring,* *lead by foot*)	**привезти** (*to bring,* *transport by vehicle*)
FUTURE	я ты они́	принесу́ принесёшь принесу́т	приведу́ приведёшь приведу́т	привезу́ привезёшь привезу́т

✳ Упражне́ние 25ж

Using the preceding chart as a model, conjugate the following verbs, indicating their stress in each form: **поднести**, **вы́вести**, and **увезти**.

These perfective transitive verbs of motion express one movement in a single direction, when the consequences of movement are still in effect (until otherwise explicitly stated).

Она́ **принесла́** нам одну́ кни́гу в сре́ду и сказа́ла, что **принесёт** другу́ю в пя́тницу.	*She brought us one book on Wednesday (and left the book with us), and said that she would bring (will bring) another (book) on Friday.*

ТЕКСТ 25а

Read the excerpt from Grossman's novel *Life and Fate* about people caught up in World War II in the former Soviet Union. In this excerpt an old Jewish doctor writes to her son, who is serving in the Red Army, about the resettlement of Jews into a ghetto during the Nazi occupation.

Note: Some people may find the text disturbing.

Pre-reading Task

What do you know about the resettlement of Jews into ghettos by the Nazis? What sorts of events do you think this doctor might describe in her letter?

...Когда́ я собрала́сь в путь[1] и ду́мала, как мне дотащи́ть корзи́ну до Ста́рого го́рода,[2] неожи́данно <u>пришёл</u> мой пацие́нт Щу́кин, угрю́мый и, мне каза́лось, чёрствый челове́к.[3] Он взя́лся[4] <u>понести́</u> мои́ ве́щи, дал мне три́ста рубле́й и сказа́л, что бу́дет раз в неде́лю <u>приноси́ть</u> мне хлеб к огра́де.[5] Он рабо́тает в типогра́фии, на фронт его́ не взя́ли по боле́зни глаз. До войны́ он лечи́лся у меня́,[6] и, е́сли бы мне предложи́ли перечи́слить люде́й с отзы́вчивой, чи́стой душо́й,[7] я назвала́ бы деся́тки имён, но не его́. Зна́ешь, Ви́тенька, по́сле его́ <u>прихо́да</u> я сно́ва почу́вствовала себя́ челове́ком, зна́чит, ко мне не то́лько дворо́вая соба́ка[8] мо́жет <u>относи́ться</u>[9] по-челове́чески.

Он рассказа́л мне—в городско́й типогра́фии печа́тается прика́з:[10] евре́ям запрещено́[11] <u>ходи́ть</u> по тротуа́рам,[12] они́ должны́ носи́ть на груди́ жёлтую ла́ту в ви́де шестиконе́чной звезды́,[13] они́ не име́ют пра́ва по́льзоваться[14] тра́нспортом, ба́нями,[15] посеща́ть амбулато́рии,[16] <u>ходи́ть</u> в кино́, запреща́ется покупа́ть ма́сло, я́йца, молоко́, я́годы,[17] бе́лый хлеб, мя́со, все о́вощи, исключая́[18] карто́шку; поку́пки на база́ре разреша́ется[19] де́лать то́лько по́сле шести́ ве́чера (когда́ крестья́не <u>уезжа́ют</u> с база́ра). Ста́рый го́род бу́дет обнесён колю́чей про́волокой,[20] и <u>вы́ход</u> за про́волоку запрещён, мо́жно то́лько под конво́ем на принуди́тельные рабо́ты.[21] При обнаруже́нии[22] евре́я в ру́сском до́ме хозя́ину— расстре́л, как за укры́тие партиза́на.[23]

Тесть[24] Щу́кина, стари́к крестья́нин, <u>прие́хал</u> из сосе́днего месте́чка Чудно́ва[25] и ви́дел свои́ми глаза́ми, что всех ме́стных евре́ев с узла́ми[26] и чемода́нами погна́ли[27] в лес, и отту́да в тече́ние всего́ дня <u>доноси́лись</u> вы́стрелы и ди́кие кри́ки,[28] ни оди́н челове́к не верну́лся...

Как печа́лен[29] был мой путь, сыно́чек, в средневеко́вое[30] ге́тто. Я шла по го́роду, в кото́ром прорабо́тала 20 лет. Сперва́ мы <u>шли</u> по пусты́нной[31] Свечно́й у́лице. Но когда́ мы <u>вы́шли</u> на Нико́льскую, я уви́дела со́тни[32] люде́й, <u>ше́дших</u> в э́то прокля́тое[33] ге́тто. У́лица ста́ла бе́лой от узло́в, от поду́шек.[34] Больны́х[35] вели́ под руки. Парализо́ванного отца́ до́ктора Маргу́лиса несли́ на одея́ле.[36] Оди́н молодо́й челове́к <u>нёс</u> на рука́х стару́ху, а за ним <u>шли</u> жена́ и де́ти...

В. С. Гро́ссман, «Жизнь и судьба́», 1960

1. Когда́... When I had gotten myself ready for the trip (to the ghetto)
2. как... how will I get my basket to the Old City (location of the ghetto)
3. неожи́данно... suddenly my patient, Shchukin, came by, a sullen and callous man, it seemed to me
4. took it upon himself
5. fence (of the ghetto)
6. он... I treated him
7. е́сли... if I were asked to name people with a kind-hearted and good soul
8. дворо́вая... mutt (stray dog)
9. relate to me
10. печа́тается... an order is being printed
11. евре́ям... Jews are forbidden
12. sidewalks
13. на... yellow patch on their chest in the form of a six-pointed star
14. не... do not have the right to use
15. public baths
16. посеща́ть... visit outpatient clinics
17. berries
18. excluding
19. поку́пки... purchases at the bazaar are permitted to be made
20. колю́чей... barbed wire
21. под... under armed guard for forced labor
22. При... upon the finding of
23. хозя́ину... the home owner will be executed just as if for the hiding of a partisan
24. father-in-law (of a man)
25. из... from the neighboring little town of Chudnov
26. bundles
27. chased
28. отту́да... from there during the course of the entire day, were heard shots and wild screams
29. sorrowful
30. medieval
31. deserted
32. hundreds
33. cursed
34. pillows
35. the sick
36. blanket

Post-reading Tasks

1. Write a five-sentence summary of the text in Russian.
2. Identify the aspect and tense of the underlined verbs of motion (both transitive

and intransitive) and the words derived from verbs of motion. Explain if they are used to convey frequent motion in a single direction, one round-trip, or one trip in a single direction.

3. Write a response to this letter from the son to whom it was written.

RUSSIAN

Saying

Обвести́ кого́-нибудь вокру́г па́льца.

To twist someone around one's little finger.
[To wrap someone around one's little finger.]

✳ Упражне́ние 25з

Fill in the blanks with a correct form of one of the following verbs of motion: **ходи́ть, идти́, пойти́, выходи́ть, вы́йти, выезжа́ть, вы́ехать, относи́ть, отнести́, подвози́ть, подвезти́, выноси́ть, вы́нести, уводи́ть,** and **увести́.**

Мы с дру́гом реши́ли встре́титься на ста́нции метро́ «Изма́йловская» в 12 часо́в в суббо́ту и _____ в парк на пикни́к. В 9 часо́в я проснулся и на́чал ду́мать о том, что мне на́до сде́лать до на́шей встре́чи. Я реши́л, что как то́лько я _____ йз дому, по доро́ге в метро́, я _____ снача́ла в продукто́вый магази́н и куплю́ хоро́ший сыр и све́жие я́блоки. Да ещё мне на́до бы́ло _____ боти́нки бра́та в мастерску́ю, потому́ что каблуки́ слома́лись.

✳ Упражне́ние 25и

Discuss with your classmates the strategies you used to complete **Упражне́ние 25к.** Did you find it challenging or easy? How did you figure out which verb to use? Compare notes with your classmates and try using a new strategy for the exercises in the *Workbook* that continue this story.

♪ Зада́ние 25а

Pick a starting point familiar to many students at your school and select a secret destination on your campus or in the city or town where your school is located. Prepare a three-minute presentation explaining how you led someone from that point to your secret destination.

♪ Зада́ние 25б

Pick a starting point familiar to many students at your school and select a secret destination on your campus or in the city or town where your school is located. Prepare a three-minute presentation explaining how you carry something from that point to your secret destination on a frequent basis.

PART 3
Idiomatic Expressions with Transitive Verbs of Motion

The transitive verbs of motion are featured in a great many idiomatic expressions. Here is a list of some of the most commonly used expressions with these verbs.

вести́ дневни́к, обсужде́ние, ле́кцию	to keep a diary, to conduct a discussion or lecture
вести́ себя́ (хорошо́, пло́хо)*	to behave oneself (well or poorly)
доводи́ть/довести́ кого́-нибудь до чего́ (до отча́яния)	to drive someone to something (to a state of despair, for example)
доноси́ть/донести́ на кого́-нибудь кому́-нибудь	to inform on someone to someone
своди́ть/свести́ кого́-нибудь с ума́	to drive someone crazy
подводи́ть/подвести́ кого́-нибудь	to deceive, to disappoint, to let someone down
подвози́ть/подвезти́ кого́-нибудь куда́	to drive someone to a destination, to give someone a ride somewhere
сноси́ть/снести́ что́-нибудь	to tear something down
относи́ть(ся)/отнести́(сь) что к чему́? (non-reflexive) к чему́ как? (reflexive)	to relate something to something else, to have an attitude toward something
произноси́ть(ся)/ произнести́(сь)	to pronounce something, to be pronounced
переводи́ть/перевести́ с како́го языка́ на како́й язы́к	to translate something
приводи́ть/привести́	to cite
приводи́ть/привести́ кого́-нибудь в себя́	to bring someone to, to revive someone
ввози́ть/ввезти́ что́-нибудь (отку́да, куда́?)	to import
вывози́ть/вы́везти что́-нибудь (отку́да, куда́?)	to export

1. Я ра́ньше вёл/вела́ дневни́к, но бо́льше его́ не веду́.

   I used to keep a diary, but I don't anymore.

2. Э́ти де́ти пло́хо себя́ веду́т. Веди́те себя́ хорошо́!

   These children are behaving poorly. Behave yourselves (well)!

3. Они́ меня́ довели́ до отча́яния.

   They have driven me to despair.

---

*In English it is possible for parents to say to their children, *Behave yourselves!* But in Russian, parents must say, *Behave yourselves well!*: «**Веди́(те) себя́ хорошо́**». Without an adverb (such as *well* or *poorly*) the expression *to behave oneself* has no meaning.

4. Эти профессора́ сво́дят нас с ума́!

These professors are driving us crazy!

5. Сейча́с сно́сят ста́рый дом на
    Тверско́й.

They're tearing down an old building
    on Tverskaya (Street) now.

6. Я пло́хо отношу́сь к ним, а они́
    пло́хо отно́сятся ко мне. У нас
    плохи́е отноше́ния.

I relate poorly to them, and they to
    me. We have a poor relationship.

7. Э́то явле́ние отно́сится к
    пробле́ме безрабо́тицы.

This phenomenon is related to the
    problem of unemployment.

8. Как произно́сится э́то сло́во?

How is this word pronounced?

9. Мы ча́сто перево́дим таки́е
    статьи́ с япо́нского языка́ на
    англи́йский язы́к.

We often translate such articles from
    Japanese into English.

10. Я привожу́ э́ту стати́стику в
    доказа́тельство.

I am citing this statistic as proof,
    evidence.

❉ Упражне́ние 25й

Fill in the blanks with the correct form of the verb as required by context.

1. Я ду́маю, что президе́нт (will cite) _____ в ка́честве приме́ра уда́чи в о́бласти
    вне́шней поли́тики перегово́ры с Япо́нией.
2. Когда́ (will they tear down) _____ э́тот дом?
3. Профе́ссор (conducted) _____ обсужде́ние по э́тому вопро́су вчера́.
4. Де́ти о́чень хорошо́ себя́ (behaved) _____ в музе́е.
5. Ты меня́ (will give a lift) _____ на вокза́л?

❉ Упражне́ние 25к

Translate the following sentences into Russian.

1. These children are behaving themselves very well.
2. It drove me to despair.
3. This is related to Andreeva's plan.
4. You are driving me crazy!

ТЕКСТ 256

This is Pasternak's poem, "Hamlet," one of the poems included at the end of *Doctor
Zhivago* and supposedly the work of Zhivago himself.

Pre-reading Task

What do you know about Shakespeare's *Hamlet*? Make some predictions about which
three or four facts from Shakespeare's tragedy might play an important role in a poem
by a twentieth-century Russian poet and see if you're right.

Гамлет

Гул затих.[1] Я вышел на подмостки.[2]
Прислонясь к дверному косяку,[3]
Я ловлю в далёком отголоске,[4]
Что случится на моём веку.[5]
5 На меня наставлен сумрак ночи
Тысячью биноклей на оси.[6]
Если только можно, Авва Отче,[7]
Чашу эту мимо пронеси.[8]
Я люблю Твой замысел упрямый
10 И играть согласен эту роль.
Но сейчас идёт другая драма,
И на этот раз меня уволь.[10]
Но продуман распорядок действий,[11]
И неотвратим конец пути.[12]
15 Я один, всё тонет в фарисействе.[13]
Жизнь прожить—не поле перейти.[14]

Б. Л. Пастернак, 1946

[1] Гул... *The roar has subsided*
[2] на... *on the stage*
[3] Прислонясь... *Leaning against the door frame*
[4] в... *in the distant echo*
[5] Что... *What will happen in my lifetime*
[6] На... *the gloom of the night is focused on me in a thousand binoculars*
[7] Авва... *Abba, Father*
[8] Чашу... *take this cup away from me*
[9] Твой... *Your stubborn design*
[10] меня... *leave me out*
[11] продуман... *the order of the acts of the play has been thought out*
[12] неотвратим... *the end of the path is inevitable*
[13] всё... *everything is drowning in hypocrisy*
[14] *Find this proverb in Unit 24!*

Post-reading Tasks

1. Write a two- or three-sentence summary of the poem.
2. What is the root of the Russian word meaning *echo*? Do you know any other words with this root?
3. What is the root of the Russian word meaning *to happen*? Do you know any other words with this root?
4. Find all the verbs of motion in the poem and identify whether they are multidirectional, unidirectional, or perfective. Then determine their spatial meaning.
5. Assume the point of view of an actress playing Hamlet's mother or Ophelia and write a response to the Hamlet who is the narrator of this poem.

✳ Упражнение 25л

Continue your list of all the "connecting" words and phrases (such as *because, but, in the first place, then,* and so forth) with those you can find in the texts of this unit. Next to each "connecting" word or phrase, write out the clause or sentence in which they are used.

✳ Упражнение 25м

Add the verbs of this unit to your lists of first- and second-conjugation verbs, noting the stress pattern of each verb as you do so.

Classroom Expressions and Grammatical Terms

Повтори́те, пожа́луйста.	*Please repeat.*
Говори́те гро́мче, пожа́луйста.	*Please speak more loudly.*
Прочита́йте пе́рвое предложе́ние.	*Read the first sentence.*
Подойди́те к доске́, пожа́луйста, и напиши́те...	*Please go to the board and write...*
Сади́тесь в гру́ппы и поговори́те ме́жду собо́й о то́м, что...	*Sit down in groups and talk among yourselves about...*
Поговори́те с партнёром/сосе́дом о том, что...	*Talk with your partner about...*
Извини́те, я не по́нял/поняла́.	*Excuse me, but I didn't understand.*
Я не понима́ю тре́тье сло́во сле́ва/спра́ва.	*I don't understand the third word from the left/right.*
Я не понима́ю второ́е сло́во на четвёртой стро́чке све́рху.	*I don't understand the second word on the fourth line from the top.*
Я не понима́ю пя́тое сло́во на шесто́й стро́чке сни́зу.	*I don't understand the fifth word on the sixth line from the bottom.*
Подними́те ру́ки, е́сли...	*Raise your hands if...*
глаго́л	*verb*
Как спряга́ется э́тот глаго́л?	*How is this verb conjugated?*
инфинити́в	*infinitive*
перехо́дный глаго́л	*transitive verb*
неперехо́дный глаго́л	*intransitive verb*
пе́рвое лицо́	*first person*
второ́е лицо́	*second person*
тре́тье лицо́	*third person*
еди́нственное число́	*singular*
мно́жественное число́	*plural*
императи́в, фо́рма повели́тельного наклоне́ния	*imperative*
глаго́лы движе́ния	*verbs of motion*
глаго́лы движе́ния с приста́вками	*verbs of motion with prefixes*
сослага́тельное наклоне́ние	*conditional (subjunctive) mood*

прошéдшее врéмя	*past tense*
настоя́щее врéмя	*present tense*
бу́дущее врéмя	*future tense*
совершéнный вид	*perfective aspect*
несовершéнный вид	*imperfective aspect*
и́мя существи́тельное	*noun*
Как склоня́ется э́то (и́мя) существи́тельное?	*How is this noun declined?*
Како́го рóда э́то слóво?	*This word is of what gender?*
(Онó) мужскóго рóда.	*It's masculine.*
(Онó) жéнского рóда.	*It's feminine.*
(Онó) срéднего рóда.	*It's neuter.*
мя́гкое окончáние	*soft ending*
твёрдое окончáние	*hard ending*
В какóм падежé стои́т э́то слóво?	*This word is in what case?*
(Онó стои́т) в —ом падежé	*It's in the — case.*
имени́тельный падéж	*nominative case*
вини́тельный падéж	*accusative case*
роди́тельный падéж	*genitive case*
предлóжный падéж	*prepositional case (locative case)*
дáтельный падéж	*dative case*
твори́тельный падéж	*instrumental case*
местоимéние	*pronoun*
и́мя прилагáтельное	*adjective*
крáткой фóрмы	*short form*
пóлной фóрмы	*long form*
сравни́тельной стéпени	*comparative degree*
превосхóдной стéпени	*superlative degree*
Как пи́шется э́то слóво?	*How is this word written (spelled)?*
Как произнóсится э́то слóво?	*How is this word pronounced?*
предлóг	*preposition*
Какóй падéж употребля́ется пóсле этого предлóга?	*Which case is used after this preposition?*
нарéчие	*adverb*
Э́то—исключéние.	*This is an exception.*
причáстие	*participle*
страдáтельное, действи́тельное	*passive, active*
деепричáстие	*verbal adverb*
междомéтие	*interjection*
сою́з	*conjunction*
части́ца	*particle*

APPENDIX 2 Literary Terms

худо́жественная литерату́ра	belles lettres, *literature that is "creative writing" (poetry, drama, prose fiction)*
про́за	*prose (not poetry)*
расска́з	*short story*
по́весть	*short novel*
рома́н	*novel*
содержа́ние	*content*
фа́була	*plot*
сюже́т	*story (how the plot is reworked in the course of the novel or story)*
те́ма	*theme*
зачи́н	*introduction*
завя́зка	*the creation or setting of a conflict or problem*
развя́зка	*the denouement*
концо́вка	*conclusion, ending*
эпизо́д	*episode*
отступле́ние	*digression*
моти́в	*motif*
ме́стный колори́т	*local color*
расска́зчик	*narrator*
повествова́ние	*narration*
де́йствие (происхо́дит где? когда́?)	*the action (takes place where and when?)*
хара́ктер	*personality or temperament*
геро́й/герои́ня	*hero, protagonist*
де́йствующее лицо́	*character (in a work of art)*
собы́тие/собы́тия	*event*
(чья) то́чка зре́ния на…	*(whose) point of view on… (+ acc.)*
Их конфли́кт заключа́ется в том, что	*Their conflict consists of the question…*
фигу́ра ре́чи	*figure of speech*
о́браз	*image*
о́бразная речь	*figurative speech*

сравне́ние	*simile, comparison*
сравни́ть/сра́внивать что с чем?	*to compare something* (acc.) *with something else* (instr.)
мета́фора	*metaphor*
метони́мия	*metonymy*
сино́ним	*synonym*
анто́ним	*antonym*
си́мвол	*symbol*
олицетворе́ние	*personification (the rendering of something inanimate as living)*
метаморфо́за	*metamorphosis*
переска́з	*paraphrase*
иро́ния	*irony*
остране́ние	*estrangement, the making strange of something*
поэти́ческий си́нтаксис	*poetic syntax*
параллели́зм	*parallelism*
литерату́рный приём	*literary device*
поэ́зия	*poetry*
ли́рика	*lyrics, lyrical poetry*
стихотворе́ние	*lyric poem (one work of literature)*
стихи́	*poetry, verse*
поэ́ма	*long, narrative poem*
о́да	*ode*
эпигра́мма	*epigram*
эпи́граф	*epigraph*
сати́ра	*satire*
ба́сня	*fable*
балла́да	*ballad*
пье́са	*play*
дра́ма	*drama*
траге́дия	*tragedy*
коме́дия	*comedy*
моноло́г	*monologue*
де́йствие	*act (of a play) or action (of a work of prose fiction)*
ска́зка	*fairy tale*
зага́дка	*riddle*

APPENDIX 3 Declension Charts

Nouns

**Таблица 1 Masculine Nouns with Stem Stress
(except masculine nouns ending in -ий)**

SINGULAR ENDINGS					
	INANIMATE HARD STEM	**ANIMATE HARD STEM**	**INANIMATE SOFT STEM**	**ANIMATE SOFT STEM**	**ENDINGS**
NOMINATIVE кто/что	учёбник	филóсоф	музéй	стройтель	Ø
ACCUSATIVE когó/что	учёбник	филóсофа	музéй	стройтеля	Ø, -а/-я
GENITIVE когó/чегó	учёбника	филóсофа	музéя	стройтеля	-а/-я
PREPOSITIONAL о ком/чём	учёбнике	филóсофе	музéе	стройтеле	-е
DATIVE комý/чемý	учёбнику	филóсофу	музéю	стройтелю	-у/-ю
INSTRUMENTAL кем/чем	учёбником	филóсофом	музéем	стройтелем	-ом/-ем
PLURAL ENDINGS					
	INANIMATE HARD STEM	**ANIMATE HARD STEM**	**INANIMATE SOFT STEM**	**ANIMATE SOFT STEM**	**ENDINGS**
NOMINATIVE кто/что	учёбники	филóсофы	музéи	стройтели	-ы/-и
ACCUSATIVE когó/что	учёбники	филóсофов	музéи	стройтелей	-ы/-и -ов/-ев/-ей
GENITIVE когó/чегó	учёбников	филóсофов	музéев	стройтелей	-ов/-ев/-ей
PREPOSITIONAL о ком/чём	учёбниках	филóсофах	музéях	стройтелях	-ах/-ях

PLURAL ENDINGS					
	INANIMATE HARD STEM	**ANIMATE HARD STEM**	**INANIMATE SOFT STEM**	**ANIMATE SOFT STEM**	**ENDINGS**
DATIVE кому́/чему́	уче́бникам	фило́софам	музе́ям	строи́телям	-ам/-ям
INSTRUMENTAL кем/чем	уче́бниками	фило́софами	музе́ями	строи́телями	-ами/-ями

Табли́ца 2   Masculine Nouns with End Stress

SINGULAR ENDINGS					
	INANIMATE HARD STEM	**ANIMATE HARD STEM**	**INANIMATE SOFT STEM**	**ANIMATE SOFT STEM**	**ENDINGS**
NOMINATIVE кто/что	каранда́ш	певе́ц	ого́нь	царь	Ø
ACCUSATIVE кого́/что	каранда́ш	певца́	ого́нь	царя́	Ø, -а́/-я́
GENITIVE кого́/чего́	карандаша́	певца́	огня́	царя́	-а́/-я́
PREPOSITIONAL о ком/чём	карандаше́	певце́	огне́	царе́	-é
DATIVE кому́/чему́	карандашу́	певцу́	огню́	царю́	-у́/-ю́
INSTRUMENTAL кем/чем	карандашо́м	певцо́м	огнём	царём	-о́м/-ём

PLURAL ENDINGS					
	INANIMATE HARD STEM	**ANIMATE HARD STEM**	**INANIMATE SOFT STEM**	**ANIMATE SOFT STEM**	**ENDINGS**
NOMINATIVE кто/что	карандаши́	певцы́	огни́	цари́	-ы́/-и́
ACCUSATIVE кого́/что	карандаши́	певцо́в	огни́	царе́й	-ы́/-и́ -о́в/-éв/-éй
GENITIVE кого́/чего́	карандаше́й	певцо́в	огне́й	царе́й	-о́в/-éв/-éй
PREPOSITIONAL о ком/чём	карандаша́х	певца́х	огня́х	царя́х	-а́х/-я́х
DATIVE кому́/чему́	карандаша́м	певца́м	огня́м	царя́м	-а́м/-я́м
INSTRUMENTAL кем/чем	карандаша́ми	певца́ми	огня́ми	царя́ми	-а́ми/-я́ми

Табли́ца 3   Neuter Nouns with Stem Stress and End Stress
(except neuter nouns ending in *-ие*)

SINGULAR ENDINGS					
	INANIMATE HARD STEM STEM STRESS	**INANIMATE SOFT STEM STEM STRESS**	**INANIMATE HARD STEM END STRESS**	**INANIMATE SOFT STEM END STRESS**	**ENDINGS**
NOMINATIVE кто/что	де́ло	побере́жье	письмо́	бельё	-о, -е
ACCUSATIVE кого́/что	де́ло	побере́жье	письмо́	бельё	-о, -е
GENITIVE кого́/чего́	де́ла	побере́жья	письма́	белья́	-а/-я
PREPOSITIONAL о ком/чём	де́ле	побере́жье	письме́	белье́	-е
DATIVE кому́/чему́	де́лу	побере́жью	письму́	белью́	-у/-ю
INSTRUMENTAL кем/чем	де́лом	побере́жьем	письмо́м	бельём	-ом/-ем (-ём)
PLURAL ENDINGS					
	INANIMATE HARD STEM STEM STRESS	**INANIMATE SOFT STEM STEM STRESS**	**INANIMATE HARD STEM END STRESS**	**INANIMATE SOFT STEM END STRESS**	**ENDINGS**
NOMINATIVE кто/что	пи́сьма	побере́жья	дела́	питья́*	-а/-я
ACCUSATIVE кого́/что	пи́сьма	побере́жья	дела́	питья́	-а/-я
GENITIVE кого́/чего́	пи́сем	побере́жий	дел	питéй	Ø
PREPOSITIONAL о ком/чём	пи́сьмах	побере́жьях	дела́х	питья́х	-ах/-ях
DATIVE кому́/чему́	пи́сьмам	побере́жьям	дела́м	питья́м	-ам/-ям
INSTRUMENTAL кем/чем	пи́сьмами	побере́жьями	дела́ми	питья́ми	-ами/-ями

* Nouns of this type are highly infrequent.

Табл#ица 4   Masculine and Neuter Nouns Ending in -*ий* or -*ие*

SINGULAR ENDINGS				
	ANIMATE MASCULINE	**INANIMATE MASCULINE**	**NEUTER**	**ENDINGS**
NOMINATIVE кто/что	Дмѝтрий	планетѝрий	упражнѐние	Ø, -е
ACCUSATIVE когѝ/что	Дмѝтрия	планетѝрий	упражнѐние	Ø/-я, -е
GENITIVE когѝ/черѝ	Дмѝтрия	планетѝрия	упражнѐния	-я
PREPOSITIONAL о ком/чём	Дмѝтрии	планетѝрии	упражнѐнии	-и
DATIVE комѝ/чемѝ	Дмѝтрию	планетѝрию	упражнѐнию	-ю
INSTRUMENTAL кем/чем	Дмѝтрием	планетѝрием	упражнѐнием	-ем

Nouns of this type take soft endings (as demonstrated in the ENDINGS column) and use a different ending for the prepositional case than the other masculine and neuter nouns.

Masculine nouns ending in **-ой (герѝй), -ей (музѐй), -ай (трамвѝй)** decline according to the pattern for soft masculine nouns with stem stress as depicted in **Таблѝца 1**.

PLURAL ENDINGS				
	ANIMATE MASCULINE	**INANIMATE MASCULINE**	**NEUTER**	**ENDINGS м/с**
NOMINATIVE кто/что	Дмѝтрии	планетѝрии	упражнѐния	м: -и с: -я
ACCUSATIVE когѝ/что	Дмѝтриев	планетѝрии	упражнѐния	м: -и, -ев с: -я
GENITIVE когѝ/черѝ	Дмѝтриев	планетѝриев	упражнѐний	-ев, Ø
PREPOSITIONAL о ком/чём	Дмѝтриях	планетѝриях	упражнѐниях	-ях
DATIVE комѝ/чемѝ	Дмѝтриям	планетѝриям	упражнѐниям	-ям
INSTRUMENTAL кем/чем	Дмѝтриями	планетѝриями	упражнѐниями	-ями

Plural endings in the nominative and accusative cases are different for masculine nouns (**м**) and neuter nouns (**с**) as shown on the preceding chart.

Табли́ца 5   Feminine Nouns Ending in *-a/-я*

SINGULAR ENDINGS					
	INANIMATE NOUNS ENDING IN -a	ANIMATE NOUNS ENDING IN -a	INANIMATE NOUNS ENDING IN -я	ANIMATE NOUNS ENDING IN -я	ENDINGS
NOMINATIVE кто/что	шко́ла	преподава́тельница	ба́ня	ня́ня	-а/-я
ACCUSATIVE кого́/что	шко́лу	преподава́тельницу	ба́ню	ня́ню	-у/-ю
GENITIVE кого́/чего́	шко́лы	преподава́тельницы	ба́ни	ня́ни	-ы/-и
PREPOSITIONAL о ком/чём	шко́ле	преподава́тельнице	ба́не	ня́не	-е
DATIVE кому́/чему́	шко́ле	преподава́тельнице	ба́не	ня́не	-е
INSTRUMENTAL кем/чем	шко́лой	преподава́тельницей	ба́ней	ня́ней	-ой/-ей
PLURAL ENDINGS					
	INANIMATE NOUNS ENDING IN -a	ANIMATE NOUNS ENDING IN -a	INANIMATE NOUNS ENDING IN -я	ANIMATE NOUNS ENDING IN -я	ENDINGS
NOMINATIVE кто/что	шко́лы	преподава́тельницы	ба́ни	ня́ни	-ы/-и
ACCUSATIVE кого́/что	шко́лы	преподава́тельниц	ба́ни	нянь	-ы/-и/Ø
GENITIVE кого́/чего́	шко́л	преподава́тельниц	бань	нянь	Ø
PREPOSITIONAL о ком/чём	шко́лах	преподава́тельницах	ба́нях	ня́нях	-ах/-ях
DATIVE кому́/чему́	шко́лам	преподава́тельницам	ба́ням	ня́ням	-ам/-ям
INSTRUMENTAL кем/чем	шко́лами	преподава́тельницами	ба́нями	ня́нями	-ами/-ями

Табли́ца 6   Feminine Nouns Ending in *-ия*

SINGULAR AND PLURAL ENDINGS				
	ENDING IN -ия	SINGULAR ENDINGS	ENDING IN -ия	PLURAL ENDINGS
NOMINATIVE кто/что	консервато́рия	-я	консервато́рии	-и
ACCUSATIVE кого́/что	консервато́рию	-ю	консервато́рии	-и

SINGULAR AND PLURAL ENDINGS				
	ENDING IN -ия	SINGULAR ENDINGS	ENDING IN -ия	PLURAL ENDINGS
GENITIVE кого́/чего́	консервато́рии	-и	консервато́рий	-й (∅)
PREPOSITIONAL о ком/чём	консервато́рии	-и	консервато́риях	-ях
DATIVE кому́/чему́	консервато́рии	-и	консервато́риям	-ям
INSTRUMENTAL кем/чем	консервато́рией	-ей	консервато́риями	-ями

Табли́ца 7   Feminine Nouns Ending in -ь

SINGULAR ENDINGS			
	INANIMATE ENDING IN -ь	ANIMATE ENDING IN -ь	ENDINGS
NOMINATIVE кто/что	пло́щадь	мышь	-ь
ACCUSATIVE кого́/что	пло́щадь	мышь	-ь
GENITIVE кого́/чего́	пло́щади	мы́ши	-и
PREPOSITIONAL о ком/чём	пло́щади	мы́ши	-и
DATIVE кому́/чему́	пло́щади	мы́ши	-и
INSTRUMENTAL кем/чем	пло́щадью	мы́шью	-ью
PLURAL ENDINGS			
	INANIMATE ENDING IN -ь	ANIMATE ENDING IN -ь	ENDINGS
NOMINATIVE кто/что	пло́щади	мы́ши	-и
ACCUSATIVE кого́/что	пло́щади	мышей	-и/-ей
GENITIVE кого́/чего́	площаде́й	мышей	-ей
PREPOSITIONAL о ком/чём	площадя́х	мыша́х	-ах/-ях
DATIVE кому́/чему́	площадя́м	мыша́м	-ам/-ям
INSTRUMENTAL кем/чем	площадя́ми	мыша́м	-ами/-ями

Adjectives

Таблица 8   Masculine Singular Adjectives

	HARD STEM	SOFT STEM	STEM ENDING IN -г, -к, -х	STEM ENDING IN -ж, -ш, -ч, -щ, -ц, and END-STRESSED	STEM ENDING IN -ж, -ш, -ч, -щ, -ц, and STEM-STRESSED	ENDINGS
NOMINATIVE какóй	нóвый	зúмний	рýсский	большóй	млáдший	-ый/-ий/-óй
ACCUSATIVE какóй/какóго	нóвый, нóвого	зúмний, зúмнего	рýсский, рýсского	большóй, большóго	млáдший, млáдшего	-ый/-ий/-óй, -ого/-его
GENITIVE какóго	нóвого	зúмнего	рýсского	большóго	млáдшего	-ого/-его
PREPOSITIONAL какóм	нóвом	зúмнем	рýсском	большóм	млáдшем	-ом/-ем
DATIVE какóму	нóвому	зúмнему	рýсскому	большóму	млáдшему	-ому/-ему
INSTRUMENTAL какúм	нóвым	зúмним	рýсским	большúм	млáдшим	-ым/-им

Таблица 9   Neuter Singular Adjectives

	HARD STEM	SOFT STEM	STEM ENDING IN -г, -к, -х	STEM ENDING IN -ж, -ш, -ч, -щ, -ц, and END-STRESSED	STEM ENDING IN -ж, -ш, -ч, -щ, -ц, and STEM-STRESSED	ENDINGS
NOMINATIVE какóе	нóвое	зúмнее	рýсские	большóе	млáдшее	-ое/-ее
ACCUSATIVE какóе	нóвое	зúмнее	рýсское	большóе	млáдшее	-ое/-ее
GENITIVE какóго	нóвого	зúмнего	рýсского	большóго	млáдшего	-ого/-его
PREPOSITIONAL какóм	нóвом	зúмнем	рýсском	большóм	млáдшем	-ом/-ем
DATIVE какóму	нóвому	зúмнему	рýсскому	большóму	млáдшему	-ому/-ему
INSTRUMENTAL какúм	нóвым	зúмним	рýсским	большúм	млáдшим	-ым/-им

Табли́ца 10   Feminine Singular Adjectives

	HARD STEM	SOFT STEM	STEM ENDING IN -г, -к, -х	STEM ENDING IN -ж, -ш, -ч, -щ, -ц, and END-STRESSED	STEM ENDING IN -ж, -ш, -ч, -щ, -ц, and STEM-STRESSED	ENDINGS
NOMINATIVE кака́я	но́вая	зи́мняя	ру́сская	больша́я	мла́дшая	-ая/-яя
ACCUSATIVE каку́ю	но́вую	зи́мюю	ру́сскую	большу́ю	мла́дшую	-ую/-юю
GENITIVE како́й	но́вой	зи́мней	ру́сской	большо́й	мла́дшей	-ой/-ей
PREPOSITIONAL како́й	но́вой	зи́мней	ру́сской	большо́й	мла́дшей	-ой/-ей
DATIVE како́й	но́вой	зи́мней	ру́сской	большо́й	мла́дшей	-ой/-ей
INSTRUMENTAL како́й	но́вой	зи́мней	ру́сской	большо́й	мла́дшей	-ой/-ей

Табли́ца 11   Plural Adjectives

	HARD STEM	SOFT STEM	STEM ENDING IN -г, -к, -х	STEM ENDING IN -ж, -ш, -ч, -щ, -ц, and END-STRESSED	STEM ENDING IN -ж, -ш, -ч, -щ, -ц, and STEM-STRESSED	ENDINGS
NOMINATIVE каки́е	но́вые	зи́мние	ру́сское	больши́е	мла́дшие	-ые/-ие
ACCUSATIVE каки́е/каки́х	но́вые, но́вых	зи́мние, зи́мних	ру́сские, ру́сских	больши́е, больши́х	мла́дшие, мла́дших	-ые/-ие, -ых/-их
GENITIVE каки́х	но́вых	зи́мних	ру́сских	больши́х	мла́дших	-ых/-их
PREPOSITIONAL каки́х	но́вых	зи́мних	ру́сских	больши́х	мла́дших	-ых/-их
DATIVE каки́м	но́вым	зи́мним	ру́сским	больши́м	мла́дшим	-ым/-им
INSTRUMENTAL каки́ми	но́выми	зи́мними	ру́сскими	больши́ми	мла́дшими	-ыми/-ими

Pronouns and Special Modifiers

Табли́ца 12 Personal Pronouns

NOMINATIVE	я	ты	он/оно́	она́	мы	вы	они́
ACCUSATIVE	меня́	тебя́	(н)его́	(н)её	нас	вас	(н)их
GENITIVE	меня́	тебя́	(н)его́	(н)её	нас	вас	(н)их
PREPOSITIONAL	мне	тебе́	нём	ней	нас	вас	них
DATIVE	мне	тебе́	(н)ему́	(н)ей	нам	вам	(н)им
INSTRUMENTAL	мно́й	тобо́й	(н)им	(н)ей	на́ми	ва́ми	(н)и́ми

Табли́ца 13 Possessive Modifiers

	MASCULINE	**FEMININE**	**NEUTER**	**PLURAL**
NOMINATIVE	чей? мой твой наш ваш	чья? моя́ твоя́ на́ша ва́ша	чьё? моё твоё на́ше ва́ше	чьи? мои́ твои́ на́ши ва́ши
ACCUSATIVE	чей/чьего́? мой/моего́ твой/твоего́ наш/на́шего ваш/ва́шего	чью? мою́ твою́ на́шу ва́шу	чьё? моё твоё на́ше ва́ше	чьи/чьих? мои́/мои́х твои́/твои́х на́ши/на́ших ва́ши/ва́ших
GENITIVE	чьего́? моего́ твоего́ на́шего ва́шего	чьей? мое́й твое́й на́шей ва́шей	чьего́? моего́ твоего́ на́шего ва́шего	чьих? мои́х твои́х на́ших ва́ших
PREPOSITIONAL	чьём? моём твоём на́шем ва́шем	чьей? мое́й твое́й на́шей ва́шей	чьём? моём твоём на́шем ва́шем	чьих? мои́х твои́х на́ших ва́ших
DATIVE	чьему́? моему́ твоему́ на́шему ва́шему	чьей? мое́й твое́й на́шей ва́шей	чьему́? моему́ твоему́ на́шему ва́шему	чьим? мои́м твои́м на́шим ва́шим
INSTRUMENTAL	чьим мои́м твои́м на́шим ва́шим	чьей? мое́й твое́й на́шей ва́шей	чьим мои́м твои́м на́шим ва́шим	чьи́ми мои́ми твои́ми на́шими ва́шими

Таблица 14   Special Modifiers: *этот/тот, один, весь, сам*

	MASCULINE	FEMININE	NEUTER	PLURAL
NOMINATIVE	этот	эта	это	эти
	тот	та	то	те
	весь	вся	всё	все
	оди́н	одна́	одно́	одни́
	сам	сама́	само́	са́ми
ACCUSATIVE	этот/этого	эту	это	эти/этих
	тот/того́	ту	то	те/тех
	весь/всего́	всю	всё	все/всех
	оди́н/одного́	одну́	одно́	одни́/одни́х
	сам/самого́	саму́	само́	са́ми/сами́х
GENITIVE	этого	этой	этого	этих
	того́	той	того́	тех
	всего́	всей	всего́	всех
	одного́	одно́й	одного́	одни́х
	самого́	само́й	самого́	сами́х
PREPOSITIONAL	этом	этой	этом	этих
	том	той	том	тех
	всём	всей	всём	всех
	одно́м	одно́й	одно́м	одни́х
	само́м	само́й	само́м	сами́х
DATIVE	этому	этой	этому	этим
	тому́	той	тому́	тем
	всему́	всей	всему́	всем
	одному́	одно́й	одному́	одни́м
	самому́	само́й	самому́	сами́м
INSTRUMENTAL	этим	этой	этим	этими
	тем	той	тем	те́ми
	всем	всей	всем	все́ми
	одни́м	одно́й	одни́м	одни́ми
	сами́м	само́й	сами́м	сами́ми

Таблица 15   **Interrogative Pronouns:** *кто/что*

NOMINATIVE	кто	что
ACCUSATIVE	кого́	что
GENITIVE	кого́	чего́
PREPOSITIONAL	о ком	о чём
DATIVE	кому́	чему́
INSTRUMENTAL	кем	чем

Numbers

Табли́ца 16   Cardinal Numbers (Number Nouns)*

	NOMINATIVE CASE	ACCUSATIVE CASE	GENITIVE CASE	PREPOSITIONAL CASE	DATIVE CASE	INSTRUMENTAL CASE
1	оди́н одно́ одна́ одни́	оди́н/одного́ одно́ одну́ одни́х	одного́ одного́ одно́й одни́х	одно́м одно́м одно́й одни́х	одному́ одному́ одно́й одни́м	одни́м одни́м одно́й одни́ми
2	два/две	два/две двух	двух	двух	двум	двумя́
3	три	три трёх	трёх	трёх	трём	тремя́
4	четы́ре	четы́ре четырёх	четырёх	четырёх	четырём	четырьмя́
5	пять	пять	пяти́	пяти́	пяти́	пятью́
6	шесть	шесть	шести́	шести́	шести́	шестью́
7	семь	семь	семи́	семи́	семи́	семью́
8	во́семь	во́семь	восьми́	восьми́	восьми́	восьмью́
9	де́вять	де́вять	девяти́	девяти́	девяти́	девятью́
10	де́сять	де́сять	десяти́	десяти́	десяти́	десятью́
11	оди́ннадцать	оди́ннадцать	оди́ннадцати	оди́ннадцати	оди́ннадцати	оди́ннадцатью
12	двена́дцать	двена́дцать	двена́дцати	двена́дцати	двена́дцати	двена́дцатью
13	трина́дцать	трина́дцать	трина́дцати	трина́дцати	трина́дцати	трина́дцатью
14	четы́рнадцать	четы́рнадцать	четы́рнадцати	четы́рнадцати	четы́рнадцати	четы́рнадцатью
15	пятна́дцать	пятна́дцать	пятна́дцати	пятна́дцати	пятна́дцати	пятна́дцатью
16	шестна́дцать	шестна́дцать	шестна́дцати	шестна́дцати	шестна́дцати	шестна́дцатью
17	семна́дцать	семна́дцать	семна́дцати	семна́дцати	семна́дцати	семна́дцатью
18	восемна́дцать	восемна́дцать	восемна́дцати	восемна́дцати	восемна́дцати	восемна́дцатью

---

* Collective numerals (such as **дво́е**, **тро́е**, **че́тверо**, etc.) are used with objects that have no singular form (such as **очки́**, **но́жницы**, **брю́ки**, as well as with the word **де́ти**). Collective numerals in the nominative, accusative, and genitive require the genitive plural of the count noun they govern.

	NOMINATIVE CASE	ACCUSATIVE CASE	GENITIVE CASE	PREPOSITIONAL CASE	DATIVE CASE	INSTRUMENTAL CASE
19	девятна́дцать	девятна́дцать	девятна́дцати	девятна́дцати	девятна́дцати	девятна́дцатью
20	два́дцать	два́дцать	двадцати́	двадцати́	двадцати́	двадцатью́
30	три́дцать	три́дцать	тридцати́	тридцати́	тридцати́	тридцатью́
40	со́рок	со́рок сорока́	сорока́	сорока́	сорока́	сорока́
50	пятьдеся́т	пятьдеся́т	пяти́десяти	пяти́десяти	пяти́десяти	пятью́десятью
60	шестьдеся́т	шестьдеся́т	шести́десяти	шести́десяти	шести́десяти	шестью́десятью
70	се́мьдесят	се́мьдесят	семи́десяти	семи́десяти	семи́десяти	семью́десятью
80	во́семьдесят	во́семьдесят	восьми́десяти	восьми́десяти	восьми́десяти	восьмью́десятью
90	девяно́сто	девяно́сто девяно́ста	девяно́ста	девяно́ста	девяно́ста	девяно́ста
100	сто	сто ста	ста	ста	ста	ста
200	две́сти	две́сти двухсо́т	двухсо́т	двухста́х	двумста́м	двумяста́ми
300	три́ста	три́ста трёхсо́т	трёхсо́т	трёхста́х	трёмста́м	тремяста́ми
400	четы́реста	четы́реста четырёхсо́т	четырёхсо́т	четырёхста́х	четырёмста́м	четырьмяста́ми
500	пятьсо́т	пятьсо́т пятисо́т	пятисо́т	пятиста́х	пятиста́м	пятьюста́ми
600	шестьсо́т	шестьсо́т шестисо́т	шестисо́т	шестиста́х	шестиста́м	шестьюста́ми
700	семьсо́т	семьсо́т семисо́т	семисо́т	семиста́х	семиста́м	семьюста́ми
800	восемьсо́т	восемьсо́т восьмисо́т	восьмисо́т	восьмиста́х	восьмиста́м	восьмьюста́ми
900	девятьсо́т	девятьсо́т девятисо́т	девятисо́т	девятиста́х	девятиста́м	девятьюста́ми
1000	ты́сяча	ты́сячу	ты́сячи ты́сяч	ты́сяче ты́сячах	ты́сяче ты́сячам	ты́сячей ты́сячами

**Таблица 17   Ordinal Numbers (Number Adjectives):
Decline as Regular Adjectives***

	MASCULINE	NEUTER	FEMININE
1	пе́рвый	пе́рвое	пе́рвая
2	второ́й	второ́е	втора́я
3	тре́тий	тре́тье	тре́тья
4	четвёртый	четвёртое	четвёртая
5	пя́тый	пя́тое	пя́тая
6	шесто́й	шесто́е	шеста́я
7	седьмо́й	седьмо́е	седьма́я
8	восьмо́й	восьмо́е	восьма́я
9	девя́тый	девя́тое	девя́тая
10	деся́тый	деся́тое	деся́тая
11	оди́ннадцатый	оди́ннадцатое	оди́ннадцатая
12	двена́дцатый	двена́дцатое	двена́дцатая
13	трина́дцатый	трина́дцатое	трина́дцатая
14	четы́рнадцатый	четы́рнадцатое	четы́рнадцатая
15	пятна́дцатый	пятна́дцатое	пятна́дцатая
16	шестна́дцатый	шестна́дцатое	шестна́дцатая
17	семна́дцатый	семна́дцатое	семна́дцатая
18	восемна́дцатый	восемна́дцатое	восемна́дцатая
19	девятна́дцатый	девятна́дцатое	девятна́дцатая
20	двадца́тый	двадца́тое	двадца́тая
30	тридца́тый	тридца́тое	тридца́тая
40	сороково́й	сороково́е	сорокова́я
50	пятидеся́тый	пятидеся́тое	пятидеся́тая
60	шестидеся́тый	шестидеся́тое	шестидеся́тая
70	семидеся́тый	семидеся́тое	семидеся́тая
80	восьмидеся́тый	восьмидеся́тое	восьмидеся́тая
90	девяно́стый	девяно́стое	девяно́стая

---

* EXCEPTION: **Тре́тий** declines like **чей**.

	MASCULINE	NEUTER	FEMININE
100	со́тый	со́тое	со́тая
200	двухсо́тый	двухсо́тое	двухсо́тая
300	трёхсо́тый	трёхсо́тое	трёхсо́тая
400	четырёхсо́тый	четырёхсо́тое	четырёхсо́тая
500	пятисо́тый	пятисо́тое	пятисо́тая
600	шестисо́тый	шестисо́тое	шестисо́тая
700	семисо́тый	семисо́тое	семисо́тая
800	восьмисо́тый	восьмисо́тое	восьмисо́тая
900	девятисо́тый	девятисо́тое	девятисо́тая
1000	ты́сячный	ты́сячное	ты́сячная
2000	двухты́сячный	двухты́сячное	двухты́сячная

Summary of Rules Concerning the Declension of Numbers

Number Adjectives and Number Nouns

In compound number adjectives (for example, *twenty seventh*), only the last digit is declined unless that digit is zero, in which case the last two digits are declined.

Мы говори́ли о **два́дцать седьмо́м** фи́льме.	*We were talking about the 27th film.*
Мы говори́ли о **шестидеся́том** фи́льме.	*We were talking about the 60th film.*

In compound number nouns all digits are declined as required by context.

Э́ти тури́сты бы́ли в **двадцати́ семи́** ра́зных города́х.	*Those tourists were in 27 different cities*
Э́ти тури́сты бы́ли в **шести́десяти** ра́зных города́х.	*Those tourists were in 60 different cities.*

Using Number Nouns

Nominative Case and Accusative Inanimate Case

Where the number noun phrase is the subject of the sentence or when it is in the accusative inanimate case, the following rules apply.

- 1, 21, 31, 41, etc.   оди́н/одна́/одно́/одни́ are end-stressed modifiers.

- 2–4, 22–24, 32–34, etc.   Noun is genitive singular.
  Adjective is nominative plural *if* noun is feminine.
  Adjective is genitive plural *if* noun is masculine or neuter.

> **Одна́ студе́нтка** сказа́ла, что она́ придёт ве́чером.
> Э́та кни́га сто́ит два́дцать **одну́ ты́сячу** рубле́й.
> **Три интере́сных журна́ла** лежа́ло на столе́.
> **Две интере́сные кни́ги** лежа́ли на столе́.
> Я ви́жу **три интере́сных журна́ла**.
> Я ви́жу **две интере́сные кни́ги**.

- 5–20, 25–30, 35–40, etc.   Noun and adjective are genitive plural.

> Э́ти **пять у́мных студе́нтов** слу́шают курс по болга́рскому языку́.
> Там мы ви́дели **пять интере́сных книг** по э́тому вопро́су.

Oblique Cases

When the number noun phrase is in any of the other cases, both the number (in all its constituent parts) and the noun phrase are declined in the same case.

> Мы говори́ли **со все́ми двумяста́ми шестью́десятью тремя́ студе́нтами**, кото́рые у́чатся на пе́рвом ку́рсе ру́сского языка́, **о четырёх ра́зных уче́бниках**, кото́рые продаю́тся для э́того ку́рса.

Adjectives Preceding the Number Phrase

Adjectives preceding a number phrase will not be governed by the number phrase. They precede the number phrase in Russian for the same reason they do in English.

> **Э́ти пя́ть студе́нтов** счита́ют, что э́то хоро́ший телеви́зор.
> *These five students believe that this is a good television.*

> Снача́ла я бу́ду в Чика́го, а пото́м я пое́ду в Миннеа́полис **на сле́дующие два дня**.
> *First I'll be in Chicago, and then I'll go to Minneapolis for the next two days.*

Verb Agreement with Number Noun Phrases

When a number noun phrase is the subject of the sentence, the verb *must* be singular in number and agree with the noun in gender when the number ends in 1.

> **Одна́ же́нщина сказа́ла**, что э́то про́сто невыноси́мо.
> *One woman said that this was simply unbearable.*

When the number does not end in 1, the verb may be third-person neuter (standard Russian) *or* third-person plural (increasingly frequent in colloquial speech).

> **Пять студе́нтов пришло́/ пришли́** в 9:00.
> *Five students arrived at 9.*

APPENDIX 4

Library of Congress Transliteration System

RUSSIAN LETTER	ENGLISH LETTER(S)	RUSSIAN LETTER	ENGLISH LETTER(S)
а	a	р	r
б	b	с	s
в	v	т	t
г	g	у	u
д	d	ф	f
е	e	х	kh
ё	e	ц	ts
ж	zh	ч	ch
з	z	ш	sh
и	i	щ	shch
й	i	ъ	”
к	k	ы	y
л	l	ь	’
м	m	э	e
н	n	ю	iu
о	o	я	ia
п	p		

Russian-English

Arabic numerals indicate the unit or units in which the given word is presented for active use (i.e., listed in the unit glossary). Arabic numerals followed by the letter *W* refer to the thematic lexicon of the given unit in the *Workbook*. Nominative case plural forms are provided when irregular, and genitive case plural forms are provided for words that have no singular form; the latter is identified by the Russian abbreviation *род.* (**роди́тельный паде́ж**). Nouns that exist *only* in the singular are marked *sing.* Nouns ending in **-ь** are marked *masculine* (*m.*) or *feminine* (*f.*). Short-form adjectives are provided only in the masculine form if there are no stress shifts in the feminine or plural forms. Short-form adjectives with shifting stress are listed in masculine, feminine, and plural forms. Past passive participles are marked with a slash to separate the short form from the long form. Adverbs and adjectives are alphabetized according to the adverb; comparative forms are provided only when they are irregular simple forms. Regular simple forms, such as **краси́вый/краси́вее** are *not* listed. When a comparative form is required, it is noted with + *comp.* Modals are marked with the parenthetical cue (**кому́**). Place nouns with irregular prepositional case endings **-ý** are indicated. Place nouns that take **на** or both **на** and **в** are indicated; the absence of a preposition implies the use of **в**. First-conjugation verbs are marked I, second-conjugation verbs II, and irregular verbs with an asterisk (*): See Units 2 and 3 for more explanation on the meaning of these terms. Imperfective verbs are listed first, followed by their perfective mates if they have one. Verbs with temporal prefixes are marked **по-** or **с-**. Multidirectional and unidirectional perfective verbs and verbs with temporal prefixes are listed separately. Multidirectional verbs are marked M, unidirectional verbs U, and perfective verbs P.

А

абстра́ктный abstract *19W*
а́вгуст August *8, 17*
аге́нство путеше́ствий travel agency *23W*
а́дский hellish *13*
аксессуа́ры accessories (*computer*) *21W*
актёр, актри́са actor, actress *19W*
америка́нский футбо́л American football *18W*
апре́ль April *8, 17*

арти́ст(-ка) performing artist *4W, 19W*
архите́ктор architect *19W*
архитекту́ра architecture *19W*
аэро́бика aerobics *18W*

Б

бале́т ballet *19W*
ба́нк bank *25W*
ба́нковский проце́нт interest (loans, deposits) *25W*
ба́нковский счёт bank account *25W*

банкро́тство bankruptcy *25W*
баскетбо́л basketball *18W*
баю́кать (I) (кого́?) баю́каю, баю́каешь, баю́кают to lull to sleep *22W*
бег running *18W*
бе́гать (M, I) to run *23*
бежа́ть (*)/по- (U, *) to run *2, 23*
бе́жевый beige, tan *10W*
без without *8*
бейсбо́л baseball *18W*
бе́лый white *10W*

вплыва́ть (I)/вплы́ть (I) to swim into; to sail into *24*

впуска́ть (I)/впусти́ть (II) to let in *11W*

врач doctor *1*

времена́ го́да: весна́, весно́й; ле́то; ле́том; о́сень, о́сенью; зима́, зимо́й seasons of the year: spring, in the spring; summer, in the summer; fall, in the fall; winter, in the winter *12*

вре́мя (времена́) time *7*

вро́де like, similar to *8*

всегда́ (+ *imperf.*) always *5*

всё (+ *comp.*) и (+ *comp.*) -er and -er *16*

вспомина́ть (I)/вспо́мнить (II) to recall, remember; to reminisce *19W*

встава́ть (I)/вста́ть (I) to get up *22*

встре́ча: До встре́чи! meeting: Until we meet up again! *2W*

встреча́ться (I)/встре́титься (II) to meet with *2, 18*

встре́чен/-ный met *19*

вступа́ть (I)/вступи́ть (II) (в до́лжность) to take up (position) at work *12W*

вто́рник, во вто́рник Tuesday, on Tuesday *17*

второ́е second (main) course *9W*

в-тре́тьих in the third *10*

входи́ть (II)/войти́ (I) to walk into *24*

входи́ть (II)/войти́ (I) в си́лу, в де́йствие, в систе́му to go into effect *24*

вчера́шний yesterday's *17*

въезжа́ть (I)/въе́хать (I) to ride into; to drive into *24*

выбега́ть (I)/вы́бежать (*) to run out of *24*

выбира́ть (I)/вы́брать (I) профе́ссию to choose a profession *12W*

вы́боры, голосова́ние election, voting *20W*

вывози́ть (II)/вы́везти (I) to export *25*

выдаю́щийся outstanding *20*

выезжа́ть (I)/вы́ехать (I) to ride out of; to drive out of *24*

вои́грывать (I)/вы́играть (I) to win *18W*

выключа́ть (I)/вы́ключить (II) to turn off (*TV, computer*) *6, 21W*

вылета́ть (I)/вы́лететь (II) to fly out of *24*

выпива́я while drinking *21*

выплыва́ть (I)/вы́плыть (I) to swim out of; to sail out of *24*

выпуска́ть (I)/вы́пустить (II) to let out *11W*

высоко́, высо́кий (вы́ше) high *16*

выступа́ть (I)/вы́ступить (II) to perform *4W*

выступа́ть (I) с ре́чью to give a speech *20W*

выходи́ть (II)/вы́йти (I) to walk out of *24, 24W*

выходи́ть (II)/вы́йти (I) за́муж to get married (*woman*) *3W, 24*

вью́щиеся во́лосы wavy hair *15W*

Г

гало́ши galoshes *10W*

га́лстук necktie *10W*

ги́бкий flexible *16*

гимна́стика gymnastics *18W*

глаз (глаза́): голубы́е, зелёные, ка́рие, се́рые eye: blue, green, brown, gray *7, 13W, 15W*

глубоко́, глубо́кий (глу́бже) deeply, deep *16*

говори́вший one who was speaking; talking *20*

говори́ть (II)/сказа́ть (I) to say, speak; tell *2, 3, 6, 11*

говори́ть/по- (II) to say, speak; have a chat *2*

говоря́ while speaking; talking *21*

говоря́щий one who speaks or talks *20*

год, в како́м году́, в про́шлом/сле́дующем году́ year, in what year, last/next year *1, 10, 17*

голова́ head *13W*

голосова́ть/про- (I) to vote *20W*

голубо́й light blue *10W*

голубы́е глаза́ blue eyes *15W*

го́льф golf *18W*

гора́здо (+ *comp.*) much more *16*

горди́ться to be proud of *12*

го́рло throat *13W*

го́род (города́) city *7*

го́рький bitter *9W*

горя́чее main course *9W*

го́сти: ходи́ть в го́сти, быть в гостя́х guests: to go visiting (*as a guest*), be visiting (*as a guest*) *6W*

гото́в ready *15*

гото́вить/при- (II) to prepare (*cook*) *2, 9W*; — на пару́ to steam (*9W*)

гото́виться/при- (II) to prepare (*oneself*) *1W*

граждани́н (гражда́нка, гра́ждане) citizen *8W*

гражда́нство: получа́ть/получи́ть гражда́нство citizenship: to receive citizenship *8W*

греми́щий thundering, crashing *20*

гро́мко, гро́мкий (гро́мче) loudly, loud *16*

гроза́ lightning *17W*

гру́бый rude *16W*

грудь (*f.*) chest *13W*

гру́стно sad *11*

грязь (*f.*), гря́зный filth, filthy *14W*

густы́е во́лосы thick hair *15W*

Д

дава́ть (I)/дать (*) to give *2, 3, 4, 11*

давле́ние pressure (*barometric*) *17W*

далеко́, далёкий (да́льше) distantly, distant, farther *16*

дверь (*f.*) door *13*

дво́е a couple of (+ *gen. pl.*) *Appendix*

двор (в/на) courtyard *10*

двою́родный брат (двою́родная сестра́) cousin *3W*

дебито́р debtor *25W*

дезинфици́рующее сре́дство disinfectant *14W*

дека́брь (*m.*) December *8, 17*

де́лая while doing; while making *21*

де́лать/с- (I) to do; to make *2*

де́ло (дела́) matter, item, errand, thing *7*

де́нежный ры́нок currency market *25W*

день (днём) day; afternoon, in the afternoon *12, 17*

де́ньги (де́нег *род.*) money *1, 7*

держа́ть/по- (II) hold *2*

де́ти (дете́й *род.*) children *7*

дёшево, дешёвый (дешéвле) inexpensively, inexpensive *16*

дирижёр conductor (*orchestra*) *19W*

дирижи́ровать (I) to conduct (*orchestra*) *19W*

дискéта floppy disk *21W*

дли́нные вóлосы long hair *15W*

для (*designated*) for *8*

дни недéли: понедéльник, в понедéльник; втóрник, во втóрник; средá, в срéду; четвéрг, в четвéрг; пя́тница, в пя́тницу; суббóта, в суббóту; воскресéнье, в воскресéнье days of the week: Monday, on Monday; Tuesday, on Tuesday; Wednesday, on Wednesday; Thursday, on Thursday; Friday, on Friday; Saturday, on Saturday; Sunday, on Sunday *17*

до: До встрéчи! До звонкá! До свидáнья! up until: Until we meet up! Until the next call! Until we see each other next! *8, 2W*

добегáть (I)/добежáть (*) to run up to *24*

добросóвестный conscientious *16W*

доверя́ть (I)/довéрить (II) to trust *11*

доводи́ть (II)/довести́ (I) (когó-нибудь до чегó [до отчáяния]) to bring to (despair) *25*

довóлен (довóльна, довóльны) satisfied *12*

договори́ться (II) to agree *2*

доезжáть (I)/доéхать (I) to ride up to *24*

дóждь: идёт (пойдёт, бýдет идти́) дождь rain: it is (it will start to; it will be) raining *17W*

дóлго, дóлгий (дóльше) for a long time, long *5, 16*

долетáть (I)/долетéть (II) to fly up to *24*

дóлжен (должнá, должны́) (+ *infin.*) obligated, ought to *15*

дóм (домá) home; building *7*

доноси́ть (II)/донести́ (I) to inform *25*

доплывáть (I)/доплы́ть (I) to swim up to; to sail up to *24*

допускáть (I)/допусти́ть (II) (что...) to assume, suppose (that...) *5*

допускáть (I)/допусти́ть (II) to let *11*

допýстим, что let's assume that... *5*

дóрого, дорогóй (дорóже) expensively, expensive *16*

до сих пор until now *17*

до тех пор, как until *17*

до тогó, как until *17*

доходи́ть (II)/дойти́ (I) (до чегó?) to walk up to *24*

доходи́ть (II)/дойти́ (I) до тогó, что to get to the point when *24*

драматýрг playwright *19W*

дремáть (I) doze *22W*

друг (друзья́) friend *1, 7*

дрýг дрýга one another *13*

дружелю́бный friendly *16W*

дýет вéтер, дýет слáбый вéтер it's windy, there's a gentle breeze *17W*

дуэ́т duet *19W*

дышáть (II) to breathe *13W*

дя́дя uncle *3W*

Е

еврéй, еврéйка Jew *11W*

едá (*sing.*) food *7W*

еди́нственный (*adj.*) only *15W*

éдучи while going by vehicle *21*

éздить (M, II) to go by vehicle *1, 23, 24W*

éсли if (*not* whether) *18*

есть/съ- (*) eat *2, 6W, 7W*

éхать (U, I) to go by vehicle *8, 23*

Ж

жáдный greedy *16W*

жáловаться/по- (I) to complain *9*

жáрить/под- (II) to fry *9W*

ждáть/подо- (I) (*no prep.*) to wait for *3*

желáющий one who wishes *20*

желáя while wishing *21*

женá (жёны) wife *7*

жени́ться (II) to get married (*man*) *3W, 10*

жени́ться/по- (II) to get married (*couples*) *3W*

жетóн token (*subway, metro*) *24W*

жёлтый yellow *10W*

жив (живá, жи́вы) alive, living *3W, 15*

живопи́сец painter *19W*

жи́вопись painting (*art*) *19W*

живóт stomach *13W*

жизнь (*f.*) life *13*

жирáф giraffe *13*

жить (I) to live *1, 2, 3W, 10*

З

за behind, beyond; for, in the place of; in exchange for *9, 12*

за + врéмя (до тогó, как...) (*time*) before (*event*) *17*

забегáть (I)/забежáть (*) to run into, behind *24*

заболевáть (I)/заболéть (I) to fall ill *13W*

забывáть (I)/забы́ть (I) to forget *6*

забы́т/-ый forgotten *19*

заведён/-ный wound up (*watch*); started (*engine*); begun, set off *19*

зáвтрашний tomorrow's *17*

задавáть (I)/задáть (*) to pose (*question*) *2W*

зáдан/-ный assigned, posed *19*

заезжáть (I)/заéхать (I) to ride into, behind; to drive into, behind *24*

заём loan *25W*

закáзывать (I)/заказáть (I) to order (*meal*); to reserve (*hotel room*) *17*

закóнчен/-ный completed *19*

закрывáть (I)/закры́ть (I) to close *3*

закры́т/-ый closed *19*

закýски (закýсок, *род.*) hors d'oeuvres *9W*

залетáть (I)/залетéть (II) to fly into, behind *24*

заменя́ть (I)/замени́ть (II) to change, replace; to fill in *14W*

замечáть (I)/замéтить (II) to notice *2*

занимáться (I) to be busy, occupied (*homework*) *1W, 12*

занимáться (I) спóртом to engage in sports *18W*

заня́тия (заня́тий *род.*) classes *1, 10*

зáперт/-ый closed, locked *19*

запи́сывая while writing *21*

повыша́ться (I)/повы́ситься (II) to increase; to rise *25W*

повыше́ние increase, rise *25W*

пого́да: дождли́вая, о́блачная, плоха́я, со́лнечная, хоро́шая weather: rainy, cloudy, bad, sunny, good *17W*

под (+ *acc./instru.*) beneath, beyond *9, 12*

подава́ть (I)/пода́ть (*) to submit (*application*) *5W*

подбега́ть (I)/подбежа́ть (*) to run up to, approach *24*

подводи́ть (II)/подвести́ (I) to disappoint; to take *25*

подвози́ть (II)/подвезти́ (I) to take; to give a ride *25*

подде́рживать (I)/поддержа́ть (II) to support *20W*

подлета́ть (I)/подлете́ть (II) to fly up to *24*

подноси́ть (II)/поднести́ (I) to carry *25*

подо́бен similar to *11*

подогрева́ть (I)/подогре́ть (I) to reheat (*food*) *9*

подплыва́ть (I)/подплы́ть (I) to swim up to; to sail up to *24*

подходи́ть (II)/подойти́ (I) to walk up to *24*

подъе́зд driveway, entrance (*building*) *24W*

подъезжа́ть (I)/подъе́хать (I) to drive up to *24*

подъём increase *25W*

пое́здить (по, II) to be traveling around by vehicle *23*

пое́хать (Р, I) to go by vehicle *23*

по́здно, по́здний (по́зже, поздне́е) late *16*

поздравля́ть (I)/поздра́вить (II) to congratulate *12W*

позови́(те) (кого́) к телефо́ну to call to the phone *2W*

по́иск информа́ции retrieval of information *21W*

пойти́ (Р, I) to go on foot *4, 23*

пока́ не (+ *verb*) until *17*

покра́шен/-ный painted *19*

покупа́ть (I)/купи́ть (II) to buy *2, 7W*

поку́пка purchase *25W*

пол, на полу́ floor, on the floor *10*

полета́ть (по, I) to fly around *23*

полете́ть (Р, II) to fly *23*

поли́тик politician *20W*

поли́тика, полити́ческие нау́ки politics, policy; political science *20W*

полови́на half *17*

полоса́тый, в поло́ску striped *10W*

по́льзоваться/вос- (I) to use; to enjoy *12*

по́мнить/вс- (II) to remember, recall *19W*

помога́ть (I)/помо́чь (I) to help, assist *11*

понеде́льник, в понеде́льник Monday, on Monday *17*

понести́ (Р, I) to carry *25*

понижа́ться (I)/пони́зиться (II) to decrease, fall *25W*

понима́ть (I)/поня́ть (I) to understand *3, 9*

поно́с diarrhea *13W*

попла́вать (по, I) to swim around; to sail around *23*

поплы́ть (Р, I) to swim; to sail *23*

поправля́ться (I)/попра́виться (II) to get better *13W*

портре́т portrait *19W*

по́сле (+ *noun*) after *8*

по́сле того́, как (+ *verb*) after *17*

посмотре́в having watched *21*

постро́ен/-ный built *19*

поступа́ть (I)/поступи́ть (II) to apply to; to enroll in; to begin a job *5W, 12W*

посыла́я while sending *21*

потребля́ть (I) to use, consume; to waste *16W*

потряса́ющий amazing *20*

походи́ть (по, II) to walk around *23*

похо́ж (на кого́/что?) similar to (*appearance*) *15*

по́хороны (похоро́н *род.*) funeral *7*

почи́щен/-ный cleaned *19*

по́чки (по́чек *род.*) kidneys *13W*

по́чта (на) post office *10*

почти́ almost *5*

поэ́ма narrative poem *19W*

поэ́т poet *19W*

по́яс belt (*for men*) *10W*

прав (права́, пра́вы) right, correct *15*

Правосла́вие, правосла́вный (*Russian*) Orthodox faith; (*Russian*) Orthodox *11*

превраща́ться (I)/преврати́ться (II) to change, metamorphose *14W*

предлага́ть (I)/предложи́ть (II) тост to propose a toast *6W*

предложе́ние suggestion; supply (*economics*) *25W*

предполага́ть (I)/предположи́ть (II) (, что...) to assume (that . . .) *5*

представля́ть (I)/предста́вить (II) себе́ to imagine *13*

предубеждённый closed-minded *16*

прекраща́ть (I)/прекрати́ть (I) to stop (*a process*) *4W*

преподава́ть (I) to teach *1*

преполо́жим, что... let's suppose that . . . *5*

при (+ *prep.*) under the auspices of, during the administration of *10*

прибега́ть (I)/прибежа́ть (I) to run *24*

прибега́ть (I)/прибе́гнуть (I) к чему́? to resort to *24*

приватиза́ция privatization *25W*

приве́тливый outgoing *16W*

приводи́ть (II)/привести́ (I) to bring; to cite *4, 25*

привози́ть (II)/привезти́ (I) to transport *25*

привыка́ть (I)/привы́кнуть (I) to get used to *3, 5, 11*

приглаша́ть (I)/пригласи́ть (II) to invite *18*

приглашён/-ный invited *19*

пригото́влен/-ный prepared *19*

придя́ having arrived by foot *21*

приезжа́ть (I)/прие́хать (I) to arrive (*by vehicle*) *24*

прие́хавший one who arrived (*by vehicle*) *20*

приёмный (приёмная) (сын, дочь, брат, сестра́) adopted (son, daughter, brother, sister) *3W*

прилета́ть (I)/прилете́ть (II) to fly to *24*

применя́ть (I)/примени́ть (II) to apply *16W*

принесён/-ный brought *19*

принима́ть (I)/приня́ть (I) to accept *5W*; to take, accept *3*; to make (*decision*) *3*; to take (*medicine*) *13W*; to adopt (*law*) *20W*

приноси́ть (II)/принести́ (I) to carry to *25*

при́нтер: ла́зерный, ма́тричный, стру́йный printer: laser, dot-matrix, jet *21W*

приня́вший one who has taken *20*

приплыва́ть (I)/приплы́ть (I) to swim; to sail to *24*

приходи́ть (II)/прийти́ (I) to arrive (*on foot*) *24*

приходи́ться (I)/прийти́сь (I) to have to do, be compelled to *11*

прише́дший one who has arrived (*by foot*) *20*

прия́тно pleased *11*

пробега́ть (I)/пробежа́ть (*) to run through *24*

про́бовать/по- (I) to try out; to test *20W*

проверя́ть (I)/прове́рить (II) to check *11W*

проводи́ть (II)/провести́ (I) (свобо́дное вре́мя) to spend (*free time*) *4W*

прогно́з forecast *17W*

прода́жа sale *25W*

продолжа́ть (I)/продо́лжить (II) to continue *5*

проду́кты (проду́ктов *род.*) groceries, food *7*

проезжа́ть (I)/прое́хать (I) to ride through; to drive through; to miss (*bus stop, train stop*) *24, 24W*

проекти́ровать (I) to draft, draw up (*architecture*) *19W*

прои́грывать (I)/проигра́ть (I) to lose *18W*

произноси́ть (II)/произнести́ (I) to pronounce *25*

происхожде́ние: Кто вы по происхожде́нию? Вы како́го происхожде́ния? ancestry: What is your ancestry? *8W*

пролета́ть (I)/пролете́ть (I) to fly through *24*

проплыва́ть (I)/проплы́ть (I) to swim through; to sail through *24*

про́пуск pass (*document*); to go *11W*

пропуска́ть (I)/пропусти́ть (II) to let through *11W*

проси́ть/по- (II) to ask to do; to ask for *2W*

про́сто, просто́й (про́ще) simply, simple *16*

простужа́ться (I)/простуди́ться (II) to catch a cold *13W*

просыпа́ться (I)/просну́ться (I) to wake up *22W*

Протеста́нство, Протестанти́зм Protestantism *11W*

протеста́нт (протеста́нтка) Protestant *11w*

про́тив against *20W*

проти́вник opponent *20W*

протира́ть (I) тря́пкой to wipe down with a rag *14W*

профе́ссор (профессора́) professor *1, 7*

прохо́дит (пройдёт) вре́мя some time goes (will go) by *24*

проходи́ть (II)/пройти́ (I) to walk through *6W*; to cover *24*

прочита́в having read *21*

проше́дший one who passed; проше́дшее past *20*

про́шлый: на про́шлой неде́ле, в про́шлом году́ last (last week, last year) *1, 17*

проща́ть (I)/прости́ть (II): Прости́те! to forgive: Forgive me! *6W*

пря́мо straight *24W*

прямо́й рейс direct flight *23W*

прямы́е во́лосы straight hair *15W*

путеше́ствие trip, journey *23W*

путеше́ствовать/по- (I) to travel around *23W*

пылесо́сить to vacuum *14W*

пыта́ться/по- (I) to try; to experiment *20W*

пье́са play *19W*

пью́щий drinker (*alcohol*), *20*

пя́тница, в пя́тницу Friday, on Friday *17*

Р

рабо́та (на/в) work *10*

рабо́тать (I) to work *1, 12*

равви́н rabbi *11W*

рад happy, glad *15*

раз в неде́лю, два ра́за в неде́лю once a week, twice a week *17*

разбега́ться (I)/разбежа́ться (*) to run off in separate directions *24*

разводи́ться (II)/развести́сь (I) to get divorced *3W*

развора́чиваться (I)/разверну́ться (I) to make a U-turn (*driving, riding*) *24W*

разгово́рчивый talkative *16W*

раздева́ться (I)/разде́ться (I) to take off (*clothes*) *6w*

разме́нивать (I)/разменя́ть (I) to change into equivalent (*break a bill*) *7W, 14W*

разреша́ть (I)/разреши́ть (II) to permit *11*

разреше́ние permission (*written, oral*) *11W*

разъезжа́ться (I)/разъе́хаться (I) to go separate ways (*by vehicle*) *24*

рак cancer *13W*

ракетбо́л racketball *18W*

ра́но, ра́нний (ра́ньше, ра́нее) early, earlier *16*

распева́я while singing *21*

расска́з short story *19W*

расска́зан/-ный told *19*

расска́зывать (I)/рассказа́ть (I) to tell (*story*) *1, 2W, 11*

рассла́бить(ся) (II) to relax *22W*

расходи́ться (II)/разойти́сь (I) to go separate ways (*on foot*) *24*

расхо́довать (I) to use, consume; to waste *16W*

рво́та vomit *13W*

реалисти́ческий realistic *19W*

ребёнок (де́ти) child *7*

ре́гби rugby *18W*

регули́рование чего regulating; regulation *25W*

ре́дкие во́лосы thinning hair *15W*

ре́дкий (ре́же) seldom, rare *16*

ре́дко (+ *imperf.*) rarely, infrequently *1, 5*

режиссёр director (*film, play*) *4W, 19W*

режисси́ровать (I) to direct (*film, play*) *19w*

ре́зать/по- (I) себе́ что to cut oneself *13W*

English-Russian

A

abandoned брошен/-ный *19*
ability, know-how умение *3*
to be able мочь/с- (I) *1, 3*
to be able to уметь/с- (I) *2, 3*
to be able to, be able to get done
    удаваться (I)/удаться (*) (кому)
    11
about о(б/о) (+ *prep.*) *10*
above над (+ *instr.*) *12*
abstract абстрактный *19W*
to accept; *see also* **take** принимать
    (I)/принять (I) *5W*
accessories (*computer*) аксессуары
    21W
to acquaint with знакомить/по-
    (II) *2*
acquaintance знакомый (*adj. decl.*) *7*
acting игра *19W*
actor, actress актёр, актриса *19W*
adopted (son, daughter)
    приёмный/ая (сын, дочь) *3W*
advertisement or advertising
    реклама *25W*
advertising agent рекламный агент
    25W
to advise советовать/по- (I) *2, 3*
aerobics аэробика *18W*
affectionate ласковый *16*
to be afraid of бояться (II) *2, 8*
after после (+ *gen.*) *8*
against против (+ *gen.*) *20W*

ago назад *17*
to agree on, share an opinion
    сходиться (II)/сойтись (I) во
    мнении *20W*
to agree договориться (II) *2*
agreed согласен (согласна,
    согласны) *3, 15*
AIDS СПИД: синдром
    приобретённого иммуно-
    дефицита *13W*
alive, living жив (жива, живы) *3W,
    15*
almost чуть не, почти *5, 5W*
always всегда *5*
amazing потрясающий *20*
ancestry: What is your ancestry?
    (*ethnic background*)
    происхождение: Кто вы по
    происхождению? Вы какого
    происхождения? *8W*
to be angry; get angry at сердиться/
    рас- (II) *9, 18*
to answer отвечать (I)/ответить (II)
    2W
antagonistic, hostile
    неприязненный *16W*
antiglare screen защитный экран
    21W
apartment квартира *24W*
**to apply to; to enroll in; to begin a
    job** поступать (I)/поступить (II)
    5W

to appoint назначать (I)/назначить
    (I) *20W*
to approve of одобрять (I)/
    одобрить (II) *20w*
April апрель *8, 17*
architect архитектор *19W*
architecture архитектура *19W*
to arrive (*on foot*) приходить (II)/
    прийти (I) *24*; (*by vehicle*)
    приезжать (I)/приехать (I) *24*
having arrived by foot придя *21*
artist (*painter, sculptor*) художник
    4W, 19W
as ... as possible как можно
    (+ *comp.*) *16W*
as ... as ... так...как... *16*
as much as сколько..., столько *16*
to ask (*information*) спрашивать (I)/
    спросить (II); (*borrow*)
    просить/по- (II) *2, 2W*
to ask someone to the phone
    позови(те) (кого) к телефону
    2W
assigned (*homework*); **posed** (*question*) задан/-ный *19*
to assume (that ...) предполагать
    (I)/предположить (II) (, что...) *5*
to assure уверять (I)/уверить (II) *11*
At what time? Когда? Во сколько
    времени? *17*
attitude отношение *3, 25*
August август *8, 17*

aunt тётя *3W*

authorities: local, regional, federal вла́сти: ме́стные, областны́е, федерати́вные *20W*

to avoid избега́ть (I)/избежа́ть (*) *6, 8*

B

back (*body*) спина́ *13W*

backward (*direction*); **in the back or from the back** наза́д; сза́ди *9W, 10W, 24W*

bag, handbag, purse су́мка *10W*

to bake печь/ис- (I) *9W*

bald; bald spot; to go bald лы́сый, лы́сина, лысе́ть (I) *15W*

ballet бале́т *19W*

bank ба́нк *25W*

bank account ба́нковский счёт *25W*

bankruptcy банкро́тство *25W*

baseball бейсбо́л *18W*

basketball баскетбо́л *18W*

bathing suit купа́льный костю́м, пла́вки (пла́вок *род.*) *10W*

to be быть *7*

to bear, keep in mind; to be aware of учи́тывать (I)/уче́сть (I) *6*

beard борода́ *15W*

to become станови́ться (II)/ста́ть (I) *3*

to become (*age*) испо́лниться (II) *11*

to become acquainted with знако́миться/по- (II) *2*

to become (*practitioner of a certain profession*) станови́ться (II)/стать (I) *12W*

✛ **before** до, перед, за (+ *time*) (+ *acc.*) ...до того́, как *17*

to begin начина́ть (I)/нача́ть (I) *3, 5*

beginner начина́ющий *20*

begun на́чат/-ый *19*

to behave well, poorly вести́ (U-I) себя́ хорошо́, пло́хо *13, 25*

behavior поведе́ние *19*

behind, beyond за (+ *instr./acc.*); наза́д, сза́ди *9, 9W, 10W, 12*

beige, tan бе́жевый *10W*

being бу́дучи *21*

to believe in God; believer ве́ровать (I); ве́рующий *11W*

to believe in ве́рить/по- (II) *11W*

beloved, favorite люби́м/-ый *19*

belt (*men*) по́яс *10W*; (*women*) реме́нь *10W*

beneath, beyond под (+ *acc./instr.*) *9, 12*

beside, except кро́ме *8*

between ме́жду (+ *instr.*) *12*

beyond, behind за (+ *acc./instr.*) *9, 12*

big большо́й (бо́льше) *1, 16*

bitter го́рький *9W*

black чёрный *10W*

blouse блу́зка *10W*

blue eyes голубы́е глаза́ *15W*

to boil; to poach вари́ть/с- (I) *9W, 16W*

boot сапо́г *10W*

boots, shoes, high-top боти́нки *10W*

boring ску́чно (кому́?), ску́чный *11*

to be born рожда́ться (I)/роди́ться (II) *3W*

both о́ба (о́бе) *Appendix*

bottle буты́лка *22*

bow tie ба́бочка *10W*

brain мозг *13W*

to break one's leg, arm лома́ть/с- (I) себе́ но́гу, ру́ку *13W*

to breathe дыша́ть (II) *13W*

to bring подноси́ть (II)/поднести́ (I), приноси́ть (II)/принести́ (I) *25*

to bring; to cite приводи́ть (II)/привести́ (I) *4, 25*

to bring someone to himself/herself приводи́ть (II)/привести́ (I) кого́-нибудь в себя́ *25*

to bring to (*e.g., to the point of despair*) доводи́ть (II)/довести́ (I) (кого́-нибудь до чего́ [до отча́яния]) *25*

brother брат (бра́тья) *7*

brought принесён/-ный *19*

brown кори́чневый *10W*

brown eyes ка́рие глаза́ *15W*

building зда́ние *7, 13, 19W*

built постро́ен/-ный *19*

bus (trolley, tram) stop остано́вка авто́буса (тролле́йбуса, трамва́я) *24W*

businessman бизнесме́н *25W*

businesswoman бизнесме́нка *25W*

bust (*sculpture*) бюст *19W*

to be busy, occupied with (*e.g., homework*) занима́ться (I) *12*

to buy something покупа́ть (I)/купи́ть (II) *2, 7W*

by a certain time к (+ *time*) (+ *dat.*) *17*

by, in по *11*

C

café кафе́ (*indecl.*) *7W*

to call for a doctor, an ambulance вызыва́ть (I)/вы́звать (I) врача́, ско́рую по́мощь *13W*

to call (*phone*) звони́ть/по- (II) *1, 11, 18*

to cancel отменя́ть(ся) (I)/отмени́ть(ся) (II) *14W, 18*

cancer рак *13W*

cantata канта́та *19W*

cap ке́пка *10W*

capable, talented спосо́бный *16*

cardigan ко́фта *10W*

to carry носи́ть (M, II), нести́ (U, I), понести́ (P, I) *25*

to carry, transport by vehicle вози́ть (II)/везти́ (I), повезти́ (I) *2, 25*

to catch a taxi лови́ть (II)/пойма́ть (I) такси́ *2, 24W*

to catch a cold простужа́ться (I)/простуди́ться (II) *13W*

cathedral (*Christian*) собо́р *11W*

Catholic като́лик (католи́чка) *11W*

Catholic cathedral костёл *11W*

Catholicism католици́зм, католи́чество *11W*

chair стул (сту́лья) *7*

to change, alter, modify; to be changed, altered, modified изменя́ть(ся) (I)/измени́ть(ся) (II) *14*

to change (*clothing*) переодева́ться (I)/переоде́ться (I) *14W*

to change (*buses, trains, or planes*); **to make a transfer** переса́живаться (I)/пересе́сть (I) *14W*

change сда́ча (*from purchase*) *7W*

change; exchange (currency) обме́нивать (I)/обменя́ть (I) *14W*

to change, metamorphose into превраща́ться (I)/преврати́ться (II) *14W*

✛ *пре́жде чем уйти́
перед тем, как уйти́*

to change money (*within one currency*), make change разме́нивать (I)/разменя́ть (I) де́ньги 7W, 14W

to change one's mind переду́мывать (I)/переду́мать (I) 14W

to change; to relieve; to replace (*succeeding in time*) сменя́ть (I)/смени́ть (II) 14W

to change, replace переменя́ть (I)/перемени́ть (II) 14W

to change; to replace; to fill in for заменя́ть (I)/замени́ть (II) 14W

to change; to switch меня́ть /по- (I) 14

character, personality: easygoing, difficult хара́ктер: мя́гкий, тяжёлый 16W

check (*checkbook, checking account*) чек 25W

to check проверя́ть (I)/прове́рить (II) 11W

chess ша́хматы 18W

chest грудь (*f.*) 13W

child (children) ребёнок (де́ти) 7

to choose выбира́ть (I)/вы́брать (I) 12W

church (*Christian*) це́рк(о)вь (*f.*) 11W

citizen граждани́н (гражда́нка, гра́ждане) 8W

citizen of Russia (*not necessarily ethnic Russian*) россия́нин (россия́не) 7

citizenship: to receive citizenship гражда́нство: получа́ть/получи́ть гражда́нство 8W

city го́род (города́) 7

classes (*pl.*), in classes заня́тия, на заня́тиях 1, 10

to clean чи́стить/по- (II) 2

to clean up, to straighten up убира́ть (I)/убра́ть (I) 5, 6, 14W

cleaned почи́щен/-ный 19

cleanliness, clean чистота́ 14W

cleanly, clean чи́сто, чи́стый (чи́ще) 16

to close something закрыва́ть (I)/закры́ть (I) 3

closed закры́т/-ый 19

closed, locked за́перт/-ый 19

closed-minded; open-minded предубеждённый; не- 16

closet; wardrobe; chest of drawers; cupboard шкаф, в шкафу́ 10, 22

clothing (*sing.*) оде́жда 7

cloud о́блако (облака́) 17W

coarse; rude гру́бый 16W

coast of the Black Sea, of the Mediterranean Sea побере́жье Чёрного мо́ря, Средизе́много мо́ря 23W

coat ку́ртка 22

coffee ко́фе (*m., indecl.*) 7W

coin (*currency*) моне́та 7

cold хо́лодно (кому́?) 11

cold просту́да, на́сморк 13W

color: What color is it? цвет: Это како́го цве́та? 10W

to come down with заболева́ть (I)/заболе́ть (I) 13W

to come to a stop; to stop (*in a hotel*) остана́вливаться (I)/останови́ться (II) 4W

to come to mind приходи́ть (II)/прийти́ (I) в го́лову 24

to come to oneself приходи́ть (II)/прийти́ (I) в себя́ 24

to come together (*by foot*) сходи́ться (II)/сойти́сь (I) 24

to come together (*by vehicle*) съезжа́ться (I)/съе́хаться (I) 24

comedy коме́дия 19W

commuter train электри́чка 24W

to complain жа́ловаться/по- (I) 9

completed зако́нчен/-ный 19

completed, finished ко́нчен/-ный 19

compose (*music*) сочиня́ть (I) 19W

composer компози́тор 19W

computer компью́тер 13, 21W

concert, concerto конце́рт (на) 10, 19W

to conduct (*orchestra*) дирижи́ровать (I) 19W

to conduct, lead, keep a diary; to conduct a conversation, a lecture вести́ (U, I) дневни́к, обсужде́ние, ле́кцию 25

conductor (*orchestra*) дирижёр 19W

to congratulate поздравля́ть (I)/поздра́вить (II) 12W

conscientious добросо́вестный 16W

to consider счита́ть (I) 12

to consist of состоя́ть (II) 3W, 10

constipation запо́р 13W

to continue продолжа́ть (I)/продо́лжить (II) 5

to convey, pass on передава́ть (I)/переда́ть (*) 6W

corner у́гол (на, в углу́) 10

corresponding соотве́тствующий 20

cotton хло́пок, хло́пковый 10W

to cough ка́шлять (I) 13W

cough ка́шель (*m.*) 13W

couple of (*genitive plural*) дво́е, па́ра *Appendix*

courteous ве́жливый 16W

courtyard двор (в, на) 10

cousin двою́родный брат, двою́родная сестра́ 3W

to cover (*chapter*); to go through проходи́ть (II)/пройти́ (I) что? 24

creditor кредито́р 25W

to cross all boundaries переходи́ть (II)/перейти́ (I) все преде́лы 24

to cross each other (*third-person*) пересека́ться (I)/пересе́чься (I) 24W

cruise круи́з 23W

to cry пла́кать/за- (I) 3, 4

cultured интеллиге́нтный 16, 16W

curly hair кудря́вые во́лосы 15W

currency market биржево́й валю́тный ры́нок, де́нежный ры́нок 25W

to cut oneself ре́зать/по- (I) себе́ что 13W

D

dad's, mom's па́пин, ма́мин 13

to dance танцева́ть/по- (I) 3

dance та́нец 19W

dancer танцо́вщик (танцо́вщица) 19W

dark blue си́ний 10W

dark hair тёмные во́лосы 15W

day; afternoon; in the afternoon день, днём 12, 17

days of the week: Monday; Tuesday; Wednesday; Thursday; Friday; Saturday; Sunday дни неде́ли: понеде́льник; вто́рник; среда́; четве́рг; пя́тница; суббо́та; воскресе́нье 17

to fill out a form заполня́ть (I)/ заполни́ть (II) (анке́ту) *5W*

to film; to photograph снима́ть *19W*

filth (filthy) гря́зь (*f.*) (гря́зный) *14W*

finally наконе́ц *5*

finances фина́нсы *25W*

to find находи́ть (I)/найти́ (I) *3, 12*

finger па́лец (па́льцы) *13W*

to finish конча́ть (I)/ко́нчить (II) *5*

first course, appetizer пе́рвое *9W*

flexible ги́бкий *16*

floor пол (на полу́) *10*

floor, story (*building*) эта́ж (на) *10, 24W*

floppy disk дискéта *21W*

to fluctuate колеба́ться (I) *25W*

to fly лета́ть (M, I), лете́ть (U, II)/ по- (P, II) *23*

to fly across перелета́ть (I)/ перелете́ть (II) *24*

to fly around полета́ть (по, I) *23*

to fly around облета́ть (I)/облете́ть (II) *24*

to fly away отлета́ть (I)/отлете́ть (*) *24*

to fly away улета́ть (I)/улете́ть (II) *24*

to fly down off слета́ть (I)/слете́ть (II) *24*

to fly in прилета́ть (I)/прилете́ть (II) *24*

to fly into влета́ть (I)/влете́ть (II) *24*

to fly into, behind залета́ть (I)/ залете́ть (II) *24*

to fly out of вылета́ть (I)/вы́лететь (II) *24*

to fly through пролета́ть (I)/ пролете́ть (I) *24*

to fly as far as долета́ть (I)/долете́ть (II) *24*

to fly up to подлета́ть (I)/подлете́ть (II) *24*

food (*sing.*) еда́ *7W*

food (*sing.*) пи́ща *7W*

foot; leg нога́ (но́ги) *13W*

football (*American*) америка́нский футбо́л *18W*

for для *8*; (*in exchange for*) за (кого́/ что?) *9, 12, 20W*; (*with time expressions*) на (+ *time*) (+ *acc.*) *17*

for the following reasons по сле́дующей причи́не (по сле́дующим причи́нам...) *11*

for a certain time на (+ *time*) (+ *acc.*) *17*

for a long time давно́ (до́лго) *5*

for a long time, long до́лго, до́лгий (до́льше) *16*

to forgive, excuse: Forgive me! Excuse me! проща́ть (I)/ прости́ть (II), извиня́ть (I)/ извини́ть (II): Прости́те! Извини́те! *6W*

to forbid запреща́ть (I)/запрети́ть (II) *11W*

forbidden, impossible (*impersonal*) нельзя́ (кому́) *11*

forbidden, prohibited запрещён (запрещена́, запрещено́, запрещены́) *11W*

forest лес (в лесу́) *10*

to forget забыва́ть (I)/забы́ть (I) *6*

forgotten забы́т/-ый *19*

former бы́вший *20*

forward, in the front вперёд, впереди́ *9W, 10W, 24W*

found найден/-ный *19*

foursome че́тверо *Appendix*

frequently, frequent ча́сто, ча́стый (ча́ще) *1, 5, 16*

Friday, on Friday пя́тница, в пя́тницу *17*

friend друг (друзья́) *1, 7*

friendly дружелю́бный *16W*

from, down off of с(о) (+ *gen.*) *8*

from от, из, с *8*

from whose point of view с то́чки зре́ния (с чьей то́чки зре́ния, с то́чки зре́ния кого́?) *8*

from (+ *time*) **to** (+ *time*) (*gen.*) с (како́го вре́мени)...до (како́го вре́мени) *17*

to fry жа́рить/под- (II) *9W*

funeral по́хороны (похоро́н *род.*) *7*

furniture ме́бель (*f.*) *7*

future бу́дущий (*adj.*) *20*

G

galoshes гало́ши *10W*

garden сад (в саду́) *10*

generous ще́дрый *16W*

to get a wrong number не туда́ попа́сть *2W*

to get angry at серди́ться/рас- (II) *9*

to get better (*health*) поправля́ться (I)/попра́виться (II) *13W*

to get by (*without*) обходи́ться (II)/ обойти́сь (I) *24*

to get divorced разводи́ться (II)/ развести́сь (I) *3W*

to get enough sleep спа́ться/вы́- (II) *22W*

to get married (*woman*) выходи́ть (II)/вы́йти (I) за́муж *24*

to get married (*couples*) жени́ться/по- (II) *3W*

to get married (*men*) (*no perf.*) жени́ться (II) *3W, 10*

to get off at the next stop (at the stop after next, in two stops) выходи́ть (II)/вы́йти (I) на сле́дующей ста́нции, остано́вки (че́рез одну́, че́рез две) *24W*

to get on a bus or train going in the wrong direction сади́ться (II)/ сесть (I) не в ту сто́рону *24W*

to get on, take the subway, a bus сади́ться (II)/сесть (I) в метро́, авто́бус *24W*

to get tired, be tired устава́ть (I)/ уста́ть (I) *22W*

to get to the point when доходи́ть (II)/дойти́ (I) до того́, что *24*

to get up встава́ть (I)/встать (I) *22*

to get used to привыка́ть (I)/ привы́кнуть (I) *3, 5, 11*

giraffe жира́ф *13*

to give a speech выступа́ть (I) с ре́чью *20W*

to give дава́ть (I)/дать (*) *2, 3, 4, 11*

glasses frame: silver, gold, tortoise shell опра́ва: серебряная, золота́я, рогова́я *15W*

Glory (Thanks) to God! Сла́ва Бо́гу! *11*

glove перча́тка *10W*

to go by vehicle éздить (M, II), éхать (U, I)/по- (P, I) *1, 23*

to go crazy, lose one's mind сходи́ть (II)/сойти́ (I) с ума́ *24*

to go into effect входи́ть (II)/войти́ (I) в си́лу, в де́йствие, в систе́му *24*

to go on foot ходи́ть (М, II), идти́ (U, I)/пойти́ (P, I) *2, 23*

to go separate ways (*by vehicle*) разъезжа́ться (I)/разъе́хаться (I) *24*; (*on foot*) расходи́ться (II)/ разойти́сь (I) *24*

to go to and return (*by vehicle*) съе́здить (с, II) *23*; (*on foot*) сходи́ть (с, II) *23*

to go to the hospital; to be admitted to the hospital ложи́ться (II)/ лечь (I) в больни́цу *13W*

to go visiting ходи́ть в го́сти *6W*

while going by vehicle е́дучи *21*

gold frame (*eyeglasses*) золота́я опра́ва *15W*

golf го́льф *18W*

good shape (*males, females*) спорти́вная фигу́ра *15W*

goods market това́рный ры́нок *25W*

granddaughter, grandson вну́чка, внук *3W*

to grate тере́ть/по- *9W*

gray eyes се́рые глаза́ *15W*

greedy жа́дный *16W*

green зелёный *10W*

green eyes зелёные глаза́ *15W*

groceries, food проду́кты *7*

guests: to go visiting; to visit го́сти: ходи́ть в го́сти, быть в гостя́х *6W*

guilty, at fault винова́т *15*

gymnastics гимна́стика *18W*

H

hair: dark, light, straight, wavy, curly, short, long, thick, thinning во́лосы: тёмные, све́тлые, прямы́е, вью́щиеся, кудря́вые, коро́ткие, дли́нные, густы́е, ре́дкие *15W*

half полови́на *17*

hand; arm рука́ (ру́ки) *13W*

to hang (*something*) ве́шать (I)/ пове́сить (II) *22*

hanger ве́шалка *22*

to be hanging висе́ть (II)/повисе́ть (II) *22*

happy, glad рад *15*

hard drive твёрдый ди́ск *21W*

hard твёрдый (твёрже) *16*

hardworking трудолюби́вый *16W*

hat with brim шля́па *10W*

hat without brim ша́пка *10W*

to hate, come to hate ненави́деть/ воз- (II) *2, 9*

to have an attitude; to be related to относи́ться (II)/отнести́сь (I) *25*

to have to do; to be compelled to приходи́ться (I)/прийти́сь (I) *11*

head голова́ *13W*

head cold на́сморк *13W*

head is spinning (*impersonal*) кружи́ться голова́ (у кого) *13W*

to be healthy: Greetings! здра́вствовать(I): Здра́вствуй(те)! *3*

to hear слы́шать/у- (II) *2, 19*

heart се́рдце *13W*

heart attack серде́чный при́ступ *13W*

height: short, average, tall рост: ни́зкого ро́ста, сре́днего ро́ста, высо́кого ро́ста *15W*

hellish а́дский *13*

to help, give assistance помога́ть (I)/ помо́чь (I) *11*

high высоко́, высо́кий (вы́ше) *16*

high-heeled shoes ту́фли на каблука́х *10W*

hockey хокке́й *18W*

to hold держа́ть/по- (II) *2*

home, building до́м (дома́) *7*

honest че́стный *16W*

to hope for; to rely on наде́яться (I) *9*

hors d'oeuvres заку́ски (заку́сок *род.*) *9W*

horse ло́шадь (*f.*) *13*

to be in the hospital лежа́ть/по- (II) в больни́це *13W*

hotel room но́мер (номера́) *7, 17*

hour; At what hour? час: В кото́ром часу́? *10, 17*

how can I get to… как мне дойти́ (II) до чего́, как мне пройти́ (I) прое́хать (I) к чему́?, как попа́сть (I) *24w*

How much does it cost? Ско́лько сто́ит…? *7W*

humidity вла́жность *17W*

hurricane урага́н *17W*

to hurt oneself ушиба́ть (I)/ ушиби́ть (II) себе́ куда́? *13W*

to hurt (*impersonal*) боле́ть (II): боли́т/боля́т (у кого) *13W*

husband муж (мужья́) *7*

I

IBM compatible computer ИБМ-совмести́мый компью́тер *21W*

if (*not* whether) е́сли *18*

image (*public relations*) и́мидж *25W*

to imagine представля́ть (I)/ предста́вить (II) себе́ *13*

imam (*Moslem cleric*) има́м *11W*

to implore умоля́ть (I) *11W*

to import ввози́ть (II)/ввезти́ (I) *25*

imports и́мпорты *25W*

to imprison сажа́ть (I)/посади́ть (II) *22*

in comparison with what; in comparison with the fact that по сравне́нию с чем; по сравне́нию с тем, что… *12*

in connection with what; in connection with the fact that… в соотве́тствии с чем; в соотве́тсвии с тем, что… *12*

in connection with what; in connection with the fact that… в связи́ с чем; в связи́ с тем, что… *12*

in front of, before something пе́ред *12*

in light of the fact that в виду́ того́, что… *10*

in, after (*time*) че́рез (+ *time*) (по́сле того́, как…) *17*

in, at в (+ *prep./acc.*) *9, 10*; **to** на (+ *acc./prep.*) *9, 10*; в (+ *acc./prep.*) *9*; **across** че́рез (+ *acc.*) *9*

in such weather в таку́ю пого́ду *17W*

in that case в тако́м слу́чае *10*

in the first place во-пе́рвых *10*

in the mornings (in the evenings, on Mondays, on Wednesdays) по утра́м (вечера́м, по понеде́льникам, по сре́дам) *17*

in the second place во-вторы́х *10*

in the third place в-тре́тьих *10*

inasmuch as… по ме́ре того́, как *11*

incomprehensible непостижи́м/-ый *19*

increase подъём, повыше́ние *25W*

to **increase** увели́чивать(ся) (I)/
увели́чить(ся) (II) 6;
повыша́ть(ся) (I)/повы́сить(ся)
(II) 6, 25W
independent незави́симый 19
**individual building in a complex of
buildings** ко́рпус 24W
inevitable неотврати́м/-ый 19
inexpensively, inexpensive дёшево,
дешёвый (дешёвле) 16
inexplicable необъясни́м/ый 19
to **inform** доноси́ть (II)/донести́ (I)
25
information storage (*computer*)
хране́ние информа́ции 21W
infrequently ре́дко 5
insane, mad, crazy сумасше́дший 20
to **insist** наста́ивать (I)/настоя́ть (I)
10, 20W
interest (*loans, deposits*) ба́нковский
проце́нт 25W
to be **interested in**
интересова́ться/за- (I) 12
interesting интере́сно (кому́)
интере́сный 11, 16
intestines кишки́ (кишо́к *род.*) 13W
to **invite** приглаша́ть (I)/
пригласи́ть (II) 18
invited приглашён/-ный 19
irreparable непопра́вим/-ый 19
Islam Исла́м, Мусульма́нство 11W
it is possible to not ... мо́жно не
(кому́) (*impersonal*) 11W
it takes how long to get to ... е́здить
(II)/е́хать (I) ско́лько вре́мени?
24W
it's ... calling (*telephone: more
formal*) беспоко́ить (II): вас
беспоко́ит... 2W
it's windy, there's a gentle breeze
ду́ет ве́тер, ду́ет сла́бый ве́тер
17W
itches че́шется (где) 13W

J

January янва́рь 8, 17
Jew евре́й, евре́йка 11W
Judaism Иудаи́зм, Иуде́йство 11W
**judging by; judging by the fact
that ...** су́дя по чему́; су́дя по
тому́, что... 11
July ию́ль 8, 17

June ию́нь 8, 17
just in case на вся́кий слу́чай 9
just the right size как раз 15

K

kerchief плато́к 10W
kidneys по́чки 13W
kitchen; cuisine ку́хня 7W, 13
knee коле́но (коле́ни) 13W
to **know how** уме́ть/с- (I) 3
to **know; find out** знать (I)/узна́ть
(I) 3
kremlin (*Russian fortress*) кре́мль
(*m.*) 13

L

laboratory лаборато́рия 1, 13
lake о́зеро (озёра) (на) 13
landscape (*painting*) пейза́ж 19W
language язы́к (языки́) 1
last: last week, last year про́шлый:
на про́шлой неде́ле, в про́шлом
году́ 1, 17
late по́здно, по́здний (по́зже,
поздне́е) 16
to **laugh** смея́ться (I) 12
laundry detergent стира́льный
порошо́к 14W
lazy лени́вый 16W
to **lead** води́ть (M, II), вести́ (U, I),
повести́ (P, I), 25
leader вождь, ли́дер, руководи́тель
13
leading веду́щий 20
to **learn** учи́ться/на- (II) 5
having learned научи́вшись 21
lecture ле́кция (на) 10
less ме́нее (+ *adj./adv.*) 16
lesson (*class, book*) уро́к (на, в) 10
to **let** допуска́ть (I)/допусти́ть (II)
11; разреша́ть (I)/разреши́ть (II)
11
to **let go** отпуска́ть (I)/отпусти́ть
(II) 11
to **let in** впуска́ть (I)/впусти́ть (II)
11W
to **let out** выпуска́ть (I)/вы́пустить
(II) 11W
to **let through** пропуска́ть (I)/
пропусти́ть (II) 11W
let's assume that ... допу́стим, что 5
let's say that ... ска́жем, что... 5

let's suppose that ... преположи́м,
что... 5
letter письмо́ (пи́сьма) 1, 13
to **lie down** ложи́ться (II)/лечь (I)
22
life жизнь (*f.*) 13
light blue голубо́й 10W
light hair све́тлые во́лосы 15W
to **like** нра́виться/по- (II) (кому́) 11;
люби́ть/по- (II) 1, 2, 9, 18
like, similar to вро́де 8
like, resembling похо́ж (похо́жа,
похо́жи) (на кого́/что) 9
to **limit, restrict** ограни́чивать (I)/
ограни́чить (II) 6
list спи́сок 19
while listening слу́шая 21
to **live** жить (I) 1, 2, 3W, 10
lively, vibrant жив (жива́, жи́вы) 15
liver пе́чень (*f.*) 13W
loan креди́т, ссу́да, заём 25W
to be **located** находи́ться (II) 2, 10;
located находя́щийся 20
long hair дли́нные во́лосы 15W
to **look for, search for** иска́ть/по- 3
to **lose** (*game*) прои́грывать (I)/
проигра́ть (I) 18W
to **lose, misplace; to be deprived of**
теря́ть/по- (I) 2, 12W
loudly, loud гро́мко, гро́мкий
(гро́мче) 16
to **love** люби́ть/по- (II) 1, 2, 9, 18
to be **lucky** везти́ (U, I)/повезти́
(P, I) (кому́?) 25
to **lull to sleep** баю́кать (I) (кого́?)
баю́каю, баю́каешь, баю́кают
22W
lungs лёгкие 13W
to be **lying down** (*position*)
лежа́ть/по- (II) 2, 22
while lying down лёжа 21

M

main course горя́чее, второ́е 9w
to **major, specialize in** изуча́ть (I) 1W
to **make a decision; to adopt a law**
принима́ть (I)/приня́ть (I)
реше́ние, зако́н 20W
to **make a transfer** переса́живаться
(I)/пересе́сть (I), де́лать/с- (I)
переса́дку, на что (где? на како́й
ста́нции и́ли остано́вке) 24W

one who is expecting, waiting for
(*acc./inf.*) ожидáющий *20*

one who talks or speaks говорящий
20

one who was talking, speaking
говоривший *20*

one who wishes желáющий *20*

only (*adj.*) единственный *15W*

only (*adv.*) тóлько *15W*

open (*opened*) открыт/-ый *19*

to open открывáть (I)/ открыть (I)
2, 3

opera óпера (на) *19W*

opponent противник *20W*

orange орáнжевый *10W*; апельсин
7W

to order (*meal*); **to reserve** (*hotel
room*) закáзывать (I)/заказáть (I)
17

outgoing приветливый *16W*

outstanding выдаю́щийся *20*

overcoat пальтó (*indecl.*) *10W*

P

pain: sharp, dull боль (*f.*): рéзкая,
тупáя *13W*

painted покрáшен/-ный *19*

painter живописец *19W*

painting (*work of art*) картина *19W,
22*; (*form of art*) живопись (*f.*)
19W

pants, trousers брюки (брюк *род.*)
10W

parents родители (родителей
род.) *1*

parts (*times*) **of the day: morning, in
the morning; afternoon, in the afternoon; evening, in the evening;
night, in the night** чáсти сýток:
ýтро, ýтром; дéнь, днём; вéчер,
вéчером; ночь, нóчью *12, 17*

pass (*document*) прóпуск *11W*

past (*adj.*); **the past** (*noun*)
прошéдший, прошéдшее
(врéмя) *20*

pastor, minister пáстор *11*

patient больнóй (*adj. decl.*) *7*

to pay платить/за- (II) *4, 7W, 8*

pedestrian crossing (*underground*)
перехóд *24W*

perform выступáть (I) *4W*; (*music*)
исполнять (I) *19W*

performance спектáкль *4W*

performing artist артист/-ка *19W*

peripherals (*computer*) периферия
21W

permission (*written, oral*)
разрешéние *11W*

to permit разрешáть (I) *11*

person, people человéк, лю́ди
(людéй *род.*) *1, 7, 8*

photocopy machine копиро-
вáльный аппарáт, ксéрокс *21W*

photograph фотогрáфия, снимок
19W

to photograph фотографировать
(I) *19W*

photographer фотóграф *19W*

physicist физик *1*

pink рóзовый *10W*

plaid; checked клéтчатый (в
клéтку) *10W*

to plant сажáть (I)/посадить (II)
22

plate тарéлка *22*

play пьéса *19W*

to play a round сыгрáть (I) матч
18W

to play игрáть/по- (I) в (+ *acc.*)
(*game, sport*), на (+ *prep.*) (*instrument*) *9, 10*

to play a role игрáть (I)/сыгрáть
роль (I) *4W*

playwright драматýрг *19W*

pleased приятно (комý?) *11*

plump, fat тóлстый *15W*

poet поэт *19W*

politician политик *20W*

politics, policy; political science
политика; политические наýки
20W

polka-dotted в горóшек *10W*

poorly, poor плóхо, плохóй (хýже)
16

portrait портрéт *19W*

to pose (*question*) задавáть (I)/
задáть (*) *2W*

possible, impossible возмóжно/не-
(комý) *11*

post office, mail пóчта (на) *10*

poster плакáт *22*

to pray молиться (II) *11W*

to prepare; cook готóвить/при- (II)
2, 9W

to prepare oneself готóвиться/при-
(II) *1W*

prepared приготóвлен/-ный *19*

pressure (*barometric*) давлéние *17W*

price ценá (цéны) (в дóлларах/
рублях) *7W*

price includes . . . В стóимость
вхóдят... *23W*; В стóимость
включены... *23W*

price per person per day стóимость
на человéка в сýтки *23W*

priest (*Russian Orthodox, Catholic*)
свящéнник *11W*

principle: from these principles
соображéние: из этих
соображéний *7*

printer: dot-matrix, jet, laser
принтер: мáтричный, струйный,
лáзерный *21W*

private room отдéльная кóмната
14W

privatization приватизáция *25W*

professor профéссор (профессорá)
1, 7

prohibited, banned запрéтный *11W*

prohibition, ban запрéт *11W*

to pronounce something
произносить (II)/произнести (I)
25

Protestant протестáнт,
протестáнтка *11W*

Protestant church кирка *11W*

Protestantism Протестáнство,
Протестантизм *11W*

public relations пáблик рилéйшн
25W

purchase покýпка *25W*

purchased кýплен/ный *19*

purple фиолéтовый *10W*

to put on (*clothing*) надéт/-ый *19*

to put in the hospital класть (I)/
положить (II) когó в больницу
13W

to put, place класть (I)/положить
(II) *22*

to put, stand стáвить/по- (II) *22*

Q

quickly бы́стро *16*

quietly, quiet тихо, тихий (тише) *16*

quit, abandon бросáть (I)/брóсить
(II) *4W*

R

rabbi равви́н *11W*

racketball ракетбо́л *18W*

rain: it is (it will start to, it will be) raining до́ждь: идёт (пойдёт, бу́дет идти́) *17W*

raincoat плащ *1, 10W*

rarely, seldom ре́дко *1*

rate of exchange курс *25W*

having read прочита́в *21*

to read чита́ть/про- (I) *2*

while reading чита́я *21*

ready гото́в *15*

realistic реалисти́ческий *19W*

to recall, remember; to reminisce вспомина́ть (I)/вспо́мнить (II) *19W*

to recognize узнава́ть (I)/узна́ть (I) *19W*

recommended рекоменду́ем/-ый *19*

reconfiguration of a computer измене́ние конфигура́ции компью́тера *21W*

red кра́сный *10W*

to reduce уменьша́ть (I)/уме́ньшить (II) *6*

regulating регули́рование (чего) *25W*

to reheat (*food*) подогрева́ть (I)/подогре́ть (I) *9*

to relate относи́ть (II)/отнести́ (I) *25*

to relax рассла́бить(ся) (II) *22W*

reliable; unreliable надёжный; не- *16W*

religious faith вероиспове́дание *11W*

to remember; to fix in one's memory запомина́ть (I)/запо́мнить (II) *19W*

to remember; to mention упомина́ть (I)/упомяну́ть (I) *19W*

to remember, recall по́мнить/вс- (II) *19W*

to remind напомина́ть (I)/напо́мнить (II) *19W*

to request (*favor*) проси́ть/по- (II) *2W*

to reserve (*hotel room*); **to order** (*a meal*) зака́зывать (I)/заказа́ть (I) *17*

reserved сде́ржанный *16W*

to resort to прибега́ть (I)/прибе́гнуть (I) (к чему́?) *24*

to respect уважа́ть (I) *9*

respected уважа́емый (много-) *19*

to rest, relax отдыха́ть (I)/отдохну́ть (I) *22*

retail price ро́зничная цена́ *25W*

reticent молчали́вый *16W*

retrieval of information по́иск информа́ции *21W*

to return возвраща́ться (I)/верну́ться (I) *2*

having returned верну́вшись *21*

while returning возвраща́ясь *21*

richly, rich бога́то, бога́тый (бога́че) *16*

to ride across, drive across переезжа́ть (I)/перее́хать (I) *24*

to ride away, drive away отъезжа́ть (I)/отъе́хать (I) *24*

to ride away, drive away уезжа́ть (I)/уе́хать (I) *24*

to ride down off, drive down off съезжа́ть (I)/съе́хать (I) *24*

to ride, drive (*arrive*) приезжа́ть (I)/прие́хать (I) *24*

to ride into, drive into въезжа́ть (I)/въе́хать (I) *24*

to ride into, behind; drive into, behind заезжа́ть (I)/зае́хать (I) *24*

to ride out of, drive out of выезжа́ть (I)/вы́ехать (I) *24*

to ride through, drive through; to miss (*bus/train stop*) проезжа́ть (I)/прое́хать (I) *24*; (ско́лько ста́нций, остано́вок?) *24W*

to ride up to доезжа́ть (I)/дое́хать (I) *24*

right, correct прав (права́, пра́вы) *15*

to roast; to stew туши́ть/по- (II) *9W*

roommate, suitemate сосе́д/-ка (по ко́мнате, по бло́ку) *14W*

to root for боле́ть (I) за кого́ *18W*

ruble of the Russian Federation росси́йский рубль *25W*

rugby ре́гби *18W*

to run (*somewhere and back*) сбе́гать (с, I) *23*

to run (fingers over keyboard, eyes over page) пробега́ть (I)/пробежа́ть (*) чем по чему́? (па́льцами по кла́вишам, глаза́ми по страни́це) *24*

to run бе́гать (М, I); бежа́ть (U, *)/по- (Р, *) *2, 23*

to run across перебега́ть (I)/перебежа́ть (*) *24*

to run around (*something*) оббега́ть (I)/оббежа́ть (*) *24*

to run around побе́гать (по, I) *23*

to run away отбега́ть (I)/отбежа́ть (*) *24*

to run away убега́ть (I)/убежа́ть (*) *24*

to run down off сбега́ть (I)/сбежа́ть (*) *24*

to run into вбега́ть (I)/вбежа́ть (*) *24*

to run into, behind забега́ть (I)/забежа́ть (*) *24*

to run late, be late for опа́здывать (I)/опозда́ть (I) *18*

to run off (*in different directions*) разбега́ться (I)/разбежа́ться (*) *24*

to run out of выбега́ть (I)/вы́бежать (*) *24*

to run through пробега́ть (I)/пробежа́ть (*) *24*

to run to прибега́ть (I)/прибежа́ть (I) *24*

to run up to добега́ть (I)/добежа́ть (*) *24*; подбега́ть (I)/подбежа́ть (*) *24*

running (*sport*) бег *18W*

rush hour час пик *24W*

Russian Orthodox faith, (*Russian*) **Orthodox** правосла́вие, правосла́вный *11*

Russification of a printer руссифика́ция при́нтера *21W*

Russified printer руссифици́рованный при́нтер *21W*

S

sad гру́стно *11*

having said, told сказа́в *21*

sale прода́жа *25W*

salted солёный *9W*

sanitarium санато́рий *13*

throat го́рло *13W*
thundering, crashing греми́щий *20*
Thursday, on Thursday четве́рг, в четве́рг *17*
ticket биле́т *4W*
time вре́мя (времена́) *7*
time goes (will go) by прохо́дит (пройдёт) вре́мя *24*
timid, shy ро́бкий *16*
to, by, toward к (+ *dat.*) *11*
today's сего́дняшний *17*
toes па́льцы на ноге́ *13W*
token (*subway, metro*) жето́н *24W*
told расска́зан/ный *19*
tomorrow's за́втрашний *17*
toner cartridge то́нер-ка́ртридж *21W*
tongue, language язы́к (языки́) *13W*
too big вели́к (велика́, велики́) (что? кому́?) *15*
too small мал (мала́, мало́, малы́) (что? кому́?) *15*
tooth зуб *13W*
tornado смерч *17W*
tortoise-shell frame (*eyeglasses*) рогова́я опра́ва *15W*
track and field лёгкая атле́тика *18W*
trade торго́вля *25W*
trade торг *25W*
tragedy траге́дия *19W*
train station (*metro, subway*) ста́нция (на) *10*
train station (*not for metro, subway*) вокза́л (на) *10, 24W*
transferred, conveyed пе́редан/-ный *19*
to translate переводи́ть (II)/ перевести́ (I) *25*
translator перево́дчик *1*
to transport вози́ть (М, II)/ везти́ (U, I)/повезти́ (P, I) *25*
travel agency аге́нство путеше́ствий, туристи́ческое аге́нство, тураге́нство *23W*
to travel around by vehicle пое́здить (по, II) *23*
to travel by conveyance е́здить (II)/ е́хать/по- (I) *8*
to travel on foot ходи́ть (II)/идти́ (I)/пойти́ (I) *8*
to travel путеше́ствовать/по- *23W*

trip, journey путеше́ствие *23W*
to trust доверя́ть (I)/дове́рить (II) *11*
to try; to test, sample про́бовать/по- (I) *20W*
to try стара́ться/по- (I) *20W*
to try; to experience пыта́ться/по- (I) *20W*
Tuesday, on Tuesday вто́рник, во... *17*
to turn off (*light, television, computer*) выключа́ть (I)/вы́ключить (II) *6, 21W*
to turn on (*light, television, computer*) включа́ть (I)/включи́ть (II) *6, 21W*
to turn out to be ока́зываться (I)/ оказа́ться (I) *3, 12, 18, 24*
to turn right or left повора́чивать (I)/поверну́ть (I) (напра́во, нале́во, куда́?) *24W*
to type печа́тать/на- (I) *5*

U

ugly некраси́вый *16*
umbrella зонт (зо́нтик) *10W*
unbearable невыноси́м/-ый *19*
uncle дя́дя *3W*
under, beneath под (+ *acc./instr.*) *9, 12*
under the auspices of, during the administration of при (+ *prep.*) *10*
to understand понима́ть (I)/поня́ть (I) *3, 9*
underwear бельё *13*
uninteresting неинтере́сный *16*
united: United Nations объединённый: Организа́ция объединённых на́ций *19*
united: United States of America соединённый: Соединённые Шта́ты Аме́рики *19*
up until: Until we meet up. Until the next call. Until we see each other. до: До встре́чи. До звонка́. До свида́нья. *2W*
upgrading of a computer модерниза́ция компью́тера *21W*
to use (*grammatical constructions, e.g., "What case is used with…"*) употребля́ться (I)/употреби́ться (II) *16W*

to use употребля́ть (I)/употреби́ть (II) *16W*; испо́льзовать (I) *16W*
to use, apply применя́ть (I)/ примени́ть (II) *16W*
to use, consume; to waste потребля́ть (I) *16W*
to use, consume; to waste расхо́довать (I) *16W*; тра́тить/ис- *16W*
to use; to enjoy по́льзоваться/вос- (I) *12*
to use; to take advantage of злоупотребля́ть (I) *16W*
to use; to take advantage of; to enjoy по́льзоваться/вос- (I) *16W*

V

to vacation at the sea, at a resort отдыха́ть (I) на мо́ре, на куро́рте *23W*
to vacuum пылесо́сить (II) *14W*
vegetables о́вощи (овоще́й *gen.*) *22*
verse (*poem*) стихотворе́ние *19W*
to visit with guests быть (I) в гостя́х *6W*
vocal music вока́льная му́зыка *19W*
volleyball волейбо́л *18W*
vomiting рво́та *13W*
to vote голосова́ть/про- (I) *20W*

W

to wait ждать/подо- (I) (+ *no prep.*) *3*
to wake up просыпа́ться (I)/ просну́ться (I) *22W*
to wake someone up буди́ть/раз- (II) *22W*
to walk ходи́ть (М, II) *23*
to walk across переходи́ть (II)/ перейти́ (I) *24*
to walk around обходи́ть (II)/ обойти́ (I) *24*
to walk (*for a while*) походи́ть (по, II) *23*
to walk away отходи́ть (II)/отойти́ (I) *24*; уходи́ть (II)/уйти́ (I) *24*
to walk down off сходи́ть (II)/сойти́ (I) *24*
to walk into входи́ть (II)/войти́ (I) *24*
to walk into, behind заходи́ть (II)/ зайти́ (I) *24*

Index of Grammatical Terms

Italicized page numbers refer to charts or tables on the page(s) indicated.
Terms indexed in Russian follow the English.

English Index

Russian Index

Literary Index

This index includes authors of literary texts (listed alphabetically by last name), as well as first lines of poetry.

Grateful acknowledgment is made for use of the following.

Texts:

19–20 From "Shchenok kavkazskoi ovcharki," *Argumenty i fakty*; *23* From *Complete Poems of Anna Akhmatova* (Somerville, MA: Zephyr); *30–31* From "Sotrudnichat' ili konfliktovat'?" by Aleksandr Libin, *Argumenty i fakty*; *48* From *School for Fools* by Sasha Sokolov (New York: Four Walls, Eight Windows); *49–50* From *First Circle* by Aleksandr Solzhenitsyn (Paris: YMCA-Press); *56–57* From *Wives of the Kremlin* by Larisa Vasil'eva (Moscow: Vagriys); *65–66* From *Collected Works of A. Belyi* (Oakland, CA: Berkeley Slavic Specialties); *71* From *Complete Poems of Anna Akhmatova* (Somerville, MA: Zephyr); *72* Adapted from "Pitanie v sem'e" by M. M. Gurvich, in Proshina, L. V. et al., *Sem'ia: 500 voprosov i otvetov* (Moscow: Mysl); *78* From *Peterburg* by Andrei Belyi (Moscow: Khudozhestrennaia literatura); *93* From "Bolen SPIDom" by Aleksei Demidov, *Rossiiskie vesti*; *108–109* From "Liza Minnelli u russkikh poprosila l'da" by Natalia Kilesso, *Moskovsksii komsomolets*; *116–117* From *Complete Poems of Anna Akhmatova* (Somerville, MA: Zephyr); *154* From "Igra v klassiki" by Andrei Gaev and Natalia Khorshavina, *Kommersant*; *156* From *Sochineniia* by Marina Tsvetaeva (Moscow: Khudozhestrennaia literatura); *163–164* From *Struna; stikhi* by Bella Akhmadulina (Moscow: Sovetskii pisatel'); *184* From *Sobranie sochinenii* by Vladimir Nabokov (Ann Arbor, MI: Ardis); *201* From *Izbrannoe* by Isaak Babel' (Moscow: Khudozhestrennaia literatura); *204* From *Tsvet vereska* by Natalia Gorbanevskaia (Tenafly, NJ: Hermitage); *233* From *Complete Poems of Anna Akhmatova* (Somerville, MA: Zephyr); *273* From *Complete Poems of Anna Akhmatova* (Somerville, MA: Zephyr); *281* "The Little Paper Soldier" by Bulat Okudzhava; *309–311* From *Irony of Fate* by E. Riazanov and E. Braginskii (Moscow: Sovetskii pisatel'); *335* From *Life and Fate* by Vasilii Grossman (Moscow: Knizhnaia palata); *339* From *Doctor Zhivago's Poems* by Boris Pasternak (Westport, CT: Greenwood).

Photos:

1 Michael Groh; *13* Benjamin Rifkin; *25* Benjamin Rifkin; *36* Michael Groh; *43* Benjamin Rifkin; *62* Nikita Smirnov; *73* Benjamin Rifkin; *89* Benjamin Rifkin; *111* Benjamin Rifkin; *122* Benjamin Rifkin; *134* Nikita Smirnov; *150* Benjamin Rifkin; *161* Michael Groh; *178* Michael Groh; *186* Benjamin Rifkin; *195* Benjamin Rifkin; *207* Benjamin Rifkin; *223* Michael Groh; *238* Nikita Smirnov; *250* Benjamin Rifkin; *266* Walter Gilardetti; *274* Michael Groh; *285* Benjamin Rifkin; *307* Benjamin Rifkin; *325* Benjamin Rifkin.

Connecting words

a

но

потому что

так как, как